MR. CHAIRMAN

MR. CHAIRMAN

POWER IN
DAN ROSTENKOWSKI'S
AMERICA

James L. Merriner

SOUTHERN ILLINOIS UNIVERSITY PRESS
Carbondale and Edwardsville

Library of Congress Cataloging-in-Publication Data
Merriner, James L., 1947–
    Mr. Chairman : power in Dan Rostenkowski's America / James L.
Merriner.
        p. cm.
    Includes bibliographical references and index.
    1. Rostenkowski, Dan.   2. Legislators—United States—Biography.
3. United States. Congress. House—Biography.   4. United States—Politics
and government—1945–1989.   5. United States—Politics and government—
1989–.   I. Title.
    E840.8.R66M47   1999   98-54247
    328.73'092—dc21   CIP
    [b]
    ISBN 0-8093-2280-3 (alk. paper)

To Irene Klay Merriner

Who ran with courage the race set before her,
always looking unto the Author of her faith

CONTENTS

ILLUSTRATIONS

PREFACE

In 1976, as the political editor of the *Atlanta Constitution*, I accompanied Jimmy Carter to a Capitol reception in Washington. Carter had secured the Democratic presidential nomination by running an anti-Washington campaign but had not yet been nominated. He was meeting congressmen to deny that he was running an anti-Washington campaign.

The subdued crowd was unconvinced. Thomas P. "Tip" O'Neill of Massachusetts tried to pump it up when Carter entered the chandeliered room, saying, "Let's show some enthusiasm, fellas!" A hulking Pole from Chicago, Daniel Rostenkowski, eyeing Carter warily, appraisingly, professionally, seemed to be as dominant a force in the room as the more famous O'Neill, the hulking Irishman from Boston. I knew Rostenkowski only as Mayor Daley's man in Washington but made a mental note to keep track of his career.

Time and circumstances moved me to Chicago, where I often covered Rostenkowski as a reporter for the *Sun-Times*, usually in Chicago, now and then in Washington or at a political convention. Aside from an editorial role in a few stories, I was not a member of the newspaper's investigative reporting team whose disclosures of Rostenkowski's financial affairs predated and formatted many of the eventual Justice Department indictments. Those disclosures, of course, inform much of this biography.

Why a biography of yet another crooked congressman? I became a political journalist because I find politics fun and also because I was tickled by the idea of getting paid to figure out how the world works. I believe the story of Rostenkowski's rise and fall reveals much about how power is sought, won, exercised, and distributed in contemporary America.

The style in modern political biography is to portray the subject as complex and contradictory and multifaceted, torn between ambition and conscience, at once ruthless and sensitive, possessing both a public face and a hidden private face, and so on. Rostenkowski spares a biographer much of the trouble of such analysis. Some of it will be indulged herein, but for a politician Rostenkowski was candid, straightforward, and authentic—except when it came to his own finances. Indeed, it is a mystery why political writers feel assigned to endeavor amateur psychoanalysis. The desire for power is not an opaque human characteristic. Nor is the desire for wealth.

Dan Rostenkowski all but wore a sign around his neck that flashed "I want power." He knew who had it, how to get it, and how to implement it. He was the "tall bold slugger" of Carl Sandburg's 1916 poem about Chicago. In Chicago this did not especially set him apart, but in Washington he came to be regarded both as a patriarch and a refreshment after all the media-obsessed "blow-dried guys" (his term) who came to inhabit the city. One reason for his popularity, among voters and reporters alike, is that he usually gave straight answers to straight questions. He knew what he thought without consulting polls, focus groups, handlers, and spinners until new arrangements of power that he did not understand contrived to hammer home the primeval lesson that all power is fleeting. Then he fell hard and fast.

Power here is not meant only in the ordinary political science sense of A getting B to do something that B otherwise would not have done. That exercise is primary—and Rostenkowski had a genius for it—but power in this book also is considered as a conflict between persons and institutions, historical forces, culture, or fate—call it what you like. Normally the institutions win. They beat Danny.

Institutional conflict in public affairs usually is personalized, defined by a bipolar model of Republican versus Democrat, or liberal versus conservative, or president versus Congress. Despite the tempting convenience of this bipolar outlook, a theme of *Mr. Chairman* is that it is largely an illusion. The forces in play overwhelm mere partisan and ideological division. In particular, the weakness of the bipolar model is shown in Rostenkowski's primary realm of exerting power, the most pervasive imposition of mass governmental coercion: the exaction of taxes. The tax bills he passed were bipartisan products.

Preface

Rostenkowski's life ascended from power in the political-science sense to tragedy in the classical sense. Again, tragedy is not used here in the loose, figurative meaning of a story about personal sorrows, or even in the night-school, great-books sense of a great hero laid low by a tragic flaw. Rather, tragedy is meant literally, from its most ancient denotation: a form of ritual sacrifice accompanied by a choral song.

The United States Justice Department and Rostenkowski's electorate in effect sacrificed him as an embodiment of the excesses of big government, to the accompaniment of a chorus of big media reportage of scandal. Rostenkowski did his part both to create big government and feed big media, which, with the inevitability of classical drama, destroyed him for it.

Don't be alarmed—the following narrative does not strain to fit such a classical schema. But neither does it reduce to a simple fable of the proverb "Pride goeth before a fall." It is the story of a great man who was also a little man, a statesman and a crook, an emotional man, an American original.

Rostenkowski did not look with favor on this study and declined the author's interview requests after June 1995. The book is sourced by previous interviews with him, interviews with others, and the public record.

A word about reporting technique: The public rightly suspects the use of anonymously sourced reportage of public affairs. All quotations and statements of fact are taken from the public record or from interviews conducted by the author. All interviews were on the record, with two major exceptions. The exceptions provided no uncorroborated account of anyone's thoughts, remarks, or actions.

ACKNOWLEDGMENTS

When I was young and foolish, I would glance at acknowledgments sections and wonder why the author seemingly felt the need to thank everyone he or she ever met. Now I know that any serious nonfiction book is a collaborative effort requiring help, freely given, from many people.

Much of this book was written at Ohio State University in Columbus, Ohio, while I was the James Thurber Writer in Residence in autumn 1996. Research was supported by a grant from the Everett McKinley Dirksen Congressional Research Center in Pekin, Illinois.

My agent, Connie Goddard, was encouraging and diligent. Others who propped me up with their faith in the project include Sharon Davis, Peggy Boyer Long, Mike McCluggage, Charles M. Merriner, Charles T. Merriner, Stan Palder, and a few who would prefer I not name them.

Librarians at the Polish Museum of America in Chicago graciously translated documents from the Polish. Librarians at the *Chicago Sun-Times*, the Chicago Historical Society, and the Oak Park, Illinois, Public Library can find any fact recorded about anything at any time anywhere.

To the sources I interviewed, including some who thought the *Sun-Times* had gone totally over the edge in its pursuit of the Rostenkowski scandal, many thanks.

Political specialists at Southern Illinois University reviewed the manuscript and made constructive suggestions, nearly all of which I followed, and concerning those I did not, I still recognize and value their insights.

Finally, thank you, Milanne and Rebecca. You put up with a lot.

MR. CHAIRMAN

PROLOGUE

A PUBLIC high school and an ethnic banquet hall near Chicago's O'Hare Airport share the peculiar fate of seeing regular processions of presidents, senators, governors, candidates for those offices, and other grandees. Both institutions happen to be located just a ten- or fifteen-minute hop by police-escorted motorcade from O'Hare's terminals. That means the potentates of politics and television can hit O'Hare, score a quick photo opportunity at the school or the restaurant, zip right back to the airport, and attain a "wheels up" for the next media market with a swiftness to gladden the soul of any campaign scheduler or TV news producer.

If the campaign message of the day is education, the motorcade points southwest to Fenton High School, where students are willing, if bored (they are getting used to this empty show), camera props. If the message of the day is the importance of ethnic communities, the motorcade heads northeast to the White Eagle, there to greet the Poles.

The auditorium at Fenton High School and a banquet room in the White Eagle look pretty much the same on television—the photo ops tend to blur together—but in fact they represent different Americas. Fenton is not located in Chicago, not even in Cook County, the ancestral fount of political clout and corruption. It is in upscale and mainly white DuPage

County. Fenton students come from, among other pastorally named developments, Wood Dale, an archetype of the suburbs that have sprung up across the land in the past half century. For that matter, the White Eagle is not in Chicago, either, but in an old adjacent suburb named Niles. Even still—in fact, maybe in part *because* it is in a suburb—it has become the front parlor of what is left of the urban working-class Democratic political organization.

If it is a clear day, a candidate descending to O'Hare for a Fenton High or a White Eagle photo op might peer out the window of the chartered jet. Obviously, that is Lake Michigan and the spikes of the Loop skyline glistening back to the east, but the landscape below appears featureless, drab. If the candidate's eyes and his sense of social history alike are sharp, though, he might discern the way the industrial parks and the two- and three-flats on the street grid of the old city "morph" into the low-slung tract houses on the curvilinear streets of the newer suburbs. And if the wind should flow from the southwest so that the jet is approaching Runway 22L, the pilot might descend directly over Niles. Of course, there would be no way to distinguish its old-fashioned grid of streets from the grids of the adjoining city and older suburbs, but the candidate still might notice two immense cemeteries. Both are in Niles, and working-class Catholics repose in both. The southern one, St. Adalbert's, is bordered on the north by an old folks' home and on the east by Milwaukee Avenue. Across the avenue, just yards from a wooded preserve, is the White Eagle.

For a politician of either party to run for high office without paying his or her respects at the White Eagle would be considered bad form. But these pols properly are seen as interlopers, visiting firemen. The senators from Washington and the governors from Springfield are treated as guests and associates with whom one might seal a deal, but they don't "own" the place.

Dan Rostenkowski walks in; he still owns it. To the hundreds of people who line up to shake his hand, the fact that he is under federal indictment for stealing $724,267 through various schemes is incidental. He remains the sovereign of Polonia.

Chicago was built on unrelenting flatland, permitting its streets to be laid out in an uncompromising grid, except that there are a few diagonal streets, following old Indian trails, for variety's sake. Along those radial avenues, the ethnic migrations have taken place. The *wychodzstwo polski*, the immigration from Poland, settled along Milwaukee Avenue on the northwest side of the city. As the Poles prospered, they, or their children, sent the moving vans on out Milwaukee Avenue into outlying precincts of the city and then into nearby suburbs such as Niles. Taking their place in the bungalows and two- and three-flats in the city neighborhoods were Hispanics, Asians, and others, but not, the precinct captains and block clubs and real estate agents saw to it, blacks.

As the Poles dispersed, they took care to retain their political power. In an uncomfortable alliance of European Catholics, there was always a Daley, an Irishman, and a Rostenkowski, a Pole, in office to look after them. The adverb *always* there is not entirely fanciful. Daleys in power in Chicago go back to 1936, and Rostenkowskis in power go back to 1912. And every once in a while, since it opened in 1946, the clans have gotten together at the White Eagle. It was named after the flag of the 1863 Polish uprising against the Russians, an uprising that failed—national defeats are part of the patrimony of the Poles. The White Eagle's architecture is basic cinder block, and its sound system sounds gravelly, like an old high school PA circuit. So much the better, for the sake of Chicago symbolism: brawny, no-frills, large, and plain.

The White Eagle proprietor gets his customers, it is said, "coming and going." Newlyweds celebrate their nuptials in the banquet halls, wearing aprons bearing baby toys, an Old Country custom to signify fertility and long life. The restaurant also serves luncheons to the funeral processions that file steadily out of the wrought-iron gates of St. Adalbert's. Motorists whipping past on Milwaukee Avenue pay no notice, but a quantity of the American immigrant experience is interred in that cemetery. It was founded in 1872. Rostenkowski knows the place. His parents and grandparents lie among the inhabitants.

On this unseasonably warm Chicago winter night, Rostenkowski is at the White Eagle to receive an award from the Polish National Alliance for being (to condense much PNA verbiage) a great American. "The most influential elected official of Polish descent in the history of the United States," as the toastmaster introduces him. A small historical irony is in operation. The Polish National Alliance used to fight a bitter family quarrel with the Polish Roman Catholic Union, among whose founders was Father Vincent Barzynski of St. Stanislaus Kostka Roman Catholic Church, which sits across the street from Rostenkowski's three-story brick home. Among the PRCU's first presidents was Peter Rostenkowski, the congressman's grandfather, who built that house across from St. Stanislaus. The PRCU was established in Chicago in 1874. The PNA was founded in Philadelphia in 1880 and was open not just to non-Catholics but to unbelievers, and not just unbelievers but anarchists. The rift between the two organizations was not closed until after World War I. Who remembers such ancient feuds? Probably not the young Republican governor of Illinois, who is joining Rostenkowski on stage. He does not have to be here: It is not an election year.

In the previous election, the governor won reelection in a landslide while Rostenkowski was defeated after thirty-six years in Congress. A Baptist, Jim Edgar comes from a small town in central Illinois and joins his suburban confederates in treating Chicago as something like an outdated, expensive nuisance. Big cities are doomed, is their unspoken credo. Governor Edgar was part of the Republican Risorgimento of 1994. His philosophy of limited government is ascendant; Rostenkowski's party of urban ethnic spoils is descendant.

Funny thing, though. It is the governor who seems pinched and uptight, Rostenkowski who seems expansive and gregarious. Folks with deliciously, defiantly non-Anglicized names such as Edward Lataowski and Wanda Wejlarc—including some who never did join the Milwaukee Avenue diaspora, who stuck close to what they call "St. Stan's" church, as did the Rostenkowskis—these folks want to shake Rostenkowski's hand, hug him, play do-you-remember-the-time-when, get their photos taken together. Edgar, lean and bland, one of the modern media politicians with never a blow-dried hair out of place, works the crowd with an air of strained cheer. Rostenkowski, tall and fleshy, works the crowd with the flair of an old-fashioned, back-slapping pol.

And yet, is it just an observer's imagination that places a scrim of sadness over Rostenkowski's visage, the sadness of a man who has hung on past his time, who fell as he prepared to run his final lap? For all his charm, his face, the shape of a canned ham, seems to wear a scowl that invariably gets him labeled "gruff" in newspaper personality profiles; his jowls have grown positively Nixonian.

Prologue

The Polish National Alliance crowd here is fading, passé. The few young couples give the impression of having come merely to indulge their parents, those lifetime PNA members who take these things so seriously. Many of the older folks wear thick, heavy-rimmed glasses and carry canes, including silver-tipped walking sticks in old continental style. A cable television news crew follows "Rosty" briefly through a receiving line, though there is no real news here—this will make just a few seconds on the local, late-evening newscast. Still, the older people are impressed. They remember when politicians showed up without scruffy kids in T-shirts holding boom mikes over their heads alongside other kids with shoulder-mounted video cameras. This crowd might not be able to define the term *photo op*. After the hubbub has subsided a bit, a priest offers an invocation in Polish. Much of the audience understands every word.

At this point the toastmaster introduces Governor Edgar's press secretary and deputy press secretary, both of Polish descent. This is a happy coincidence even though both have Anglicized surnames, Lawrence and Mack. Nobody points out that the guest of honor called himself "Danny Rosten" as a schoolboy, scrubbing the ethnicity off his name, or that the statesman's daughters call themselves "Rostens."

The governor says nice things about him. He says nice things about the governor. The temptation is to interpret the moment cynically, but in truth both men are sincere, not just going through the motions. There is an overlay of formal ceremony, to be sure, the political purgatory that public men endure without flinching, the incessant blah-blah of innumerable events in innumerable banquet halls—nevertheless, these guys really do admire each other. The history of Rostenkowski's partnerships with Republican presidents and governors would dismay those who believe the United States has a strong two-party system. Republicans and Democrats, always kicking each other in the shins! Rather, they often shake hands and clap each other on the back, seeking the sweetness of compromise and familiarity, just as in a marriage.

In the governor's eyes, Rosty is the guy who got the federal cash to rebuild the expressway here named after John F. Kennedy, who was the president installed in office by, legend has it, Rostenkowski's patron, Mayor Richard J. Daley. Rosty also got federal cash for the enormous Deep Tun-

nel flood control project, single-handedly scooping it out like some political Paul Bunyan. And so on. In Rostenkowski's eyes, the governor is . . . a
potential character witness in his upcoming criminal trial?

The governor is of the land of the Fenton High Schools, the suburban
middle classes. Rostenkowski is of the land of the White Eagle, the urban
working classes. He left Milwaukee Avenue to write the nation's tax laws,
play golf with presidents, jet around the world with billionaires. When he
was indicted on charges of official corruption, there was much head-
scratching over the question of why, when he was in a position to steal millions of dollars if he wanted, he would get himself in trouble over pilfering
some postage stamps. Some pundits harrumphed and opined that Rosty
was a classic Chicago hack who could not shake off the squalor of his native Thirty-second Ward, not even in the marble corridors of Washington.
The possibility that Washington had corrupted Milwaukee Avenue more
than the other way around did not seem to cross many minds.

Which world did this spectacularly gifted politician more inexcus-
ably betray, that of the professional classes or that of his origins? Which
world was more thoroughly corrupt—and corrupting? Those are questions this book will seek to answer by tracing the life and times of former
House Ways and Means Committee Chairman Daniel D. Rostenkowski.
He was a man who loved to have a gavel in his hand. They called him
"Mr. Chairman."

1

BIG JOE RUSTY

And they tell me you are crooked and I
answer: Yes, it is true I have seen
the gunman kill and go free to kill
again.

— Carl Sandburg, "Chicago"

ON AN August night in 1938, Leo "Cowboy" Mosinski told his wife he could not sleep and was going for a midnight stroll. How far he walked is not known, but he ended up snoozing in a car with his buddy, Bruno "Jeff" Switaj, parked outside the home of Joseph P. Rostenkowski, the alderman and Democratic party committeeman of Chicago's Thirty-second Ward. A large man and a forceful personality, Rostenkowski had earned his nickname, "Big Joe Rusty." He was the employer of Mosinski and Switaj.

Mosinski lived with his young wife and daughter about a block away on the same side of the same street as the alderman. Switaj lived with his widowed mother, also about a block away on a different street, Potomac Avenue, in what was then known as "Polish Downtown." Asleep at 1349 Noble Street were Rostenkowski and his wife, their twin daughters, and the kid brother, ten-year-old Danny.

Shortly after 6:30 A.M. a car pulled alongside Switaj's parked car. The driver sat with the motor idling while another man got out on the passenger side. He fired five shots—two into Mosinski, two into Switaj, and a fifth that missed. Then he returned to the getaway car, whose driver obligingly departed.

Alderman Rostenkowski, awakened by the shots, ran to the scene.

Soon he went to the Racine Avenue police station for questioning. Yes, he said, the two men were "lieutenants" in his political organization. No, he didn't know why they were killed. "I haven't the faintest idea what happened or why," Rostenkowski told the press. "Both men worked for me, but I don't know of any enemies they might have had and I haven't any myself who might have wanted to get them." [1]

Although Mosinski was on "relief," the Depression term for welfare, he had in his pockets seventy-six dollars, a significant piece of money at that time. He had been a policeman for the state highway department. Three newspapers in town variously reported his age as thirty-four, thirty-two, and twenty-seven. The coroner listed him as twenty-seven.

Jane Mosinski, dabbing her eyes or covering her face with a handkerchief, was an emblematic figure for the newspapers: Widow Weeps at Inquest into Mysterious Slaying of Husband. Still, it would be a mistake to imagine that the press went into its customary frenzy of headlines, given this story of a double murder in front of a politician's house. The question of why the car was parked at the curb of 1349 Noble Street scarcely was pursued. Coverage was, by standards of newspaper sensationalism, restrained. Perhaps it was not that big of a story. Since 1920, the city had had an average of forty-three gangland murders every year.

Switaj had been unemployed since his candy and notions store went bust two years earlier, his sister told the press. "I want his name cleared," she said. "I know he wasn't mixed up in anything." The coroner said he was thirty-four years old and an "alley inspector," presumably a city job that Rostenkowski got for him. He was Chicago's ninety-seventh murder victim of 1938 and the sixth classified as an organized crime assassination. There would be eight more that year—with a total of just fourteen, it was an off year for mob hits.

Mosinski and Switaj had been familiar figures in the taverns of the Near Northwest Side. Earlier that summer, police had questioned Mosinski about some window smashings in connection with a Democratic primary election campaign, routine stuff (such incidents characterized Chicago ward elections into the 1990s). Also questioned at that time was Mosinski's brother-in-law, a bartender in a saloon on the ground floor of Joe Rostenkowski's three-story home. This versatile saloon also housed the Thirty-second Ward Democratic headquarters. There was nothing uncommon about this. Back then, many saloonkeepers served as alderman, and vice versa.

The brother-in-law lead quickly turned cold as police were told he had been out of town on the night of the shootings. Police turned their attention elsewhere, and by the Monday after the Saturday morning murders, they had collared John "Donkey Ears" Wolek. He had been among companions of Mosinski and Switaj on a tavern tour in the night hours before they were killed.

Milwaukee Avenue runs southeast to northwest through the North Side of Chicago. Further northwest is the Chain-o'-Lakes region of what was then the still-rural expanses of outlying Cook County and adjoining Lake County. Some of the resort towns by these small lakes were hospitable to illegal slot machines. Mosinski and Switaj, informants told Cook County investigators, stole slot machines from these places, took them to Milwaukee Avenue saloons, and strong-armed the saloonkeepers to set them up. If so, this activity was unwise. Not even during the heyday of Al Capone in the 1920s had organized crime been able to install slot machines inside the city limits of Chicago. When it came to illegal gambling, this was just about the only shred of probity the city clutched to itself.

Gambling money was the wellspring of the political machine of Mayor Edward J. Kelly and Cook County Democratic chairman Patrick A. Nash. Operators of handbooks, the term for illegal off-track betting supervised by organized crime, made regular monthly payments to the Democratic ward committeemen. A fifty-fifty profit split between the operator and the politician was considered fair. A well-run handbook might give ward headquarters a thousand dollars a month, while a crumby little craps parlor might yield three hundred. This was not a matter of pockets of corruption: it was citywide and systemic. Just about anyone could place a bet just about anywhere, from newspaper city desks to corner taverns to the exclusive dining halls of businessmen's clubs. By tradition, Democratic committeemen chose the local police captains and the captains in turn took charge of collecting the payoffs. Vice on such a scale could not have thrived without the covert cooperation of the police department and the business establishment.

Supposedly, Mosinski and Switaj had been using Alderman "Big Joe Rusty" Rostenkowski's name in pushing their slot machines along Mil-

waukee Avenue. On collection days, a rakeoff was taken by two police detectives. When the police department heard this, it threw up the predictable defenses. Any such detectives were free-lancing and not part of any
allegedly endemic police corruption—grim expression of outraged innocence here—and the Cook County investigators agreed.

If the informants' account was true, Mosinski, Switaj, and their detectives were paragons of audacity. The detectives were crossing police brass
by horning in on the gambling dough. As for Rostenkowski's two ward
heelers, they were inviting vengeance from any of four parties: first, the
mob, from whom the slots were hijacked; second, the saloon owners, who
feared both mob reprisals and police raids; third, handbook operators,
whose income was undercut by the unsanctioned slots, and finally, Rostenkowski himself, if indeed they were falsely citing his name to push their
scheme. Furthermore, gambling interests had been trying for years to make
slots, or at least off-track betting, legal in Chicago and would not have appreciated any independent entrepreneurs.

Rostenkowski, by the way, was an advocate of legal off-track betting.
"Race betting is much like liquor," he explained. "The government can
handle it better by regulation than prohibition. Some of my people cannot
afford to go to the tracks, but like to bet a little on the ponies."[2] Mayor
Kelly favored legalization, too, figuring that legitimate gambling taxes
could bail out his nearly broke, Depression-era city. Rostenkowski always
was a loyal soldier of the Kelly organization and the notion that he would
strike out on his own, using Mosinski and Switaj to set up a personal gambling empire, seems unlikely.

Coincidentally, that same month, August 1938, saw the launching of
a spasm of gambling raids by the Cook County state's attorney, who had
his own police force. Though his credentials as a reformer were dubious,
if not downright phony, State's Attorney Thomas J. Courtney sent his
cops smashing into handbooks, axes swinging, to arrest attendants and patrons. Some places greeted ten raiding parties within two weeks. However,
the prosecutor absentmindedly neglected to obtain judicial warrants. The
number of raids was more than six hundred. The number of convictions
was zero. Courtney was grabbing headlines to run against Kelly in the 1939
mayoral primary (Courtney lost). The mob did not seem to take the raids
seriously, and they apparently were unrelated to the string of murders.

Two months before the killings outside Rostenkowski's house, a bomb was planted at a tavern in the Near Southwest Side controlled by Alderman Hugh B. "Babe" Connelly. The tavern's patrons, who included a young Richard J. Daley, spoke of it as "Babe's place." Connelly denied that he owned the tavern, though, and actual ownership of real estate can be a legally ambiguous question in Illinois to this day. Connelly represented the Eleventh Ward, a neighborhood called Bridgeport, home of the Daleys. An outsider, driving casually through the Near Northwest and Near Southwest sides then, would have trouble telling the locales apart. Small frame houses, brick bungalows, and two- and three-flats on narrow lots as far as the eye could see. But the difference was nothing short of the cultural split between two nations. The Eleventh Ward was mostly Irish, the Thirty-second, Polish. In time, these duchies would see rivalries and reconciliations between their respective royal families, the Daleys and the Rostenkowskis.

Mosinski, it seems, had been employed by Connelly in gambling quarters above the tavern. They quarreled, and Mosinski was fired. Maybe that attempted bombing back in June was construed by Connelly as a retaliation from Mosinski. Maybe that is the event that marked Mosinski and his pal, Switaj, for death. Maybe Connelly or mob higher-ups were behind their murders. In any case, the suspect, "Donkey Ears" Wolek, was released. Nobody was charged with the murders. The killers still are listed in files of the Chicago Crime Commission as "unknown." It is likewise for every gangland murder of 1938.

Summer turned to fall on the upper midwestern prairie, and the grayness of late November descended on Rostenkowski's Noble Street home. His wife, Percella (later Anglicized to "Priscilla"), owned the saloon on the ground floor, and the family lived on the third floor. One morning, the papers reported that a car had pulled up in the night and somebody fired five shots, smashing the windows of the tavern. An odd coincidence: Bullets also were fired that night into the real estate office of Rusty's Polish pal on the city council, Alderman Frank Konkowski Jr. of the Twenty-sixth Ward. Like Rusty, Konkowski lived over his place of business, a normal circumstance for Chicago politicians until the professionalization of the middle classes that followed World War II sent them into high-rise offices downtown.

The press said that two police detectives dug bullets out of the rear wall of Rostenkowski's tavern to compare them with those fired into Konkowski's place. Back to the Racine Avenue cop shop went Rusty. He asked police not to release details of the shooting to newspapers. That afternoon, he told reporters he didn't know of any shooting. "A number of holes" were in the windows, he allowed. "They might have been made by steel balls or stones from a slingshot. I haven't any idea what might have caused their being tossed." He said he had notified his insurance company but not the police. "The police declared they had no report on the incident," duly noted the evening editions of the *Chicago Daily News*.[3]

There you have it, a stereotypical episode from the legendary days of gangsterism in Chicago: two murders, a slot machine racket, a tavern bombing, lots of gunfire, and three aldermen—Rostenkowski, Connelly, Konkowski—all apparently connected somehow. "Donkey Ears" and "Cowboy," indeed, not to mention Ward Bosses and Corrupt Cops. The force of such stereotypes shakes the leaves on a thick branch of popular culture yet today.

History deals in facts, but many facts get lost under legends. The facts behind the Mosinski and Switaj murders have never emerged. The legend of Chicago's political criminality thrives. Perhaps the location of the victims' car outside his house was just a terribly unfortunate coincidence for Alderman Rostenkowski. Maybe Joe Rusty was unfairly tainted by his city's reputation for crookedness. Dan Rostenkowski, later in his own life, would have occasion to reflect on the extent of that reputation.

Chicago wears a collective smirk that masks a small, illicit pride in the city's reputation for melodramatic wickedness. Both the romance of the legend and the smirk that confronts it make it difficult for a researcher to separate the historical portrait from the popular cartoon. This is at least as true for an obscure politician such as "Big Joe Rusty" as for more locally famous politicians of those days such as "Bathhouse" John Coughlin, Michael "Hinky Dink" Kenna, or Mathias "Paddy" Bauler.

Bauler's career is worthy of a moment's review if only to illustrate the degree by which, in the history of Chicago politics, caricature overlaps reality. Paddy was the most cartoonish of all ward bosses because, for starters, he ran the Forty-third Ward out of his saloon as the last of the great saloonkeeper-aldermen and because he had the face of a red balloon and because he once shot and wounded a policeman who was trying to get into an illegal party at his saloon at four o'clock in the morning. Paddy, despite his nickname, was not Irish but German, and he said the cop had called him a "big Dutch pig." Nothing much came of the shooting except that the cop got fired, even though he once was a bodyguard of Mayor Anton Cermak, who, incidentally, was assassinated. During the height of World War II food rationing, Bauler held an election rally and gave out as door prizes a wartime cornucopia of twelve canned hams, twenty-seven-dozen eggs, and thirty-five pounds of frankfurters. Two of his brothers had been aldermen, and another brother was a cop, and anyone else even distantly related somehow seemed to get city jobs. One of his bartenders was a city "ghost payroller" nominally in the employ of the city council License Committee, which was chaired by Joe Rostenkowski. Paddy's only child, Harry, became one of the closest friends of Dan Rostenkowski, who used to go to his house to hear Harry play the drums.

Good government types are known in Chicago parlance as goo goos, and the goo goos were trying to get rid of Paddy as late as the mid-1950s; when they failed, he made his immortal remark, "Chicago ain't ready for reform," which still is cited by out of towners writing about Chicago politics. Unrepentant even at the age of eighty-seven, he said, "I'll bet you one hundred bucks to any Goddamn thing you want that you will never see Chicago reformed until every son of a bitch in the town leaves the place"— a statement that, when you stop to think about it, is actually profound, even Augustinian, in its evaluation of human sinfulness.[4]

Paddy and Rusty were two ward bosses from decades now overlaid with Hollywood stereotypes and theme-park nostalgia, with "Capone's Chicago" a tourist attraction in the city, as if corruption and violence are somehow quaint. In truth, those were hard times lived by hard people. Conventioneers taking bus tours past gangster haunts might reflect that after the 1928 primary, the *New York Times* reported on its front page that "Chicago went to the polls today with sluggings, kidnappings and other forms of violence accompanied by the murderous rat-tat-tat of machine guns." So many bombs were thrown that day that it became known as the "Pineapple Primary." It was also the election in which a black candidate for Republican committeeman was chased in his car for a mile, curbed, and shot to death. In 1935, a state representative was shot to death in front of his wife, mother, and eight-year-old son on the doorstep of his home. In

1936, another state representative was killed by a shotgun blast while riding in his car. Hard times lived by hard people, and they produced a culture that developed Joe Rostenkowski's son, Danny.

In decades to come, when asked about the murders on Noble Street, Dan Rostenkowski would say that he scarcely remembered the day that two guys got shot in front of his house. He obviously disliked the question. He resented the stereotypes associated with his background. He never fully succeeded in shaking them off.

Peter Rostenkowski was born in Poland in 1868 and is believed to have emigrated to Chicago at the age of eighteen in 1886. A 1937 biographical dictionary of local Poles called him "a pioneer Chicagoan," but that is hyperbole. Dan Rostenkowski's grandfather was rather one man among the European masses who fell in waves upon American shores after the Civil War, when the Industrial Age hungered for labor and the pioneers' frontier had traveled far west of the Mississippi River. Chicago was forty-nine years old and already a city of consequence when Peter Rostenkowski arrived.

The story of immigration to America has been told often and well. The point here is merely to note the astonishing expansion of Polonia in Chicago. The city was chartered in 1837 with 4,006 souls. In the first election, two men with Polish surnames cast votes for mayor. The 1890 census counted fifty-three thousand Poles, but these figures are unreliable because Poland did not then exist as a country and many Poles were tallied as Austrians, Germans, or Russians. By 1930, after World War I had reinvented Poland, the count was more than four hundred thousand. It was the largest congregation of Poles anywhere except Warsaw. The removal of Poles to America usually is considered as just a facet of the story of a "nation of immigrants," but it was in itself a major migration.

And yet these multitudes, the four hundred thousand, were only 12 percent of the Chicago population of 3.4 million. Nearly two out of every three residents then were either foreign-born or second-generation "white ethnics." The liberal revolt against bossism has tended to dismiss the political genius required to govern a farrago of nationalities, to superintend something new under the sun: a polyglot democracy. True enough, violence and vice were ingredients of such politics.

Maybe something about the eternal flatlands and the wet, cold winters of the Great Lakes area reminded Poles of the plains of their homeland and drew them west from New York City. In any case, modern pietism toward Ellis Island, the Statue of Liberty, and the melting-pot ideal has tended to obscure the hardships that nineteenth-century immigrants endured. Chicago, for all its allure to immigrant Slavs and Celts, swiftly became a nucleus of nativism. Within two years of Peter Rostenkowski's arrival, there appeared a local magazine, *America: A Journal for Americans*, which during its brief heyday published anti-immigrant screeds remarkably similar to the "angry white male" literature of a century later. Doggerel entitled "I Wish I Was a Foreigner" and signed anonymously by "An American" used irony to utter long-familiar resentments. Two stanzas will suffice to convey the sentiment:

I wish I was a foreigner, I really, really do
A right down foreign foreigner, pure foreigner through and
    through
Because I find Americans, with all of native worth,
Don't stand one-half the chances here with men of foreign
    birth . . .
The Spaniard and Bohemian, the Russian and the Pole,
Are looking toward America with longings in the soul,
Because the politicians will receive with open arms,
And the goddess of our freedom bid them welcome to her
    charms.[5]

The fortitude required by immigrants to prevail against nativist resistance was surely exceptional, a fortitude underscored by the fact that a large proportion of immigrants eventually repatriated. The means by which Polonia succeeded in Chicago were self-guarding and not devoted to winning the approval of the host society. Lenin is reputed to have said that he saw power lying in the street and picked it up. In that vein, it might be said that American immigrants saw power residing in the ballot box and learned how to fill it.

Politics was not the first institution to protect Polonia, though. The first institution was the church. When the Poles started pouring in, both city hall and the Catholic archdiocese already were pretty much run by the Irish, with help from Germans, Scandinavians, and Anglos. The Poles from the start demanded their own parishes. Leaders of Polish Downtown formed a Society of St. Stanislaus as early as 1866. The next year, the society formally petitioned the local Irish bishop for a priest, and by 1869 a priest was serving a parish of 150 families in a small frame church of Saint Stanislaus Kostka at Noble and Bradley (now called Potomac) streets.

However, the bishop refused to dedicate the church until its property title was transferred from the St. Stanislaus Benevolent Society to the Catholic Bishop of Chicago, Corporation Sole. Under "corporation sole," all church property legally was owned personally by the bishop himself, who usually was Irish, which irked the Poles. "St. Stan's" was dedicated on 18 June 1871. Services were conducted in three languages—English, Polish, and German (many of the local Poles were German-speaking Kashubes). The Irish bishop appointed to St. Stan's a priest who was not Polish but Lithuanian. Displeased by this circumstance, six Poles beat the priest senseless, encouraging him to decamp to Pennsylvania. The bishop got the point and named a Polish priest to succeed him.

The importance of St. Stan's, the mother church of Polonia in general and the Rostenkowski family in particular, is supreme. Barely thirty years after its founding, it claimed to be the largest Catholic parish in the world, with forty thousand members. Alongside this astounding growth, the church midwifed the creation of the Polish Roman Catholic Union, a rampart of immigrant fraternity against nativist opposition. Also, the church sired St. Stanislaus College, later known as Weber High School, as well as a grammar school, attended by Rostenkowskis unto the fourth generation. Dan Rostenkowski, a first-rate raconteur, used to delight in telling reporters that his grandmother climbed the bell tower of old St. Stan's to look south and watch the Chicago Fire of 1871. (It was the original wooden church, not, as reporters tended to assume, the current stone basilica, begun in 1877.)

After the fire, the city rebuilt itself, inventing modern architecture during the process, within fifteen years. Chicago exploded from a half-million to a million inhabitants in a single decade, the 1880s. This is the Chicago of the big shoulders and brawling huskiness and roaring energy and other cliches that have entered American mythology. It was the Chicago that young Peter Rostenkowski encountered.

He set up a real estate and building and loan office in the heart of Polish Downtown, or *Stanislawowo* as the residents called it. There were concentrations of Poles elsewhere in Chicago, notably around the Union Stock Yard of the Near Southwest Side and the steel mills of the South Side, but Polish Downtown was the seat of Polonia in the same way that New York's Lower East Side was the seat of American Jewry. Both places nurtured legends of shared adversity and family solidarity. About three-fourths of a mile long and a half-mile wide, Polish Downtown was centered at the intersection of Division, Milwaukee, and Ashland avenues. Here, as in much of the rest of the city, goats kept in the backyard and privies kept under the raised sidewalks were commonplace. Saloonkeeping, insurance, and building and loans were favored routes away from the goats and privies and into the middle class. Peter Rostenkowski, with his younger brother, Albert, got involved with both the St. Joseph Building and Loan Association and the Polish Roman Catholic Union.

Building-and-loan associations provided mutual aid to immigrant clans denied by the host society. Coming from an Old Country where few peasants could own land, the immigrant saw home ownership as the fulfillment of the American promise. A building and loan association member would put aside a slice of his wages—twenty-five or fifty cents a week, maybe a dollar, out of an average unskilled weekly wage of eight dollars—for a number of years to build up a down payment on a home. When finally able to acquire a mortgage, he got a low-interest loan from the same association. Fraternal benefit societies such as the Polish Roman Catholic Union did the same and more, and the PRCU survives today, offering its members discount life insurance and home mortgages.

The front parlor of the house that Peter Rostenkowski built at Noble and Evergreen streets for a time housed a building and loan, where immigrants would drop by once a week, drop a quarter in a slot, and take home a receipt. Rostenkowski also was a director, then one of the first presidents, and later the treasurer of the PRCU. In his official PRCU portrait, he looks something like President William McKinley, standing soberly with starched collars and vest-pocket watch chain, round-faced with the portly self-satisfaction associated with that late-Victorian era. He prospered, married Katarzyny Giersch, and on 15 September 1892 their son Joseph was born in the house across from St. Stan's.

After the parish and the fraternal lodge, politics was the third route to community power. This was the route Joe Rostenkowski would take after the example set by his Uncle Albert. Albert, born in Poland in 1875, lived a block down the street from Peter and won election to the Illinois House of Representatives in 1912. A photograph in the state archives shows, not exactly a handsome, but a substantial-looking man on the threshold of middle age, with the slicked-down hair stylistic of that period, eyes set wide apart under dark brows, a strong, straight nose, and impressive jowls—a face remarkably resembling one in another official photo, down to the three-quarters left profile, that his nephew, Joseph, would submit when he won his own house seat eighteen years later. Albert Rostenkowski was a deputy tax collector and deputy tax assessor for Cook County. At that time, it was not considered bad form to hold local and state offices at once. Indeed, it multiplied one's access to job patronage. Generations bred in the prosperity and welfare statism that followed World War II might not appreciate the paramount importance of landing a job for immigrants before the Depression and for everybody during the Depression. Politics was a massive hiring hall.

Direct democracy was not a familiar idea to immigrant European peasants. The American electoral process, conducted in a foreign language, must have been mysterious to them. In the fatherland, affairs of state had been the distant business of courtiers, clerks, and armies. In *Stanislawowo*, a politician who was right at hand and who could provide a municipal job, offer to pay your rent during a personal emergency, bail a miscreant relative out of jail, gain another relative's admission to Cook County Hospital, get the curbs fixed and the alleys cleaned, and, again, provide a job—this was a formidable personage. To vote as instructed whenever election days rolled around must have seemed an eminently fair price for these services.

More than one historian has remarked that the ward boss was the linear descendant of the feudal lord in the Old Country. This quality helps explain the paradoxical importance of old family ties in a young city. When Joe Rostenkowski took his seat in the Illinois General Assembly, the Cook

County legislative roster already read like a political social register for a city too young to boast the real thing. There were seated the Italian, Roland Libonati; the Irishman, Thomas Keane; the Pole, Benjamin Adamowski—names that would be important in the later career of Dan Rostenkowski. After first-generation immigrant leaders created parish churches and mutual aid societies, second-generation leaders already had formed an establishment, a guild, a political club, with its own rites and dues. This in a city less than a century old.

The city ward boss was a respected and influential man, hardly the petty figure of derision painted by reformers from the Progressive Era until now. True, the press often scolded the bosses for their crookedness, but their constituents seldom read the English-language press, and anyway the ability to deliver jobs and favors was what mattered. This delivery service required long hours and hard work, personal rigors that developed keen insights into human nature. It did not require formal education.

Paddy and Rusty sometimes attended wakes together, as appearances at constituents' wakes were a hallowed duty of the ward boss. On one occasion, Rostenkowski took along his eight-year-old son, Danny, to pick up Bauler at his tavern at 343 West North Avenue for a joint visit to the wake of a local politician. Bauler refused to go. Asked why, the estimable Bauler explained: "I ain't going to his wake, because he ain't coming to mine."[6]

Just as Paddy Bauler was a caricature of the white-ethnic pol, Stanley H. Kunz was likewise, and his career was, if anything, even more lurid. He was not the first Polish alderman, but he was the first Chicago Pole in the state senate and later in Congress and perforce the first outstanding Polish political boss. The papers called him "Stanley the Slugger" and even "the terrible Pole." Not the least of his claims to our notice is that he provided a foil for Joe Rostenkowski's start in politics.

Kunz was born in 1864 in Pennsylvania—like the factory cities of the upper Midwest, the mines and mills of Pennsylvania attracted immigrant Polish labor. When Kunz was twenty-four, Polish Downtown sent him to the state house. Politics and horse racing consumed the rest of his life.

Photographs show a solemn-looking politician, with slicked-down hair parted near the exact top of his head, wearing pince-nez, a moustache, and a goatee. In later years, the goatee turned a dignified white and Kunz carried a cane. The somber photos are deceptive for Kunz was a brawler and a shouter who banged his cane on tables for emphasis. He became an alderman in 1891 and served as alderman or Democratic ward committeeman or both for most of the next thirty years.

The jobs of alderman and committeeman overlap but are not the same. The alderman handled complaints about city services and took care of the ward's official needs in the city council. The committeeman was a party leader, then elected by the precinct captains, later by voters in primary elections. He sat on the county's central committee and slated candidates for city council, the legislature, and the judiciary. These formal duties often were secondary to the committeeman's real power and function in society. The ward organization sponsored its own picnics, Fourth of July parades and fireworks, softball leagues, dinner-dances, and charity food pantries.

Under the system then in place, Polish Downtown was part of the Sixteenth Ward and each ward sent two aldermen to city hall. Kunz's counterpart alderman for a time was John F. Smulski, a Republican. This bipartisan arrangement was not unusual. Albert Rostenkowski was a Republican when he served in the house from 1913 through 1916 and again from 1923 through 1926 ("But he was a Republican!"[7] Dan Rostenkowki has said, with an air of headshaking at the curious ways of our ancestors). "Big Bill" Thompson, mayor during much of the Al Capone regency, was a Republican. Republicans, after all, dominated national politics from the Civil War to the Depression, and Chicago had an actual two-party system. The Republican appeal to urban immigrant communities was never significant, though, especially because the Catholic clergy tacitly aligned itself with the Democratic party.

In 1903, Smulski became the first Pole elected city attorney. He exposed fraudulent personal injury claims against the city and in the course of an otherwise dry, lawyerly report offered this lamentation: "One cannot avoid a feeling of intense disgust at the inattention and the seemingly willful neglect in the performance of public duty in this city. I wonder frequently if there is anyone in Chicago who really looks after its public affairs."[8] Similarly, after Congressman Kunz was acquitted of bribery in 1929, the prosecutor said, "I have come to the conclusion that it is useless to indict and try public officials in this city. It is a waste of the public money because it seems impossible to get convictions."[9]

An anthology of such lamentations by Chicago reformers probably could fill a small volume. The tradition goes back at least to 1872, when respectable citizens formed a Committee of Seventy, which broke up in fights and devolved into the Committee of Twenty-Five, which broke up in fights and then formed a Committee of One Hundred, which accomplished nothing.

In 1930, Boss Kunz was brought down by a stolen election. It was a heavily Democratic year, the first national elections since the stock market crash of 1929, in a heavily Democratic city. In ten wards along the North Branch of the Chicago River, the Republican candidate got a total of 3,727 votes to 53 for Kunz. Even in a city whose voting returns often were romantic, especially in the "river wards," this disparity was egregious. Kunz said the police department had sent machine guns into some precincts, but that not even this precaution had stayed Al Capone's henchmen from strong-arming election officials to switch ballots and tallies.

The winning candidate, Peter C. Granata, was chief clerk in the city attorney's office, and his brother, Kunz said, was Al Capone's secretary. Kunz demanded an investigation. During a congressional hearing on the disputed election, Kunz jumped to his feet and yelled, "You're a liar!" to Granata, prompting an uproar with congressmen shouting over one another, providing another instance of unsatisfactory congressional decorum. In 1932 the House of Representatives took the rare action of overturning an election, with a vote of 190 to 168 along party lines. Kunz was sworn back into office, but only nine months were left in the two-year term.

As for Granata, he was elected that fall to the state legislature, where he served for forty years, welcoming a young Dan Rostenkowski to the Chicago delegation in the 1950s. Granata remained a consistent legislative leader of the so-called West Side Bloc, the political arm of organized crime in Chicago, then dominated by Italians, who were among the last of the white ethnics to switch from the Republican to the Democratic party.

There were no more election wins for Kunz, whose career elided from squalor into pathos. In one of many legal proceedings, Mrs. Kunz testified that the couple's income was limited to sales of mineral water from their home. Impoverished or not, Kunz still was fighting for control of his ward, which he was losing to Joe Rostenkowski.

Polonja Amerykanska never achieved the broad political power of the Irish or attained the plane of bourgeois respectability reached by, say, the Germans. A review of Chicago's Polonia prepared for the 1937 city centennial, an exercise in filiopietism, included a subchapter headed "Our Youth Will Uphold Democratic Ideals," and presented this piquant apophasis: "They are not afflicted with any inferiority complex." [10] Unfortunately, an inferiority complex, to use an old-fashioned psychological term loosely, afflicted Polonia persistently. A Polish American scholar, in a study of political Polonia, judged Joe Rostenkowski to be "somewhat limited in intelligence and cunning, blunt, straightforward and emotional . . . not the man to appeal to respectable America" [11]—in other words, the natural heir of the embarrassing "Stanley the Slugger" Kunz and an impediment to assimilation.

Nationally, the Polish community worried the respectability problem endlessly. As early as 1881, a Polish American intellectual lamented, "From among so many Polish emigrants not only not a single powerful personality has risen, but the average level has not even reached that of the most downtrodden European people, the Irish. The problem is thus with how much dignity will the Poles wear on their heads the crown of American citizenship. Will they remain behind the Irish and be only voting cattle, will they eternally continue to break stones, dig in mines, chop wood, drive mules, etc., or will they stand on the same level as Germans, Frenchmen, Englishmen in the higher professions, in literature, commerce, politics and the arts?" [12] Nine decades later, in 1969, another Polish American intellectual observed that many Poles in America "changed their name. An inferiority complex was often found among them, as well as the loss of a sense of togetherness with the Polish ethnic group." [13] In that same year, still another scholar noted, "There was timidity and self-consciousness among the [college] students about their ethnic background. Their academic performance was generally above average, even superior, but in class they were the last to speak up. They identified themselves as Polish-Americans only after several weeks of classes and only in private." [14]

From the realm of popular culture, consider Stanley Kowalski, the protagonist in Tennessee Williams's 1947 play, *A Streetcar Named Desire*, objecting to being regarded as "some kind of ape." Or consider young Dan Rostenkowski, hoping for a minor leadership post early in his congressional career, fretting that his colleagues would have trouble pronouncing his "ridiculously long name." [15] One need not venture far into the murky depths of amateur psychobiography to speculate that Rostenkowski was tempted later to overcompensate for any such ethnocentric self-doubts.

The defensive communalism of Polish parishes and the preoccupation of Polish bosses with running their own wards, no matter their unsavory reputation in the civic mainstream, probably hindered the rise of Polonia into the bourgeoisie. Insisting on having their own priests and political bosses brought gains to Polonia, but there was a price to pay as well. Poles did not win cultural assimilation or political power commensurate with their numbers.

Maybe if Joe Rusty's rebellion against Stan Kunz had occurred forty years later, the press could not have resisted portraying it as a struggle of a Reform Democrat against a Regular Democrat, light versus darkness. As it was, the "reform Democrat" scarcely existed outside the precincts of academia, and the notion of "conflict of interest" troubled few brains. The Rostenkowski-Kunz fight was just a generational power struggle, a leadership squabble within one of the Irish machine's constituent groups.

The mechanics by which Rostenkowski pulled it off were not out of the ordinary. Kunz meant to bestow his committeeman's post on his son and claimed their joint bribery indictment had been a plot by their enemies to prevent it. There is no evidence that Rostenkowski was involved or even that any such scheme was afoot. Techniques of a higher level of finesse were at hand.

Chicago has a national reputation for ballot fraud, but the priority level of fraud, the connoisseur's fraud, so to speak, lies in the nominating petitions required to gain access to the ballot in the first place. Both the precinct workers who circulate the petitions and the petition signers, who by law must be registered voters, have opportunities to fake it. Each side then might legally challenge the other's petitions in an effort to knock the opposition off the ballot. In such contests, bet on the machine candidate. The run-of-the-mill character of Rostenkowski's fight for Thirty-second Ward committeeman is conveyed by a 17 March 1936 *Chicago Tribune* report:

Charges of intimidation by deputy sheriffs, threats of bombing, proffers of jobs and money yesterday enlivened the election commissioners' hearings of objections to the nominating petitions of ward committeeman candidates . . . Mrs. Margaret Gorgola, 1733 Blucher St., a Kunz worker, testified that a week ago Justin Antonovitch, deputy bailiff of the Municipal Court and Rostenkowski precinct worker, threatened to send her to jail or bomb her home unless she signed a false affidavit denying she had circulated Kunz petitions. Her husband, John, testified he had been offered a $150 job to persuade her to sign the affidavit.

Threats, bribes, subornation—a typical Chicago election.

Nothing came of this, of course, and to be fair, larger forces than back-alley politics were in play, and Rostenkowski had the wit to exploit them. Kunz traditionally was enemies with whoever was mayor, but Rostenkowski aligned himself with Mayor Kelly to gain the backing of the Kelly-Nash machine. This was a troublesome bargain, for while it placed Rostenkowski in power, it also reinforced the subordination of Polonia to the Irish hegemony.

Anyway, Joe Rostenkowski had the sense to take the side of the mayor of Chicago over the governor of Illinois. Governor Henry Horner had sinned against Chicago by vetoing the "Bookie Bill" to legalize handbooks. Meanwhile, the New Deal had created the Works Progress Administration, providing public jobs to unemployed men, and the possibility that ranks of WPA workers might be a political asset did not elude politicians. Rostenkowski professed shock that Kunz was enlisting WPA men on the governor's behalf. "Kunz, I am told," Rostenkowski harrumphed, "has been informing these unfortunates that failure to attend Horner meetings may be detrimental to their interests."[16] In exchange, Kunz accused Rostenkowski of the crime of consorting with Republicans. He said a deal was cut with Thirty-second Ward Republican committeeman Casimir Gorny and Gorny's clout, a Circuit Court judge, guaranteeing Gorny a clear field for reelection in return for GOP help for a slate of Democrats that included Rostenkowski. Kunz's defeat closed his public life; he died in 1946.

Three months after Alderman Rostenkowski's election as committeeman in 1936, Peter Rostenkowski died at the age of sixty-eight. Peter had become something of an elder statesman in Polonia, serving as treasurer of the Polish National Committee, which raised funds for relief for the Old Country in World War I and lobbied for that nation's liberation. The committee's leaders included Ignace J. Paderewski, the international star pianist. In 1916, Peter Rostenkowski was among a delegation of Polish irredentists who met with President Woodrow Wilson in Washington. World War I was epochal for Polonia, which foresaw the fulfillment of the dream of Polish nationhood after 146 years of partition. Poland won its independence with the Armistice and was established as a republic after another year of fighting with Russians. About ten thousand Poles from Chicago served under the American flag in the war, and another three thousand volunteers fought in France with the Polish Army, which the Polish National Committee helped organize. In 1926 Paderewski, who had become independent Poland's premier, returned to Chicago to award Peter Rostenkowski the *Polonia Restituta*, the new nation's highest civilian decoration.

The funeral procession for Piotra Rostenkowskiego included five hundred cars, and St. Stan's was "packed to the rafters," the Polish-language press reported. The officiating priest honored Rostenkowski for his lifelong credo, "In everything and always, I am a Pole." The priest added (in Polish), "Yes, it is true, we are Americans, but nobody deprives us of our Polishness." [17] The eulogist put in a pitch to maintain church services strictly in Polish, taking the losing side of a lengthy cultural battle with the Irish-led church hierarchy, which favored English.

Rostenkowski was buried at St. Adalbert's Cemetery next to his first wife, Katarzyny, who had died in 1916. Shortly after the ceremony, Joseph Rostenkowski went to Municipal (now called Midway) Airport for a flight to Philadelphia, where he was a delegate to the Democratic National Convention that first renominated President Franklin D. Roosevelt. In the 1930s, hardly anyone ever dashed to an airport to catch a plane for anywhere, and Rostenkowski's winged departure climaxing an epic-scale family funeral must have impressed his eight-year-old son, Danny.

Peter's death left Joe, Priscilla, the sixteen-year-old twins, Gladys and Marcella, and Danny living in the upper two floors over the tavern on Noble Street. Joe had married Priscilla Rose Dombrowski, the sister of a prominent doctor, in 1918. He had attended, of course, St. Stan's grammar school and high school and also took courses at Metropolitan Business College. It did not take him long after the war to set himself up in the insurance and real estate business.

The affinity of Chicago politicians for the insurance business can be simply explained. If local businesses bought their policies from a politician-broker, those businesses would encounter few problems with city fire, safety, and health inspectors and would find that their annual business licenses were easily renewed. So it came to pass that in the year 1967, Dan Rostenkowski set up his own insurance business. For many years, when filling out political questionnaires, he listed his occupation as "insurance."

Insurance was the pols' favored manner of making a living, enabling them to send their sons to law school to take part in the professionalization of the political class so that they could make their fortunes in turn by legally fixing property tax assessments. Into the 1990s, an examination of the *vitae* of members of the Cook County Democratic Central Committee would find it dominated by a few elders who still brokered insurance and real estate and by several middle-aged lawyer-politicians who specialized in assessment appeals.

Joe Rostenkowski served his apprenticeship in the insurance office and in Kunz's precincts until breaking with his patron to make his first run for office, a seat in the Illinois House of Representatives, which in the milieu of Chicago politics was small potatoes. The Legislative Voters' League, a goo goo group, rated him "an active man, well spoken of in his community, appears to be deserving." [18]

Rostenkowski took his seat in Springfield in January 1931 and two weeks later introduced a resolution asking public officials to commemorate each October 11 as the anniversary of the death of Casimir Pulaski, the Polish hero of the American Revolution. A second Rostenkowski resolution, honoring a former representative who had died, was offered in May. That was pretty much the totality of his legislative contribution. Rostenkowski's term was unremarkable except as a springboard for a job that counted, alderman.

When he sought his second aldermanic term in 1935, the Muncipal Voters' League, another aggregate of goo goos, assessed him as "timid about participating in council and committee discussions, but shows improvement over previous record." [19] This condescension carries the unmistakable sniff of nativists looking down their noses at immigrants, and perhaps it is no wonder that ethnic bosses such as Rostenkowski disdained to seek their approval. The *Chicago Daily News* showed a sharper understanding of Chicago politics, commenting that Rostenkowski "has taken little part in council activities, but businessmen in the ward report that he has been attentive to the needs of his district." Now that is what an alderman is for.[20]

It was the Depression. Even Al Capone, who among other personal attributes had a sense of public relations, set up a soup kitchen with a large sign over the doorway: "Free Soup, Coffee, and Doughnuts for the Unemployed."[21] For its part, the Thirty-second Ward Democratic organization steadily distributed baskets of food, coal, and clothing. A photograph survives showing Danny as a broad-faced boy in overalls, leaning on parcels of clothing as a stocky Rusty, looking jaunty in a white shirt, vest, and fedora, stands behind him. Several ward workers, similarly attired, stack boxes on the floor and a table to complete the scene.

At Christmas time, Danny would accompany his father as Big Joe delivered a ham or a duck with all the trimmings to the unemployed. Sometimes on the upper floors of two- and three-flats, they left a bushel basket stuffed with food outside a doorway, only to hear neighbors yelling, "No, not there! He has a job!" It was, Congressman Rostenkowski reflected much later, a "self-policing" welfare system.

During the Depression, the Thirty-second Ward office every now and then would transport foreign-born Poles to the federal building in the Loop for their citizenship tests. The test question "Who is the president of the United States?" sometimes elicited the answer, "Joseph Rostenkowski." This reply was not so ludicrous as it now might appear. At that time, the Democratic administration in Washington was remote, geographically and operationally, from the Chicago machine. The income tax applied only to the well-to-do; Social Security was just being set up, and there was no military draft, no federally supported home mortgages. It was Joe Rostenkowski who could bestow such beneficences as government provided. Not coincidentally, he then would get the newly endowed citizens registered to vote. Six decades later, a longtime neighbor remembered with fondness, "Old Joe, he was always for the boys." Asked to elaborate, he declined, saying the Rostenkowski family "has been hurt enough."[22]

Just as jobs and welfare were elements of the community power of the church and fraternal aid societies, they were the elements of urban political power. Indeed, the parishes and the lodges embodied the private-sector welfarism for which Republicans would express such nostalgia in the waning decades of the twentieth century. But they tended to forget that charity was a three-legged stool that included the government along with the church and fraternals. It was distasteful that the floor under the government leg included planks of corruption and even violence.

The organizations of Rostenkowski and others were sustained by the saloon vote. "Every saloonkeeper was the 'mayor' of his community," Dan Rostenkowski reminisced. "It was the natural meeting place of people to sit around and have a five-cent schooner of beer and talk about politics."[23] That was true enough, but saloons housed activities more serious than neighborly conversation. The saloons were not strangers to the criminal underworld. Still, Joseph Rostenkowski never faced serious public charges of personal corruption. The murders of Mosinski and Switaj passed without political consequence. A year later, an assistant state's attorney complained that a judge had released a burglary defendant as a favor to Rostenkowski, but the judge was transferred, and that was the end of it.

"He was a crude guy, just a product of the streets and the alleys," John J. Hoellen, who served in the city council with Rostenkowski in the 1940s and 1950s, and whose father had served with Rostenkowski in the 1930s, said of him.[24] Tom Drennan, a former city hall reporter who covered Rostenkowski, said, "He was of the old breed of Polish-American politicians. He was not held in very high regard by the powers that be . . . Joe was a great two-fisted drinker, a shot-and-a-beer guy."[25] These assessments should not overshadow the fact that Rostenkowski possessed the political skills to run a Chicago ward for twenty-four years while his base, the Poles, kept slipping away.

The Thirty-second Ward's demographics constantly shifted. Polish Downtown became known as Wicker Park as Poles leapfrogged northwest to the neighborhood of Avondale and even into adjacent suburbs. Rostenkowski represented about seventy thousand people who formed a virtual Little Europe of Poles, Ukrainians, Lithuanians, and Bohemians. He looked out for them. Charles A. Freeman, an alderman who later became a respected judge, said he could not remember Rostenkowski giving a single speech on the council floor. Rostenkowski's interests were the needs of his ward and his party.

He helped get a Milwaukee Avenue rapid transit line built. (It is now called the Blue Line and terminates at O'Hare Airport.) Every year, he pitched in to stage the "Night of Stars" gala, a citywide fund raiser for the Kelly-Nash Machine. He was a delegate to the 1940 Democratic National Convention in Chicago, which nominated FDR for a third term by virtue of machinations directed by Mayor Kelly.

Rostenkowski remained unconcerned with the protocols of bourgeois respectability. In 1947, he returned a *Chicago Sun* candidates' questionnaire, then as now a favorite newspaper device to pretend it is covering issues and not just personalities and scandals. Most of the questions and his responses are presented here:

> *Please state your views on:*
> *1. Housing and city planning.*
> "I am in favor of it."
> *2. Public schools, with reference to freedom from political control and interference.*
> "I am definitely in favor of having the school system free of any political interference or control."
> *3. Civil service and its application and extension to city employees.*
> "I am in favor of civil service and its extension to city employees."
> *4. Police Department, with reference to freedom from political control and interference.*
> "I am for that." [26]

While these answers have the rare political virtue of simple directness, they are hardly the kind of public policy formulations typically wrought to win editorial blessings. Perhaps Rostenkowski understood the rules of this game and refused to play. The press was not about to back him anyway. The *Sun* later merged with the *Times* and the *Sun-Times* listed him and Paddy Bauler as among "some of the council's worst specimens." A few years later, the *Sun-Times* rubbed it in even more, calling Rostenkowski "an undeviating member of the plunderbund which now controls the council." [27]

Concerning this "plunderbund," it should be noted again that city hall corruption was not a matter of a few bad apples; it was systemic and even something close to compulsory. Paul H. Douglas, a liberal intellectual who became one of the most important U.S. senators of the midcentury, served a stint in the city council from 1939 through 1942. "As alderman, I was introduced into a strange new world," he wrote in his memoirs. "Gambling was prevalent all over the city, and it was commonly known that City Hall, the ward organizations, and the police all shared in the payoffs." After describing similar graft in city departments and the public schools, Douglas considered his seatmates: "[F]ew of my new associates had ever gone to college. But in terms of innate intelligence most of them would have held their own with my colleagues on the Midway [the University of Chicago]. I liked them and believed them better persons than most of the well-educated and wealthy utility lawyers."[28]

Douglas quickly found that an honest man could not live on an alderman's pay. After office expenses, he wrote, "there was only $200 left from my monthly salary of $417." Requests from "churches and charitable organizations to support their benefits" took the rest and more, and "the last straw came when a solicitor for a church benefit demanded $50. I explained my problem, which did not impress her in the least. She repeated that she wanted the money, and if I didn't give it, the members of her church would be told and would act accordingly at the next election."

This episode merits some elaboration, for it illustrates the tacit complicity of reformers in corrupt power. Douglas made a public appeal for goo goos to "help me be an honest alderman," and "what frustrated many," he wrote, "was not just their failure to get the money, but that they, good, pious church people, were being given a lesson in ethics by a despised politician. My situation was not unique, for, talking to my [aldermanic] colleagues, I found that they gave many thousands of dollars a year to churches and charities. Evidently, the 'good' people of the community contributed to the moral downfall of the politicians as much as did the 'bad.' The 'bad' gave money to the politician; the 'good' took most of it away."[29] Such ethical ambiguity colored the career of a later chairman of the House Ways and Means Committee who donated handsomely to charities.

"Joe Rostenkowski never had any money. Joe gave away more money than he made," a longtime friend said.[30] In this light, stories of Joe's alleged crookedness carry a dimension beyond simple larceny, though the stories are dismal enough. When the time came for the local power company to renew its municipal franchise, thousand-dollar payoffs perfunctorily were handed to aldermen. Somehow Rostenkowski missed out. Having heard that his colleagues all got the thousand bucks, Rostenkowski shouted in "where's-mine?" outrage to everyone in the room. Even for aldermen, this was egregious behavior, and it became a joke among city hall insiders.

Whether Rostenkowski could have gone farther in politics is debatable. His pal Kelly suggested he run for Congress in 1942, but Rostenkowski instead put Thomas S. Gordon, nephew of the founder of the *Polish Daily News*, in the seat. In 1945, Rostenkowski stepped down as a candidate for the Cook County Board to help heal a rift in the Polish-American Democratic Organization. Occasionally, he was mentioned as a potential candidate for sheriff, city clerk, or circuit court clerk, but he never left the starting blocks.

During this period, Rostenkowski experienced a family tragedy. Priscilla Rose Rostenkowski died of cancer on 6 June 1949 at the age of fifty-one in the house her father-in-law had built. The funeral was held at St. Stanislaus Kostka, and she was buried at St. Adalbert.

Whatever his ambitions might have been, Rostenkowski's reputation outside his ward would have been a stumbling block to higher office. Former Alderman Hoellen recalled an incident involving Rostenkowski: "Of course, we didn't associate, but I got to know him. When his wife died, he was going out with a girl who was working for one of the [city council] committees. Her name was Polly, and he was supposedly giving Polly a ring. I was introducing a resolution to congratulate him on his engagement to Polly. And he almost blew a gasket. He didn't want anybody to know about it or hear about it or anything else. He convinced me that it was in poor taste, so I didn't do it." In fact, Rostenkowski never remarried, but his reputation for unsavoriness and secretiveness endured.

In 1955 Rostenkowski supported an Irishman, Richard J. Daley, against a Polish candidate for mayor. The Thirty-second Ward duly punished him by bouncing him from the city council, whereupon he landed a "ghost payroller" job with the city sewer department. As soon as Democrats won back the White House from Eisenhower Republicans in 1961, enabling federal patronage to flow anew, Rostenkowski was awarded the post of customs collector for the Port of Chicago. He was sponsored for the sinecure by a liberal hero of no less stature than Senator Douglas and appointed by a liberal demigod, President Kennedy. The separation between Reform Democrats and Regular Democrats may be less of a distance than is commonly supposed.

But this is getting ahead of the story. In the early 1940s, America was heading into another world war, and Joe Rusty was thinking about sending his son, Danny, off to military school.

Dan Rostenkowski, who like his father was called "Rusty"—the nickname "Rosty" was not affixed until midlife—was a big kid, something of a bully, the sort of guy who owns the bat and ball and always insists on pitching. "Joe sent Dan to military academy to get him out of the neighborhood," said former city hall reporter Drennan. "And out of the influence, you know, the problems of being a ward boss's son."

It was a tough, crowded, and grimy urban neighborhood, the Thirty-second Ward, and second-generation Poles worried about their children. Somewhat mockingly, the kids had started calling the heart of Polonia, the intersection of Milwaukee and Division, "dzia dzia's corner," grandfather's corner, because that was where the old folks hung out. Neighborhood toughs were turning away from Old Country traditions and toward the vice that flourished under the Kelly regime.

Even before he was old enough to shave, Danny was learning the rites and techniques of machine politics and saloon society. Sometimes the Rostenkowsi tavern would feature barbershop harmony singers, and the boy could hear them in the family residence upstairs. Down to the ground floor he would go, mingling with the older folks, charming them with his physical poise and big grin. He was tall for his age, with large hands and feet even in proportion to his size, hands made for an athlete's grip and a politician's handshake. He was the leader of his gang, spearheading forays downtown to State Street, where a pal who worked as an usher in the massively ornate Chicago Theater would kick open a side door, letting the boys in to watch free first-run movies. As Rostenkowski grew older, that ordinary boyish mischief threatened to escalate into more troublesome transgressions. "Danny was a hard kid to handle. His father spoiled him," said a family friend.[31] There came a time when Rostenkowski, then one of the most powerful people in the country, wept at the unveiling of his portrait on Capitol Hill. "My parents always wondered if I would ever amount to anything," he said.[32]

The boy had just turned thirteen when Joe took him to Washington to witness the inauguration of President Roosevelt for a third term in 1941, the sequel to the Democratic convention in Chicago the previous summer. A visit to the national capital to accompany a major ceremony of state certified Big Joe as a big shot and Dan as a big shot's son. This was twenty years or more before television conferred on everyone the mass illusion that they are present at all important public occasions. The boy was profoundly impressed by the majesty of the inauguration, the pomp and circumstance, the flags and colors.

Roosevelt wore a top hat to the ceremony on the East Portico of the Capitol but took the oath of office bare-headed in the January cold. His inaugural address made no note of the fact that Europe and Asia already were at war, but the speech was redolent of a call to arms: "There are men who believe that democracy, as a form of government and a frame of life, is limited or measured by a kind of mystical and artificial fate; that, for some unexplained reason, tyranny and slavery have become the surging wave of the future—and that freedom is an ebbing tide. But we Americans know that this is not true."[33]

Then, just before the inaugural parade began on Pennsylvania Avenue, the armed forces put on what must have been for the time a stunning display of 235 airplanes in flight. Not a cloud smudged the azure sky as thirty-six B-17 Flying Fortresses overflew Lafayette Park, launching an aerial cavalcade of heavy bombers, medium bombers, and fighters from Langley Field in Virginia and two aircraft carriers offshore. For a nation officially at peace, it was quite a rattling of sabers, an efflorescence of militarism, which perhaps lodged in Congressman Rostenkowski's mind during the Vietnam War a quarter-century later. Back home, young Rostenkowski thought he might go to West Point. "Polish people are great for uniforms and parades," he observed.[34]

The elder Rostenkowski decided his son should go to military school "to do something for some discipline," Drennan said, "and not have him susceptible to the kind of temptations that you could imagine he could have."[35] In the fall of 1942 a cadet enrolled as Daniel David Rosten arrived at St. John's Military Academy in Delafield, a small town 25 miles west of Milwaukee, Wisconsin, a 120-mile drive from Chicago.

Lopping syllables off your ethnic surname to speed assimilation in America was a common practice. The city boy, born the day after New Year's in 1928, whose boyhood was spent on city streets in the Depression, found himself at a prep school in the boondocks in the company of sons of the privileged upper-middle class. He reveled in it. The fact that Joe could afford to ship Dan off to a prestigious boarding school proved that the Rostenkowskis had made it. Let the respectables rail against the "plunderbund." Dan "Rosten" would show them all.

St. John's had been founded in 1884 by an Episcopal priest, and its shield carried the motto *Labore, Ludere, Orare* (work hard, play hard, pray hard). Rosten checked into DeKoven Hall, newly remodeled after a 1940 fire, one of the limestone buildings resembling fortresses on the 150-acre campus. "I loved it there," Rostenkowski remembered. "It was one of the greatest things my father ever did for me. I wasn't the alderman's son anymore. I was on my own. I started even. It taught me responsibility and how to make my way on my own." [36]

We can imagine a rough-edged lad from Polish Downtown thrust into a pastoral Episcopalian redoubt and wonder at his agile escalade of its class walls. The primary explanation surely lies in Rostenkowski's possession of an immense store of the highest currency of popularity among young males: athletic prowess. Power for social cohesiveness, for smashing class and even racial walls, is exerted by sports teams with their shared sacrifices and goals.

At the same time, Dan was a gregarious, hail-fellow sort. A reputation gained later for ruthlessness notwithstanding, he always was quite the sentimental fellow. A few were put off by his cockiness, but in the main, people liked him, wanted to be around him.

A third trait, which he shared with Big Joe, is one that has always characterized leaders in Western culture—extraordinary personal energy. Dan Rosten was constantly in motion. He was the guy to see to get a dance or a banquet organized, to lead cadets through a parade drill, to compile the senior class's mock "will" of bequests. He talked fast. He combed his hair fast. He did everything fast.

Rosten's high school career was academically undistinguished but a spectacular success in athletics and leadership. The handsome, six-foot-two, 180-pound boy starred in football, basketball, baseball, and track. He was chosen captain of "A" Company. One of seven cadet companies, it comprised many of the school's top athletes. "In athletics, 'A' Company men were the saviours of the academy," the *Trumpeter*, the 1946 cadet yearbook, recorded. "What would the football team do without the sturdy linebacking of Bender, the loose-limbed grace of Palmer and the pass-catching ability of Rosten?"

As captain, Rosten was entitled to wear three chevrons on his gray uniform sleeves. He liked uniforms, drill, and discipline. Throughout his life, he was fastidious about his clothes (yet another trait he shared with Richard J. Daley). Young Captain Rosten commanded cadet ranks of a lieutenant, first sergeant, five staff sergeants, five sergeants, nine privates first class and thirty-one new cadet privates. Although the company did not win drill competitions—"pitiful looks of despondency covered the men's faces when the parade was over and they had lost," if the yearbook can be believed—Rosten was a popular leader. He was elected president of the school's Officers Club.

St. John's promoted its cadet corps as self-governing, with student officers responsible for much of the day-to-day campus life, and in an all-boys school, the jocks pretty much run the place anyway. Rosten was not a young politico but rather the personification of the Big Man on Campus. "He wasn't political back then. None of us were," a classmate recalled at the fiftieth reunion of the class of 1946. Rosten's stature as a BMOC endowed him with a sense of command and privilege that would guide the rest of his career, suppressing whatever "inferiority complex" he might harbor as a "Polack."

At St. John's, the privileged athletes had an informal "Swagger Stick Club" of jocks who acted in the school plays (they were recruited by the drama coach). They also had their own formal organization, the "S Club." They were allowed to wear their S sweaters instead of the uniform of the day at special events—basketball games or weekly on-campus movies. "Special privileges are accorded members of the 'S' Club and those rightfully so," to quote the yearbook once again. In his adult years, Rostenkowski never regarded the ceremonies and perquisites of elite clubs as anything other than his rightful due, including the club known as the House

Ways and Means Committee. And he always felt at home in all-male settings—the environment of testosterone, the milieu of booming laughter and good-natured insults, the grown-up version of the boys' club in the treehouse.

Asked to cite his pet peeve, senior cadet Captain Rosten wrote, "People who don't stand when the national anthem is played at parade." If a student of the Vietnam era wrote such a thing, it would be suspected of irony or sarcasm, but there is no reason to think Rosten was anything other than sincere. Student leadership in the wartime 1940s meant an unquestioning acceptance of authority and its attendant rites. He thrived at St. John's, in part because he was as respectful of authority there as he was in later life. In Congress as in St. John's, and as in Catholic St. Stan's, there was a chain of command and elaborate, formal and informal systems of symbolic deference. Members of his generation, not at all sure that World War II would end before they got out of school, believing they would be called to wear the uniform and likely placed in harm's way, accepted this as their duty. They believed in the received hierarchy.

In fact, the war did end just before the fall semester of Rosten's senior year, which he breezed through as the school's top jock. In football, the team was undefeated, with five wins and two ties. In basketball, Rosten played center and usually was the team's top scorer, as it compiled a record of eight wins and three losses. In baseball, the Lancers were the Midwest Conference champs, with a fifteen-and-three record. "The 'Keystone' [second base] was covered by Dan (Duper) Rosten," the *Trumpeter* recorded. "'Duper' was the big noise of the infield and a demon on the short grounders. Dan was also a powerful hitter with a .346 average and two homers." Rosten also found time for track, competing in the discus and shot put. He won a total of three varsity letters in baseball, two in basketball, two in track, and one in football.

Small wonder, then, that in senior mock elections Rosten was voted the "best athlete," "best all around fellow," and "most popular captain," although he placed only third in the balloting for "most popular cadet." That tertiary standing perhaps is explained by another designation, his position as runner-up for the title of "most conceited cadet." The arrogance of the ward boss's son did not abandon him at St. John's.

He was graduated with a class of 106 seniors on 13 June 1946. Many of his classmates were headed for Northwestern University in Evanston, Illinois, or the University of Wisconsin in Madison, or the University of Michigan in Ann Arbor—campuses that symbolized the Midwest, its hard-headed pragmatism and its open-handed cheer. Rostenkowski had considered applying for West Point. With his father's connections, he easily could have won a congressional appointment. Instead, the young graduate decided to enlist in the United States Army.

A HOUSE FOR ALL PEOPLES

Most people figure that all politicians are crooks. The truth
of the matter is that the people are crooks themselves. A
workman is stealing tools, hammer, nails; an office girl is
taking pencils, fountain pens, paper clips home . . . the honest
bankers who will take your eye teeth out, the real estate men,
the union agents. You name them.

—former Illinois legislator James C. Kirie, quoted in Rakove,
We Don't Want Nobody Nobody Sent

CHRISTMAS of 1946 found eighteen-year-old Private Dan
Rosten in cold Korea with the Seventh Infantry Division. Its
job was to patrol the thirty-eighth parallel of latitude. At the
time, it was just a line on a map. Nobody foresaw it as the
battleline of the Korean War of 1950–1953.

Despite the cold, Rosten had a warm job. Assigned to the kitchen on
the night shift, he baked bread in batches of forty loaves. It must have been
tedious, unwelcome work for a prince of St. John's by way of the Thirty-
second Ward. Further, for a boy of the prairies, the dreary mountains of
South Korea, denuded of forests, must have seemed alienating.

Later, he was transferred to Kangming, near the beaches on the Japanese Sea. Baker Rosten, still working nights, whiled away the afternoons
swimming or playing baseball. Some professional ballplayers, in army uniform because of the postwar draft, appreciated Rosten's talent and urged
him to try out for the big leagues when he got home. I'll do just that, "Dan
(Duper) Rosten" thought.

The fact that he was in Korea at all was the consequence of a kink in
America's acceptance of world leadership after World War II. Korea had
been largely an afterthought for Roosevelt, Churchill, and Stalin, carving
up the postwar world during their Big Three conferences. It was decided

that Russian and American troops would occupy Korea for the purpose of disarming and repatriating the Japanese, who had conquered the peninsula early in the century.

That line of latitude was intended merely to divide separate areas of responsibility for Americans and their Russian allies, nothing else. The American command, suffused with the can-do certitude derived from having just conquered half the world in the biggest war ever fought, estimated the job would take from eight to twelve weeks. Then, of course, there would be free elections, supervised by the newly formed United Nations. Three days after the war ended, the Seventh Division sailed to Korea to accept the surrender of Japanese soldiers south of the thirty-eighth parallel. The stipulated eight to twelve weeks notwithstanding, the division was still there a year later when Private Rosten joined it. In one of the first maneuvers of the Cold War, the Russians had denied the UN election commission access to North Korea.

Perplexed by the way the occupation was dragging out, an American commander observed, in an official history of the division published in 1948: "Korea, although a nation with four thousand years of civilization behind it, was backward, undeveloped, poverty stricken, and completely torn down as a result of forty years of Japanese occupation which almost completely stripped the country of its natural resources and individual initiative. The Korean people were quite anxious to learn, but they were not capable of absorbing Western culture in great amounts in a short period of time."[1]

A half-century later, those comments vibrate with the American capacity for self-delusion and disappointment in Asia. Koreans, like the Vietnamese later, had their own views about the value of "absorbing American culture," quickly or otherwise. However, if Rostenkowski ever applied any lessons he learned as a soldier in Korea to the Vietnam War, or to any other public policy issue, he never discussed it in public.

Rostenkowski's silence regarding his military service is odd, given the penchant of politicians of that era to preen over their military records, however undistinguished. A candidate's billboard would proclaim "veteran" in large block letters, especially if his opponent had not served. For Rostenkowski, his two army years apparently were a nonevent, aside from the discovery that grunt-level soldiering entailed more than flags and parades. One friend, close enough to exchange annual Christmas phone calls with Rostenkowski, was surprised to realize, when asked, that he didn't even know in which branch of the military Rostenkowski had served. Another close friend recalled, "We never dwelt on it. With Rosty it was just, 'We did our time.'"[2] We do our time, we fulfill our obligation—the same attitude Rostenkowski would take into federal prison in 1996.

In May 1948, Dan Rosten came home from Korea. Chroniclers of his career have assumed that Joe gleefully groomed his son for a life in politics and waited only for a suitable office to open for him. Rather, it seems that Joe and Priscilla envisioned Dan as a college graduate, a military officer, and then an entrant into one of the professions. Joe might have seen himself as one of the saloonkeeper-aldermen whose sons were cleansed of their ethnic grubbiness by virtue of having graduated from the Loyola or Northwestern University law schools. (The roster of any Chicago City Council of the last fifty years would offer examples of such typically American, filial ascent.) Perhaps Rostenkowski's reticence about his prepolitical years reflects his disappointment over having disappointed Joe and, while she lived, Priscilla.

In any case, after knocking around for a summer, Dan went to the University of Kansas on a basketball scholarship. The Kansas coach assigned him in practice to guard Clyde Lovelette, a six-foot-nine center who became a professional star in St. Louis and Boston. Dan was seven inches shorter than Lovelette but scrappy and aggressive enough to hold him to a measly seven points that day.[3] Afterward, he was bruised and sore, feeling as battered as after football games at St. John's, where he played both offensive end and defensive back. Congressman Rostenkowski once indulged this reverie of the St. John's gridiron: "There is nothing quite like the awful quiet which seems to descend when you see the opposing back break away and you are the only man between him and the goal. You know the stands are roaring but you don't hear them. There's just you and he and no one else and that terrific silence."[4] (Rostenkowski has an unappreciated gift of eloquence.) But guarding Lovelette offered no such glory, no terrific silence. Plus, Rosten was indifferent to the academic pursuits of the university. After a few weeks he shook the dust of Lawrence, Kansas, off his gym shoes.

Back in Chicago and fumbling for a career—in contrast to the stereotype of the postwar Silent Generation, whose members plodded without question down the beaten paths of academia and the professions—Rosten pitched in with the 1948 gubernatorial campaign of Adlai E. Stevenson. Rosten's role was minimal, but this was an important election for both Illinois and the nation.

Cook County Democratic chairman Jacob M. Arvey, the son of Eastern European Jewish immigrants, held the odd precept that it was better to win with a reformer than to lose with a regular. He slated the liberal intellectuals Adlai Stevenson for governor and Paul Douglas, Joe's former colleague in the city council, for senator. Arvey was prescient enough to understand that Democrats needed to appeal to returning veterans who were just starting to flood into the suburbs in a deliberate renunciation of the crowded, corrupt city. When Joe was starting out, the Cook County suburbs had a population of 606,000. When Stevenson ran, the suburbs already were up to 885,000.

Fine, the machine said, we'll have two clean faces on the ticket, but we don't want that economics professor, Douglas, as governor. Arvey made a deal. If Stevenson would run for governor and Douglas would accept exile to Washington—who in the machine cared about the United States Senate?—both would have the party's support. After a characteristic period of solitary agonizing over his decision, Stevenson accepted. He campaigned against corruption in Springfield. It was he who coined the term *plunderbund* and also quoted the Scripture (Micah 6:8) later adopted by Daley in his mayoral campaigns, that if elected he would do justly, love mercy, and walk humbly with his God.

Stevenson accused Governor Dwight H. Green of tolerating illegal gambling and slot machines in Illinois. This was accurate, although Green had been the prosecutor who put Al Capone in jail on income tax charges. Probably Douglas, if anyone did, appreciated the ethical ironies. Stevenson won by a record 527,067 votes, enabling President Truman to carry Illinois by 33,612 votes on his way to his monumentally surprising reelection.

Joe and Dan did their part. The Thirty-second Ward carried for Stevenson and Douglas with 79 percent of the vote for each and for Truman with 76 percent.

Dan cared less about the election than he did about baseball. In the spring of 1949 Chicago White Sox scouts took a look at the aspiring second baseman but took a pass. Using contacts he had made playing army ball in Kangming, Dan won a tryout with Connie Mack's Philadelphia Athletics. He was with the team's farm club at its Sarasota, Florida, training camp when Joe called.

He told his son, "Look, you've been away from home for six years. Your mother is sick. You're not going to be a Lou Gehrig or a Babe Ruth. Come home and go back to school. "Go back to school. An overbearing father, a dying mother, an unrealized dream of playing major league baseball—surely the conflicting claims of self and family tore at the heart of young Rosten. He always maintained that Joe did him a favor. Swinging a phantom bat, he would say, "He was right. I wasn't going to be a baseball star. I was a late swinger." [5]

Priscilla died later that spring. In the way of many Eastern European couples, she had been a quiet and gentle antipode to Joe's loudmouth swagger. Also in the way of traditional wives, her feminine modesty masked a backbone of steel. She was a sharp card player who knew how to manage an urban saloon. At the same time, personifying another feminine virtue of the times, she was a first-rate cook. Her pineapple French toast was acclaimed throughout the Northwest Side. She even had something of a public life, to the extent countenanced by those times. Like Joe, she belonged to the Polish Roman Catholic Union and the Polish National Alliance, and the mayor named her to the Committee on Veterans Centers. She was only fifty-one when she died. Joe was fifty-six. The twin daughters, professional dancers, were twenty-seven. Dan was twenty-one.

Priscilla had been adamant that she didn't want her boy going into politics. She knew how its demands had kept Joe away from the family. Likewise, Joe had a program for his son: Go back to school. Dutifully, Dan signed up for night classes at Loyola. Living at home, he also continued hanging out with his buddies.

In January 1950, Joe got Dan a job as an "investigator" with the office of the corporation counsel, which is what Chicago calls its city attorney. Traditionally, this was a no-show, "ghost payroller" patronage job. Investigator Rostenkowski might have become acquainted in the early 1950s with Harold Washington, who also had obtained a corporation counsel's investigator job because his father was a machine loyalist. Washington would drop by the office every two weeks to pick up his paycheck, then once a month to pick up two checks, and then, when even that became too burdensome, he asked to have the checks mailed to him.[6] In 1983, Washington, a child of the machine, became the first black mayor of Chicago by running on an antimachine platform. Paul Douglas, alas, was dead and not around to appreciate the irony.

In September 1950, a former acting police chief of Chicago was murdered while federal protection was being arranged prior to his testimony before a U.S. Senate investigating committee. Within forty-eight hours, a lawyer who had been gathering evidence for the Republican candidate for Cook County sheriff also was murdered. Democrats took a beating in the November elections, but municipal elections were not at stake, and Joe won his customary reelection to the city council the following spring.

Meanwhile, Dan was taking night-school courses in economics, history, and political science, presumptive preparation for a political career. On the side, he pursued a real estate license at Pearson Real Estate School.

He also was something, by unsophisticated midwestern standards, of a boulevardier. On a blind date, he met a slim, attractive blond with laughter in her bearing, LaVerne Pirkins. He took her to a downtown restaurant called "Barney's." Her blond hair complemented a purple dress, and purple was Dan's favorite color. When the check came, he turned to a pal and exclaimed, "Hey, I just wanted to date this girl, not buy her!"[7]

But he "bought" her after all. The couple was married on 12 May 1951. Dan's best man was Robert J. Sulski, a young lawyer and Korean veteran who became an alderman, judge, and son-in-law of Congressman Gordon, who was put in office by Joe.

The Rostenkowski union produced four daughters and survived decades of stresses that sundered many political marriages of their era. LaVerne, like Priscilla, was modest, demure, and never swore. The proficiency of Joe's and Dan's cussing must have been a strain for her. She and Dan moved into a small bedroom, sharing the second floor of the home place at Noble and Evergreen with Joe. Their first child, Dawn, was born the next year.

In 1952, Dan ran for a seat in the Illinois house, restoring thereupon the "-kowski" to his name, lest voters be confused about his ethnicity. According to Laverne, "His father told him, 'Danny, you've got to make your move. There's a seat open. Now's the time.'"[8] By Dan's account, "My father told me he could get me onto the dance floor, but I would have to learn to dance on my own."[9] Still, by friends' accounts, Joe may well have wanted his son to finish college first.

In the primary election, John P. Touhy got 9,288 votes; Dan, 7,724; Bernard C. Prusinski, 6,457.5; a has-been, 1,673.5, and a little-known housewife, 598. The half-votes are accounted for by the complex, proportional representation system then in place. In the 4 November general election, Rostenkowski led the field with 14,271 votes. Two Republican candidates, although they had good Polish names ending in "-ski," won fewer than 14,000 votes combined.

At the St. Nicholas Hotel in Springfield, a tall young man in a cowboy hat stomped in, took a seat, and announced for all to hear, "I'm the Sombrero Kid!" After glowering in turn at several customers, he snarled to a man at the far end of his table, "Draw!"

The recipient of this challenge merely put his hands on the table. "Go ahead and draw," he calmly said. "But it'll be murder. My hands are on the table."[10]

A staredown commenced, and in the ensuing silent moments other customers, in a state somewhere between befuddlement and alarm, backed off from the scene. But it was all in fun. Rostenkowski, the "Sombrero Kid," and his house colleague and pal, Kenneth R. Wendt of Chicago's North Side, were playacting a scene from a Western movie they had just watched.

Rostenkowski, a big man full of physical energy, and Wendt, another big man who had played professional football with the old Chicago Cardinals and who was given to extravagant emotions and gestures, were an unofficial Springfield comedy act in those years. Rostenkowski was a witty sort, though not possessed of the verbal wit expressed in one-liners and sharp retorts. Rather, he was a general all-around kidder, always joshing and japing. Each New Year's Eve, he, Wendt, Representative George W. Dunne, and another buddy or two—a Polish-Irish clique, as it were—went over to Harry Bauler's basement. The guys would rib one another mercilessly. "Danny would get up and make a few words and people would howl and holler at him," Dunne recalled.[11]

In the 1950s the entire Cook County delegation took the train to

Springfield. The journeys became parties on wheels, especially after the sessions adjourned and Mayor Daley took the troops down for the annual Democratic Day at the state fair in August. Rostenkowski and Matthew Danaher, Daley's neighbor and closest friend (until he was indicted in 1974), entertained a trainload of pols and their families by singing Irish songs together. No wonder Rostenkowski was finding politics more fun than classes at Loyola.

After Rostenkowski was elected to the state senate in 1954, his new colleagues adopted a resolution in his "honor." It is presented here in full, not because it is especially interesting or amusing, but because it exemplifies the boys-club har-de-har that vivifies legislative bodies. Students of legislatures seldom write about it.

Senate Resolution No. 73

Whereas, In Anno Domini 1953, the title of youngest Senator was conferred upon the distinguished Senator from the 43rd Senatorial District—Albert Scott; and

Whereas, Senator Scott bore his diaper-adorned distinction with jaunty grace for a biennium; and

Whereas, As it must for all men, time went marching on, and as the Sessions of the Sixty-ninth General Assembly opened, a new contender for the title of Senatorius Juvenilius appeared in the person of a genial young man who respresents the 27th Senatorial District; and

Whereas, To date, no citizen, irate or otherwise, has suggested that Junior Rostenkowski be obliged to prove compliance with Section 3 of Article IV of the [Illinois] Constitution which provides that "no person shall be a senator who shall not have attained the age of twenty-five years"; nor has anyone questioned Junior's right to vote; and

Whereas, The age of Senator Rostenkowski, as of that of the female sex in general, is a military secret, but with characteristic philosophy and with full appreciation of Father Time, Senator Scott is ready, willing and able to yield up his title to the youthful contender; and

Whereas, Senator Scott has in his possession "The Barefoot

Boy With Cheek," emblematic of the title of Senatorius Juvenilius, which in free-style translation means "Baby Senator"; therefore be it

Resolved, By the Senate of the Sixty-ninth General Assembly
of the State of Illinois, that the title of Senatorius Juvenilius, or
"Baby Senator" is hereby conferred upon Senator Daniel D. Rostenkowski, together with all accoutrements, paraphernalia, rights,
titles, appurtances, duties and immunities thereunto appertaining;
and be it further

Resolved, That a copy of this preamble and resolution be
spread upon the pages of the Journal of the Senate; and that a suitable copy thereof be furnished to Senator Rostenkowski as evidence of his title and authority.[12]

This resolution was introduced by Senator Roland V. Libonati of Chicago. A card, that Libonati. He was a leader of the West Side Bloc, organized crime's delegation in Springfield.

Coincident with such "barefoot boy with cheek" tomfoolery was the
ceremonial and ritualistic face of the legislature. This was the program for
7 January 1953, Rostenkowski's first day as a lawmaker: The Illinois secretary of state called the house to order. A local divine offered a prayer. The
secretary of state designated a provisional clerk, who called the roll. A committee was deputized to call on an Illinois Supreme Court justice and ask
him to administer the oath of office to house members. The members were
sworn in. The house elected a temporary Speaker, with the Republican
nominee winning, 86–66. The secretary of state appointed a committee of
seven to escort the temporary Speaker-elect to the chair. He was sworn into
office. The house adopted a resolution agreeing to meet with the senate to
perform their constitutional duty of canvassing the election returns for
statewide officers. The house elected a temporary chief clerk, doorkeeper,
and postmistress. The house created a committee on credentials to review
the certificates of election of its members. The house elected a permanent
Speaker, with the identical 86–66 result. A committee was formed to escort the Speaker-elect to the chair. He was sworn into office. The temporary chief clerk, doorkeeper, and postmistress were elected as permanent officers. The committee on credentials offered its report, which was

adopted. The house directed the clerk to notify the senate that the house was duly organized. The house named a committee to "wait upon the governor" and advise him that the house was "ready to receive any communications which he may have to present." The Speaker was directed to appoint a Rules Committee. The house adopted temporary rules. The house ordered the Committee on Contingent Expenses to provide all members with copies of the Illinois Revised Statutes. The house authorized the Speaker to appoint a Standing Committee of Correspondents to supervise the press gallery. The house created a Committee on Elections to resolve contested elections for house seats. The senate sent over a message that it, too, was duly organized and ready for business. The committee to wait upon the governor reported that the governor had expressed his thanks and stated that he would deliver his remarks in person.[13]

And then, and only then, after a couple of hours of this saraband, the house and senate convened in joint session to hear the governor speak, whereupon a joint senate-house committee was appointed to wait upon the governor, and so forth and so on. The press and academia normally dismiss these rituals as superfluous or even ludicrous—the very idea of politicos putting on airs, assuming the pompous trappings of a House of Lords.

Just as analysts of legislatures tend to disregard the members' kidding around, they tend to disregard the stagecraft and ceremony. The persiflage is deemed too informal to matter, just gossip-page stuff, while the protocol is deemed too formal to matter, just civics-textbook stuff. The real dynamics of legislatures must lie elsewhere.

In reality, both the informal and the formal dimensions of legislating contribute substantively to the legislative product. On the formal side, ceremony and ritual make up an essential cement for any culture. All great legislators develop an inordinate love for the institution they serve and a fierce jealousy for its prerogatives and customs. This is true for Speakers of the House and presidents of the senate on the state and federal levels alike. U.S. House Speaker Sam Rayburn once scolded President-elect Kennedy so severely for presuming to interfere with the makeup of a certain House committee that Kennedy could only clear his throat and change the subject.

Dan Rostenkowski, who became a superb legislator, was adept at both dimensions, the formal and the informal. His informal, just-between-us-guys side is well known, but he was a practitioner of the formal as well. His tenure as the U.S. House Ways and Means chairman would demonstrate that he knew better than to disdain formal procedures as mere rigmarole. He insisted on observing the niceties of holding hearings even though the hearings were supererogatory to the actual cutting of deals. Ordained legislative procedures are not, as often thought, an aesthetic overlay, a tuxedo clothing a mechanic. Rather, they are the mechanic's proper suit of clothes. He is conducting the public affairs of a free people. If the people want to tolerate corruption in government, that is their privilege.

In 1953, of course, legislative expertise lay far in Rostenkowski's future. He was sent to Springfield, a prairie town two hundred miles south of Chicago, to do the machine's bidding, and he did it. He was no legislative innovator, though he attached his name as a cosponsor on measures sought by the city. For instance, he offered legislation to relax the requirements for voting and to grant the franchise to eighteen-year-olds, a repeated machine ploy to expand its voter base to gain leverage against the downstate Republican machine. Downstate snorted and biennially buried the bill. Chicago also tried to allow the ill and disabled to vote by absentee ballot; Republicans said forget it.

At that time, the General Assembly met only in odd-numbered years and was rigged for downstate control. Since 1901, the state constitution had allowed Cook County but 37 percent of the legislative districts, even though Cook County by 1950 had 52 percent of the state population. This was a decade prior to the U.S. Supreme Court's one-person-one-vote ruling and decades before the hegemony of suburbia. The old bipolar legislative process was largely reactive and defensive. Chicago blocked downstate bills deemed injurious to it, and vice versa. Now and then the mayor of Chicago and the governor of the state would make a deal and something significant would get passed. Usually it was a tax increase.

Despite the Chicago-downstate struggle, Chicagoans felt at home in Springfield in the sense that the legislature provided an environment of corruption and attendant violence. In February 1952 Charles Gross, Republican committeeman of the Thirty-first Ward, which neighbored Rostenkowski's, was killed in a shotgun assassination. In June 1953, while the legislature was sitting, Representative Clem Graver of Chicago was abducted from a garage near his home and never seen again. In August 1953,

Theodore Roe, the last black holdout who insisted on running his own numbers racket, was murdered, permitting the final takeover of that racket by the First Ward and the West Side Bloc.

Less dramatically, the legislature notoriously was bought off by lobbies, in particular the racing and trucking industries. In 1964 state senator Paul Simon, later a U.S. senator and presidential hopeful, earned a "Benedict Arnold Award" from his Springfield colleagues because Simon published in *Harper's* magazine an account of the legislature's corruption by the racing industry and the West Side Bloc. "Cold cash passes directly from one hand to another," Simon wrote.[14]

Such was the General Assembly that Rostenkowski encountered as he hung out at the St. Nicholas Hotel, drinking with buddies such as Ken Wendt; Alan J. Dixon, later a U.S. senator; and a few reporters. Statehouse newsmen then were considered part of the "club" and were not paragons of what is known as adversary journalism; many, before the practice was exposed, even had simultaneous spots on the state payroll.

With St. Nick's full of Democrats, Republicans hung out at the Hotel Abraham Lincoln, named for their party's patron saint and apotheosized Illinoisan. This geographic partisan division of lodging and partying was less than stringent, though. There were bipartisan dinners and drinking sessions. Portraits of Lincoln and Stephen A. Douglas, Lincoln's Democratic opponent, flanked the House Speaker's rostrum in bipartisan veneration. The parties got together when it counted. Rostenkowski drew a legislative salary of five thousand dollars, enjoying a 67 percent pay raise enacted under a bipartisan deal by the previous legislature.

To review Rostenkowski's roll call votes is unproductive because he always voted with the machine. Democrats perennially offered a weak bill to foster nondiscrimination in employment; it died. Republicans tried to impose "court reform" to lessen the machine's control of the judiciary; Chicago killed it. A Republican effort to rewrite the Chicago city charter to break up what was called "the alliance between crime and politics" there was buried. Representative Anthony J. "Busy Busy" DeTolve, another of those First Ward guys with funny nicknames, sponsored a bill to ban broadcast coverage of proceedings in which a witness may be subpoenaed to testify—a reaction against the televised U.S. Senate organized crime hearings, which so embarrassed Chicago—and the senate shelved it after it passed the house. The Republican governor tried to create a state commission to investigate crime; it was torpedoed by Peter C. Granata, the one-time opponent of Stanley Kunz. The legislature was being asked to investigate everything except "how to take the smell out of limburger cheese and the hole out of the doughnut," one member griped.

The 1953 session ended on 27 June, the first time in twenty-four years it quit before the stipulated 30 June closure. The two chambers even banged the gavels and went home with some decorum, refraining from the customary final-night hijinks. The local paper reported in some wonderment that only a single firecracker had been set off beneath the seat of a single senator.[15] The stage was being set for collusion between the Republican governor and the Democratic mayor, which characterized Illinois politics for the rest of the 1950s.

After a single term, Rostenkowski wanted to move up to the senate. The machine dumped a fourteen-year incumbent to make way for him. In the April 1954 primary Rostenkowski ran unopposed. In the November general election he won 83 percent of the vote.

The 1955 legislative session met for less than two months before Chicago had itself a new mayor and Joe and Danny had themselves a new Boss.

To attend St. Stanislaus Kostka Roman Catholic Church, the Rostenkowski family merely had to cross the street. For the Daley family, the stroll to the Nativity of Our Lord Roman Catholic Church was just a little farther. They would exit their home at Thirty-sixth Street and South Lowe Avenue, head down Lowe, and turn right at Thirty-seventh Street. Richard J. Daley would say his earliest memory was of being taken to that church by his mother, and he attended Sunday services there all his life. He was baptized there, married there, held funeral services for his parents there, and himself was buried from there. Every year, just before Easter, Daley's wife "Sis" joined the other neighborhood women in the traditional scrubbing of the church floors. Like St. Stan's, the Nativity of Our Lord was a large, stately building whose steeple towered over the small homes of the neighborhood. Like St. Stan's, it was the social center of a tough neighborhood peopled by European Catholics who were scorned by the native society. The parishes were founded just a year apart—St. Stan's in Polish Downtown in 1867, the Church of the Nativity in the Bridgeport neighborhood, about six miles south of St. Stan's, smack in the geographic center of Chicago, in 1868.

The Poles of St. Stan's and the Irish of Nativity parish would find cause to forge political alliances. But the Irish had priority in Chicago, in terms both of time and of power. The Irish trickled into Chicago as laborers building the Illinois and Michigan Canal starting in 1836, then poured into Chicago starting in 1845, the beginning of the Great Famine. Caused by a blight that turned Ireland's potatoes to slime, the famine killed 1 million Irish, out of a population of 8 million and sent another 1.5 million abroad. Poles did not start pouring into Chicago until after 1871, when Otto von Bismarck brutally "Germanized" his Polish provinces. The Poles arriving in Chicago found the Irish in charge of the Roman Catholic Archdiocese and taking charge of city government. Indeed, the Irish dominated the city's religious and political life for more than 125 years, even though they were outnumbered during much of that period—at least by official census counts, which are questionable[16]—by native-born Americans, German Americans, Scandinavian Americans, and Polish Americans.

Richard J. Daley, "last of the big-city bosses," came to personify the Irish politician in America—colorful; by reputation a supervisor of corruption; and by personality, unapologetically ethnic. The punchy, single-word titles of popular biographies of Daley convey something of his persona: *Boss. Clout. Legend. Requiem.*

Born 15 May 1902, Daley was ten years younger than Joe Rostenkowski and twenty-six years older than Dan Rostenkowski. Both Rostenkowskis would be important in his career, the father helping to install him in the mayor's office, the son helping to keep him there. Daley and Dan Rostenkowski both were the only sons of ethnic families—among Catholics of the time, small, single-son families were uncommon. Daley and Rostenkowski both understood the supreme value of the old neighborhood and of the Old Country as well. Both attended Catholic parishes that were clannish and promoted nationalism in their fatherlands. Both grew up in hard times on wicked streets.

Daley's Bridgeport grew out of a settlement of Irish who came to dig the canal and lived in shanties along the South Branch of the Chicago River. When the uptown society ventured there for groundbreaking ceremonies for the canal, amid much excitement and speechmaking, on the

Fourth of July 1836, the *Chicago American* reported: "The steamboat Chicago, on her way down, was assailed by a small corps of Irishmen, who stationing themselves at the stone quarry on the banks of the river, showered full volleys of stones amidst the thick crowd of ladies and gentlemen on the upper deck. Some fifty passengers leaped ashore, some with bludgeons, and the assailants were soon led, covered with blood and wounds, captive to the boat . . . though the capture of a dozen Irishmen is no great feat." The Irish sense of grievance against such nativist contempt festered deep into the next century, and it never exited Richard Daley's bones.

The canal, connecting Lake Michigan to the Illinois River and thence to the Mississippi, was born in 1835 when the legislature agreed to underwrite the construction bonds. Voting with the majority on the crucial 28–27 vote was a young state representative, Abraham Lincoln. Completed in 1848, the canal had a heyday of just six years—railroads were supplanting it by 1854. Yet those bonanza years were enough for Chicago to establish itself as the hub of the Midwest, surpassing St. Louis. Navvies who had excavated the canal next applied their strong backs in Bridgeport's new brickyards, breweries, meatpacking firms, and eventually a steel mill.

In 1865 the slaughtering and packing industry was concentrated in the Union Stock Yard just to the south of Bridgeport. These were the Chicago stockyards that entered national folklore, a 355-acre constellation of cattle pens. The stockyards were worked by the Irish (including, briefly, a young Richard Daley) and Germans, joined in turn by Italians, Poles, and Lithuanians. Each group set up its own residential enclave within sight and smell of the stockyards. Bridgeport stayed Irish.

The first Irish alderman was elected in 1846, forty-two years before the first Polish alderman. The Irish aptitude and appetite for politics has fascinated scholars and furnished a parlor of popular culture for many decades. This parlor is shelved with novels such as Edwin O'Connor's *The Last Hurrah* (1956) and decorated with mythology surrounding the Kennedys. The Irish political prowess has been so celebrated that their relatively tardy progress in socioeconomic status is frequently overlooked. A national Irish bourgeoisie did not emerge until after World War II.

For that matter, the Irish did not just step off the boat and walk up the street to take over every city hall in the country. They did not invent the political machine or hold an exclusive franchise on it. A generation or two was needed after the arrival of the Famine Irish for the Irish to dominate urban governments. Then they showed an undeniable flair for machine politics, and once they acquired power, they were good at keeping it. The Irish pioneered the way into politics for every non-Anglo ethnic migration.

The legendary importance of "blarney" aside, the Irish had at least two major advantages over other immigrant groups. First, except for some country folk who spoke only Gaelic, they knew the English language. Second, they had experience in the homeland with both democratic institutions and village-pub vigilantism. An Irish tradition of village-level self-government was constrained by an occupying foreign power, the English, much as American immigrant Irish found the government controlled by native Anglo Protestants. Irish immigrants and their sons might lack economic assets and education, but they found two escape routes from digging canals and living in shanties: politics and the rackets. In Chicago, these were pretty much the same thing.

As the Irish blazed this trail, nativist opposition grew fiercer. The *Chicago Tribune* thundered: "Who does not know that the most depraved, debased, worthless and irredeemable drunkards and sots which curse the community are Irish Catholics?"[17] The *Chicago Evening Post* editorialized: "Scratch a convict or a pauper and the chances are that you tickle the skin of an Irish Catholic, an Irish Catholic made a criminal or a pauper by the priest and the politician who have deceived him and kept him in ignorance, in a word, a savage, as he was born."[18] Just as the collected handwringings of frustrated Chicago reformers might fill a book, a compendium of nativist invective against the Irish would make a sizable anthology.

By 1870 there were forty thousand Irish in Chicago, roughly double the number of Poles at that time. The first Irish mayor, John Patrick Hopkins, was elected in 1893. Hopkins's tenure was typically Chicagoan. He set up a dummy gas company for the purpose of blackmailing utilities by threatening to compete with them. He then retired after one term in office, selling his fake corporation for more than $6 million. Meanwhile, there were so many Irish policemen that it became traditional for a mayor to name an Irish police superintendent. In Chicago as in New York and Boston, mayors recruited Irish cops in the belief that only they could control the Irish gangs. In less than half a century, the Irish, America's first great urban underclass, had achieved political prominence. Then, starting in

1933, the mayors of Chicago for forty-six straight years all were sons of Bridgeport. After an interval of black control in the 1980s, Bridgeport, in the person of Daley's son, Richard M. Daley, took the mayoralty back.

Corruption, violence, and bigotry were not strangers to Bridgeport any more than they were to Polish Downtown. The paramilitaristic Clan-na-Gael, a secret society sworn to promote Irish nationalism, included among its members Mayor Hopkins and ranking police and fire officers. Other Irish groups were little more than gangs of thieves and street fighters who learned to develop political muscle. A gang called "Ragen's Colts" preyed on Canaryville, the neighborhood housing the stockyards. Bridgeport was home to a somewhat more respectable youth group, the Hamburg Social and Athletic Club. It still exists, the oldest chartered organization in Illinois.

On a July Sunday in 1919, a fourteen-year-old black boy was swimming off the Twenty-fifth Street beach and floated south until he was off the Twenty-ninth Street beach. This was a fatal mistake, for he had crossed an invisible line separating the Negro beach from the white beach. Race riots lasted for four days. Twenty-three blacks and fifteen whites were killed, and a thousand homes were burned—the worst American race riots of the century. The enmity between Irish Americans and African Americans, an open sore since the Civil War draft riots in New York in 1863, forms one of the most gruesome chapters of the American experience. The chapter was still being written when Mayor Daley confronted protest demonstrations led by the Reverend Martin Luther King Jr. in the 1960s.

An official study of the 1919 Chicago riots concluded that 41 percent of the clashes occurred in and around Bridgeport. The study also declared that white athletic clubs such as Ragen's Colts and the Hamburg Club fomented much of the anarchy.

At the time, Hamburg Club member Richard Daley was seventeen years old, a fresh graduate of De La Salle Institute, a Christian Brothers high school. Daley never discussed his memories of the 1919 riots with interviewers, and it is not known whether he participated in them. In any event, Daley certainly had a hard-headed understanding of South Side Irish tribalism. In 1924 he became president of the Hamburg Club and served in that office for fifteen years.

As in Polish Downtown, the priest, the saloonkeeper, and the politician were key neighborhood figures, and all were committed to the Democratic party. The party's reliable stance was antinativist and antitemperance, and it provided a reliable hiring hall. In turn, the street gangs and the saloon vote supported the party. The important saloons included two on Thirty-seventh Street, Babe Connelly's—the same Connelly who had briefly employed Joe Rostenkowski's ward heeler, Leo "Cowboy" Mosinski—and Schaller's Pump. Daley eventually became a law partner of the founding Schaller's grandson. (Schaller's also was a hangout for Dan Rostenkowski once Daley had anointed him, in effect, as an honorary Celt.) One street over, on Thirty-eighth, was a third central Irish saloon, Sheehan's. Mayor Daley once told an aide that at Sheehan's, "everyone had to check his gun when he came in—the policemen and the hoods." [19] That's how tough the neighborhood was. It was patrolled and defended against ethnic incursions by the Hamburg Club.

About the time Daley became club president, he also was hired as the personal secretary to Eleventh Ward alderman and Democratic committeeman Joseph "Big Joe" McDonough, who stood just three inches over five feet and weighed three hundred pounds. The alderman liked the kid and made him a precinct captain and a city council clerk. Meanwhile, he attended night classes at the DePaul University Law School and, after nine years of plugging away, won his law degree in 1933.

The American vernacular includes the terms *lace-curtain Irish* and *shanty Irish*, but the lace-curtain Irish in the more well-to-do areas of the South Side regarded McDonough's crowd with an earthier epithet—as *pigshit Irish*. In much the same way that Joe Rusty was shrewd enough to ally himself with an Irish mayor while other Polish factions fought city hall, the "pigshit Irish" McDonough was shrewd enough to ally himself with a Bohemian mayor while the rest of the Irish clan tore itself up with political infighting.

The Bohemian, Anton "Pushcart Tony" Cermak, was an uneducated political genius. Finding common cause in all saloonkeepers' opposition to Prohibition, Cermak touted his organization as a "house for all peoples," assembling a coalition of Italians, Poles, Germans, Scandinavians, Jews, and Bohemians (Czechs), who outnumbered the Irish. First Cermak got himself elected Democratic party chairman, then his coalition overwhelmed the old Irish cadre in the 1931 mayoral election. This putsch enthroned the first truly multiethnic urban political machine. Daley inherited and refined it a quarter-century later.

As an overture to disaffected Irish at the 1932 Democratic National Convention, held in Chicago, Cermak favored the renomination of the Catholic candidate, Al Smith, of New York. On the third convention ballot, Franklin D. Roosevelt overcame Smith to win the nomination. Federal patronage did not flow Chicago's way after Roosevelt defeated President Herbert Hoover. Cermak was being punished for coming late to Roosevelt's support. Plainly, the mayor would have to eat some crow. He traveled to Miami to meet with the president-elect and plead for peace.

On 15 February 1933, seated in an open car with Roosevelt, Cermak was fatally shot by a gunman who apparently meant to kill Roosevelt instead. With the mayor's office vacant, Chicago's Irish succeeded in a swift counterputsch, installing Edward J. Kelly as mayor. Kelly kept together the ethnic jumble that Cermak had built, including "Big Joe" McDonough as an Irish stalwart and "Big Joe" Rostenkowski as a Polish stalwart. Facing the voters for the first time in the 1935 election, Kelly figured a large victory would persuade Roosevelt that he would need the Chicago machine to win reelection in 1936. Cermak had defeated his Republican mayoral opponent in 1931 by 194,000 votes, an impressive margin. The machine went throttle-to-the-firewall, and Kelly beat his Republican opponent in 1935 by 632,000 votes, an astounding margin.

FDR got the point. Bypassing his White House political apparatus, he put Kelly in charge of federal patronage in Chicago (a pattern that would be repeated thirty years later with President Lyndon B. Johnson and Mayor Richard J. Daley). Roosevelt's New Deal set up the Works Progress Administration in 1935. The WPA in time put 68,400 workers in Chicago, a machine bonanza. These were the WPA workers whom Governor Horner was trying to get his mitts on and who precipitated a campaign issue between Joe Rusty and Stanley Kunz.

Alderman Rostenkowski deployed his precinct captains for Kelly. The Thirty-second Ward carried for the mayor with 84 percent of the vote, better than Kelly's citywide average of 76 percent. As a thank-you gesture to Polonia, Kelly supported changing the name of Crawford Avenue to Pulaski Avenue. The renaming was resisted by avenue merchants, supposedly because of the expense of printing new stationery but more likely because businesses did not want a "foreign-sounding" street address (the actual name change to Pulaski required another nineteen years and a ruling by the Illinois Supreme Court). Kelly remained the political patron of Joe Rostenkowski and of Dick Daley through most of the 1930s and 1940s.

Daley's career, which was characterized by diligence more than brilliance, ascended steadily up the Democratic structure in Illinois, Cook County, and Chicago political offices. From 1937 through 1944, Daley served as Kelly's man in the General Assembly of Illinois—the same role that Dan Rostenkowski played for Daley in the 1950s.

In 1947 Daley replaced "Babe" Connelly as ward committeeman. That same year, the scandals of the Kelly administration became too much even for the Democratic Central Committee to put up with, and he was dumped in favor of a figurehead reformer, a Bridgeport businessman, Martin Kennelly. As usual, Paddy Bauler introduced an epithet that conveyed the regular organization's attitude. He called the mayor "Fartin' Martin." [20]

Daley's maneuvers to depose Kennelly in 1955 were calculated and methodical. Also, Daley was lucky. When it came time to choose a new Cook County Democratic chairman in 1953, Daley's selection was stalled by a clique of four South Side Irish pols. The leader of this faction was the chairman of the city council Finance Committee, who pretty much ran the city under the ineffective Kennelly. Opposition to Daley dissipated, though, when the finance chief was killed in an automobile accident. Once installed as party chairman on 21 July 1953, Daley could not be dislodged until he died, twenty-three years later.

In 1954 Kennelly blithely declared his candidacy for a third term. The party's nominee for mayor would be recommended by a slate-making committee that was named and stacked by Daley. Among the members were Joe Gill, a Daley supporter and his predecessor as chairman; William Dawson, the South Side black political boss and a fierce enemy of Kennelly; William J. "Botchy" Connors, Democratic leader of the Illinois senate and a Daley pal from their Springfield days; and Joseph Rostenkowski. Kennelly appeared before this committee, read a brief statement of candidacy, and then waited for questions. There were none. At length Gill said, "Thank you, Mr. Mayor," and the flustered Kennelly departed. Five days later Gill announced that the slating committee had "drafted" Daley to run; the choice was made official by the Central Committee, 49–1.

"They were interested in getting the right kind of candidate to knock out Kennelly," said Benjamin S. Adamowski, a Polish politician and another Daley pal from the state senate, although he became a Daley foe. "They had to have an Irish candidate," Adamowski explained. "If they had run anyone other than an Irish candidate, they would have raised the ethnic question. And you never raise the ethnic question in a primary."[21]

But why were they so eager to "knock out" Kennelly? The question is an embarrassing one for Daley's defenders, for the intuitive answer is that the carnivores of the machine wanted to feast without the restraints imposed by the do-gooder mayor. The conventional answer for many years, one promoted by Kennelly himself, was that his ouster was engineered by William Dawson for reasons of racial politics.

A one-legged, secretive, and profane man, Dawson was yet another Chicago politician, steeped in the culture of corruption, who would figure in the congressional career of Dan Rostenkowski. Through personal drive and discipline, he took control of six wards at a time when a black man was fortunate enough to control a precinct. "A church is highly organized, isn't it?" Dawson said. "So is a business. Why not politics?" In the early 1950s, when Daley was Cook County clerk, he would pause now and then on his way home from work to schmooze at "Dawson College," the Second Ward political headquarters on Indiana Avenue. Such an outreach was unthinkable to Kennelly, and it paid off for Daley—though the day would come when he would crush Dawson without remorse.

In 1950 the U.S. Senate Committee to Investigate Organized Crime in Interstate Commerce, the so-called Kefauver Committee, held hearings in Chicago as part of its national fact-finding tour. Revelations about crooked police and illegal gambling in the city embarrassed Kennelly. He had been trying to clean up gambling by sending cops from downtown to arrest policy wheel operators in the South Side black ghetto.

Blacks would place daily "policy" bets of a nickel, dime, or quarter on a "gig," a three-digit number that paid off if drawn from a canister called a "wheel." This numbers racket was controlled by Congressman Dawson. Like his counterpart Irish, Polish, and Italian committeemen, Dawson put in place the neighborhood police commanders who protected the gambling. Dawson personally appealed to Kennelly to call off the raids by his downtown cops, but Kennelly haughtily refused.

If the mayor's intention was to eliminate ghetto gambling, he failed. The South Side numbers racket was taken over by organized crime led by Italian Americans. Black gambling profits were removed from black hands and passed to the criminal overlords of the First Ward.

The First Ward, which encompassed the Loop, formed the political superstructure of organized crime in the city. This fact is not a matter of insider knowledge, chuckled over by political operatives, lawyers, and reporters sharing after-hours drinks. It was common knowledge, understood by Chicagoans in the same way they knew that the Cubs were the National League team and the White Sox the American League team. The mob's control of the First Ward, especially after its 1947 merger with the "Bloody Twentieth" Ward on the Near West Side, was part of the civic landscape, like Lake Michigan and Grant Park. When Jane M. Byrne, mayor from 1979 to 1983, came to write her memoirs, she cited the crime syndicate's domination of the First Ward as an all-but-casual observation, in the same manner as mentioning that the Tenth Ward was the home of the South Works steel mills.

Perhaps Kennelly did not even know his raids were abetting the white mob's acquisition of the black numbers racket. In any case, Dawson led a revolt against Kennelly's renomination in 1951. It fizzled, but to senior politicians, including Daley, Kennelly's second term obviously would be his last, and 1955 would see a new mayor.

The publicity generated by the Kefauver hearings—the first televised congressional investigation—and its political fallout foreshadowed the era of big media and big scandal, which eventually would destroy Dan Rostenkowski. One of the first byproducts of the crime-hearing scandals was the surprise victory of the Republican candidate for the U.S. Senate, Everett M. Dirksen, over the Senate Democratic majority leader, Scott W. Lucas, in 1950. Dirksen went on to become the powerful Senate Republican leader under President Johnson. In 1956 the fame won by Senator Estes Kefauver of Tennessee boosted him to the Democratic vice presidential nomination, despite Mayor Daley's efforts to put fellow Irishman John Kennedy on the ticket that year. The Kefauver hearings had pervasive consequences, but the defeat of Mayor Kennelly over the gambling issue was not among them.

Kennelly was unenlightened on racial issues. He quietly supported segregation in public housing, reversing Kelly's position, and nakedly tried to appeal to white voters by naming a "dark conspiracy" of Dawson and Daley together. The pitch was that Kennelly had angered Dawson by undercutting his rackets and power and that the black insurgent Dawson and the Irish challenger Daley, members of the same machine, perforce were in cahoots. To publicize the point, Kennelly stepped up his South Side gambling raids, much as State's Attorney Courtney had showboated his gambling raids in the mayoral race of 1939, with similar results.

Daley unseated Kennelly in the Democratic primary with a citywide plurality of 49 percent of the vote. Dawson carried his own wards for Daley with a stratospheric 87 percent. Historians have noted that the black vote accounted for three-fifths of Daley's winning margin, but the corollary, that whites provided two-fifths of it, is overlooked. The white machine had its reasons to turn against Kennelly, quite apart from the matter of South Side gambling.

Kennelly cared little for politics, leaving it to the "gray wolves" such as Joe Rostenkowski in the city council, but he did care about a goo goo issue, civil service reform. In his two terms, Kennelly slashed the number of city hall patronage jobs controlled by the machine from thirty thousand to eighteen thousand. This was intolerable enough, but Kennelly actually was intending to extend civil service protections to sanitation crews.[22]

Sanitation jobs were controlled by the Italian American bloc, a critical component of the machine. The protection of patronage, as much as the protection of ghetto gambling, was the thrust behind the fall of Kennelly and the rise of Daley. Patronage in exchange for votes was the lifeblood of the party. The Italian American First Ward nearly matched Dawson's voting output, carrying for Daley with 86 percent. Richard J. Daley, the paramount big-city mayor of the twentieth century, owed his ascension in part to organized crime figures striving to maintain their dispensation of garbage jobs. As mayor, Daley never moved to clean up the First Ward. (His son, Mayor Richard M. Daley, partially solved the public relations problem by redistricting the First Ward as the Forty-second Ward in 1992. No longer could the First Ward be cited as a metonymy for the crime syndicate.)

Adlai Stevenson endorsed Daley over Kennelly in 1955—Daley had served in Governor Stevenson's cabinet as state revenue director. Stevenson's embrace was a liberal-intellectual smooch of the machine similar to Senator Douglas's sponsorship of Joe Rostenkowski for customs collector. In the primary, candidate Adamowski carried four Polish wards, including Rostenkowski's Thirty-second, for a citywide total of 15 percent of the vote. But in the general election against the Republican nominee, Rostenkowski redeemed himself with the Irish, carrying his ward for Daley with 59 percent of the vote, better than Daley's citywide average of 55 percent. Thus coalesced Daley's odd amalgamation of Stevensonian liberals, blacks, and white ethnics including the Poles and Italians.

The perspicacious Paddy Bauler, on the same night that he made his celebrated "Chicago ain't ready for reform" remark, indicated that he understood the importance of Daley's victory. He named three Democratic big shots—Tom Keane, Jake Arvey, and Joe Gill—and scoffed that "they think they are gonna run things . . . They're gonna run nothing. They ain't found it out yet, but Daley's the dog with the big nuts now that we got him elected. You wait and see; that's how it's going to be," Bauler prophesied.[23] Sure enough, Daley was reelected five times before dying in office in 1976. His performance in office provided crucial lessons to a young Dan Rostenkowski.

The first lesson would have lodged in the persistence of the machine itself. Other than in Chicago, there hardly was an Irish-led urban working-class political machine standing. The ones in Boston, New York, Jersey City, San Francisco, and elsewhere had passed into history by the end of World War II if not before. But Chicago's working-class democracy was kept nailed together under Kelly, the policeman's son; Kennelly, the packinghouse worker's son; and Daley, the sheetmetal worker's son. Ethnocentricity was the heartbeat of this working-class machine. Dan Rostenkowski in 1955 might have observed that the Irish ran the city even though the Poles supposedly outnumbered them, that the Italians had taken over the Negro gambling racket and controlled the city sanitation department, and that Richard Daley was the Irishman who told the Poles, the Negroes, and the Italians when to go to lunch.

Daley's machine comprised a mosaic of European nationalities with little in common besides economic status, Roman Catholicism, and Anglophobia. Rostenkowski matured politically in a single-party system obsessed with ethnicity, social class, and political spoils, dominated by Irishmen. He also had a long practice in deferring to Irish mentors—Daley and U.S. House Speakers John W. McCormack, Thomas P. "Tip" O'Neill, and Thomas S. Foley—and even, back when Rostenkowski was an aspiring major leaguer, Philadelphia Athletics manager Connie Mack (Cornelius McGillicuddy).

Politics as wrought by the Irish was concerned with power and patronage more than ideology. In a famous 1963 book, *Beyond the Melting Pot*, coauthor Daniel P. Moynihan, an academic who later became a U.S. senator from New York, complained that the Irish did not know what to do with power once they got it because "they never thought of politics as an instrument of social change."[24] He meant that local Irish bosses thought about jobs and favors far more than they did about the programmatic liberal enthusiasms that animated intellectuals such as Moynihan. Daley, perhaps more than Moynihan, understood perfectly what the Great Society programs under President Johnson meant. They meant that he was given a lot more jobs and contracts to control, even if such control vitiated the ostensible social purposes of the "power-to-the-people" programs themselves.

A hallmark of the Daley machine was the handshake deal behind closed doors. Again, this was an Irish political penchant, nurtured through centuries of conniving to get around their English masters. As one old-time Boston Irish pol put it, "Never write when you can speak; never speak when you can nod."[25] Or as a hostile Daley biographer, Mike Royko, wrote, "The first lesson [in city hall] is always the same: never repeat what you see or hear, or somebody might get indicted."[26] Playing secretive insider politics was not an occasional tactic to advance an end but practically the game in itself. It was a game Rostenkowski perfected in writing the national tax reform law of 1986. But it was a game that provoked a beast, the media-driven culture of scandal. Daley and Rostenkowski alike, absorbed in playing the game, belatedly realized the rapacity of this beast prowling the sidelines.

One of Daley's first actions as mayor was to ram through the Illinois legislature a bill—supported of course by Senator Rostenkowski—stripping the city council of its power to prepare the annual budget and granting the mayor the power to veto specific items of spending bills. Far from a dull point of governmental mechanics, this was an act of audacity. In a free republic, the power to write the public budget is the essential political power—that is why the framers of the Constitution stipulated that revenue measures must originate in the House of Representatives, the chamber closer to the people than the Senate. That the budget is the critical allocation of power might seem to be a truism, but many politicians, liberal reformers in particular, are inexplicably slow in grasping it. The time came when Rostenkowski had to choose between taking the chairmanship of the Ways and Means Committee, which writes tax laws, or becoming House majority whip, a stepping-stone to the speakership he coveted. The fact that he took the Ways and Means chair telegraphs that he had studied under Daley.

Daley also might have impressed him with the importance of public works. This lesson had been learned by twenty-five-year-old state representative Abraham Lincoln, who switched his position to support public subvention of the Illinois and Michigan Canal. When Daley's turn came, he built nearly five hundred miles of expressways, developed O'Hare International Airport, laid subway and rapid transit lines, and erected a University of Illinois campus. Tangible, highly visible improvements to the face of the city carried almost no end of political benefits, except for an upward creep of property tax rates, the impact of which usually could be delayed and which tended to fall on property-owning Republicans anyway. Labor was happy with the construction jobs, capital was happy with the contracts and bond issues, and politicians were happy with the patronage and publicity. Everyone was happy. In an interview years after Daley's death, Rostenkowski remembered with glee the mayor's early years in office: "We completed the Eisenhower [Expressway]! We put lights up! We fixed curbs!" [27]

After decades of liberal vituperation, Daley's career is widely misunderstood. From the riots of the 1960s, he acquired a national reputation for conservative repression. Actually, he was a key leader of postwar liberalism, in the sense that liberalism is identified with the derisive, polemical term, *tax and spend.* Just as the liberal revolt against bossism has tended to overlook the remarkable political skills of the bosses, it has tended to disregard the machine as the cradle of the modern welfare state. The machine established the idea—for practical rather than ideological reasons, to be sure—of activist government, of government as an agent of economic assistance. This machine ethos was nationalized under Franklin Roosevelt. Since then the degree of support for welfare statism has varied, but the basic redistributionist concept, while frequently challenged and slowed, has not been reversed.

Daley's edifice of welfarism cemented both labor unions and Loop businesses to the pursuit of government dollars. Contrary to some conservative mythology, public revenues were not spent mainly on Democratic client groups such as blacks and the poor. They were spent to benefit the lords of the Loop and the Daley machine. The Loop business establishment—even, in time, the *Chicago Tribune*, a Republican mouthpiece—consistently backed Daley over his Republican challengers. The challengers would squawk, but to no effect. As Rostenkowski's career progressed, his financial support was similarly bipartisan, and toward the end his backing from Republican industrialists was little short of adulatory. Conservative Republicans viewed Rostenkowski, the machine Democrat, as indispensable.

Daley, supposedly a crude Irish throwback to the days of bossism, in reality modernized the office of Boss. He was the boss not just of a hodgepodge of ward organizations but of a blend of big government, big labor, and big business. Even the establishment punditry saw his as a forward-looking, business-oriented administration. For a 1963 article cutely headlined "Clouter with Conscience," Daley told *Time* magazine: "The old bosses were not interested in what was good for the public welfare. They were interested only in what was good for themselves . . . We're the first of the new bosses." [28] He took for granted that the provider of public welfare was big government as secretively manipulated by him. His identification of his person with his city acquired epic proportions. Surveying the desolation of the West Side ghetto after riots in 1968, he asked, "Why did they do this to me?" [29]

The persistence of urban ethnocultural politics, the focus on power and patronage at the expense of ideology, the brokerage of insider deals and the control of public budgets as the basic mechanisms of power, the provision of pubic works as the rewards of power, the mistaking of the needs of personal ego for the public welfare—all these were features of the Daley and Rostenkowski suzerainties. Faith in politics as the fount of money, jobs, and power was a heartfelt conviction for both men.

Likewise, it was a conviction of Speaker Tip O'Neill, like Daley a stereotypical Irish pol. "More than any other group I know of, the Irish in this country used the ballot box to improve their lives . . . It was the politicians who made the difference, who took their people out of the menial jobs and gave them better opportunities," O'Neill wrote in his memoirs.[30]

If this ethnic preening and faith in politics were well founded, then the Irish, with their unsurpassed political success, should have climbed quickly up the economic staircase. In reality, sociological studies show that it took several generations for the Irish to invade and occupy the American middle class. One school of thought even holds that, by doling out working-class public jobs, Irish bosses helped keep their people out of the entrepreneurial mainstream.

By contrast, two groups that deliberately shunned electoral politics, Japanese Americans and Chinese Americans, made swifter advances in economic status—even though the Irish had the advantages of white skin and the native tongue. Irish American economic advancement primarily occurred after, not during, the heyday of Irish American urban political machines.[31]

Such a phenomenon raises a question of the efficacy of politics and government as an agent of the economic advancement of an ethnic group. This is a question that apparently did not trouble Daley or his protégé, Rostenkowski. True believers, they pursued the politics of insider deals with fervor and certitude.

The pair also appeared untroubled by questions about the extent of crookedness in their machine. This indifference doubtless derived in no small part from the hauteur and insensitivity of the opponents of the machine. The hostility between "regulars" and "reformers" was not generated just by disagreements over government operations but by a cultural gulf as well. Reform causes normally were led by upper-income, well-educated people ignorant of the desires and fears of the immigrant working class. To quote Paddy Bauler once again, "Them new guys in black suits and white shirts and narrow ties, them Ivy League guys, them goo goos." Reformers tended to be well-to-do Protestants who presumed to know how Catholic laborers should behave: Catholics such as those who filled the pews at St. Stanislaus Kostka and the Nativity of Our Lord.[32]

Throughout his adult life, Daley attended mass every day, usually at St. Peter's Church on Madison Street near city all, sometimes at the Church of the Nativity. The puzzle of how a devout man could preside over corruption so pervasive has often been posed. Daley's defenders present him as a kind of one-man regulatory agency restraining the total amount of thievery, rather in the sense that the Immigration and Naturalization Service puts a crimp on illegal immigration but can't even think of stopping it. If Daley had such an attitude, its roots were in the Catholic services and grammar school classrooms of his youth.

The 1960 election of Kennedy as the first Catholic president supposedly liquidated the Protestant-Catholic division as a political issue, and since then it has been considered rather bad form even to inquire into a politician's "religious affiliation," as Kennedy phrased it. A kind of prudery has descended on journalistic and academic discussion of individual faith. In a secular and pluralistic climate, an effort is needed to appreciate not only how seriously previous generations took religious differences but also their enduring vestiges. When Daley was growing up, sectarian divisions sundered even baseball loyalties. The White Sox, playing near his home in Comiskey Park, built by Irish American Charles Comiskey, were the "Catholic" team, whereas the Cubs, playing in the North Side stadium, built by William Wrigley, were regarded as the "Protestant" team.

That Daley and Rostenkowski and most of their friends were Catholics is a fact of significance. It provides a societal and philosophical kinship beyond the two politicians' similarities of governmental practices. Protestants and Catholics held different ideas of rectitude. Daley was totally intolerant of adultery among his associates. Upscale Protestants in public life—say, Adlai Stevenson—had a more relaxed view of it.

The church of Daley's and Rostenkowski's generations taught that sin is personal and individual, not collective and social, and that human nature is depraved. The business of politics is jobs and power; the business of the church is saving souls. The "social gospel" of upscale Protestant churches, the meliorism of the do-gooders, would not find a welcome in the pulpits of old St. Stan's and Nativity.

Before the 1955 campaign, the *Tribune* waved the alarm flags: "grafters and fixers, the policy racketeers and others who can't do business with Mayor Kennelly and his department heads are yearning for a city administration they can do business with. Mr. Daley is no hoodlum, but if he runs he will be the candidate of the hoodlum element."[33]

Daley, with some justice, took this as a personal affront. "I would not unleash the forces of evil," he said. "It's a lie. I will follow the training my good Irish mother gave me—and dad. If I am elected I will embrace mercy, love charity, and walk humbly with my God."[34]

Notice that he felt impelled to defend his Irishness against an assault from an Anglo organ such as the *Tribune*. Notice also that he did not say he was unaware of evil. He just said he would not unleash it.[35] In like manner, when Dan Rostenkowski discovered evidence of the frailty of human beings, he did not appear scandalized. Some things did outrage him, though. He was outraged when his grown daughters would swear.

Joe Rusty fell on his sword for Dick Daley. For the crime of supporting the Irishman, Daley, over the Pole, Adamowski, voters of the Thirty-second Ward booted Joe from the city council after twenty-four years. His ouster proved that even in those times the machine, which loyally backed Rusty, was not omnipotent.

"At least the boys know Rusty didn't take a powder," Joe said in his insurance office adjoining the family home after the defeat. "I represented my people for a long time. And they were satisfied. But when Adamowski came along, they thought I should drop the organization and support him. Well, I've got a lot of men in middle age—fifty-five to sixty-five—in my organization. I couldn't just say, 'Boys, you're on your own.' I owed it to them as a leader to stick by them, and I did . . . I'm going to rebuild with youth. I'm going to get young men and young women into the organization, to give it life. And I'm going to build around my son, the senator."[36]

Joe was beaten by Bernard Prusinski, a civil engineer and House colleague of Dan's, who said that politics, even at its best, stinks. Perhaps because of that goo goo attitude of Prusinski's, Republicans in the ward supported Joe.

In 1952 Joe got caught in a ghost-payrolling miniscandal, but it probably had no effect on his 1955 defeat. Rusty was chairman of the License

Committee, which employed three "investigators." One was a precinct captain who drove Rusty to work at city hall every day for $275 a month. Another was a part-time bartender at Paddy Bauler's saloon who drew $200 a month from the city. These two men supposedly made spot inspections of stores and bakeries, checking for valid city licenses. A third ghost, paid $225 a month, was an unmarried woman (not the "Polly" of the 1940s).

"She does my correspondence and goes on special investigations," Rusty said. Such as? "Once in a while I go out with her. I might go to a night club with her to see if they have a license for the number of musicians working," he explained. Also, the city council had passed an ordinance banning the employment of barmaids unless they were wives, mothers, daughters, or sisters of saloonkeepers. "We did a lot of work in that barmaid situation," Rusty told the press. "We saw a lot of barmaids in back of bars, and I didn't think it was ladylike." [37]

Unimpressed by such regulatory diligence, Republicans exposed Rusty's three ghosts. Nothing, of course, came of it. After losing his council seat, he went to Daley for a job. He was offered a perch as superintendent of sewer repairs but considered it unsatisfactory. "I told the mayor what he could do with the job," Rusty huffily told a friend. [38] But he ended up taking it, joining the payroll on April Fool's Day of 1957 at $763 a month. In 1958 Republicans charged it was a no-show job and submitted evidence to the state's attorney, who by then was Adamowski, who had turned Republican. Nothing, of course, came of it.

Joe was as good as his word about building the organization around "my son, the senator." Having served as a delegate to five straight Democratic National Conventions, Joe stepped down from the Chicago delegation in 1956, although he and Dan both attended the convention as hangers-on. Both their roles were negligible, but the convention, held in Chicago, is memorable for Daley's exertions on behalf of Kennedy. In March 1956 Kennedy endorsed Adlai Stevenson for renomination and told reporters he was not seeking the second spot, but politicians knew he was lying. In July Speaker Rayburn told Stevenson, "Well, if we have to have a Catholic, I hope it's not that little pissant Kennedy." [39] Stevenson, who seemed frosty toward Kennedy or at least to the idea of running with a Catholic, met with the young Massachusetts senator on the third day of the convention and invited him to make the speech nominating Stevenson for president. This was interpreted as a face-saving consolation prize signaling that Stevenson would not place JFK on the ticket.

After Stevenson was nominated on the first ballot, he stunned the convention by refusing to name a running mate. "The choice will be yours. The profit will be the nation's," he told the astounded delegates. Daley and others quickly went to work for Kennedy, but Kefauver won the spot on the third ballot under circumstances still disputed.

Stevenson later put out the word to liberals that he privately had wanted Kennedy over Kefauver, although for the record he said, "I expressed no preference and had none."[40] Daley, a cannier politician than Stevenson, came to believe that Stevenson secretly had told Rayburn, who chaired the convention, to keep Kennedy off the ticket. In any event, the most important fallout of the convention was that television made JFK a national star.

Down in the wards, the cliché "Television is the new precinct captain" had not yet been coined. Having thrown Joe out of the city council in 1955, Prusinski challenged him for the bigger job of ward committeeman in 1956. Typically, the challenger charged that the incumbent's supporters had tossed beer bottles through the window of his campaign office. Typically, the incumbent denied it and offered a one-thousand-dollar reward for proof to the contrary. "A baby act seeking a sympathy vote," Rusty sneered at the bottle-throwing allegation.[41] And besides, he said, four cars had their tires slashed at his own annual St. Patrick's Day party. In turn, Prusinski said two of his precinct captains had been beaten by Rusty's guys in a tavern fracas. Assault charges were filed and counterfiled. Nothing, of course, came of it. Joe won reelection with 53 percent of the vote. Dan won reelection to the Senate with no trouble.

By this time Dan and LaVerne had three daughters, Dawn, Kristie, and Gayle. Dan had left the corporation counsel's office in 1953 and needed income. He took a job as president of the local Auto Salesmen's Association, which enabled House Speaker Carl Albert later to disdain him as a "big-talking, big-living former car salesman"[42]—in upscale midcentury American precincts, a slur. Rostenkowski also was the public relations agent for Teamsters Local 705 in Chicago. These were the only private-sector jobs he ever held, aside from the insurance business he set up as an auxiliary political office in the 1960s and the consulting work he acquired after leaving

Congress. In November 1956 Rostenkowski got another plum as assistant director of public information for the Chicago Park District, which nominally was separate from city hall but naturally was controlled by Daley.

In Springfield Dan's service as one of Daley's messengers was dominated by two themes that were to define and shape his public career. The first was taxes. The second was corruption.

A major part of the perennial bickering between Chicago and downstate involved the issue of raising the sales tax. Cities had been given authority to levy a half-cent tax back in the 1940s, but it was meaningless because voter approval in a local referendum was required. Voters were indisposed to raising their own taxes. The city kept trying to lift this provision—Rostenkowski had cosponsored such a bill in 1953—but Republicans kept shooting it down. They didn't want the Chicago machine to get any more money, even though downstate communities needed the extra revenue as well. The stalemate persisted until the new mayor, Daley, and the first-term Republican governor, William G. Stratton, made a deal.

Stratton, a former congressman elected governor in 1952 at age thirty-eight, had a typically Illinoisan career. As state treasurer, he had loaded the payroll with pals and also spent the entire two-year appropriation for his office in just eighteen months, whereupon he sought a special supplement from the legislature, which routinely granted it. These were ordinary and legal practices. After he left the governor's office, Stratton was indicted on charges of evading income taxes on political contributions, but he won an acquittal.

In 1955 Stratton agreed that cities could impose the sales tax on their own. Also, a ceiling on Chicago's power to levy property taxes was removed. Further, cities could tax utility revenues. Finally, Daley got bonding authority to build a huge convention center, which became McCormick Place.

In exchange, Daley agreed that the state could raise its own two-cent sales tax by a half-penny, the first state sales tax increase since 1941. Stratton delivered his Republican votes. Daley delivered his Democratic votes. It was supposed to be a temporary, two-year sales tax measure. In 1957 it was extended indefinitely.

Daley in addition granted Stratton a free ride to reelection. The Democratic nominee for governor in 1956 was the treasurer of Cook County,

Herbert C. Paschen. The press revealed that he had taken a trip to Europe paid for by an illegal "flower fund" kept in his office. Daley dumped Paschen and replaced him with an obscure judge, Richard R. Austin, who had no chance against the incumbent governor.

The Stratton administration was noteworthy for building highways. He set up a Toll Highway Commission for the suburbs and financed freeways through Chicago. (It was Prusinski who put the kink in the Northwest Expressway that curved around St. Stan's, saving it from demolition, but reporters later credited Rostenkowski.) Stratton's chairman of the toll highways, an old buddy from Congress named Evan Howell, quit a cushy federal judgeship to take the plum. He charged contractors one thousand dollars each for a bogus "contractors' club" and also used public funds to set up a personal apartment on Chicago's posh Lake Shore Drive. The legislature didn't much care, but then Howell was overheard in a Springfield bar making a disparaging remark about a legislator. That was going too far. The next day the legislature voted an inquiry into his actions, which Stratton earlier had succeeded in blocking. Rostenkowski was one of eight cosponsors of the resolution calling for the probe. Something, but not much, actually came of it. Howell had to resign.

Still, the salient point is that the highways got built. The lessons of the sales-tax and highway episodes were clear, although rarely remarked: Republicans and Democrats conspire to raise taxes and provide pork. If a constant thread links Dan Rostenkowski's forty-two years in elective office, it is that Republicans and Democrats alike raise taxes and provide pork. There are partisan differences, to be sure, but they are matters of degree, not of kind. Rostenkowski became a nonpareil provider of tax revenues and pork, and Republican executives loved him. "Governor Stratton was as friendly with him, and Dan Rostenkowski was as friendly to Governor Stratton, as if they'd been members of the same political party," a colleague said.[43] Later GOP governors of Illinois and even President George Bush openly supported Rostenkowski's reelections.

First, though, Springfield had some more scandals to serve up. In 1956 the press revealed that state Auditor Orville E. Hodge, a Republican, had stolen $2,500,008. Even by Illinois standards, this was excessive. Hodge was a high-living man about town, the sort who was everyone's pal. He was especially friendly with members of the West Side Bloc such as Libonati and Granata. In 1955 he had spent his department's two-year fund in eighteen months, just as Stratton had done when he was state treasurer. The house, with only two "nays," voted Hodge an emergency appropriation of $525,000. He stole every nickel of it.[44] The Hodge scandal was a liability for Stratton's reelection campaign, making him all the more grateful to Daley for putting up a patsy such as Austin.

In 1955 the legislature passed a bill exempting Union Electric, a utility based in St. Louis, from paying thirty-five thousand dollars a year in Illinois franchise taxes. The price was a one-time bribe of thirty-five thousand dollars handed to Hodge, which a Union Electric consultant thought was fair. "We got what we wanted," he said. "The fee was in line with what we were used to paying."[45] The exemption bill had been cosponsored by Senator William J. Lynch, who had been Daley's law partner. After the Union Electric payoff made headlines, Lynch cosponsored a resolution in the 1957 session creating a joint senate-house committee to investigate the matter. Nothing came of it, of course.

For the ticklish step of installing Lynch as Senate Democratic leader, Daley had designated Rostenkowski, a sign that the young Polish senator was climbing quickly in Daley's favor. A caucus of Chicago senators met in a Loop law office to select the 1955 leadership. The actual votes would be taken later at a caucus of all senate Democrats in Springfield, but that was a technicality. Rostenkowski nominated Lynch for the job over "Botchy" Connors, a Daley pal who moreover was the patron of Rostenkowski's close friend George Dunne.

In the senate chamber, Lynch reasoned that he could keep track of his members more easily by watching them from the back than by constantly turning around from a seat in the front, so he took a seat in the very last row. He was flanked by two other machine senators. Rostenkowski, in his har-de-har mode, called the trio "Hart, Schaffner and Marx." The tag stuck.

In 1957 Rostenkowski shared a Springfield apartment with three other legislators. He would do an "Odd Couple" routine, boisterously complaining that Senator William G. Clark washed his socks every night— every night!—and the constant drip-drip-drip as they dried over the sink drove the other roommates nuts. Taking the train home on weekends, Rostenkowski met each Saturday at Won Kow, a restaurant in Chicago's Chinatown, with Wendt, Dunne, Harry Bauler, and another North Side pol, Jack Merlo, to chew over Cook County politics. It was the "young Turks" group, with Rostenkowski the youngest by a decade or more.

By this time Rostenkowski was confident enough to champion a bill on his own. He proposed a $150 million bond issue to provide bonuses for the "dogfaces who fought the Korean War." War veterans would receive $15 for each month of overseas service, up to a maximum of $555, with the bonds retired by taxes on harness racing and liquor. The bill passed the senate handily in 1955 but Stratton killed it. In 1957 Rostenkowski came back with half a loaf—a $75 million bond issue, this one financed by a one-cent cigarette tax. It passed, though voters rejected it in a 1958 referendum. The bonus issue got Rostenkowski quoted by name in the capital newspaper, the *State Journal-Register*. This was a minor coup because ordinarily the paper did not identify individual members of the Chicago delegation. Why bother to distinguish among robots?

In addition Rostenkowski successfully pushed a bill to extend for two years the state-funded provision of free polio vaccine to children. He also supported benefits for old folks, offering bills to fight age discrimination, set up a state commission on the aged, and the like; to regulate utilities, to regulate the sale of paints and oils, and the like: instruments of the traditional Democratic "compassion" and "consumer" issues. On one "compassion" bill, Rostenkowski joined hands with the West Side Bloc.

Libonati had a pet project, the Americana Boys' Camp for underprivileged children in Wisconsin. Governor Stevenson had vetoed a bill subsidizing the camp on the ground that spending public money for private purposes was unconstitutional. Libonati, with lobbying help from Hodge, tried again under Stratton. With Rostenkowski and three others, Libonati introduced an appropriation for the camp in 1957. It got hidden in a routine welfare department funding bill and signed into law.

By the end of Rostenkowski's six years in the legislature, he was acquainted with the murder of politician Charles Gross, the presumed murder of politician Clem Graver, the Paschen scandal, the Hodge scandal, the Howell scandal, the Union Electric scandal, and his father's ghost-payroll scandal. He understood that John Kennedy had been denied the vice presidential nomination at least in part because of anti-Catholic bias. Moreover, he knew the Irish boss, Daley; the black boss, Dawson; the Jewish boss, Arvey; the Italian boss, John D'Arco (who controlled Libonati); the Republican boss, Stratton; union leaders through Teamsters Local 705; and business leaders through the car salesmen's trade group. A house for all peoples indeed. It had been a singular, an astonishing, a thorough political apprenticeship, one that could have been acquired, in such breadth and in such head-knocking, arm-twisting, back-scratching pragmatism, nowhere but Chicago.

IF DANNY SAYS IT'S TRUE

Whatever one may think about democratic government, it
is just as well to have practical experience of its rough and
slatternly foundations. No part of the education of a
politician is more indispensable than the fighting of elections.
Here you come into contact with all sorts of persons and
every current of national life. You feel the Constitution at
work in its primary processes.

—Winston Churchill, *Great Contemporaries*

I N 1959 an eighteen-year-old Cadillac was speeding west at night
on the Pennsylvania Turnpike en route to Chicago from Washington,
D.C. The car contained three young United States congressmen.
Two were Republicans who were trying to get some sleep. In the
front passenger seat was Harold Collier, his head resting on a pillow nes-
tled between the door and the backrest of the bench seat (front bucket seats
at this time were found only in sports cars favored by the young and the
rich). Sprawled in the back seat was Bob Michel. The Caddy was large, the
king of the General Motors hierarchy of car models, indeed the very em-
blem of American superiority, but still, it was not a comfortable sleeping
berth. Michel stretched and yawned. Behind the wheel, merrily whizzing
down the turnpike, was a Democrat, Dan Rostenkowski. Like his dad, he
was called "Rusty."

Collier and Michel were a bit uneasy about Rusty's pedal-to-the-metal
driving, but what the heck; they were in a hurry, and at the same time they
needed sleep. At least Rostenkowski's turn in the driver's seat was less
nerve-racking than Collier's. He had a penchant for variable foot pressure,
speed up and slow down, speed up and slow down, such that Bob and
Danny would grit their teeth.

The three lawmakers left Washington every Thursday evening, making the seven hundred miles to Chicago in twelve hours, maybe eleven and a half. LaVerne Rostenkowski, Corinne Michel, and Carol Collier all had refused to move to Washington, asserting the matriarchal right to bring up the kids at home. Their husbands drove home every weekend to see their families and attend to the politics of their home districts. Genial politicians, they liked one another, joked and gossiped on the road, sometimes shared the moody silences familiar to anyone who has undertaken long automobile journeys, but in the main they slept.

Collier represented the northwest suburbs of Chicago, the land of the Wood Dales and the Fenton High Schools, still subordinate at that time to the Chicago monolith. Michel came from Peoria, the prairie precincts far enough south of Chicago to elude its wickedness, populated by farmers and shopkeepers and small-town burghers who made up the mythopoeic essence of heartland America, then and now. Rusty represented Poles and Italians—eastern and southern European Catholics—along with some Russian Jews and Scandinavian Protestants in Chicago's Northwest Side. Everyone knew he was Mayor Daley's guy in Congress, accepted it as an unremarkable fact.

On Monday nights the congressmen reversed the commute, taking that 1941 Caddy east to Washington to meet the legislative calendar. The House timetable smiled on such members of the "Tuesday Through Thursday Club." On Monday afternoons House leaders "rolled" onto the legislative journal the pending "suspension calendar" of routine matters. On Tuesdays and Wednesdays the legislators actually considered legislation. Thursday morning sessions convened early, though, so that members could speed home after lunch. Each wall clock in the Capitol was encircled by small electric lights that illuminated when a roll call was being ordered; on Thursday afternoons they normally remained dark. On Fridays a speaker pro tem banged the gavel just long enough to vouchsafe another suspension calendar.

Before long the Caddy was judged inadequate and bequeathed to Collier's son, a high school student who was thrilled to acquire such a gem in which to tool around and impress the girls. Rusty got a beaten-up, white 1955 Chevrolet station wagon and threw a mattress in the back. Then while one man would drive, another would stretch out on the mattress, and the third would snooze in the passenger seat. They switched positions twice so that each drove about one-third of the way.

The long drives were necessitated by personal economy. Congressmen at that time were reimbursed for only one trip to their home district and back a year. A fair number of congressmen went home every Thursday, but mostly they were lawyers who took the train to New York, Philadelphia, or New England. There they practiced law or kept district office hours, meeting constituents who lined up in anterooms awaiting an audience with their congressmen, fulfilling traditional roles as government ombudsmen (this was before immense congressional staffs took care of such chores). That Illinois trio in the Chevy was an anomaly and now seems quaint in its bipartisanship. The Illinoisans did not practice law or run surrogate city halls. What they did was fill the tank with gas for about four gallons a dollar, split three ways.[1]

Rostenkowski's poor-mouthing was one of the points he raised to persuade Daley to send him to Washington. Daley had set aside a terrific plum to reward both Dan for his service in Springfield and Joe for his sacrifice in the 1955 election. He was going to make the boy the clerk of the Cook County civil and criminal courts, the largest unified court system in the country. Not only did the position offer ample patronage, but Rostenkowski's taking it would certify the job as a Polish entitlement.

The Irish had to fill the top two jobs: mayor and county assessor. The assessor determined property tax assessments, providing employment for machine lawyers who got them reduced for clients with clout. (*Clout*, a wonderful Chicago word, has been corrupted. It meant improper political influence or the bearer of it. Now it is just a synonym for power.) Offices below mayor and assessor were proffered by Daley under his program of keeping non-Irish ethnicities always fighting one another. Because of the Poles' numbers, once one of them grasped an elective office it became a Polish legacy. Such has been the status of the Chicago city clerkship for decades. Daley proposed making the clerks of city hall and Cook County courts both Polish.

That Rusty spurned the court clerkship for Congress must have shocked Daley. Why would the boy aim his sights so low? The Chicagoan belief that aldermen are bigger than United States representatives and senators is a staple of local political humor, but to the machine it was no joke.

The Irish-led machine's disregard for the federal legislature is expressed by the fact that so many Poles were put out to pasture there: Congressmen Kunz, Schuetz, Kocialkowski, Maciejewski, Gordon, Kluczynski, Pucinski. When Maciejewski died in 1949, the headline on his *Tribune* obituary read, "Anton Maciejewski Dies; Ex-Head of Sanitary Board." The text noted that, oh yes, he went to Congress for a spell. The Metropolitan Sanitary District, though, parceled out patronage and contracts. It mattered. Washington had not yet become Leviathan. Still, Rostenkowski had his reasons.

The Cook County Central Democratic Committee slated candidates for office in December 1957, eleven months before the November 1958 general election. Early selection of the tickets and early spring primaries were a scheme to maximize boss control and minimize voter and reformer influence. Raising money to challenge a machine candidate for long months before the general election was nearly an insuperable barrier. It remained largely so even when Rostenkowski finally was defeated for Congress in November 1994. In 1957 Daley had the ticket drawn up: for Circuit Court clerk, Dan Rostenkowski.

Rusty fretted that Republicans controlled the state legislature and still were pushing court reform, which might eliminate the clerk's position. Then he would be just another out-of-office pol, scraping by with the Teamsters and Park District jobs.

"Dan, do you have your petitions ready?" Daley asked, referring to the nominating petitions to gain ballot access.

Daley always insisted that families must come first. "Mr. Mayor, you told me not to make a big decision without talking to my wife. Well, I spoke to LaVerne, and she doesn't want me to run," Rostenkowski said.[2] It was not the last time he would use this ruse against Daley.

U.S. Representative Thomas S. Gordon, put in office by Joe, was stepping down after sixteen years because of ill health. He lined up his son, Tom Jr., an attorney for the Sanitary District, to succeed him. Alderman Thomas E. Keane of the Thirty-first Ward, which neighbored Joe's, gave forth rumbles that he wanted the post. This probably was just a maneuver to push both the junior Gordon and the Illinois state senator from Keane's ward, who also wanted the congressional seat, out of the picture so that

Daley could make his own pick. Keane was the brains behind Daley and remained so until he went to jail in 1974.

The Gordon family history paralleled that of the Rostenkowskis. The congressman was a product of Weber High School, building and loan associations, Polish and Catholic institutions, and nepotism. He ran the *Polish Daily News*, founded by his uncle, a priest. Public jobs as a parks official, commissioner of public vehicle licenses, and city treasurer fell his way. By rights, by all that the machine held sacred, he should have been able to put his son in Congress.

Except that Daley insisted on naming his own guy, and Rostenkowski made a good argument. Look, Rusty said, southerners control the congressional committees that dole out pork. Why? Because southern districts send their congressmen to Washington and keep them there until they die, meaning that they acquire key committee chairmanships by virtue of seniority. He made a reference to the South's still fighting—and winning—the Civil War by grabbing all that pork. Chicago's congressional delegation was made up of superannuated coots, average age seventy-two. Time for the city to send a young man to Congress, so it could develop its own poobah, its own key chairman. Okay, said Daley.

First, though, Rostenkowski had to overcome opposition from, of all people, Joe. The father wanted to keep the son close to home. The family argument was so fierce that, according to a friend, Joe actually threatened to put up a candidate of his own against his son in the Democratic primary. In the event, the machine slated Danny on 16 December 1957, a free ride with no opposition in the primary. Republicans went through the motions of fielding a candidate, but Rostenkowski won the general election with 75 percent of the vote. He was two months shy of his thirty-first birthday.

And so when that white 1955 Chevy wagon pulled into Chicago after a long night on the highways, the occupants went their separate ways, Michel southwest by train to Peoria and Collier northwest by Carol's car to the 'burbs. Rusty headed straight downtown to the LaSalle Street entrance to city hall, an ugly gray fortress that occupies a square block along with the Cook County offices. Rostenkowski took the elevator to the fifth floor to see the mayor, known then as "The Man on Five." He briefed Daley on what was going on in Congress. Before long, Daley was introducing his Polish Wunderkind as "the future Speaker of the House." He meant it. So did Dan.

If Churchill was right when he said, "No part of the education of a politician is more indispensable than the fighting of elections," then Rostenkowski was ill educated. He was handed a seat in the Illinois house in 1952, the Illinois senate in 1954, the U.S. House in 1958, and never broke a sweat to keep his seat until 1992. True, he had to overcome Joe's objections to his moving to Congress, but that was in the nature of a son's establishing independence from his father, a universal struggle for young men and not part of the electoral process. Rostenkowski liked to spin a story of working his way up the ranks. He boasted of having funded his 1958 campaign almost entirely from his own pocket, six to seven thousand dollars. But he had no primary opposition and risible Republican opposition. He received the office as something like an inherited title of nobility. He might as well have knelt before Daley and been tapped on the shoulder by his liege's sword. An election was not a prize to be won in open contest but an endowment, a birthright. The arrogance of power was planted early in the season of Rostenkowski's career.

However, he had the foresight to go to Washington and launch a national career when Daley wanted to keep him around as another Cook County hack. He found that Congress did not daunt him. The machine was antidemocratic, presuming to pick the people's elected leaders for them, but the U.S. House was antidemocratic in many of its operations as well. Committee chairmen ruled by seniority, not by merit. Rostenkowski's combination of arrogance toward peers and deference to seigneurs served him well there. He grasped the congressional culture quickly, swimming as naturally in its waters as he had at St. John's and in the General Assembly.

Ironically, much of the good that Rostenkowski eventually did for his country depended on the fact that he was the antithesis of a popularly elected leader. He could ascend the House Democratic hierarchy and take tough, unpopular stands on policy precisely because his seat was so secure he could not possibly be beaten in a free election. But the time came when Rostenkowski paid a brutal price for his miseducation in democratic processes.

Rostenkowski trod the plush blue carpet in the majestic, 139-by-92-foot House chamber to make his first floor speech on 22 January 1959. The speech satisfied two congressional folkways: freshmen normally do not speak up, but members must be eulogized. Rostenkowski announced the death of his predecessor, Thomas Gordon, with proper ceremony and somberness.

Rostenkowski shined in the informal, joshing congressional folkways along with the formal and solemn. The House has 448 tan leather seats, broader than first-class seats in modern jumbo jets, and unlike the Senate's chairs, they are not individually assigned. Indeed, the chamber is seldom filled except for presidential State of the Union addresses and other House-Senate joint sessions. During day-to-day business, only a few members are on the House floor. They gather in chaired clusters exactly as high school cliques aggregate around lunch tables in the school cafeteria. Al Gore Sr., part of a southern clique, said that Rusty "was always smelling something"—that is, he kept his nose in the air—and his arrogance inevitably offended some people. Rostenkowski did not hang around much with the ten-member Cook County Democratic delegation on the floor, comprising as it did feuding ethnicities. In the cloakrooms and along the brass railing at the back of the House, he gravitated to potential mentors. One of them was Hale Boggs of Louisiana, another big, brusque guy.

"Hey, isn't there a Polish museum in your district?" Boggs once asked him, wearing an expression of earnest solicitude.

"Yeah, the Polish Museum of America," Rostenkowski said, referring to a section of the Polish Roman Catholic Union building on Milwaukee Avenue near his home.

"I just heard there was a fire in the library there," Boggs said, woebegone to bear such sad tidings.

"Really?" said Rusty.

"Yeah. Both books burned up."[3]

Rostenkowski took the joke well, just as he did when, campaigning through his district for reelection in 1960 in that 1955 Chevy, a friend remarked that it was no wonder he drove a station wagon—no sedan could fit his lengthy Polish surname along the side. But years later, when a summer intern ventured to crack a Polish joke, a roaring chairman of the Ways and Means Committee physically tossed him out of the office. Polish jokes were accepted from mentors and friends, but not from some hireling kid.

Nowadays the constraints of political correctness forbid ethnic jokes to everyone. That is just one small way in which Congress and the country were different forty years ago.

Historians report that World War II transformed Washington from a sleepy southern town to a thriving world capital. Granted. Nevertheless, Washington at the tail end of the Eisenhower presidency still offered many features of a small town, just as the Thirty-second Ward did. The House in effect was a village of 435 people with its own castes, gossip grapevines, and common knowledge of each resident's social standing and personal strengths and weaknesses.

When Rusty, Michel, and Collier commuted to the capital, none of them had a press secretary—only a handful of legislative leaders employed such a creature. Today not even the greenest backbencher would dream of serving without one. When Rostenkowski arrived in Congress, the average member's budget for staff salaries was $20,000; when he left it was $515,760. A congressman's salary increased from $22,500 to six times that figure. The number of Washington lawyers rose from scarcely one thousand to sixty-one thousand, and the number of national trade organizations—lobbies—from five thousand to twenty-four thousand. An ethics resolution passed in 1957 had no force of law and was ignored; every member by law had to declare the value of every T-shirt given to him or her. By the time Rostenkowski left Congress, the income tax code had ballooned from two hundred thousand words to eight hundred thousand. The federal budget of $92 billion had become $1.6 trillion. Entitlements and interest payments on the national debt that had consumed one-third of the federal budget now gobbled up two-thirds. The proportion of Americans who told pollsters that they trusted the government "to do what is right most of the time" was 76 percent; now, on a good day, it might approach half that figure.

The 1950s often are regarded as a time of smugness and torpor. Their confidence and brio are overlooked. *Life* magazine declared in a 1959 editorial—without an atom of irony attached to any word—that American civilization "ought to be freer and bolder than the Greek, more just and powerful than the Roman, wiser than the Confucian, richer in invention and talent than the Florentine or Elizabethan, more resplendent than the Mogul, prouder than the Spanish, saner than the French, more responsible than the Victorian, and happier than all of them put together."[4] This was the country that Rostenkowski recognized.

Perhaps his Thirty-second Ward constituents would not have recognized it even at the time. Polish Downtown was dying, though the nation scarcely had noticed yet the decay of its inner cities. The ward, part of a larger community designated by city planners as West Town, had been losing population since Joe was elected alderman. A city study said West Town's housing was antiquated and run down, "frame cottages and shanties [and] dilapidated old apartment buildings," mostly built before 1900 during the prime of Peter Rostenkowski. Meanwhile the outflow of people to outlying neighborhoods and suburbs was enabled by a frenzy of highway building fostered by President Eisenhower, Governor Stratton, and Mayor Daley—highways that eased the cross-country commutes of Rostenkowski, Michel, and Collier. All of these men were politicians, not seers. They did not foresee the political and social supremacy of the suburbs.

To the contrary, the 1958 elections enhanced the status of urban Democrats. Rostenkowski joined a Democratic House majority that grew by forty-eight seats in the final midterm election under Eisenhower. Republicans took such a blow that the party did not fully regain its lost legislative strength until 1980. Large numbers of liberal, non-Southern Democrats went to both houses, prefiguring the Congresses of the early 1960s. In Massachusetts, Senator Kennedy took heart from the 1958 returns. He figured they could only help in his drive to be president.

That Dick Daley stole the 1960 election for Jack Kennedy has become an American political legend. As with other presidential legends—Ulysses Grant's drunkenness, George Washington's wooden teeth—it is now considered amusing. In 1996 John F. Kennedy Jr. said in Chicago, "In the 1940s my grandfather bought the [Chicago] Merchandise Mart, and in the 1970s my family bought the Apparel Center, and of course in the 1960 election my family bought 20,000 votes in Cook County."[5] Even Republicans laughed. As with other presidential legends, it endures in a realm insulated against fact. A historian as careful as David Farber has written, "Illinois had been the difference between victory and defeat for Kennedy."[6] No, it hadn't. Kennedy would have won the Electoral College even if he had lost Illinois. Still, the genesis of the legend is instructive.

In September 1959 Daley spoke at a party fund raiser in Troy, New York. After mass the next morning a Kennedy operative asked, "How is our boy doing out there in Chicago?"

With wide-eyed innocence, Daley said, "Who's our boy?"

"Jack Kennedy, of course. Who else?"

"I don't know how he's doing," Daley grumped. "I haven't heard from him in six months."

This exchange immediately was conveyed to a campaign higher-up, Kenneth P. O'Donnell. "I know he wasn't lying," the operative said, "because I met him at the five o'clock [A.M.] mass. We don't tell lies to each other at the five o'clock mass. Maybe at an eleven o'clock mass or a twelve o'clock mass, but not at a five o'clock mass."[7]

Impressed by this parsing of veracity, the campaign dispatched JFK to make a proper obeisance in October, catching a World Series game in Comiskey Park with Daley and his son Rich. Afterward, each man said the other just watched the game and didn't talk much.

Daley was sitting pretty, having won reelection that spring with 71 percent of the vote. The mayor considered running for governor, but he abhorred putting two Catholics atop the ticket. He made sure a Protestant, Otto Kerner, was slated for governor. "I was thinking of my four sons and I wanted John Kennedy to be their president," Daley told an aide. (He also had three daughters.) But he delayed endorsing JFK as long as possible to enhance his potential clout.[8]

Joe and Dan Rostenkowski had business of their own to take care of in 1959. Bernard Prusinski, who beat Joe in 1955, was up for reelection as alderman. Like Adamowski, he had switched parties to the GOP. State's Attorney Adamowski had purged Robert J. Sulski, Congressman Gordon's son-in-law and best man at Dan's wedding, from a job in his office. The Rostenkowskis ran Sulski against Prusinski. Prusinski campaigned by speaking in Polish, which Sulski could not do. Sulski creamed him anyway.

In the spring of 1960, Kennedy marched through the primaries, winning even in heavily Protestant West Virginia. After that crucial primary, Lyndon Johnson paid a secret visit to Daley to seek his help at the Democratic National Convention. Daley replied, "Lyndon, all of us here like you. We think you've done a great job as majority leader in the Senate, and you would make a fine president. But Jack Kennedy will get more votes for us in Illinois than you can get, so we've got to be for Kennedy." [9] Still he did not endorse.

On 6 July Johnson publicly admitted that he was a candidate for president. On Sunday, 10 July, a group including Dan Rostenkowski, "Botchy" Connors, and others gathered at the Union Pacific train station in Los Angeles to welcome Daley and the rest of the Illinois delegation to the convention. But the Daley family had slipped away early to attend 9:00 A.M. mass at a nearby church. The band the welcomers had hired later tracked down Daley at his hotel and saluted him with "Chicago, Chicago."

After the band was shooed away, Daley held an Illinois caucus. In an elevator he encountered Adlai Stevenson, who was making noises that he wanted a third nomination. But Daley previously had gone to Stevenson's northern Illinois farm and the former governor had disavowed interest, so goodbye Adlai. Daley strode to the caucus podium, looked over the front rows, and said casually to an astounded Rostenkowski, "Danny, why don't you nominate Kennedy?"

As Rostenkowski stood, cleared his throat, and wondered what the heck he should say, Daley pronounced, "And now the youngest congressman will introduce the name of the young senator." Rostenkowski himself had not declared a preference, awaiting Daley's cue, and he perceived the subtlety that Daley as yet had not specifically, personally endorsed Kennedy. After Rostenkowski obediently spoke, Daley reclaimed the podium and went blah-blah, concluding with: "I'm for Kennedy." [10]

Scott Lucas, who was for Missouri Senator Stuart Symington, hinted that a Catholic nominee would hurt the Illinois ticket. Lucas had no more clout. The caucus voted 59.5 for Kennedy, 6.5 for Symington, 2 for Stevenson. Illinois voters had not known of Daley's commitment, but the Kennedy camp did. They had counted on at least 57 votes from Illinois.

Daley refused to take Stevenson's calls until he yielded to Jake Arvey's argument that talking with the former governor was a matter of protocol. Stevenson wondered whether his minuscule two caucus votes merely reflected Daley's fence-straddling. No, said Daley, you're dead. On the convention floor, as a Stevenson boomlet expanded, Stevenson approached Daley and tried to strike up a conversation. Television viewers saw Daley shun him.

Kennedy endured a scare from Stevenson and from LBJ at the convention, but he was nominated on the first ballot. Then he picked Johnson for his running mate, among circumstances still disputed. When Daley got a call from Kennedy with the news, he said, "Listen, you're the nominee and I don't care if you put Snow White on the back end of that ticket." He hung up and told Rostenkowski, "It's Johnson." Rostenkowski shouted, "No, no, no!" Daley did not reply.[11]

But at a separate Democratic summit in the nominee's hotel suite, the mayor had favored Symington for veep, telling Kennedy he could not guarantee the usual 9–1 margins from William Dawson's black wards with a southerner on the ticket. Kennedy, though, knew what he was doing. "Not you, nor anybody else, nominated us. We did it ourselves," Kennedy told Daley.[12] This was so: Kennedy owed relatively little to the urban Catholic bosses, Daley of Chicago, Carmine DeSapio of New York, David Lawrence of Philadelphia, or Pat Brown of California.

Election night, 8 November 1960, was excruciating for Kennedy and his Republican opponent, Vice President Richard M. Nixon. Illinois Republicans still can recite from memory Kennedy's margin in the state: 8,858 votes. Nationally he won by 112,803 votes, the closest presidential election of the century.

The Kennedy camp in Hyannis Port called Daley as many as fifteen times during that long election day and night, including a call from the candidate himself. "Mr. President, with a bit of luck and the help of a few close friends, you're going to carry Illinois," Daley assured.[13] Steve Smith, a Kennedy brother-in-law, put it more clearly. "Well, we can always count on Mayor Daley. And if the ballot boxes downstate aren't in, why, he'll hold out a few ballot boxes in Chicago to equal them," Smith told an underling.[14]

Nixon stated in his memoirs, "The Daley machine was holding back the Chicago results until the downstate Republican counties had reported and it was known how many votes the Democrats would need to carry the state."[15] That was standard operating procedure for Chicago. Indeed, it is a wonder that Illinois election totals got compiled at all, as the Chicago and GOP machines strived to outwait each other to see how many votes needed stealing, each seemingly willing to hold out until next Groundhog Day if necessary. Perhaps Republicans in 1960 were guilty of impatience, releasing their returns too early. In time there developed a rumor that Daley had made a deathbed confession of stealing 1960. But there was no deathbed— Daley died suddenly of a heart attack.

No time log exists of which Illinois precinct, ward, township, and county returns were reported when in 1960. The true outcome of that presidential election will never be known. Yes, JFK would have won without Illinois. But he would have lost without Illinois and either Texas or Missouri, and pervasive vote fraud was a strong tradition in all three states.

A 1988 academic inquiry into the 1960 election in Chicago concluded that while there was widespread fraud, Kennedy's win was a byproduct of the machine's foremost objective: to defeat Republican State's Attorney Adamowski.[16] The machine did not care about goo goos, but it feared an ambitious Cook County politician with subpoena powers. Adamowski had filed suit against thirty-eight state legislators, including Rostenkowski, for "double dipping" by holding state and local government jobs at once. The suit was dismissed, of course, but the machine hated such nuisances. Thus, Daley got rid of a Republican prosecutor (his son, Mayor Richard M. Daley, achieved the same in 1996). The presidential nominee's votes alongside those of the Democratic nominee for state's attorney were *lagniappe*, as it were, a bouquet from the machine to the national party.

Certainly, Kennedy owed Daley. The president-elect claimed that he offered William Dawson the postmaster generalship, traditional dispenser of White House patronage, but that the elderly congressman had refused. This almost surely was a Kennedy-Daley ruse to attract black approval.

Rostenkowski attended the Kennedy inauguration, the first weekend he spent in Washington following his 1958 election. He had taken a bachelor pad that he called the "Junkyard" near Capitol Hill. LaVerne was appalled to open the refrigerator door and find therein only a carton of orange juice and some stale sausage. Kenny Wendt and his wife, Eleanore, took the train to the inauguration, and the two couples stumbled over each other in the cramped Junkyard, getting formally dressed for the ceremonies. Kennedy gave his celebrated inaugural address bare headed in the January cold, just as FDR had done before Danny's eyes exactly twenty years earlier.

On 28 April 1961, Daley brought the new president to Chicago to speak to the annual one-hundred-dollar-a-plate Cook County Democratic banquet. A hundred dollars was a piece of money in those days. When donors approached Daley with cash for these and other fund raisers, he would arise from his throne, walk around the desk, shake hands, and offer effusive thanks. When donors handed over a check, Daley remained seated and muttered a curt "thank you." [17]

President Kennedy first went to New York to meet such luminaries as General Douglas McArthur and Adlai Stevenson, whom he had named his envoy to the United Nations. For the *Air Force One* flight from New York to Chicago, JFK took along two Chicagoans, Dan Rostenkowski and Roland Libonati.[18] Libonati had preceded Rusty to Congress, winning a special election in 1957.

With his porcine, wattled face and blustery ways, Libonati was another caricature of a Chicago pol. The city honored such ambulatory caricatures—Paddy Bauler, Dick Daley, Roland Libonati. The congressman's "Chinaman" or "rabbi," Chicago slang for a political patron, was First Ward Committeeman John D'Arco. D'Arco in turn was controlled by organized crime boss Sam Giancana of Oak Park, a suburb flanking the city on the west.

Libonati was yet another son of the immigrant class who essayed entry into respectability by graduating from Northwestern University Law School. He became a lawyer for Al Capone, not a client recommended by the bourgeoisie. In 1931 Libonati famously was photographed at Comiskey Park with Capone and "Machine Gun" Jack McGurn, who was a top suspect in the 1929 "St. Valentine's Day massacre." Libonati's wife, Jeanette, was a classmate of Elliot Ness at Chicago's Fenger High School. With the endemic malice of adolescents, he was called "Elegant Mess." Ness became the federal agent who destroyed Capone, according to mythology spun by the television series and movie *The Untouchables*.

Sam Giancana had big plans for Libonati's young congressional aide, attorney Anthony Tisci. First he would marry Tisci to his eldest daughter.

Then he would dump Libonati and install Tisci as the mob's voice in Congress. But Antoinette Giancana spurned Tisci. Eventually he married a younger Giancana daughter, Bonnie, but health problems cut off his career.

In February 1960, Frank Sinatra introduced Judith Campbell (later Exner) to Kennedy in Las Vegas. Campbell and Kennedy began an affair. In March Sinatra presented Campbell to Giancana, who also began an affair with her. In April Campbell visited Kennedy at his townhouse (Jacqueline was away) in Georgetown, the upscale Washington enclave. Jack asked Campbell if she could set up a meeting with Giancana. "I think I may need his help in the campaign," he explained.[19] On 12 April, JFK and Giancana met secretly. Years later, FBI wiretaps were released, revealing large mob contributions to the Kennedy campaign in the West Virginia primary. The cash was disbursed to county sheriffs through Sinatra and an Atlantic City gambling figure run by Giancana.

Richard Cardinal Cushing of Kennedy's native Boston claimed credit for the West Virginia triumph. He had met with the president's father, Joseph P. Kennedy, to allocate payoffs to Protestant clergymen in that state, "contributions" of one to five hundred dollars. "It's good for the Lord. It's good for the church. It's good for the preacher, and it's good for the candidate," Cushing philosophized.[20] Joe and the cardinal took care of the clergy, while the mob took care of the sheriffs.

This was the background behind that *Air Force One* flight of Kennedy, Libonati, and Rostenkowski to Chicago. Alas, no record of their conversation was kept.

They deplaned to meet a greeting party of Governor Kerner, Mayor Daley, Senator Douglas, and the president's sister, Eunice, wife of R. Sargent Shriver, who ran the family's Merchandise Mart until Kennedy put him in charge of the Peace Corps. It was a mild spring day of sixty-one degrees except for Chicago's eternal raw wind. Kennedy motorcaded to the Conrad Hilton on Michigan Avenue and stayed there ninety minutes, according to White House logs, but actually he sneaked out for sex with Campbell.[21]

Five thousand Democrats cheered Kennedy with a roar that night at Exposition Hall, the lakefront convention center built by Daley under a deal with Stratton. No congressmen were seated at the head table, a telltale of their status in the machine. Rostenkowski needed several years to get Daley to reverse that lowly placement.

Kennedy, in his speech, said 1960 should be remembered not as a partisan win—far from it!—but as "the time when the United States began to move forward with a vastness of effort and a boldness of imagination to match the urgency and magnitude of its dangers." After that Kennedyesque rhetorical flourish, the president named a country many had hardly heard of, Vietnam—or rather, in the fiction maintained by the United States, South Vietnam—noting that Communists controlled much of the countryside. "We are prepared to meet our obligations, but we can only defend the freedom of those who are determined to be free themselves." [22]

Later, still paying off his debt to Daley, Kennedy appointed Joe Rostenkowski as Chicago customs chief. Joe, grown portly and sporting a pencil-thin mustache at age sixty-eight, attracted three hundred well-wishers to his swearing-in at the old Customs House on Canal Street. Because of Hatch Act restrictions on political work by federal employees, Joe had to cede his ward committeeman's seat. Dan took it over in October 1961.

Now a full-fledged member of the Central Committee, Dan devoted nearly equal time to cultivating his two fields, Chicago and Washington. As in Congress, Rostenkowski's stature in Cook County skipped a generation. The committee, comprising fifty city wards and thirty suburban townships, was run by a senior clique of Daley, Keane, Dunne, assessor P. J. Cullerton, and a few others. Then there were scores of young guys, with no "middle management" in between. "Rostenkowski controlled that bloc, that one era, damn near all by himself," a veteran committeeman said. "It didn't appear there was anybody else that had the same kind of easy access, the same kind of purchase with the old timers." [23] Before long Daley put Rostenkowski in charge of the slating committee, which counted among its duties the quadrennial rite of slating Daley for mayor.

At home, he and LaVerne had their fourth daughter, Stacy Lynn. Dan soon wore a gold shamrock around his neck, inscribed on one side with his wedding date and on the other with the birthdates of his girls. He never took it off, although he switched other personal items according to which city he was in.

As congressional payments for trips home steadily were liberalized, members of the Illinois trio sometimes commuted by Ozark Airlines at forty-seven dollars a ticket. When Rostenkowski drove, the man sleeping on the mattress in the back might be his executive secretary, Walter Nega, or administrative assistant, Clarence Sochowski. When flying home, Rostenkowsi developed a ritual: pluck the Washington office keys from his left shirt pocket, place them in a briefcase, transplant the Chicago office keys from the briefcase to the shirt pocket. He even switched wallets for Chicago. However, never did he adjust his watch off Chicago time, one hour earlier than Washington's.

In the early years, Rostenkowski and Michel drove to suburban Virginia for lunch at the Chicken Shack, ordering beer and whatever was the cheapest special of the day. As Rostenkowski grew accustomed to lobbyists' luncheons, he also availed himself of congressional junkets, visiting Australia, Indonesia, Hong Kong, Singapore, and Saigon. He continued to move fast, punching buttons on his office telephone as if they might attack him unless subdued, hailing confederates in the halls as if they had been roommates at St. John's. In February 1963, Hale Boggs got him named an assistant Democratic whip over the twenty members whose name began with "R," one of whom was Franklin Roosevelt's son James, a member from California, whom Rusty invited to a Polish banquet in Chicago. His pursuit of mentors was exceptional.

In April 1963, Dan and Joe faced a test—to carry their ward for Daley despite another challenge from Adamowski, running this time on the Republican ticket. Like Dan, Adamowski was the son of a saloonkeeper/alderman and a boy-wonder Polish politician. Daley was elected to a third term with 56 percent of the vote, by the machine's yardstick a frighteningly close election. He won the Rostenkowskis' ward, though barely. Daley's winning margin came from black wards.

Also that spring, Alderman Benjamin F. Lewis of the West Side, an African American, was shot three times in the back of the head while handcuffed to a chair in his office. No arrests were made, no charges filed.

On 22 November 1963, President Kennedy was murdered. Gloom still hung over the United States three weeks later as Christmas approached. In particular, the president's widow was grieving, shut off from the world in her Georgetown home.

Charles Daly, the Kennedy administration's liaison with Congress, received a call from Kenny O'Donnell, JFK's close friend and political strategist. "Chuck, we need to get a real person to stop by and say hello," O'Donnell said.

Daly mentally reviewed the roster of congressmen, and as a candidate for a "real person" hit on the young Polish guy from Chicago. O'Donnell, Daly, and Danny were admitted to Mrs. Kennedy's home the next evening. Probably she and Rostenkowski alike wondered at first what he was doing there. The encounter started awkwardly, the visitors speaking in hushed, formal phrases as if in church.

Before long Rostenkowski relaxed a bit, and then some more. He described the adulation Kennedy received whenever he visited Chicago, which segued into a droll recitation of some of the city's political battles. Rostenkowski was charming and funny and he made Mrs. Kennedy laugh.

Turning to Robert Kennedy, she asked, "Bobby, is this true?"

Bobby smiled. "If Danny says it's true, it's true." [24]

Rostenkowski hit his stride during the Johnson presidency, though national prominence was still twenty years hence. Paradoxically, he was both Daley's puppet and a rising operator with whom a member might roll a log. "Why ask me? I'm just a slave," Rostenkowski would wisecrack in alluding to Daley. But he also was a comer, a member with a future.

Once Rostenkowski took LaVerne to Washington for dinner at the White House. "Bird!" Johnson barked to his wife, Lady Bird. "Why don't you take the women upstairs and show them the private quarters. Show them the closets, show them the swimming pool. Let them know how we live here." This invitation was a Johnson specialty. Throughout his eight-year presidency, Eisenhower never took his own vice president, Nixon, upstairs.

"Now, ordinarily, a president would not do that," Rostenkowski said. "For me to have that experience—it is just exciting!" [25] He never disguised the kick he got out of rubbing shoulders with presidents, gaining entry to the sancta of power, whereas a typical congressman might declaim, "Ahem, yes, I was talking to the president last night and I told him . . ." Rostenkowski's open frankness, his no-baloney style, was a big component of his popularity and leadership.

"When I think of Dan," said Jim Wright of Texas, who became

Speaker, "I think of the old Roman words that became our English word 'sincere.' They were two words, *sine cera*. They meant 'without wax,' and if you had them stamped on an article, it was exactly what it intended to be or appeared to be, nothing patched up about it."[26] (Wright's etymology was charming but erroneous—sincere derives dully from *sincerus*.)

Rostenkowski had penetrated the congressional garden far enough to grasp one of its innermost fruits when it ripened in 1964. In April Representative Thomas J. O'Brien of Chicago died at age eighty-six. It was O'Brien who had placed Rostenkowski on the Commerce Committee, a choice spot for a freshman. The dean of the Chicago delegation, O'Brien was heavily influential in Congress, though not with Daley, who did not control him. When O'Brien turned seventy, he observed, "It used to be you had to go out and fight to get elected all by yourself. Now the organization does it for you."[27] This was a complaint, not a boast, as Churchill would have understood. Thin, stooped, and taciturn, O'Brien was among the few unsung heroes who make Congress function at all. He would lean on the back wall of the House, foot up on the brass railing, or sit languidly in a seat on the floor. He could "with the slightest nod of his head decide the fate of many a bill; he did not have to say a word to do it. He did not even have to stand to show the votes that he carried around in his back pocket," recalled Speaker Carl Albert.[28]

O'Brien's death opened his seat, traditionally held by Illinois, on the Ways and Means Committee. This panel writes laws on taxes and trade and makes the rules for welfare, health care, and Social Security. Members spend their entire careers trying to break into Ways and Means. Rostenkowski was a young third-termer. He got the seat.

By seniority, Dawson might have claimed it, but he already was chairman of Government Operations, and moreover, Daley had frozen him out of Cook County politics. Roman Pucinski already was busily pitching pork from the highways subcommittee of Public Works, and anyway, his seat was less safe than Rostenkowski's. Melvin Price of downstate had been in Congress for decades and thus was in line to chair Armed Services. By a process of elimination, if nothing else, Daley promoted Rusty to the seat.

Taxes and Social Security and the rest were important but not primary. In terms of internal congressional power, Democrats on Ways and Means assigned all other Democrats to their committee seats.

So it was Rusty whom Daley took along to meet Johnson in the White House on the morning of 6 August. LBJ called them upstairs, where, in pajamas, he monitored TV sets for each of the three networks. Daley asked for a beer. A steward was summoned. No beer was in stock, but Chivas Regal was, and even though Daley liked it, he took offense at the offer of the upscale Protestant drink in the appalling absence of the working-class Catholic drink. Sitting on the high presidential bed with his feet dangling off the floor, Daley complained, "When Jack Kennedy was here, they had beer." [29] Actually, Daley grew much closer to Johnson than he ever did to Kennedy.

Johnson took a liking to Daley's young sidekick and gave him a spot on the Democratic National Convention stage in Atlantic City in late August. First he played all kinds of games selecting a vice president, much as FDR had screwed around with naming Truman in Chicago in 1944. Johnson tantalized multiple aspirants, delaying the announcement to the last minute, then breaking precedent by appearing before the delegates to anoint Senator Hubert H. Humphrey of Minnesota. In a telltale of the stature of the presidency then, the *New York Times* portrayed Johnson's machinations as a display of shrewd statesmanship to unify his party, not as crude wheeling and dealing. Later coverage of Johnson was less charitable.

On the day before Johnson and Humphrey were nominated by acclamation, Rostenkowski was summoned to see Johnson's aide Walter Jenkins in Atlantic City. In a command center under the stage, Jenkins said Johnson wanted him to make a seconding speech for his running mate and in fact was waiting on a White House phone. Rusty told the president he would be honored and so forth. Upon hanging up, he realized he did not know whom he was seconding.

"Didn't he tell you?" asked Jenkins. Told no, Jenkins was reluctant to divulge the secret. "Look, I've got to write a speech," Rostenkowski said. Okay, said Jenkins, it's Humphrey.

Rostenkowski had said, "The trouble with Hubert is that he gives long-winded answers to questions no one had asked." [30] But then, this was not an uncommon observation. Rostenkowski walked back to the Illinois delegation on the floor, sat down next to Daley, and remarked by the way,

"I'm making a seconding speech for the vice president." A nice honor for you, Daley replied, what will you say? "Oh, the usual thing, great guy and all that." Daley squirmed. Rusty, gloating, said, "Well, I better start working on my speech," stood up, and sauntered away. "Come back here!" Daley commanded. "Who is it?"[31] Having forced Daley to ask, Rostenkowski told him and walked off, probably grinning like a schoolboy who has outwitted the dean with a prank.

Flying to Atlantic City the next day, Johnson called Rostenkowski again. "How can he call me? He's on an airplane," Rostenkowski naively wondered. However, he was not naive about Johnson's motives. He deduced that the "nice long Polish name 'Rostenkowski' was being displayed at the bottom of the screen. And that Poles all over the country were watching me and thinking, 'What a good Polish name.'"[32]

As it happened, the networks did not telecast either Daley's seconding speech for Johnson or Rostenkowski's for Humphrey. The proceedings went far into the night, as they did before television producers took control of the conventions, and there was no conflict, the realm of human interaction the media consider newsworthy. Rostenkowski gave his speech before the delegates and Johnson and Humphrey and their wives, seated in honor in the galleries. A mere four years later, Johnson did not dare show up at his own party's convention.

The 1964 convention was the zenith of the Democratic party and its philosophy of interventionist government at home and abroad. The conservative Republican nominee, Senator Barry Goldwater of Arizona, had no chance. The bushel baskets of turkey and all the trimmings left outside two-flat doorways by Joe and Danny during the Depression were fully nationalized by the overwhelmingly Democratic Congress that LBJ swept into office in 1964. Johnson promised a Great Society with "abundance and liberty for all," along with "an end to poverty and racial injustice." There was no laughter at the grandiosity of these claims. Congress enacted the War on Poverty, medical care for the aged, civil rights and voting rights, federal aid to education, and Model Cities.

Even Rostenkowski had some difficulty swallowing all this. Once he encountered Johnson and worried that "you're going to bankrupt the country with all these programs."

"Danny, all we do is open the door ajar a little, but you open the door. The American people will decide how far we should let it go," the president replied.[33]

If Johnson really believed that, he misunderstood the zeal of politicians to spend public money, and he did not misunderstand politicians. For their part, the American people wanted the door of government benefits flung wide open. They just did not want to be taxed to pay for them.

Another Great Society moment occurred when Johnson called Rostenkowski with the happy news that he was authorizing millions of dollars to build a mass transit line in the median strip of the Kennedy Expressway in northwest Chicago.

"So I called Dick Daley," Rostenkowski said.

I was excited, and I told him, "This is fantastic, we're going to have surface transportation out to Jefferson Park on the Kennedy."

He said, "Is that so? The Kennedy? Really."

I said, "Yeah."

"Oh."

So about twenty minutes later I get a call from Lyndon Johnson. "Dan, you know I told you about that money for that highway in Chicago? I made a mistake. It's for the Dan Ryan [Expressway]."

I said, "The Dan Ryan? What do you know about the Dan Ryan?"

"I made a mistake."

"Is that a fact?"

"Yeah."

"You know, the Dan Ryan goes through Dick Daley's neighborhood."

"Well, if you want to pick a fight with Dick Daley, you go right ahead."

I called Dick Daley back. I said, "You just talked to Lyndon Johnson."

"Oh, no, Dan, oh, no, no, no, it was just a mistake."

Daley had snared the money for his own Southwest Side instead of Rostenkowski's Northwest Side. "The fact of the matter is, we got the money [for the Kennedy], but it took about two more years," Rostenkowski said.[34]

This anecdote became Rostenkowski's all-time favorite. The Jackie anecdote he told only to close friends, but the transit anecdote he told to lecture audiences across the country for decades, always with warm affection for Johnson and Daley alike. That the story illustrated manipulative abuses of big government eluded him.

Many of the worst abuses were not revealed for many years. At the 1964 convention, civil rights figures assisted by Martin Luther King Jr. challenged the credentials of the all-white Mississippi delegation. On White House orders the FBI bugged King's Atlantic City hotel room. An FBI agent kept LBJ aides Walter Jenkins and Bill Moyers informed of the dissidents' activities; a compromise allowing the seating of the white delegates was struck before the president arrived.

In October 1964, Jenkins was arrested in a public men's room for homosexual activity. Johnson believed he had been set up by the Goldwater campaign. He ordered information on the sexual practices of Goldwater's staff. The Republican campaign plane was bugged.

Neither big-government spending nor its police-state abuses was the moral issue of the 1960s. The moral issues were white racism and the Vietnam War.

The Thirty-second Ward and Washington, D.C., shared many traits of small towns, and one of them was racial segregation in residency, restaurants, shopping, and lodging. These practices were outlawed, but not therefore eliminated, in the 1960s. During that period, frank expressions of white ethnocentrism were accepted with an equanimity that is unthinkable now. When a Chicago radio station switched from Italian, German, and Polish programming to full-time Negro programming in 1963, Rostenkowski and Pucinski felt no compunction about protesting the change, even though there was no all-black station at the time. Hints were dropped about putting congressional pressure on the Federal Communications Commission to override the station's decision.

Both congressmen supported the civil rights bills of 1964 and 1965, as did the entire Chicago delegation. Indeed, after Libonati had double-crossed Kennedy on the president's civil rights bill in 1963, Daley called Bobby Kennedy to inform him that Libonati would not seek reelection. And so it came to pass. During their dutiful support for the White House, Daley and Rostenkowski endured racially troubled years in their city.

Three phenomena defined the era. First, white flight and "panic peddling" by real estate agents transformed the city as whites fled in fear, block by block, neighborhood by neighborhood in assembly-line fashion, mostly on the South and West Sides. Second, Daley demanded and got personal command over federal War on Poverty and Model Cities money for Chicago, to the immense frustration of community advocates. Third, King came to Chicago to launch his first civil rights campaign in a northern city.

The "white backlash" gave hope to Republicans. In 1964 Rostenkowski's GOP opponent was Eugene Embrom. Adamowski traveled through the district assuring voters that Embrom, despite his ambiguous surname, was Polish through and through. Rostenkowski creamed him with 66 percent of the vote. Two years later, at the height of the backlash, Republicans found a candidate with a "ski" name, John H. Leszynski, who said, without fear of opprobrium: "If the Negroes move in, property values will go down. Some Negroes may be fine people, but it's the riffraff we don't want and are afraid will move in. The coloreds make no effort to keep their property up. You know, a little soap and water never hurt anybody." [35] Rostenkowski had to content himself with a so-so landslide of 60 percent.

Rostenkowski was becoming a Polish knight in Chicago. At 1:30 A.M. on a June night in 1964, he heard a crash of thunder and spied the south tower of St. Stan's afire. As a neighbor called the fire department, Rostenkowski ran across the street, smashed his shoulder into the door, and broke it down for the firefighters. The blaze destroyed the cupola on the tower, which never was replaced (although Rostenkowski led the fund raising to renovate the church interior in the 1980s). The congressman's role in the fire escaped notice by the mainstream press, but the press did report in repeated election seasons that Rostenkowski had turned down a major league baseball contract, was a Korean War veteran, and had graduated from Loyola. All three points were inaccuracies, which Rostenkowski did not trouble himself to correct.

Daley also enjoyed a good press—even the *Tribune* gushed with praise—as racial pressures steadily increased. On 26 July 1965, King led a march to city hall. On 1 August, civil rights protesters marched along Daley's block in Bridgeport. The mayor's neighbors tossed vegetables, profanities, and slurs at the demonstrators. Police arrested marchers but no residents. Daley blamed the ruckus first on Communists, then on Republicans. Civil unrest in his city rattled him to a degree the public never saw. He was so unsettled that Rostenkowski actually feared for the mayor's mental stability.

On 11 August, Johnson's aide Larry O'Brien reported in a memo to the president that Rostenkowski was "most concerned" about Daley and had suggested that "you could have an assignment for [Daley] to take him out of the country for a week or two" until the situation cooled.[36]

That very night, a crowd gathered to watch police arrest a drunken-driving suspect in the Watts section of Los Angeles. Police allegedly abused a pregnant onlooker, and the first murmurs of riot echoed down the streets. The next night, in Chicago, a fire truck accidentally killed a young black woman on the West Side. Riots lasted four nights in both cities. Chicago avoided any fatalities; Watts, with thirty-four deaths, shocked the nation and its president. Both cities rioted just a week after Johnson signed the Voting Rights Act.

Although Johnson did not send Daley abroad, the mayor went to the White House for the signing of a housing bill in September. In October Daley met with the president in New York and raged because $32 million in Chicago education funds had been held up over the mere matter of non-compliance with desegregation guidelines. Johnson swiftly appeased him, and Daley had little trouble in getting his hands on Great Society pork thereafter.

In January 1966, King moved into a West Side slum apartment to direct a crusade in Chicago. Historians of the duel between King and Daley generally conclude that Daley outwaited and outfoxed his adversary. The city had no tradition of organized black dissent. Black aldermen were so servile to Daley they were known as the "Silent Six," though it was a misnomer in the case of one of them, who regularly arose on the city council floor to proclaim, "God bless Richard J. Daley, the greatest mayor in the history of the world, the best friend the black man ever had." From black wards Daley installed aldermen who were prominent civic figures, as distinct from politicians, and who were loyal Catholics, as distinct from the Protestant clergy who led the civil rights revolt. After a long, hot summer of rallies, marches, and riots, King settled for little more than a face-saving, open-housing document at a 26 August summit with Daley.

In January 1967, Rostenkowski was elected chairman of the House Democratic caucus, the junior fourth of the leadership quartet: caucus chair, whip, majority leader, Speaker. Immediately he was confronted with an explosive racial issue, the caucus hearing on Representative Adam Clayton Powell of Harlem. Powell committed various acts of peculation, nepotism, and absenteeism, but his real crime was violating protocol by taunting the white majority with his deeds. John McCormack of Massachusetts, who became Speaker after Rayburn died in 1961, did not want to strip Powell of his chairmanship of the Education and Labor Committee. The Democratic caucus, with Rostenkowski banging the gavel, met behind closed doors—secretiveness did not stir much of a fuss in those times—and witnessed a rare coalition of southerners and northern liberals that demanded that Powell be dumped from his chair.

When this dump-the-chairman resolution was taken to the floor, the full House shockingly repudiated its leadership and actually expelled (technically, "excluded") Powell from Congress. The vote was 248–176, with Rostenkowski voting with the leadership. Pucinski, with more Republican backlash in his district to worry about, voted for expulsion.

The Powell decision foreshadowed the House revolt against seniority in the 1970s and moreover expressed the racial trauma of the 1960s. The leadership was out of touch with what members were hearing about race from their constituents—and not just the aged Speaker McCormack, but also Majority Leader Carl Albert, a heavy drinker who had suffered a heart attack the previous year; Whip Hale Boggs and their Republican counterparts who had signed on to the Democratic caucus deal: Minority Leader Gerald R. Ford of Michigan and Whip Leslie C. Arends of Illinois. The era of Great Society good feeling had fallen apart in only two years. As for Powell, he promptly won a special election to return to the House, and later a Supreme Court ruling fully reinstated him, but he lost the 1970 primary and died in 1972.

Another long, hot summer saw Detroit, Newark, and many other cities erupt in ugly and lethal riots in 1967. Democrats were much more alarmed about potential racial disturbances than about antiwar protests as they considered where to hold their national convention in 1968.

Antiwar chroniclers often postulate Johnson's Gulf of Tonkin resolution, nearly unanimously adopted by Congress in 1964, as the original sin of the Vietnam War. Actually, Eisenhower's Formosa resolution of 1955 had established the principle that in taking the country into foreign wars the president can pretty much do whatever he wants. The congressional record of the 1960s was one of prostration before three presidents on war matters. Johnson ran as the peace candidate against the alleged warmonger Goldwater in 1964. In March 1965 the first American combat troops waded ashore at DaNang. In March 1966 the House took its first up-or-down vote on war funding, recording exactly three nays, none from Illinois.

Nonetheless, liberal Democrats were tormented by the war. On one of his numerous visits to the White House—he was practically a staffer there—Daley told Johnson to get out of Vietnam. Rostenkowski was taken aback that a mere mayor would brace the president so firmly. Johnson beckoned his military aides, who laid maps and charts over the Oval Office desk. "It was quite a sight, seeing the president with the maps spread across his desk, waving his arms and excitedly trying to explain to Dick why the LBJ position on the war was right," Rostenkowski said years later.[37] Daley, meeting reporters after conferring with Johnson, said nothing about Vietnam. One does nothing to tear down the party or its president.

In the spring of 1968, a prominent Chicago lawyer who had served in the Kennedy administration was granted an audience with the Man on Five. Daley said a son of a good friend had died in Vietnam and the loss seemed senseless. "When you have a bad hand, you should throw in your cards," the mayor told his visitor.[38] Urged to make his views known to Johnson, Daley said he could not, out of loyalty to the president. This was disingenuous—Daley had spoken up to Johnson, though he never made his antiwar opinions public.

As early as 1965 the government was becoming alarmed about draft dodgers. Daley's U.S. attorney, Edward V. Hanrahan, made a show of meeting with the FBI and with Chicago police intelligence—the "Red Squad," which, as later court proceedings proved, was an illegal political espionage unit. Hanrahan's stated aim was to stamp out the draft-evasion movement organized by Students for a Democratic Society. At the same time, Rostenkowski called for a congressional investigation of SDS. "I think it is important to know if there is any enemy connection with the fomenting of this movement," he said. "I'm sure that many students are being duped in this matter, though they themselves think they merely are voicing legitimate protests against American foreign policy."[39] Such was the establishment boilerplate of the time.

In 1967 Rostenkowski gave the annual Fourth of July oration on the grounds of the Chicago Historical Society in Lincoln Park. Entitled "Is Patriotism Necessary?" the speech avoided the holiday's customary flag-waving to express in some limited measure the anguish of those years. "It seems to me that love of country is one of the great and indispensable virtues," Rostenkowski said, but, "No people are so thoroughly prepared to think ill of themselves as Americans. In this we are aided and encouraged by our characteristic love of exaggeration and our lack of perspective." Then Rostenkowski, who almost never spoke publicly of his religious faith, quoted his "favorite verse," Hebrews 12:1: "Seeing that we are compassed about by so great a cloud of witnesses . . . let us run with endurance the race that is set before us."[40] He did not mention race relations or Vietnam.

Rostenkowski had chaired the slating committee that renominated Daley for mayor that year. Daley's opponent was yet another Polish Republican, John L. Waner (originally, Wojnarowski). It was assumed that Daley would be elected to a fourth term. Sure enough, he carried 73 percent of the vote and all fifty wards—no longer could black wards claim they put him over the top. It was assumed that Daley would bring the Democratic National Convention to Chicago in 1968.

THE WHOLE WORLD IS WATCHING

> The previously distinct genres of journalism, literature, and
> theater gradually fused into something known as media. The
> amalgam of forms resulted in a national theater of celebrity.
> —Lewis H. Lapham in *Harper's*, August 1994

D ALEY'S defenders contend that he never wanted the convention in the first place. The case is unpersuasive. No doubt
there were times after the West Side riots of April 1968 that he
wished this cup might pass from his lips. But he had energet-
ically sought the convention.

Although the era now is compressed in the national mythology as the
sixties, there was an immense cultural difference between, say, 1962 and
1967, or even 1967 and 1968. As cities across the country burned in 1967,
Chicago was relatively peaceful. The message taken by the Democratic ruling class was, Daley can control his blacks.

Not only that, but Chicago had become the leading business convention city, and Daley was praised nationwide as a rare Democrat who was
both an efficient administrator and probusiness. The convention would
showcase the greatness of the city and its mayor.

And then there were the political factors: Johnson sentimentally
wanted the convention in Houston in his home state, but with escalating
riots at home and American deaths in Asia, he was deeper in political peril
every month. He could carry Texas automatically in 1968, but Illinois was
problematic. The presumably favorable publicity from Chicago would

help Johnson win Illinois and also, from Daley's standpoint, boost his state and local tickets.

On Saturday, 6 October 1967, Daley flew his courtiers to a World Series game in St. Louis, thence to Washington for a one-thousand-dollar-a-plate fund raiser for Johnson's reelection. Johnson "worked the tables" at the banquet, approaching the Illinois delegation with special animation. LBJ stood behind Daley's chair, gave the mayor's shoulders a Texan-sized squeeze, and boomed, "The greatest of them all!" Then he leaned forward and said something into Daley's ear.

"What'd he say?" Rostenkowski asked as soon as LBJ moved on.

"He gave us the convention."

"Dick, we can't take that convention! For Christ's sake, those civil rights people will crucify us!"

Daley looked at Rostenkowski blankly and said, "He gave it to us. We'll handle it." [1]

The mayor was correct in one respect. "Those civil rights people" did not disrupt the convention.

The next day, the site selection committee of the Democratic National Committee formally announced the selection of Chicago.

That Johnson was running for reelection was assumed, although his presidency was disintegrating. In a minor episode, Rostenkowski on the previous Tuesday had defied Johnson and the House leadership on an important tax bill. Rostenkowski attended too few meetings of Ways and Means then to have a real influence on fiscal policy, but his defection still was a shock.

Johnson had proposed a 10 percent income tax surcharge to finance the war. When the committee met behind closed doors, a move to table the surtax until Johnson presented a detailed list of spending cuts naturally was favored by Republicans, such as Harold Collier, Rusty's old driving partner, who had taken a seat on Ways and Means in 1963. But when even Rostenkowski voted aye, Boggs glared at him in anger. The final tally listed twelve of seventeen Democrats voting against their president. In the end, Rostenkowski supported Johnson when the matter reached the floor, but the full House rejected the president's position, 238–164. As in the Adam Clayton Powell case, the Democratic leadership was repudiated.

"You might say I'm not exactly welcomed with fond embraces at the

White House any more," Rostenkowski said. "The president isn't happy with any of us."[2] In the insular world of Washington, the fact that Johnson was so weakened that he no longer was feared in Congress was impressive. In the nation at large, the events of the next year shook the earth.

On 29 January, Communists in Vietnam launched their Tet offensive. Prowar conservatives have never tired of insisting that Tet was a military defeat for the Communists. But that outcome was not clear for months afterward. The early offensive, with enemy troops scaling the walls of the U.S. embassy in Saigon and tramping the grounds, was an immense psychological victory for Hanoi.

On 27 February Walter Cronkite, a respected news reader on network television, spoke out against the war. Watching on one of his many TV sets, Johnson at once concluded he had lost middle America's support for the war.

On 31 March Johnson shocked the nation by announcing in a televised speech he would not seek or accept "the nomination of my party" for reelection. After signing off, he walked from the Oval Office to the residence with his wife, their two daughters, and a son-in-law. Johnson's memoirs relate that he then was called by Humphrey, his Texas crony John B. Connally, and Daley. The memoirs do not reveal that the first call he took was Daley's.

The next morning, Johnson flew to Chicago for a speech to a broadcasters' convention. Riding in the presidential limousine to the Conrad Hilton Hotel on Michigan Avenue were Daley; Rostenkowski; Tom Foran, the acting U.S. attorney; and Frank Stanton, president of CBS (and Cronkite's boss). The atmosphere was tense and silent. At length Rostenkowski piped up, "You know, today's April Fool's Day. You could say that you were just early with your speech last night." No response.[3]

The trip was undertaken in such secrecy and security that Chicago hardly knew the president was visiting. As LBJ entered the hotel, a nineteen-year-old cried out, "Why don't you negotiate with the Viet Cong?"[4] He was arrested for disorderly conduct. In St. Louis that same day, an antiwar activist said Johnson's abdication had ruined plans to disrupt the Democratic convention.

On 4 April, Martin Luther King Jr. was murdered in Memphis, Tennessee.

On 8 April, Rostenkowski took a half-hour helicopter tour over the consequent riotous destruction of twenty blocks of the West Side. Stunned by what he saw, he said, "Negro leadership has to formulate a policy on situations like this. They have to find solutions to avert things like this." That he had put the onus on "Negro leadership" indicates that he did not accept the clerisy's blanket explanation of white racism.[5]

Two days earlier, Daley had made the same aerial inspection of devastation. Nearly writhing in pain, he said, "Why did they do this to me?"[6] On 15 April, Daley said police had defied his orders "to shoot to kill any arsonist" and "to shoot to maim or cripple anyone looting."[7]

On 24 April, honoring a promise to Daley, Johnson arrived for the Cook County Democratic fund raiser—still costing, even under wartime inflation, one hundred dollars a plate. It was a Daley operation par excellence. Police exchanged uniforms with Conrad Hilton waiters so that they might carry placards into the ballroom reading, "God Bless You Mr. President" and the like. Two bands played "Hello Dolly," altered to "Hello Lyndon," the 1964 convention anthem, and "Happy Days Are Here Again," the enduring FDR anthem. Johnson avoided demonstrators chanting, "LBJ, LBJ, how many kids did you kill today?"[8] by arriving late and through the back entry and kitchen of the hotel. He then teased the audience with hints that he might run after all, only to deflate them with quips.

On 27 April, Chicago police brutally attacked peaceful antiwar marchers at the Civic Center (now the Daley Center) across from city hall. Police misconduct at the August convention should not have been such a shock. On that same day, Humphrey declared his candidacy for president, conjuring "the politics of joy." The slogan did not embarrass him. Filing deadlines for the primaries, contested by Senators Eugene J. McCarthy of Minnesota and Robert F. Kennedy of New York, had passed. Humphrey reckoned the party bosses would nominate him anyway.

On 4 June in Los Angeles, having just won the California primary, Kennedy was murdered.

On 24 August, delegates started flying into Chicago for the convention. Rusty's mentor Hale Boggs had the baleful job of chairing the platform committee, which would adopt a Vietnam plank. Working in the Blackstone Hotel, Boggs was startled one day when a plainclothes detective working for the committee motioned for silence by placing a finger to his lips, then pointed out two hidden microphones. Whoever planted the bugs was never discovered.[9] Later, Boggs charged on the House floor that the FBI was bugging his congressional office.[10] Most of the House thought he had gone nuts. The very idea that the FBI would do such a thing!

If Carl Albert and Dan Rostenkowski had ever sat down to compare their backgrounds, they might have learned that they had much in common. Albert was a Dust Bowl kid and Rusty a city kid, but both were shaped by the Depression and shared a hearty faith in the New Deal. Both men's mothers died of illness in middle age. Both men joined the public payroll young—Albert as a federal housing lawyer who went to Congress at age thirty-eight. For a time, he had practiced law in Matoon, Illinois.

Of all things, Albert, like Rusty, was acquainted as a boy with a fatal shooting near his house. The victim was named Frank Miller, like the villain in the Western movie masterpiece *High Noon*. Albert's neighbor returned home one morning to find Miller in bed with his wife. Taking offense, the man shot Miller as he was running through Albert's yard. A jury acquitted the killer.

In the 1940s, Albert found his Oklahoma farmers penalized by peanut allotments set in Washington. Crop quotas had been established by Henry A. Wallace, agriculture secretary and later vice president, who was an admirer of Soviet central planning. Virginia and North Carolina, because of their congressmen's clout, got special breaks on the peanut allotments. Just a junior congressman, Albert moved mountains and got the same break for Oklahoma. His constituents "could judge whether they had a congressman worth keeping,"[11] Albert preened in his memoirs. The idea that a free people might plant whatever acreage they liked without governmental edict did not cross his mind.

In 1968 Speaker McCormack was considered too old to chair the Democratic convention, so the job fell to Albert, the majority leader. He was eager for it. Though his frame stood barely five feet tall, it packed an ego the size of an aircraft carrier.

The convention opened on 26 August in the International Amphitheater, a thirty-four-year-old, cramped, ugly building in an old, cramped, ugly part of town near the stockyards and Daley's house. Federal, state, and local soldiers, police, and law enforcement personnel, including undercover agents infiltrating the antiwar groups, numbered 28,200. Delegates and alternates numbered 5,011. Such was the setting for the quadrennial gathering of the majority party, the oldest sustained political party of a free country.[12]

Albert, hardly visible over the podium, wielded a gavel of wood from Thomas Jefferson's home. The first night, Monday, featured multiple challenges to state delegations' credentials and adjourned at 2:45 A.M. Though he never admitted it, Albert looked to Daley, seated near the platform, for signals on when to recognize and cut off floor speakers.

Playing his 1960 games, Daley delayed an Illinois endorsement of Humphrey until the last minute, plotting a possible draft of Johnson or, much more likely, of Senator Edward M. Kennedy of Massachusetts. But Johnson wisely stayed at his Texas ranch, and the "Teddy" boomlet fizzled.

On Tuesday, Daley led the arena in singing "Happy Birthday" to Johnson, who turned sixty. Years later, Daley told a friend that he twice had to tell Johnson "that he could not come to Chicago — once when he was sitting in *Air Force One* on the runway with the engines running," during his birthday.[13] Johnson fantasized swooping into town and winning nomination by acclamation.

Also that Tuesday night, the convention abolished the unit rule and created a commission to change the way future nominees would be chosen. These were the most radical things the convention did, but because they were procedural and institutional, not personal, the media paid little mind. The unit rule required that state delegations vote as one, regardless of internal divisions. It was the device by which southern governors and northern mayors ruled.

After midnight the convention opened debate on the platform, or rather on the Vietnam plank. Johnson and Daley scheduled this event for after all sane television viewers had gone to bed. Debate was invidious and anarchic, with Daley angrily drawing a finger across his throat to telegraph adjournment at 1:17 A.M.

Wednesday, Albert gaveled the convention to order at noon. Humphrey, Daley, Rostenkowski, and Keane were having dinner in the vice president's hotel suite when word came that protesters intended a march on the Amphitheater. The Chicagoans left at once for the arena.[14] This decampment enabled Rostenkowski to tell an interviewer later that he had witnessed the "Battle of Chicago."

That evening saw the largest clash of police and protesters. Fewer than ten thousand demonstrators, perhaps as few as six thousand (they included Harvard student Al Gore Jr.), had provoked the establishment into something tantamount to a brain seizure. It happened in Grant Park and on Michigan Avenue outside the Conrad Hilton, miles from the Amphitheater. Demonstrators stormed the hotel to chant, "Dump the Hump!" Humphrey, on the twenty-fifth floor, thought they were cheering him and went to an open window to wave gleefully. Perhaps, after three decades, that scene is funny.

LBJ's forces defeated the peace plank handily, and the convention was set to consider nominations for president. A moment of history now was born from—seriously—air conditioning. The AC system in the grungy Amphitheater blasted chilled air straight at the podium. On the first night, a shivering Albert developed a cold, which he said stuffed his sinuses, weakened his voice, and impaired his hearing. By the third night, he was weak and confused. The floor was crowded, angry, exhausted, and raucous. An actual brawl broke out among the New York delegation. Johnson, watching the action at his ranch, called the Amphitheater in rage. Manning the phones on the platform was Dan Rostenkowski.

Johnson, in full, profane Texas cowboy mode, demanded that the convention be brought to order. "He started screaming his head off at me," Rostenkowski said.[15] So Rostenkowski went up to Albert and said, look, it's my hometown crowd, my friends are here, it would mean a lot to me if I could preside for a moment. Sure, said Albert, handing over the Jeffersonian artifact. Rostenkowski banged the gavel with vigor and called for the convention's sergeant at arms to clear the aisles. This was code for Chicago police to clear the aisles, which they sternly did. Then Rostenkowski introduced Governor Harold Hughes of Iowa, who nominated McCarthy. McCarthy delegates chanted, "We want Gene!" but the floor was returned to a semblance of decorum. Rostenkowski gave the totemic gavel back to Albert and left the platform surrounded by Democrats congratulating him for rescuing the convention from meltdown.

By this time news reports of the violence up in Grant Park were seeping into the convention fortress. Albert called to the podium Senator Abraham A. Ribicoff of Connecticut, who nominated Senator George S. McGovern of South Dakota. Ribicoff said that under McGovern, "we wouldn't have to have Gestapo tactics in the streets of Chicago."

Daley, purpling with passion, leapt to his feat and screamed insults at Ribicoff, as interpreted by a professional lip reader, to wit: "Fuck you, you Jew son of a bitch! You lousy motherfucker! Go home!" [16] The question of whether Daley actually said that divides Chicagoans still. Rostenkowski and others devoutly insist that Daley merely called Ribicoff a "faker." Whichever, the videotape shows the mayor nearly convulsed with rage.

Attaining heights of sanctimony, Ribicoff looked at Daley and intoned, "How hard it is to accept the truth." [17] Daley's rage surpassed that of a mere personal affront. A powerful Democrat had attacked another powerful Democrat in public. Ribicoff was blaspheming in the temple.

At sorrowful length, Humphrey was nominated, after Daley and most of his Illinois delegates stalked out in indignation. Rostenkowski perfunctorily retook the podium to call for the benediction at 12:10 A.M.

Some "what ifs." Johnson privately had told Connally that if the platform or Humphrey himself renounced his war policy, he would descend on Chicago to claim renomination. What if Boggs's Vietnam plank plottings had not been bugged when Humphrey briefly wavered and indicated he might accept a stop-the-bombing plank? What if Rostenkowski had lacked the aggressiveness to take command of the podium and the finesse to sweet-talk Albert out of it? What if Albert had refused to yield the gavel to him? What if the convention descended into utter chaos and Johnson had called for *Air Force One* and pointed it north to Chicago? What if Steve Smith, the Kennedy brother-in-law who had set up a secret Kennedy command post in Chicago's Standard Club, had heard a positive word from Teddy?

But for those brief moments at the podium on 28 August, Rostenkowski may well have become Speaker of the House. Soon enough, Albert was hearing reports of Rostenkowski's bragging that he had overpowered him, grabbing the gavel to salvage the convention. Rostenkowski denied spreading this story. Still, the image of the hulking Rostenkowski wresting the gavel from the dwarfish Albert became so fixed in Washington lore that Tip O'Neill reported it as fact in his memoirs. Albert was not amused. He barred Rostenkowski from rising in the House leadership for as long as he could—eight years.

On 29 August, Humphrey gave his acceptance speech to a convention hall packed with Daley henchmen. That the convention host would stack the galleries with his supporters was expected, even almost mandatory after the previous day's warfare, but evicting legitimate delegates to pack the floor with ringers was something else. Fearing a mass walkout by delegates protesting the street violence and the Humphrey railroad job, Daley chartered six buses to carry in four hundred fake delegates, mostly patronage workers in cheap, dark suits. Meanwhile, at the arena entrances, other flunkies handed out "We Love Mayor Daley" signs. Delegates who refused them were denied entrance. Of all the abuses of power during that horrible week, this one was hardly noticed.

Albert and Daley took satisfaction in the fact that they got Senator Edmund S. Muskie of Maine nominated for vice president and Humphrey on stage for his acceptance speech before prime time on television ran out. That will show them, they thought. That will show them that we have this thing under control.[18]

Daley's defenders point out that nobody was killed or even severely injured during the convention in Chicago, whereas police killed three people in Miami in July while Republicans nominated Richard Nixon. But those deaths occurred during a race riot in Miami that was separate from the GOP convention in Miami Beach. For sustained collective violence in electoral politics, America saw nothing like Chicago in 1968, before or since.

"The whole world is watching!" provocateurs behind the front ranks chanted happily as demonstrators bracing Daley's police got clubbed and kicked. And so it was—television by now was ubiquitous. A prevalent belief is that telecasts of the riots ensured Humphrey's defeat. The entire drama made *New York Times* columnist Tom Wicker rather weak in the knees. After mourning his refusal of an invitation to join an antiwar march to the Conrad Hilton—"I had believed always that I belonged with the young and the brave and the pure in heart"—he concluded that Chicago was "the place where all America was radicalized."[19]

Perhaps the media were radicalized. Forty-three reporters, photographers, and TV cameramen were assaulted by security personnel during the convention, incidents that were, at least to the media, shocking and unforgivable. The country at large took a different view. A national poll found that 71.4 percent believed the Chicago police conduct was justified and 61.7 percent thought that Daley did a good job.

Rostenkowski took an informal sounding of his district and found the same sentiments, only more so. "The people of my district have told me they would have acted exactly as Mayor Daley did," he said.[20] Rostenkowski hardly would have reported that his constituents thought Daley an ogre. But, doubtless, he was speaking the truth. His district still was probably the most heavily Polish in the country, comprising older Poles resisting the suburban flight, holding to respect for Catholic and civil authority, grieving for an Old Country enslaved by communism.

The United States was, week after week, month after month, losing the Vietnam War—at the least, failing to win it, despite years of official statements to the contrary. Johnson proclaimed in his October 1967 fund raiser that the war would be won in 1968, and then came Tet. America does not like losers, or riots, or as Carl Albert put it, "ill barbered, ill clothed, and ill tempered" antiwar demonstrators. The public wanted the war ended and at the same time thought the hippies and yippies in Chicago got what was coming to them.

The influence of television in that era remains a matter of argument. It is doubtful that television radicalized the nation or stopped the war. Nevertheless, the expanding takeover of the American political process by television is undeniable.

At this point, Paddy Bauler makes another appearance in our narrative. Considered a buffoon, a role he relished, Bauler was shrewd. As astonishingly early as 1950, he noticed that his precinct captains were having trouble rousing voters from their televisions. Few households owned sets at the time, politics was not televised anyway, and the machine took no notice of Bauler's oracular complaint.

Over the next few decades, television steadily annexed American electoral institutions in ways still not clearly understood—perhaps TV is so pervasive it defies understanding. In effect, politics became a branch of television news and ads, and television news and ads became a branch of the mass entertainment industry. Any entertainment industry must have a repertory of heroes and villains.

A slogan of the 1960s counterculture was "The personal is political." That has been turned on its head so that now the political is merely personal. The media are obsessed with personal anecdotes, preferably pathographic, of politicians. The assumption is that life experiences determine personality and that personality determines public policy. Institutional or societal determinants of public policy are disregarded.

If your life experiences are revealed on television, then you are by rights a celebrity. An essential power of television is the power to confer celebrity. In bestowing it, the media cannot resist placing their celebrities on stock shelves of good guys and bad guys.

That is what happened to Dick Daley in 1968. The convention ripped the rubber mask of bourgeois respectability off the round, scowling face of the old Irish boss of "the city that works." Previously a progressive Democrat, Daley overnight became Boss: crude, ill-spoken to the point of mangling the English language, paranoid, racist, probably corrupt. A stock celebrity bad guy for the clerisy. Rostenkowski's turn in the "national theater of celebrity," a game show with winners and losers, was years away, but his time came.

Chicago 1968 was a turning point in the mass mediation of public affairs. But the fallout of that week in August might have caused an even larger phenomenon—a continental drift of the national psyche. After that televised trauma, the shores of the polity seemed to harden and exude toxins. Public life became more personal, more suspicious, more polarized, more cynical. Mistrust and cynicism grew so universal that they scorched everything they touched, smudging with caustic soot even what was good and beautiful in America. In this sense, perhaps Tom Wicker was right after all. Chicago is the place where all America was radicalized.

Edmund Muskie, son of an immigrant Polish tailor, was the first Polish governor, senator, and vice presidential nominee. He never made much of his ethnicity until the 1968 campaign. On 2 October, he stumped through the three Polish congressional districts in Chicago with Rostenkowski; Pucinski, who had barely survived a 1966 election challenge from John

Hoellen; and John C. Kluczynski, a genial, poker-playing builder of seniority in Congress and a Southwest Side Pole who thereby was disdained by Rostenkowski and Pucinski, the Northwest Side Poles—Poles could never close ranks like the Irish. (A fourth Pole, Edward J. Derwinski, was a suburban Cook County Republican.)

Nixon went to the Loop shortly after the Democratic convention, pointedly campaigning in an open car and appealing to the "quiet Americans." Muskie's visit was the first to the city by a member of the national Democratic ticket. Inexplicably absent from the Muskie rallies was Daley, whose crackdown on the protestors had been applauded in those districts. The old lion apparently was still licking his wounds in his lair.

After the 1968 convention, Daley withdrew further into his Bridgeport cultural cocoon, ever more isolated and suspicious. He told Walter Cronkite the extreme security of the convention was a response to law enforcement intelligence that "certain people planned to assassinate many of the leaders, including myself."[21] These remarks were derided as paranoid fantasies, but Daley's personal fear was real enough to him.

Kenneth O'Donnell, a close adviser to the Kennedys, called Jane M. Byrne, an aide to Daley, on the last morning of the convention. O'Donnell asked to talk privately with Daley. Byrne said Daley would refuse, for he was upset with the convention behavior of the Kennedy camp. Okay, O'Donnell said, but at least give him this message: The night before, he had paused at the bar of the Pick-Congress Hotel, where two of the country's foremost Democrats, enraged by the convention fiasco, told him they would "get Daley." O'Donnell thought Daley should know this. When Byrne conveyed this information to Daley, he reacted with the utmost grimness. He asked: "Is it to be physical?"[22]

Daley's defenders point out that he served eight more years and won two more elections as mayor, contrary to the media impression that his career ended in 1968. But as a national kingmaker, pal of presidents, and spokesman for urban needs, Daley was through after 1968. Rostenkowski's political biography now begins to diverge from that of his patron.

Rostenkowski prepared to return to Congress under his second Republican president. First he had business to take care of at home. He arranged a Cook County judgeship for his friend Alderman Sulski, which opened a vacancy in the city council. By now enough Hispanics had moved into the Thirty-second Ward that a Puerto Rican, Angel L. Colon, was emboldened to run for alderman. For his candidate, Rostenkowski selected Theris M. Gabinski, a thirty-year-old high school teacher and coach from the old neighborhood. Elected easily, Alderman Gabinski became a close associate of Rostenkowski for the next twenty-five years.

In 1967 Joe Rusty bought the building at 2148 North Damen Avenue. The congressman moved his district office into the building, paying rent to his father out of his congressional expense allowance. In 1968 Dan bought the adjacent storefront at 2150 North Damen. This building soon had Gabinski and the ward organization as Rostenkowski's tenants. Gabinski used city hall funds, and the ward used political funds, to pay the rent. Such back-door rental schemes were traditional in Chicago politics, but the practice helped put Rostenkowski in ethical jeopardy a quarter-century later.

At the time, Rostenkowski returned to Washington to make the Democratic caucus something more than an informal assembly. He already had strengthened his place as a combination caucus chairman and regional whip. A whip—the term comes from the "whipper-in" of the hounds on English fox hunts—does not directly enforce party discipline, although whips customarily receive a bullwhip or horsewhip as a gag gift from their supporters. The basic duty of the whip is to count the votes for upcoming legislation, an essential task. "The only thing that matters up here is votes. Everything else is bullshit," as Representative Frank Annunzio of Chicago explained.[23] The secondary duty of the whip is to persuade members to change their votes when the leadership so orders.

As regional whip, Rostenkowski noticed that his tallies of members' positions on bills were leaking to lobbyists and White House congressional aides. He promptly clamped a gag rule on his vote counts, thereby lessening the outside pressure on members to change their votes. It was a classic machine move: take care of your own, keep disputes inside the organization, dam the flow of information to outsiders.

As caucus chairman, Rostenkowski instituted regular caucus meetings. Speaker McCormack, elderly and unpopular with liberals, reluctantly assented to such meetings before he was reelected Speaker in 1969. They started out as monthly sessions and then were held every Thursday. Mc-

Cormack was not invited to the Thursday panels, a snub a stronger Speaker would not have tolerated. Each Thursday, Lindy Boggs arose at 4:30 A.M. to bake pastries for her husband, Hale, and Rusty and the guys. Between forty and sixty members might show up in a large meeting room across from the House chamber, where the whips reviewed the legislative calendar for the next week. Predictably, this gathering became a Democratic inner circle.

President Nixon was of no mind to send federal pork to Daley's Chicago, of all places, or to enhance Model Cities, a notorious Great Society boondoggle. However, Nixon wanted to extend Johnson's 10 percent war surtax for another year. Nixon called the House Democratic leaders to the White House, where Wilbur D. Mills of Arkansas, chairman of Ways and Means, agreed on the need for the revenue. But Rostenkowski declined to pledge his support, acting presumably on Daley's orders. The end of the fiscal year and a deadline of sorts, 30 June, was coming up.

Chicago's $38 million Model Cities grant had been frozen by the Nixon administration. On 28 June, the money was released. On 30 June, Rostenkowski voted for the surtax and brought five other Chicago Democrats along with him. The surtax passed with five votes to spare, 210–205. Rostenkowski had applied a lesson learned under Governor Stratton: Democratic legislators and Republican executives connive to raise taxes and provide pork.

The White House still was displeased that Daley sliced up and handed out the pork. Again the feds threatened to curtail funds because neighborhood decision making, which the program mandated, was ignored. Daley told his frustrated Model Cities administrator to reason with the feds. He said, "I already did." Daley asked, "Did you take the fellas with you?" The "fellas" were the nine Democrats representing Chicago in Congress. The administrator called the regional federal bureaucrat and asked to bring in some "citizens" to discuss matters. Sure, bring them in. "When they saw who the nine 'citizens' were, they nearly shit. The funds didn't get cut off," Daley's man said.[24] Whatever the merits of the city's position, everyone is familiar with the fun of besting a bureaucrat.

Rostenkowski also was enjoying himself chairing the machine's slating sessions. The rituals were as rigid as an archbishop's investiture. Would-be candidates appeared before the slaters to present their credentials. Rosten-kowski then asked two questions: "If we slate you for office will you sup-port the Democratic ticket?" and, "Would you be willing to run for some other office in the interest of the party?"[25] If both answers were yes, the candidate's name was submitted to Mount Olympus, where Daley would construct a Delphic slate which seers could never divine.

On 7 September 1969, Daley drove Rostenkowski and a few other courtiers to the northern Illinois farm of the late Adlai Stevenson. Exit-ing the mayor's limousine, they must have looked as out of place as labor bosses approaching a management soiree, for Stevenson's son, Adlai III, was hosting a hot-dogs-and-beer picnic for several thousand liberal Dem-ocrats. They included McGovern, other Senate liberals, and the Reverend Jesse L. Jackson. Young Stevenson, the state treasurer, hoped to run for the Senate on an antimachine platform. The atmosphere was convivial enough as Daley and prominent liberals made ceremonial speeches of mutual praise along the banks of the Des Plaines River. As the sun sank low, Mc-Govern rose with a news bulletin—"Senator Everett Dirksen has died in Washington."[26]

Stevenson turned to Jackson and asked him to pray. Jackson had brought a black choir, which, after his prayer, led the crowd in singing "The Battle Hymn of the Republic." Everyone, including Daley, held hands and swayed to the singing.

Illinois had lost an institution, the Senate its best orator and per-haps its slipperiest politician. The Republican leader's "switcheroos"—his word—on issues had helped LBJ enact his civil rights and social welfare laws. Now, with his seat vacant, Democrats had a good chance to capture it. Stevenson quickly made his peace with Daley, who in due course slated him, and Stevenson won the 1970 election.

Daley was climbing up from the pits of 1968, and Rostenkowski was planting big footprints in Congress. Though he rarely spoke on the floor, he was offering legislation on his own—antipollution bills, subsidies to lo-cal museums, a proposal to grant renters the same tax break as homeown-ers. He had an office in the Rayburn House Office Building adorned with a portrait of Franklin D. Roosevelt and, on a side table, one of Daley. Vis-itors to this sanctum never left in doubt of Rostenkowski's clout or where they stood with him. It appeared to Rostenkowski that life in Congress under a Republican president would not be so bad. The next three years would conspire to try to change his mind.

Joe Rostenkowski died on 8 February 1970 at the age of seventy-seven. He had not retired from the customs office until 1969 even though Johnson had abolished the collectors' positions as patronage outlets in 1965; LBJ kept Joe on the job. The funeral was a St. Stanislaus Kostka spectacular similar to Peter's in 1936. John Hoellen, the Daley and Rostenkowski foe, gave Dan an enlarged photo of Joe taken shipboard after the St. Lawrence Seaway made Chicago an international port in 1959. Dan was touched.

One of the penalties of being a young golden boy of an older establishment is that you start going to funerals at a fairly young age. Harry Bauler, Paddy's only child, had died back in 1962 of a heart attack at age fifty-two. Paul Powell, downstate powerhouse, legislative leader, Illinois secretary of state, and crook, died in October 1970. William Dawson died in November. Daley, who had politically emasculated Dawson, gave a eulogy and managed to say Dawson "was a great man" three times in the first eight sentences. Peter Granata died in 1973. And so on.

More pressing to Rostenkowski was the leadership of the House. The liberals of his "class of 1958" had formed the Democratic Study Group, joined by Rostenkowski, with modernizing House procedures one of its goals. In February 1970, the group launched a futile young-Turks effort to unseat McCormack. Rostenkowski, chairing the caucus, backed the Speaker—actually, McCormack was his favorite of the six Speakers under whom he served. In May McCormack surprisingly announced he would retire at the end of the year. He was seventy-eight, and his wife needed constant care.

In line to succeed McCormack was Majority Leader Albert, who started compiling pledges of support even though the Speaker would not be elected until the next congressional session in January. Every large state endorsed Albert except Illinois. Albert inquired of two friends from Illinois, Mel Price and Frank Annunzio. They said Rostenkowski was holding out.

Albert was a brilliant student, a champion orator, a Rhodes scholar, and vain about it. "I thought he [Rostenkowski] was my friend, though hardly my brainiest one," he sniffed.[27]

Daley and Rostenkowski were playing machine politics on a national scale. They wanted Boggs as Speaker and Rostenkowski as majority leader, the officer who handles floor proceedings for the party. For the rest of 1970, the Chicagoans tried to put together a Dixie-Daley coalition to achieve this coup.

Congressional Democrats fell into three camps: conservatives from the South, liberals from the North and West, and liberal-to-moderate, big-city organization men such as Rusty. The ploy for him was to assemble enough southern and urban votes for a Boggs-Rostenkowski ticket. When Albert's lock on the Speakership became clear, Rostenkowski kept at it anyway, challenging Boggs for majority leader.

By late December Rostenkowski, who could count votes, knew he did not have them. He had major disqualifications for the job: he spent half of each week running his ward back home, he lacked experience in managing floor debate, liberals resented his support for the Vietnam War and for House seniority rules, and he was regarded as Daley's stooge.

Sensible enough to cut his losses, Rostenkowski dropped out of the running shortly before Christmas, privately cutting a deal with Boggs. He would deliver at least eighteen votes to the Louisianan. Boggs, if elected majority leader, then would appoint Rostenkowski as whip, the third-ranking leadership post.

Rostenkowski called the five active candidates for majority leader to a luncheon meeting at the House restaurant to set the ground rules. They decided to hold two ballots, then drop the low man on the third ballot, and so on until somebody won a majority. Further, they barred other hopefuls from entering the race after balloting began. This device would prevent a compromise candidate—say, Rostenkowski—from breaking a deadlock.

Rostenkowski encountered Tip O'Neill at another restaurant that evening and remarked, "We gave you a screwing today," explaining the no-late-entry rule.

"I'm not running anyway. I'm with Boggs."

"Don't give me that," Rostenkowski replied. "We know you're trying to sneak in through the back door." Actually, Tip was pledged to Boggs.[28]

Meanwhile, the caucus was scheduled to meet on 19 January, with Rostenkowski and Albert still estranged. The time had come to talk business. Rostenkowski made a dinner date with the incoming Speaker for 18 January. He waited for hours, but Albert never showed up.[29]

The caucus met the next morning and elected Boggs on the second ballot. Now it turned to the presumed reelection of Rostenkowski as caucus chairman. Lo and behold, the Texas delegation suddenly put up another candidate, Olin E. "Tiger" Teague. The Texans had caucused the night before and agreed with a member who remarked, "Somebody at least ought to run against that son of a bitch" Rostenkowski.[30] Teague, a Texas football star and decorated veteran who had lost a foot in World War II combat, once raised a terrible fuss over being denied a parking space next to an elevator in the underground House parking garages. Although his own space was just a few steps away, Teague demanded the closer one by rights of seniority and status as a disabled veteran.[31] A typical congressman. However, he was modest enough not to try to depose Rostenkowski. He said that even though his delegation had placed his name in nomination, he was not a candidate. He waved his own ballot in the air to show it was marked for the Chicagoan.

Even the South was stunned when Teague won, 155–91. Northerners had banded with southerners for an unmistakable message: Screw you, Dick Daley, for 1968.

Internal House forces were also at work, to be sure. Fearing liberal advances, the oil states had assured a hegemony of Albert of Oklahoma, Boggs of Louisiana, and Teague of Texas. Congress the previous month had trimmed the oil depletion allowance from 27.5 percent to 22 percent, a move equated by oil producers to the collapse of civilization.

His first election loss devastated Rostenkowski. "It destroyed me," he said years later. "I just wanted to crawl into a corner and die. I had been riding on the crest of a wave and now I was drowning."[32]

He still had his deal with Boggs to be named whip. By tradition (scrapped in 1986) the majority leader appointed the whip, subject to a veto by the Speaker. Congress convened on 20 January and formally installed Albert. Soon Boggs came calling in the Speaker's office. Upholding his bargain, Boggs three times asked Albert to make Rostenkowski whip. Thrice he refused. Albert was armed with a neutron bomb—you couldn't have a whip who was rejected by his colleagues for caucus chairman.

"He insulted me and humiliated me at the convention. I won't have him," Albert said.[33] He presented Boggs a list of five acceptable names. The job at length went to O'Neill, in part to gratify liberals because of his early and strong stand against the war.

Congress, where saving face is more important than in an oriental palace, moved to salve Rostenkowski with a cocktail party in his honor in the ornate Ways and Means chamber in February. Rostenkowski put on a good front, but, as he said, he had got his brains kicked out.

Although Daley called Rostenkowski right after the caucus upset—"Is there anything I can do for you, Dan?"[34]—a heavy strain was put on the Daley-Rostenkowski relationship. Rostenkowski felt that Daley had not worked the phones vigorously enough in calling fellow big-city mayors to line up their delegations for him. Considering the anti-Daley quality of the vote, how much good he could have done is questionable.

This is conjecture, but Daley might have thought his congressman was getting too big for his britches. Daley tediously had clawed his way up the party ladder, while Rostenkowski had had positions of power handed to him. Plus, Daley didn't need to go through Rostenkowski to gain instant access to the Oval Office and probably assumed it would ever be thus. Maybe he deliberately restrained his efforts on Rostenkowski's behalf.

In any case, the influence of the Chicago machine was waning. An antimachine lawyer, Michael L. Shakman, filed suit in 1969 contending that requiring city employees to do political work and firing them at will for their political affiliation were unconstitutional. The federal courts agreed. The machine found ways to get around this, but in time the successive Shakman Decrees put a severe crimp on patronage.

More immediately and dramatically, Chicago police murdered—the verb is accurate—two Black Panthers and wounded four others in a raid on their West Side apartment on 4 December 1969. Guns blazed for eight minutes, with one bullet, possibly, fired by one of the victims. The raid was sanctioned by Daley's state's attorney, Edward V. Hanrahan. Far from the first exercise of terrorism by a unit of government in America, this one shocked even Chicago. In 1972 Hanrahan was defeated by a Republican, giving Daley another hostile state's attorney. More important, the electoral defeat of Hanrahan was the first uprising of black political power in Chicago.

Daley had his woes at home, but Rostenkowski was trying to save his career in Washington. To build an alternative power base, he identified 183 members of both parties who represented cities or were sympathetic to city needs and began sending "Dear Colleague" letters proposing an urban coalition. Also, he came out against the war.

His excuse was that while campaigning for Daley's reelection early in 1971, "the people didn't want to hear about the campaign. Sure, they were enthusiastic about the mayor, but what they wanted to know was when we were going to get out of the war. That's when I started to reevaluate my position. I noticed that the kid in my district who goes to vocational school does not get an exemption [from the draft]. He goes to Vietnam while the college kid stays home."[35] Apparently it took him six years to notice this.

To be fair, the arc of Rostenkowski's position on the war tracked that of middle America—initial support followed by frustration followed by revulsion. Representing his constituents' views, he made a 1970 speech in Chicago denouncing "revolutionary freaks—a product of affluence, not poverty, a product of romantic thinking," who urged America's youth to become "freaky, crazy, irrational, sexy, angry, irreligious, childish, and mad."[36] On a candidates' questionnaire, asked to select one of five war policies, Rostenkowski checked the middle, moderate view—"gradual troop withdrawals geared to the training of the South Vietnamese army"—the stated Nixon policy and essentially the one proposed by Humphrey late in the 1968 campaign.

In March 1971, Rostenkowski joined O'Neill and two other congressmen to demand total withdrawal of military forces by the end of the year. This was the first serious rupture of House leadership on the war, as Albert and Boggs still supported Nixon (the Senate was more antiwar). Rostenkowski also moved far ahead of Daley on the issue. Daley merely had called for Nixon to divert resources from the Pentagon to the cities—he still would not publicly attack a president, even a Republican one.

As the 1972 election cycle came around, Rostenkowski tweaked Daley again by endorsing Representative Abner J. Mikva, an antimachine liberal, for reelection. (Mikva later became a federal appeals judge and White

House counsel to Clinton.) Rostenkowski also thought that Daley's support of Hanrahan was crazy. Daley horsewhipped Rostenkowski's slating committee to force a unanimous endorsement of Hanrahan, though he later was persuaded to dump him for an alternate, but Hanrahan still won the primary, only to lose the general election.

On the presidential level, Daley as usual withheld his endorsement while the peace candidate, McGovern, won primary after primary. McGovern had chaired the commission that rewrote party rules to dethrone the bosses, elevate primary voters, and strive for racial, sexual, and generational balance in state delegations.

Daley dismissed the McGovern Commission with an obscenity as his slatemakers met in party headquarters on the second floor of the Sherman House hotel on 24 February.[37] Rostenkowski had taken the precaution of placing two women and a Hispanic on his eight-delegate Eighth Congressional District slate, but Daley ignored the new rules. In the 21 March primary, the citywide Daley slate was elected over an antimachine slate. Visions of kingmaking at the upcoming convention danced in Daley's head. He assured his committeemen that no one would dare throw them out. For insurance he had a machine judge enjoin the anti-Daley delegation from participating in the convention. The rebels went to federal court and got the U.S. Supreme Court to overturn the machine judge on 7 July. Daley still wasn't worried.

On 30 June, the party's Credentials Committee had voted in Washington to seat the rebels and evict the Daley delegates, who had, after all, won a popular election. It was an undemocratic, screw-you-Dick-Daley decision that punished his white working-class supporters. Daley went to his vacation home in Michigan to sulk, while sending Rostenkowski and the rest of his forces to the convention in Miami Beach, where surely—how could they not?—the floor delegates would reject the Credentials Committee ruling. McGovern and his strategists tried to work out a compromise, but the convention embraced the rebels, 1,486–1,372. An astounded and pained Daley stayed in Michigan. In November, the white working class repudiated McGovern for Nixon.

Rostenkowski had tried to see Larry O'Brien, by now the Democratic national chairman, to rescue the convention. Put off by a receptionist—Mr. O'Brien is much too busy!—Rostenkowski at length just barged through the office door. He found O'Brien and Joseph A. Califano, another Democratic major domo, nonchalantly munching apples. At this point, Rostenkowski deduced that the Daley delegates were doomed, and he did not deign to set foot in the convention hall that week.

The convention was a mess, a fiasco, with McGovern unable to deliver his acceptance speech until well past midnight on 14 July. The insurgent Illinois delegation happened to clinch the nomination for him during the roll call. McGovern chose as his running mate Senator Thomas F. Eagleton of Missouri, rejecting a private entreaty from Georgia Governor Jimmy Carter, which went unreported. When Eagleton's history of electroconvulsive therapy for depression was revealed, McGovern sought a new nominee for vice president. Turned down by Ted Kennedy and many others, McGovern picked Sargent Shriver, the Kennedy brother-in-law from Chicago.

Shriver had wanted to run for governor in 1956 and 1960, for vice president in 1964, and for the Senate in 1966. He always was supported by his friend Rostenkowski but somehow never won Daley's blessing—or, by implication, that of the brothers Kennedy. Early in 1972 Rostenkowski had touted Shriver for the Senate, perhaps to evade Daley's urgings that he run for the Senate himself. "Your father would be so proud of you," Daley coaxed, "a nice Polish name in the Senate." Rostenkowski used the old LaVerne-won't-let-me-run ploy to get out of that one—why give up his seniority in the House?[38]

When Daley suggested Pucinski for the Senate, Rostenkowski made no effort to keep his Northwest Side Polish rival by his side in the House—during their years in Congress, the two men had dinner together only twice. Pucinski lost the Senate race and was "promoted" to alderman.

On 8 August, Rostenkowski nominated Shriver for vice president at a special meeting of the Democratic National Committee in Washington. The Illinois rebel leaders were not there. The proceedings were formal and sober, in contrast to Miami Beach. The country did not care and reelected Nixon overwhelmingly. But Daley carried Cook County for McGovern. Let the goo goos rage—he would prove he was still a good, loyal Democrat.

Nonetheless, Daley's machine was steadily coming apart. The new governor was an anti-Daley Democrat, Daniel J. Walker. Walker had headed a commission that investigated the 1968 convention disturbances and labeled them a "police riot." Strictly speaking, the term applied only to police behavior in Lincoln Park on Sunday and Monday nights, not the "Battle of Chicago" in Grant Park on Wednesday night, a distinction swiftly lost and never recovered. Daley now confronted a hostile governor, a hostile state's attorney, and a hostile black power movement. His health was not good, though this was kept secret.

On 17 October 1972, Rostenkowski's friend and mentor Hale Boggs died in a plane crash in Alaska. O'Neill moved up to majority leader and Jim Wright of Texas to whip. Rostenkowski's rise in the leadership appeared foreclosed.

By virtue of Daley's clout and his own talents, Rostenkowski had been, for a junior congressman, in the thick of urban politics, national politics, even presidential politics for more than a decade. Now it seemed his luck had turned. He considered going home to prepare to succeed Daley when the mayor retired or died. His daughters were growing up, and it seemed he never saw them. For Dawn's sixteenth birthday, he gave her a new car. A car was an unthinkable luxury when he was a kid, and he was appalled when Dawn said, thanks, Daddy, but she really didn't like the color. Maybe there was something to this generation gap business after all. Maybe materialism and hedonism had supplanted the self-discipline of his Depression generation. Maybe he belonged home with LaVerne and the girls. Rostenkowski thought he had done good things in Congress, but if he went home he might achieve something truly historic. He might become the first Polish mayor of Chicago.

5

PIGS GET FAT

> There are men in this city who pose as reformers who
> regularly permit the assessors to value their whole property
> for less than they paid for the pictures on their walls, who
> cheat the city, then thank God they are not thieves, like the
> aldermen.
>
> —Chicago mayor Carter Harrison, 1893

JAMES R. "Big Jim" Thompson (somehow Illinois politicians are never nicknamed "little") had the machine on the run in the early 1970s. A shambling, overweight six-foot-six, Thompson was a man of large appetites with a tall, imposing presence, although, like Lyndon Johnson's, it lacked the easy carriage and coordinated gait of a natural athlete like Rostenkowski. Again like Johnson, Thompson became a chronic, flesh-pressing, cornpone campaigner.

The son of a Chicago doctor, Thompson announced to a classmate at age eleven that he intended to become president of the United States. After law school he got his prosecutorial start under State's Attorney Adamowski. Then the Nixon administration named him the U.S. attorney for northern Illinois.

When Secretary of State Paul Powell died in 1970, $800,000 in cash was found stuffed in shoeboxes and a bowling bag in his Springfield hotel suite. Powell used to bid farewell to visitors in his office by merrily handing over a $100 bill, advising them to buy a U.S. savings bond for $87.50 and use the remainder for a good steak dinner. After his death, the cached $800,000 attracted the notice of the Internal Revenue Service.

The IRS followed the money trail and soon was investigating a corral of Illinois political figures who had profited from horse racing. They included former governor Otto Kerner, Daley's former law partners Thomas J. Lynch and George J. Schaller, and, among many others, Dan Rostenkowski.

In Illinois the sport of kings was the sport of crooks. When payoffs were offered, politicians came spinning out of the turn, cloppity-clop as eagerly as the racehorses themselves. In 1962 the head of the state racing board, acting as emissary for racing impresario Marjorie Lindheimer Everett, paid a visit to the governor at his Springfield office. He offered a sweetheart deal on racing stock.

"That's awfully nice of Marje," Governor Kerner commented. The remark reflected his view of the windfall. It was merely a personal favor, irrelevant to public policy. He was foolish. Just as, then and later, Rostenkowski was foolish.

State government licensed the racetracks, levied their taxes, subsidized promotions of the industry, and sanctioned each track's all-important racing calendar. The racing dates determined when high purses and prime mounts would be available. Mindful that its profits depended on governmental action, the industry dispensed cut-rate stocks to politicians like a gumball machine.

Parimutuel betting was legalized in Illinois in 1927, and—surprise—the Capone syndicate was behind some of the tracks. In 1951 the executive secretary and former campaign manager of Governor Stevenson was ousted in a racetrack stock scandal. Later in the 1950s, the legislature and Governor Stratton cut taxes on downstate tracks during a state fiscal crisis. Secretary of State Powell was an unabashed beneficiary of racing stocks. "The only mistake I made was that I didn't get more [stock]," he once lamented. In 1963 the press revealed a major bookie ring at Sportsman's Park in Cicero, a town adjoining the city's West Side which once was Capone's headquarters. Tracks throughout the state regularly chartered buses to convey legislators to the races, where they enjoyed drinks, dinner, and tips on likely winners, all on the house. But the horse droppings did not really hit the fan until the 1970s.

In due course, the IRS findings were turned over to the U.S. attorney's office. Big Jim Thompson perused them with fascination. He particularly was interested in Kerner's stock.

"Marje" Everett had given $45,000 to Kerner's 1960 campaign, a large sum at the time. In 1962 she offered Kerner and his old army buddy, the state revenue director, stock options in her Chicago Thoroughbred Enterprises. That was mighty nice of her, and in 1966 the two men exercised the options. Kerner backdated a promissory note to 1962 for twenty-five shares of Chicago Thoroughbred at $1,000 a share. Ten months after getting the stock, Kerner traded it for 5,000 shares in a unit of Chicago Thoroughbred, the Balmoral Jockey Club, worth $30 a share. He and his buddy each had made a net profit of $144,721 from dividends and stock sales.

Grand juries were empaneled, subpoenaes were issued, testimony was taken, indictments were promised. The press speculated that as many as twelve politicians might be indicted, based no doubt on leaks from Thompson's office as part of a normal strategy to pressure targets of the investigation to "flip"—to testify for the government in exchange for leniency. Thompson's tactics gave the machine fits.

The cases of Lynch and Kerner were especially touchy. Daley had gotten LBJ to place both of them on the federal bench, from which perch Lynch had blocked appeals from antiwar protesters for city permits to sleep in the parks and march in the streets during the 1968 convention.

As for Kerner, he had been U.S. attorney in the 1950s, during which he stated, "There is no such thing as organized or syndicated crime or gambling. It is only newspaper talk." As governor, Kerner had chaired Johnson's National Advisory Commission on Civil Disorders, the "Kerner Commission," with its celebrated finding in 1968 that "white racism," producing "two societies, black and white," caused the 1960s urban riots.[1]

Meanwhile, more stockholders' names were appearing in the press, including those of Rostenkowski's pal George Dunne and then of Rusty himself. Back in 1957, state senator Rostenkowski bought 2,500 shares in the Egyptian Trotting Association for $500, or twenty cents a share. As part of the deal, he also had to buy debenture bonds costing between $1,000 and $1,300. The corporation lost money that year with harness racing at downstate Cahokia. In 1958 it was idle, but in 1959 it shifted to a suburban Chicago track controlled by Everett. Soon it redeemed the debentures and started paying dividends. Rostenkowski made a quick $42,000 profit on the $500 investment.

No problem, he told reporters, I sold that stock long ago. "I do recall that the stock was in someone else's name, but I don't remember if I made any money on the later sale of the stock or even who bought the stock," he said.[2] (The "someone else" was Chicago attorney Leonard L. Levin as nominee for Rostenkowski's shares, a common ploy.) But the press persisted. On 3 October 1971, Rostenkowski called a *Chicago Daily News* reporter and said, "I have checked my records, and it is a fact that I do own 2,500 shares of Egyptian Trotting Association stock."

Reporters live for such moments. Popping questions, the reporter heard Rostenkowski say, "That's all." Click.[3]

Decades later, Thompson said, "I remember [Rostenkowski's] name but I don't remember any more than that he had stock. They all had stock."[4] He said Rostenkowski was not called as a witness or targeted for prosecution. He was small fry.

The only big fish indicted was Kerner. At trial his stiff-necked, WASPish how-dare-you-impugn-my-integrity demeanor did not aid his defense. Thompson had a problem in that he initially was not sure of what crimes Kerner was guilty.[5] Kerner had stolen no money from the state or its taxpayers. Prosecutors could not prove that gift X to politician Y produced public policy Z. That is the dilemma of public watchdogs to this day, including those who prosecuted Rostenkowski in the 1990s, no matter how many "campaign financial reform" laws are passed.

Thompson found a century-old 1872 mail fraud statute to indict Kerner for depriving the citizens of his "loyal and faithful service," namely, by showing favoritism in awarding racing dates and other matters. It worked. For good measure, there also were indictments for conspiracy, tax evasion, and perjury. Kerner went to jail in 1973, was released for ill health, and died in 1975.

Rostenkowski was not altogether unscathed. Daley disliked any bad publicity for the machine and upbraided his protégé for it. Daley publicly denied having scolded him, but the denial was of no consequence—he also had denied issuing the 1968 "shoot to kill" order, even though it was recorded on tape. After Rostenkowski's 1971 loss to "Tiger" Teague followed by the racetrack mess that fall, Daley was turning more to Annunzio and less to Rostenkowski for Chicago delegation business. The Italian community was delighted, the Polish community disturbed.

Considering the negative publicity, Daley's defenders believe that President Nixon and his attorney general, John N. Mitchell, politically prosecuted Kerner to punish Daley for stealing the 1960 election. Kerner happened to be the son-in-law of Anton Cermak, and, supposedly, jailing him would damage Daley and his machine. For all the manifold sins of Richard Nixon, of this charge he is innocent. Those who level it do not understand the parochialism of machine politics. How would the conviction of Kerner, a mere governor kicked upstairs to a federal judgeship, undercut Daley's power? The record shows that the only interest Mitchell's office took in the case was to insist that Thompson himself, not his deputy, Samuel K. Skinner, personally conduct the trial. "If you're going to indict a federal [appellate] judge for the first time in history, the U.S. attorney's going to be sitting at the [courtroom] table," as Thompson later said.[6]

The machine did not unduly grieve over the jailing of Kerner, but it was troubled by Thompson's successful prosecutions, on nonracing corruption charges, of Daley's closest Bridgeport pal, Circuit Court Clerk Matthew Danaher; Daley's press secretary, Earl Bush; and Daley's brains, City Council Finance Committee Chairman Thomas E. Keane. Big Jim became an inevitable Republican candidate for governor, although Daley feared that he wanted to run for mayor.

Political consultants advised Thompson to get married, get a dog, and lose weight. He complied with all three directives. Meanwhile, Daley's choice to oust the renegade governor, Dan Walker, in the 1976 Democratic primary was Michael J. Howlett, the secretary of state. For the recruitment of Howlett into the candidacy, Daley assigned Rostenkowski. Howlett turned him down. Rostenkowski reported the refusal to Daley. Daley declared that Howlett owed it to the party. Soon Howlett found himself the slated candidate for governor.

Howlett accompanied presidential candidate Jimmy Carter on a flight from Chicago to Moline, and the pilot of the chartered jet keyed the intercom to say, "We're proud and happy to have Governor Carter and his lovely wife, Rosalyn, aboard," to which the reporters in the back of the plane cheered, "Yay!"

The cheer was not, despite Republican beliefs to the contrary, a telltale endorsement of a Democrat by the "liberal news media." The press corps traveling on presidential campaigns then resembled a flying fraternity house, full of hijinks and practical jokes, placing high values on irreverence and irony. The attitude expressed by that cheer was ha ha, this is just an empty show; it's all bullshit, but we're all in it together, and if this doofus pilot thinks we're honored to be flying with Carter, if he's that clueless, we'll indulge him with an ironic "yay!" just because we're so hip. Probably neither Carter, Howlett, nor the pilot understood the subtlety.

Then the pilot added, "We're also proud and happy to have aboard the slated Democratic candidate for governor, Michael Howlett," to which the reporters impishly shouted "Boo!" to signify their disfavor of the Daley machine. Howlett, riding up front with Carter, arose, thrust aside the mauve curtain separating first class from media steerage, intromitted his round face and silver hair past the bulkhead, and said with conviction, "Fuck you!"[7]

Anyone who can say that to the media deserves election, but Howlett, though he defeated Walker in the primary, thus scotching Walker's presidential ambitions, lost in November to Thompson. President Ford narrowly carried the state against Carter. Daley was zero-for-two at the top of the ticket. He had less than two months to live.

Rostenkowski remained ensconced in his Ways and Means duchy. Encountering Washington reporters for the *Chicago Tribune* in off-the-record moments, he would complain, "Aw, all you guys ever write about is me and my racetrack stock. You don't pay any attention to anything else going on here." Then he would gloat, "I've still got mine. I'm the only one with those racing stocks that's still making money on them. I didn't chicken out and get rid of it."[8] Perhaps Rostenkowski had missed the larger point.

Racetrack deals were catnip for Illinois pols, "mighty nice" transactions that yielded a swift few thousand dollars or tens of thousands. But for serious money they needed to turn from Chicago to Washington. Rostenkowski's career thus far has confirmed the verity that Republicans and Democrats collude to raise taxes and provide pork. His actions in the Presidential Towers development illustrate the corresponding bipartisanship of manipulating public policy for making money.

Early in Daley's mayoralty his machine spoke of Loop boardroom desires as "Republican interests," just another pressure group to be appeased, rather like the Poles or Italians. By the 1970s, the term had fallen out of usage. Only the closest scrutiny could distinguish "Republican interests" from Democratic interests, except during election-season rhetoric.

Concurrently the nation was trying to rebuild its forlorn inner cities. The area just west of the Loop was Skid Row. Bums along Madison Street tossed empty bottles of Thunderbird wine in the gutters. Flophouses painted large letters on their ancient dirty brick outer walls, "Transients Welcome." The new developments did not erect neon signs flashing "Yuppies Welcome," but they might as well have. On six acres of Skid Row, within shouting distance of the walnut-and-skylights boardrooms of the Loop, four apartment buildings, each forty-nine stories tall, were built largely on Rostenkowski's clout. The free market, so loudly venerated by Republicans, would not have constructed these towers. The development occupied the presidencies of Carter, Reagan, Bush, and Clinton, two Republicans and two Democrats, consuming close to $200 million in subsidies, tax breaks, and defaulted loans. Had he lived, Otto Kerner, jailed for a mere $150,000 stock swap, might have looked with envy on such perfectly legal churning of cash.

In addition to Rostenkowski, other players were involved in Presidential Towers. Daniel J. Shannon was an accountant who had headed the Park District, which once employed Rostenkowski, and he operated Rostenkowski's "blind trust," which returned him a huge profit on a minimal investment. Shannon had helped Rostenkowski and others set up the Garfield Ridge Savings and Trust Bank in 1966 and had headed the Teamsters Union Central States Pension Fund, which had owned the old Sherman House hotel, headquarters of the Cook County Democratic Party. He was once hired to analyze a tax bill for the Ways and Means Committee, and his development company employed a Rostenkowski son-in-law. James P. McHugh was a contractor in whose real estate partnership Rostenkowski owned an interest, 50 percent of which was bought out by Shannon in the early 1970s, and in whose partnership, incidentally, Rostenkowski's sisters Gladys and Marcella ("Marcia") also invested. Also there were a Democratic representative, Frank Annunzio, and a Republican senator, Charles Percy; and a powerful alderman who located his law office, along with the beauty parlor of a woman friend, in Presidential Towers; and the alderman's brother, who ran a private security company that won the Presidential Towers security contract and who later became an alderman himself; and a 1960s bomb thrower who transmuted herself into a public relations entrepreneur and who represented Presidential Towers and also Daley's son and successor as mayor, Rich; and a Reagan White House official and U.S. Senate candidate who was a lobbyist for Presidential Towers and a partner in a Loop law firm that also employed Daley's son, Bill, later the U.S. commerce secretary under Clinton; and a cousin of a U.S. senator from Michigan; and a phalanx of boardroom biggies whose public spiritedness inspired them to donate campaign cash to Republicans and Democrats alike; and a Republican governor, James Thompson; and a lawyer hired to lobby Thompson for Presidential Towers who later was named U.S. attorney in Chicago; and two Democratic mayors, Jane M. Byrne and Harold Washington, the latter an antimachine mayor whose reelection campaign chairman was the proposed underwriter for some Presidential Towers bonds; and Jack Kemp, housing secretary under Bush and the 1996 Republican nominee for vice president. All this for the sake of inducing yuppies to forsake the suburbs for downtown. And to make money for Democratic and Republican elites.

The foregoing catalogue of Presidential Towers figures might appear formidably dense, so let us begin the narrative with someone not included therein, Charles Swibel. An escapee from Nazis in Poland, Swibel epitomized the hustlers of all nationalities who gravitated to Chicago, like iron shavings to a magnet, as a natural environment in which to get rich. In 1962 Daley named Swibel chairman of the Chicago Housing Authority, a shadow government that operated public housing, a city within a city because liberals of the 1950s and 1960s thought it humane to stack poor people in ugly high rises stretching for block after desolate block, or, in the case of Chicago, mile after mile.

In 1982 the Reagan housing department, itself so corrupt that it later warranted a special prosecutor (admittedly not a high hurdle in contemporary Washington), audited Swibel. The recitation of his misfeasances impressed even Chicago. For example, he had deposited housing authority funds in low-interest accounts at a local bank, which gave Swibel a $50 million personal line of credit to finance his private real estate deals. Mayor Byrne, who had campaigned against the "evil cabal" of the machine but soon ran open armed into its clutches, including those of Swibel, "reluctantly" accepted his resignation from the housing authority. Swibel remained a Byrne strategist.

Perhaps Swibel did not much care about his CHA dismissal, for he already had swung a deal for Presidential Towers, called then "Madison-Canal" after its cross streets. The genesis of Presidential Towers was in the Great Society. In 1968 Congress passed a law to allow state and local governments to issue tax-exempt bonds to subsidize residential mortgages—home ownership, the American dream! State housing authorities proceeded to float such bonds, but cities took little interest. Swibel perceived that an opportunity was being missed. In 1974 he acquired Madison-Canal at an urban renewal land price set in 1968. Absentmindedly, he neglected to pay property taxes while the land multiplied in value under the Ford-Carter inflation. In 1978 city hall sold $100 million in tax-exempt bonds to develop Swibel's land. Chicago was the first city to make a major bond issue under the program.[9]

In Washington, House Ways and Means Committee chairman Al Ullman of Oregon suspected that such bonds were being used to make developers rich rather than to provide mortgages for the working class. Not only that, but the nontaxable bonds were denying revenues to the government during what were believed at the time to be alarming budget deficits. Ullman wanted to end the mortgage bond program, but he was a weak chairman compared to his predecessor, Mills, or successor, Rostenkowski.

The committee tied itself in knots over what to do about the bonds. At length Ways and Means gave up—a rare surrender—and kicked the issue to the full House. The House then kicked it to the Senate so that the issue might be decided in a legislative conference committee comprising members of both bodies.

Rostenkowski was the second-ranking Democrat and the only Illinoisan on that conference committee during the end of Carter's term in 1980. A compromise phased out the bond program in three years, and, in the meantime, new projects had to set aside at least 20 percent of their apartments for low-to-moderate income tenants. Thus the objections of Ullman and other liberals were answered. The compromise made the news, but a Rostenkowski maneuver did not. He inserted an amendment exempting Presidential Towers from the 20-percent rule.

Freed from such a money-losing nuisance, Shannon, McHugh, and Daniel E. Levin, a cousin of Senator Carl Levin of Michigan, bought Madison-Canal from Swibel, who, slapping his forehead in remembrance, paid up the back taxes so as to transfer the title. The three developers, armed with the city's $100 million (eventually, $180 million) in tax-exempt, five-year construction bonds, also won a commitment from the Reagan administration for a forty-year, low-interest mortgage of $159 million. This was the largest mortgage the Government National Mortgage Association ("Ginny Mae") had ever made.

At about the same time, congressional reforms impelled Rostenkowski to set up a blind trust for his investments so that he could not wittingly profit from congressional action. To head the blind trust, he selected Shannon. In 1980 he gave Shannon two hundred dollars, which bought two hundred shares, a 5 percent interest, in Newco, Inc., formed that year to buy the assets of an electrical supply firm for $2.5 million. Newco evolved into Electric Supply Corporation, then into MP Electric, Inc. Fifteen months after the formation of Newco, MP Electric was sold to Crescent Electric Supply Corporation for $5 million. A $2.5 million acquisition had doubled in value in fifteen months. Rostenkowski's two hundred dollars was the only money he put into his blind trust for its first four years. That sum earned him a profit approaching ninety-five thousand. The exact amount cannot be specified because of the ambiguous nature of congressional financial disclosure records.

An officer of Newco said its buyers acquired an undervalued company and were able to sell for twice its purchase price because Crescent Electric was willing to pay extra for a foothold in the Chicago market. This explanation surely would have satisfied the House ethics committee, which never cast a glance at Rostenkowski's ninety-five-thousand-dollar profit on a two-hundred-dollar investment.

Back at Madison and Canal, Shannon, McHugh, and Levin still needed help to get Presidential Towers built. Labor leaders wanted the construction jobs the project would provide, so they went to their friend Annunzio, whose labor connections dated to the 1940s. Annunzio chaired a labor committee that had given fifteen hundred dollars to Adlai Stevenson's 1948 campaign. The governor named Annunzio state labor director but then fired him in 1952 over a conflict of interest. In 1964 Daley chose him to succeed Roland Libonati in Congress, where he continued to employ Sam Giancana's son-in-law, Anthony Tisci, as a legislative aide. Annunzio became known in the House as "Mr. Ethnic" for his efforts to make Columbus Day a federal holiday and to jawbone Hollywood against portraying Italian Americans as mobsters. More to the point, in 1982 he was a member of the House Committee on Banking, Finance, and Urban Affairs.

Annunzio slipped into a housing bill an amendment to waive certain fees attached to federal mortgage bonds. The waiver applied only to Presidential Towers, although that project was not named in the amendment— standard practice in the sinuous language of federal tax laws. The projected savings to the developers of Presidential Towers amounted to $3 million. When the press got wind of this pork, the congressman was forthright. "My job is to bring federal funds and jobs to Chicago," said Annunzio in another epigram from an unsung political philosopher.[10]

Back again at Madison and Canal, Shannon, McHugh, and Levin still needed help to get Presidential Towers built. Rostenkowski, by this time chairman of Ways and Means, helpfully inserted into a 1982 tax bill a provision that promised smaller income tax bills for the 590 limited partners in Presidential Towers. The bill required investors to spread their depreciation deductions evenly over fifteen years, a "straight line" write-off. Rostenkowski's exemption allowed Presidential Towers investors to take larger or "accelerated" deductions in the first few years. The estimated tax savings over five years were $7 million.

The developers now had five governmental boons: the city's construction bonds engineered by Swibel, Ginny Mae's low-interest mortgage, the Rostenkowski 20-percent waiver, the Annunzio bond-fees amendment, and the Rostenkowski depreciation amendment.

In a series of articles beginning 20 November 1983, Rostenkowski's and Annunzio's machinations were disclosed in the *Chicago Sun-Times* by reporter Chuck Neubauer (who later wrote many of the stories leading to Rostenkowski's indictment in 1994). Rostenkowski's public response was predictable and characteristic. "Anything I did for Presidential Towers, I did for the city," he said. "I guess I use my leverage for any kind of project that benefits the city."[11]

It was good for the city! Bring young professionals back downtown, improve the city's tax base, and ease the city tax burden on the working class. Were these not worthy goals? The 590 investors might have thanked God they were not crooks, like Carter Harrison's, or Dick Daley's, or Jane Byrne's aldermen. The old guys, "Bathhouse" John Coughlin, "Hinky

Dink" Kenna, "Paddy" Bauler, "Big Joe Rusty," were history, crude vulgarians, uneducated ethnics. Would they know how to work a K Street lobbyist's reception in Washington, college diploma intangibly placed in a well-tailored jacket pocket? Could they discuss debenture bonds, land writedowns, urban renewal studies for the Department of Housing and Urban Development, send a basket of fruit on the HUD secretary's birthday?

Those old guys, petty grafters, boodlers, would not have grasped the new system of big government, big business, big labor, the system erected by such as Dick Daley and Lyndon Johnson and the multitudes who voted for them. The trick was not in illegal peculations—that was déclassé—but in legal manipulations of legislative and bureaucratic processes. Bondholders benefited, developers benefited, unions benefited, the entire city benefited. Presidential Towers, even with public subventions, was something of a speculative gamble, but was that not the essence of the free enterprise system? And if an agent of the legislative process, Dan Rostenkowski, was aided by a pal who also happened to be a developer, what were friends for? Anyway, Rostenkowski acted for the good of Chicago. As did Governor Thompson, Mayor Byrne, and Senator Percy, who all went to bat for the project. And anyway it wasn't as if Presidential Towers were the only development in the country so favored—although, to be sure, the Towers consumed 68 percent of Ginny Mae's subsidized mortgage funds in 1983.

Still, in one respect the new manipulators were just like the old guys. Rostenkowski used to hand down a piece of inherited machine wisdom: "Pigs get fat but hogs get butchered." Or, to cite another farmyard proverb quoted by a 1920s chairman of Ways and Means: "You can shear a sheep once a year, but you can only skin him once." [12] Such folklore came straight from Hinky Dink and Bathhouse, who counseled their precinct captains to stick to the small payoffs, not gross bribery; it would add up to millions over the years but meanwhile would not incite prosecutors to convene grand juries. The developers of Presidential Towers did not steal millions of dollars. They merely got a break of a few percentage points on the interest rate and of clauses here and there in the tax code. Taxpayers might have been sheared, but they weren't skinned.

In the old days, the prosecutors of such as Stanley Kunz mourned their failure to obtain convictions. In our time, prosecutors are more apt to mourn their failure to find prosecutable offenses. The jailings of Kerner in 1973 and Rostenkowski in 1996 were anomalies, kinks in a criminal justice system bent by politics and special circumstances. Rostenkowski raised the defense of selective prosecution. He had a point. Pigs were getting fat all over the place, perfectly legally, and few knew it better than he.

The fundamental problem is not the alleged singling out of Rostenkowski for prosecution but the fact that America is confused over what constitutes public corruption in the era of big government. This confusion befuddled, for example, investigators from the media and a special prosecutor's office into the Whitewater affair involving President Clinton and his wife. When the government regulates and subsidizes nearly everything, the line separating legal from illegal interventions in governmental process blurs into mist. To get indicted, an intervener must be egregious. The actors in Presidential Towers were not. Far from it. They were reviving the inner city, a liberal enthusiasm written into laws passed by Democratic Congresses. And if these laws resulted in the evictions of men subsisting on Social Security disability checks in single-room-occupancy "Transients Welcome" hotels, well, those were the breaks.

So it came to pass that ground was broken for Presidential Towers in 1983 with Thompson turning the first spadeful of earth and Percy cutting the ribbon. Doors were opened in 1985 for four towers of putty-colored brick: yuppie heaven, 2,346 apartments, mostly studios and one bedrooms, with a health club featuring a pool, sauna, and tanning parlor; satellite television; a concierge, valets, and maids; restaurants, a drugstore, florist, and bank on the premises, all within walking distance of the law offices and investment banks in the Loop, provided the tenants were not afraid of panhandlers and the homeless and crime on the streets. Most of the tenants were single, professional men and women in their twenties. The occupancy rate was high. The place should have made money.

Vigilant in their pursuit of clout remained the developers. The Towers were insured by a firm headed by George Dunne, by now the chairman of the Cook County Board. The law firm of Michael J. Madigan, the Southwest Side Irishman who was Speaker of the Illinois house, appealed the Towers' tax assessments. Security was handled by Victor Vrdolyak, brother of Alderman Edward R. Vrdolyak, leader of the city council, who set up his own law offices in the Towers. Anton R. Valukas, Thompson's personal lawyer and later U.S. attorney, was hired to lobby the governor. As a courtesy, the developers reserved suites for Loop estimables to conduct afternoon trysts and late-night poker parties.

In August 1989, Presidential Towers asked HUD for a bailout loan of $16 million. In February 1990, the Towers missed its first $1.5 million monthly mortgage payment. Two months later, the trustee of the bonds filed with the Federal Housing Authority a notice of election to assign. That is how lawyers spell default. The amount of the defaulted mortgage by then was $171 million.

There followed tedious negotiations with housing secretaries under Bush and Clinton to salvage the project and prevent HUD from acquiring title to—and management responsibility for—four apartment towers it did not want. Back in 1987 the city under Mayor Washington had refinanced the construction bonds for $180 million over forty years. As its price the city required the developers to underwrite a new low-income housing trust fund, but under default there was no money to put into it. Testifying before a city council committee at the time, developer Levin said, "I want no sympathy. I am not a poor man. But building residential buildings is a risky business. Presidential Towers could not have been built conventionally." [13]

Indeed. That is the voice of the modern high-stakes entrepreneur, dependent on mastering government's power to condemn property, hold it, sell it cheap, and subsidize development on it. Developers were casualties of their own sway over these governmental processes. Tax laws were so favorable to commercial real estate in the 1980s that the resulting boom grossly overbuilt the Chicago market, producing an inevitable bust. Presidential Towers had to go begging for yuppies, offering various breaks on their rentals, which averaged $785 a month. By 1990 a total of nine luxury projects in Chicago had defaulted on FHA loans.

Jack Kemp, Bush's housing secretary, blew into town, blustered that Presidential Towers was a HUD "mistake," and demanded concessions for the poor in return for a bailout. Exposure to poor people would be good for yuppies in the Towers, he said in the sort of pronouncement that did not endear him to certain GOP quarters.

Rostenkowski once again was called on to defend his role and was typically defiant. Not only did he have "no regrets," but he said, "I had Jim Thompson in here begging me to do it . . . [Thompson and Percy] didn't do much. I did a heck of a lot more. But when all the accolades were pointed out they were in the front row. When all the criticism comes out I don't see them any more."[14]

The developers acquired still another arrow in their clout quiver with Rich Williamson, a former Reagan White House official in the gold-plated law firm of Mayer Brown & Platt. Williamson lobbied HUD through Kemp's aide William Dal Col (later the campaign manager for 1996 presidential hopeful Steve Forbes), along with Thompson, Senator Alan J. Dixon, and Representative Lynn Martin (later Bush's labor secretary). The developers also hired public relations consultant Marilyn Katz, who had organized antiwar demonstrations at the 1968 convention.

HUD finally agreed to pay off the defaulted mortgage after the issue was bounced from Kemp to Clinton's housing secretary, Henry Cisneros. In April 1994, HUD said it would not foreclose on the property, and the owners agreed to reserve 165 apartments—7 percent of the units—for tenants with low to moderate incomes. Such was the fallout of a 1968 Great Society program to help poor people acquire deeds to their own homes.

The Presidential Towers affair eerily seemed to smudge with misfortune anyone who stepped close to it, however innocently. Frank Annunzio was redistricted out of his seat in 1992 and later hospitalized for depression. Charles Percy, Alan Dixon, and Lynn Martin all went down in election defeats. Ed Vrdolyak, chairman of Cook County Democrats, switched to the Republican party, lost a race for mayor, and declined into oblivion. Victor Vrdolyak died of illness at age fifty-nine in 1992. George Dunne was scorched in 1988 for having group sex with two female Cook County employees. Housing Secretary Cisneros was investigated for allegedly improper payments to a former mistress. Developer Levin went through a nasty divorce. Developer Shannon's twenty-eight-year-old son committed suicide in his Presidential Towers apartment. As for the elderly tenants of the old "Transients Welcome" hotels, nobody kept track of what happened to them.

This chapter has hopscotched from a minor state-level racetrack scandal of 1962 through 1972 to a federal housing financial decision in 1994 that provided a sad anticlimax to a Great Society dream of 1968. The nucleus of corruption had migrated from Milwaukee Avenue and the Illinois Capitol to Pennsylvania Avenue in Washington. The lessons during that time frame were consistent. First, manipulate governmental processes to make yourself and your patrons and clients rich. Second, steal legally if you can—the laws invite it—but in any case steal in small sums seriatim, and nobody gets too upset.

Rostenkowski understood these lessons; still, he had journeyed far past such hometown concerns as Presidential Towers. He was too busy writing the mammoth tax laws of 1986 (a political triumph for Reagan) and 1990 (a political disaster for Bush). Periodically he would hint at coming home to run for mayor or retiring from public life altogether and make big-time money in private industry. Constantly he dealt with corporate chieftains, manifestly less talented than he, who made ten times his salary. Look, he didn't need all this grief. A mob of senior citizens, angry over his Medicare amendments, had thumped on the hood of his chauffeur-driven car in Chicago. Why, sometimes he suffered the indignity of having to run against somebody in the Democratic primary. Grumble grumble . . .

Jim Thompson stepped down from the governor's seat in 1990 to become a rainmaker lawyer-lobbyist at a Loop law firm, Winston & Strawn. Thompson paid a visit to H208, Rusty's second-floor Capitol office, adorned with portraits of the eight members of Ways and Means who had ascended (descended?) to the presidency. Thompson was there to ask for something or other on behalf of some client or other and endured one of Rostenkowski's bitching sessions. "I've put up with so much bullshit in this job," Rostenkowski mourned.

Thompson listened in amusement for a bit and then replied, "Danny, you're taking all this grief because you would never sit on the side of the desk where I'm sitting, and look across it, and call somebody else Mr. Chairman."

After a moment a smile spread across Rostenkowski's jowls. "You're right," he said.[15]

THE TUESDAY THROUGH
THURSDAY CLUB

> Is there really someone who, searching for a group of wise and
> sensitive persons to regulate him for his own good, would
> choose that group of people who constitute the membership
> of both houses of Congress?
>
> —Robert Nozick, *Anarchy, State, and Utopia*

IN March 1973, Rostenkowski sat in a rocker in his 2111 Rayburn office and winced slightly whenever he shifted position. Springtime had beckoned him to the golf course, where he wrenched his back. He took golfing seriously—or rather, obsessively—and rocked in his office in frustration, kept off the links and reduced to contemplating life as an assistant Democratic whip after Nixon's landslide reelection.

The next month Rostenkowski had another occasion to wince when Tip O'Neill whipped a survey out of his pocket and handed it over for perusal. As Watergate began to unfold, a government workers' union commissioned an early poll to gauge the scandal's potential effect on the 1974 congressional elections. The results were so startling that the pollster, a leading Democratic analyst, vouchsafed them to O'Neill. The study showed that 43 percent of the public would vote for a congressman who was in favor of impeachment, compared to 29 percent who would vote against him (the rest said it wouldn't matter). Among Republicans, fully half would vote to oust any congressman who opposed impeachment— these were voters of the president's own party. Perhaps the most disturbing number was that only 7 percent of Democrats would vote for a congressman who opposed impeachment.

This was early in 1973, before the firings of Nixon's top aides, revelations of a secret White House taping system, the "Saturday night massacre," and all the rest. At the time, the word *impeachment* scarcely was whispered, let alone debated.

The poll "turned Danny around," O'Neill said.[1] Indeed, it rattled members of both parties, forcing them to think unthinkable thoughts, which politicians hate to do as much as the rest of us. Republicans who cherish the belief that Watergate was a Democratic plot to railroad Nixon out of office have forgotten how shocking was the idea of impeachment to the entire political class. The poll—assuming it was accurate—indicated the public was far in front of that class in its judgment of Nixon.

Considering Watergate, Rostenkowski was a typical Democrat, just as he had been on Vietnam—support for the president, followed by disbelief at the appalling parade of high grotesqueries, followed by revulsion. In finally opposing Vietnam, he cited a moral reason, the plucking of working-class boys out of the Thirty-second Ward to die in Asian rice paddies while middle-class boys happily ejected college deans from their offices in antiwar protests. Watergate he evaluated wholly on political terms. If he thought the White House crimes morally reprehensible, that perspective did not inform his public statements. Impeachment was in the wind, he grudgingly allowed, but he didn't like it. His constituents, again, were older, conservative, working-class, home-owning white ethnics with respect for authority in their bones. "My district was always America first, very strong against communism," he said, and in the meantime, "most of those screaming out for impeachment are candidates for the Senate or governorships."[2] This was a tactic for politicians on the make—something he understood. Many years later he said he would not have voted to impeach Nixon.

In May 1973, Rostenkowski had yet another occasion to wince. Daley made one of his royal visits to Washington and did not even inform him in advance. Customarily, Daley would be welcomed at National Airport by the whole Chicago delegation, Rostenkowski foremost, and escorted in a procession of state to the White House or a congressional hearing room or wherever. This time Daley deigned to attend a meeting of the Democratic Advisory Committee of Elected Officials—a body with a portentous title and hence little real power—in the company of Frank Annunzio. City hall off the record blamed the snub of Rostenkowski on Democratic national chairman Robert Strauss, all the more puzzling because Rostenkowski recently had endorsed Strauss for the job. Probably the designation of Annunzio was the dual doing of Daley, who was sending Rostenkowski a message, and Speaker Albert, who remained alert for opportunities to hurt him. Characteristically, neither Daley nor Rostenkowski said anything in public about the tiny tempest, but presumably the Nixon White House picked up on it. Nixon named Rostenkowski to represent the United States at the Poznan International Trade Fair in Poland in June—a favor for a congressman whose support he might need down the road.

In March 1974, following hammer blow after hammer blow of Watergate concussions, his presidency destroyed, Nixon flew to Chicago for a speech to a business group. Although protocol would demand it, not a single Illinois Republican greeted *Air Force One* at O'Hare. Nixon was met only by Daley, an aide, the mayor's son Bill, and Pucinski.

In the limo to the Loop with Nixon, Daley brought up two things close to his heart: Chicago and America. Chicago had always led the nation in outpourings of tribute to American astronauts, he said, and in fact a celebration for the *Skylab* astronauts was coming up in a couple of weeks. How grateful Nixon must have felt toward Daley, the old enemy who had stolen Illinois from him in 1960, for discussing patriotic ceremony instead of Watergate. Daley, the Chicago Irish sheetmetal worker's son despised by the clerisy, and Nixon, the suburban Los Angeles Quaker grocer's son despised by the clerisy, both wounded old political warriors—the moment was poignant. Nixon (as Rostenkowski pointed out at the time) had visited Chicago shortly after the 1968 convention and *praised the Chicago police*. For the *Skylab* fete, Nixon promised the mayor he would send the Strolling Strings of the Air Force, a twenty-one member band he often invited to the White House for receptions for Vietnam POWs and the like.

When the astronauts arrived, only a few thousand folks—many of them city payrollers sent by Daley—turned out for the Loop celebration. People apparently were bored by the space program and in no mood for patriotic jubilation.

On 6 May 1974, four days after Jim Thompson indicted Alderman Keane, Daley's speech suddenly was slurred in a city hall meeting, and he felt his leg go numb. A mild stroke was diagnosed. Daley's courtiers gave the public a minimum of information. On 2 June, doctors performed an endarectomy, excising a blockage from an artery that fed the mayoral brain. Officially, the surgery was scheduled for 3 June. Fearing assassination by a power cutoff during the operation, Daley dispatched police to guard the hospital and went under the knife a day before scheduled. "He always has this thing about not trusting anyone," Ed Vrdolyak muttered, "but now it looks like the old man is losing his marbles."[3] Removing to his vacation home in Grand Beach, Michigan, to recuperate, Daley was out of action during that summer's impeachment proceedings against his fellow paranoiac, Richard Nixon.

Like all congressmen, Rostenkowski looked to his district for guidance on impeachment. He heard "no mention" of it there, but when he went into suburban Republican districts, voters were "really burned at the president." Maybe, Rostenkowski reasoned, he was in a position to broker a deal.

As the case for impeachment metastasized, many congressmen still longed to avoid it. Rostenkowski floated the idea that an impeachment resolution might be coupled with a grant of immunity from later criminal prosecution of Nixon. "I'd vote for that in a minute," he said. "Lots of people agree with me that we don't want to see a president of the United States go to the penitentiary, but nobody wants to put his name on a piece of legislation."[4]

Rostenkowski, holding an invulnerable seat, was available to put his name on such a resolution. He had his staff draft one. Republican representatives and some GOP senators were favorable to the ploy because it would give political cover to explain their impeachment vote to diehard partisans of the it's-all-a-plot ilk. But events quickly overtook this maneuver. As a practical matter, such a resolution still would have left Nixon subject to criminal liability in state courts and subpoenas to testify at federal Watergate trials anyway. To avoid certain impeachment, Nixon resigned on 9 August. President Ford soon nullified the prosecution scenario by granting Nixon a full pardon.

In truth, Rostenkowski had little to do with the impeachment proceedings of 1974. Not a lawyer, nor a member of the Judiciary Committee, which voted articles of impeachment, he was just another urban Democrat, moreover one apparently on the outs with his patron, Daley, who was debilitated with uncertain prospects for recovery. For all his political talents and years of experience, Rostenkowski for much of the 1970s was more or less an ordinary congressman—pork barreler, junketeer, collector of speaking fees from lobbyists' groups, avid seeker of outside income, golfer.

But Daley was still "Da Mare." On 3 September, he quit the summer palace in Michigan for city hall, where the fiction of his competence was assiduously maintained. Actually, Michael Daley each morning checked his father's schedule at city hall and at Democratic headquarters to determine whether the mayor was capable of meeting the day's events. On 9 October, Daley was called to testify at the trial of his former press secretary, Earl Bush. Coincidentally, that same day Keane was convicted, and, in Washington, Ways and Means chairman Mills took an impromptu drunken dip in the Tidal Basin with an Argentine stripper. Within two days, another Chicago alderman was convicted of tax evasion and Bush was convicted of mail fraud. Everywhere, it seemed, the giants were tumbling, and anguish lay heavily on the shoulders of the political establishment.

The congressional elections that November swept in a class of "Watergate babies," seventy-five freshman Democrats resolved to scrape the rottenness out of the seniority system. The Democratic Caucus, which Rostenkowski had done so much to empower in the late 1960s, now undercut him avidly. By a 146–12 vote on 2 December, the caucus eliminated the power of Ways and Means members (enjoyed since 1911) to assign all House Democrats to committees. This task was assigned to a new Steering and Policy Committee, from which Rostenkowski was excluded. The next day the caucus expanded Ways and Means from twenty-five congressmen to thirty-seven, diluting the power of senior members. (Two new Illinois seats went to a liberal Democrat, Abner J. Mikva, and a conservative Republican, Philip M. Crane.)

Seekers of confirmation of the dictum that power is corrupting need only look at the power wielded by committee chairmen in the prereform Congress. They could be autocratic, vain, obstreperous, irascible, arbitrary. Presidents labored mightily to get around them, often unsuccessfully. The Watergate babies swiftly deposed three despots, the chairs of banking, armed services, and agriculture (all southerners).

It must have galled Rostenkowski that, after sixteen years of accruing seniority and courting mentors, and although merely in his forties with a long career still ahead, the importance of seniority suddenly was degraded.

Early in the 1975 session the caucus overruled Ways and Means to bring repeal of the oil depletion allowance—sacrilege to the old guard—to the House floor. Reform, reform! was the watchword. Rostenkowski and Daley, eyewitnesses to decades of reform efforts in Chicago, did not shed their skepticism.

Rosty seized an opportunity to slam Senator Ribicoff of Connecticut for his "Gestapo tactics" slam at the 1968 convention. Ribicoff sought a tax provision to benefit the insurance firms headquartered in his state. For several nights, Rostenkowski boned up on insurance tax law and was able to avenge Daley by deleting the Ribicoff amendment.

Daley was seventy-two, sick, and humiliated by the events of 1968, 1972, and 1974; most of his best friends were indicted, jailed, sick, or dead (Danaher died in 1974 shortly before his scheduled trial). To show that he was still alive, still a player, still Boss, Daley journeyed to Kansas City for the Democratic party's biennial "miniconvention" in December 1974. Chairman Strauss gave him the blessing of an appearance at the podium. The applause was warm, perhaps out of deference to an old lion, perhaps because Daley by now was superannuated, no longer feared on the national stage.

He still was feared in Chicago. On the Monday after the miniconvention, 9 December, he summoned eighteen of his colonels to the La Salle Hotel for a council of war. Turning on the blarney, Daley spoke for ten minutes, offering to step down for the good of the party if anyone there wished it. One by one, the colonels—Rostenkowski, Dunne, Vrdolyak, the others—rose and affirmed that not only did they want him to run, but the citizens of Chicago devoutly, passionately willed it.

A short time later, Daley went to the Illinois Room of the hotel for the formal luncheon meeting of the fifty members of the Central Committee and publicly declared his candidacy for mayor. The urban Democrats could have used Cornhuskers Lotion that night, for they clapped their hands nearly raw. The scene was reminiscent of the standing ovations of the Politburo for Josef Stalin in the 1940s, which went on forever because everyone was afraid to be the first to stop applauding and sit down. Dunne, in a typical encomium, declared, "Almighty God must love Chicago very, very much, because he's blessed us with leadership for twenty years that's unparalleled in history or any other part of our country." [5] No other candidate sought the committee's endorsement. The meeting, chaired by Rostenkowski, unanimously approved Dunne's nomination of Daley as the mayor sat impassively, hands folded in his lap.

In the February 1975 primary, Daley easily defeated a young lakefront liberal, William Singer (later an informal adviser to Clinton), and two other candidates, one of them black. Daley won a plurality but—for the first time—not a majority of the black vote. In the April election, the sacrificial Republican nominee was John Hoellen, who went hat in hand to the Loop Republican boardrooms and raised an insulting twenty-nine thousand dollars. Daley spent more than $1 million.

Entertaining hopes of brokering national power yet again as the 1976 presidential season sprouted, Daley characteristically withheld his endorsement. Each Wednesday morning after the Tuesday primaries, Daley was called by former Georgia Governor Jimmy Carter, perhaps the most misunderstood national leader of our time. Among the White House hopefuls that year, Carter best perceived how heartsick the nation was over Vietnam and Watergate; he ran as an antipolitician who said he would never tell a lie to the American people. In fact he was a cunning politician with a politician's aptitude for dissembling, rancor, and grudges, as members of the Georgia power structure had pointedly learned. Carter called Daley weekly not to ask for an endorsement—he was too shrewd for that—but just to flatter the old man, chat about this and that. No doubt he found an opening to mention that his Georgia delegation had voted to seat Daley in the putsch of 1972. In the 1976 Illinois primary, which he won, Carter filed no delegates against Daley's uncommitted delegate slate in Chicago.

When Daley went to New York for the Democratic convention in July 1976, he was treated with the utmost respect. The McGovern convention of 1972 had evicted Daley; the Carter convention smothered him with kisses. The latter party gathering actually may have emasculated him more efficiently. Daley had little to do but attend to convention formalities. He called a meeting of the Illinois delegation on Sunday, convention eve, in a private dining room of the Waldorf Astoria.

A black woman delegate planted a loud smooch on Daley's cheek. Trying to regain his composure, ungallantly wiping his cheek with the back of his hand, Daley leaned forward toward the microphone and said, "The chair now recognizes a great congressman from Chicago, Danny Rosten-kowski."[6] Just as he had been at the 1960 convention, Rostenkowski was surprised.

The mayor of Chicago was a great man, he improvised. Senator Adlai Stevenson, son of the late, great governor of Illinois, was a great man. The delegation should recommend that Carter select Stevenson as his running mate. (Stevenson had been among six potential veeps interviewed by Carter.) The motion carried. The delegates adjourned and went to parties. Carter on Wednesday tabbed Senator Walter F. Mondale of Minnesota for vice president.

The media were fixated on the lovefest for Carter in contrast to the ugly conventions of 1968 and 1972, missing the real politicking, which involved jockeying for the House majority leader's post. Albert was retiring, finally getting out of Rostenkowski's way. Jim Wright of Texas aggressively worked the delegations to assemble support for majority leader. The other candidates, Phillip Burton of California and Richard Bolling of Missouri, were Rostenkowski's enemies, so he backed Wright. If Wright became majority leader, Rostenkowski might become whip. Bolling, who possessed perhaps the most brilliant mind in Congress, did little more than declare his availability. Burton threw parties. Wright organized a field operation in the New York delegates' hotels, inviting congressmen to his room for personal "face time."

In August 1976, Judge Lynch, nearly the last of Daley's lifelong friends, died (Schaller lived until 1996). According to insider gossip, Lynch left much of his $7 million estate in a trust for Daley's children, although his will did not name the beneficiaries.

In September, Carter made a campaign swing through Chicago. He promoted national health insurance but failed to recognize Rostenkowski, chairman of the health subcommittee of Ways and Means and a longtime advocate of national health, appearing with him. Beyond a lapse in protocol, this snub was a political blunder, a combination of naiveté and pride. Having won nomination as an anti-establishment candidate, Carter would not flatter the midlevel sons of the establishment, even though he secretly hungered for its approval, as was evident as soon as he named his cabinet, heavy with establishment luminaries.

After President Ford stupidly declared in a televised debate that Poland was free of Soviet domination, Carter returned to Chicago in October for the annual heritage dinner of the Polish American Congress. First he greeted a crowd turned out by his and Daley's advance men at Midway Airport. To deflect attention from anti-abortion picketers, Carter denounced superhighway projects that razed poor neighborhoods to benefit suburbanites. You never saw a freeway cut through a golf course, Carter said, repeating a surefire applause line. Giggle giggle went the crowd, to Carter's mystification. He didn't realize Daley was a champion of superhighways slicing up Chicago neighborhoods and even then was seeking deals for a proposed Crosstown Expressway near Midway (it never got built, despite many years of exertions by Illinois politicians). Daley hustled Carter away and put him in a limo speeding down a South Side freeway built by Daley and named after the elder Adlai Stevenson.

Daley later staged a torchlight parade for Carter, as he had done for Kennedy in 1960, except now the "torches" were battery operated and cast an eerie green glow over the sidewalk placard holders proclaiming their ward and union affiliations. The media treated it as a triumphal celebration of an old-fashioned campaign ritual. Actually it was a pallid throwback, Daley's last deployment of his ranks for public inspection.

After election day—Carter carried Chicago, but Ford narrowly won Illinois—Daley indulged one final exercise of his private power. With Rostenkowski managing his campaign, Wright defeated Burton for majority leader on the third secret ballot by a single vote in the 292-member caucus. "We owe Danny just about everything," Wright said.[7] Daley had worked the phones to his network of big-city mayors, helping Danny line up urban congressmen. "I like to think the entire Chicago delegation voted for Wright," Rostenkowski said.[8]

Nevertheless, Wright and Daley could not make Rostenkowski whip. Speaker-elect O'Neill gave the post to John Brademas of Indiana. Rostenkowski was named chief deputy whip, assigned at last a seat on Steering and Policy. Two major perks attended Rostenkowski's new status—inclusion in the weekly leadership meetings with President Carter and occupation of his own office in the Capitol. Meanwhile, Bob Michel, Rostenkowski's old driving partner from Peoria, was elevated to Republican whip.

On Monday, 20 December, one of Daley's mouthpieces on the *Chi-*

cago Tribune staff published a column puffing the mayor's masterful acquisition of clout in the new Congress and White House. His small-minded critics won't give him credit for it, the columnist sniffed.

That afternoon, Daley kept a doctor's appointment he had scheduled after feeling chest pains over the weekend, of which he informed no one outside his family. While the doctor, alarmed by the indications of an electrocardiogram, was arranging to admit Daley to a hospital, the mayor had a fatal heart attack in his office. Daley's body was taken for a final visit to the church he had attended all his seventy-four years, the Nativity of Our Lord, the omphalos of Bridgeport.

The tabloid *Sun-Times* ran a banner headline that said it all: MOURN DALEY. In the city council chamber, Daley's empty chair was draped in purple and black crepe. Speaking to the Cook County Democratic Committee, Rostenkowski gave one of many eulogies:

> Mayor Daley was a man who could put you down in a second, and he could also make you soar to heights you never believed you could attain. He was a compassionate man. On Christmas Day he'd call me up and say, "Dan, just want you to know I'm thinking of you." Mayor Daley sometimes scolded. But when you were feeling low, he would really come through. You remember I had an election in the United States Congress with a very disappointing result [an allusion to his defeat by Teague]. The phone rang. I got on the line, and his voice said, "Danny, what did they do to you? What can I do for you, Dan?" That's the kind of man he was.[9]

Mourners at the funeral included Ted Kennedy, George McGovern, Vice President Nelson Rockefeller, and President-elect Carter. After the services "Sis" Daley invited the mayor's closest friends to the family home on South Lowe. "He wanted you to have this," she told Rosty, pressing something into his palm. It was Daley's money clip. He still carries it. Daley was buried at Holy Sepulcher alongside his parents, Michael and Lillian, in a suburban Irish cemetery. On election day mornings thereafter, Rich Daley paid a private visit to his father's crypt.

Shortly after he was inaugurated in January 1977, Carter refused an invitation to speak to the annual Cook County Democratic banquet.

After Daley's death, Rostenkowski remained a member of the Tuesday Through Thursday Club, dashing to O'Hare and National airports twice a week, spending long weekends ministering to his home district, seeing his daughters into junior high, high school, and college, renovating his home at Noble and Evergreen with LaVerne, playing golf on prime courses around the country with such as Tip O'Neill and corporate heads, convinced that Daley had been a great man persecuted by liberals.

Still, Daley's death liberated Rostenkowski. For the first time since Joe sent him off to Saint John's in 1942, he was freed of an oppressive mentor. Meanwhile, Rostenkowski's diligence in Congress did not merit Stakhanovite awards, but he was attaining expertise in two critical areas of policy: health care and taxes.

At the same time, sustaining a membership in good standing in the Tuesday Through Thursday Club was becoming increasingly difficult. In 1959, Rosty's first year in Congress, the House recorded eighty-seven roll-call votes. By the mid-1970s the number was well above six hundred. Reformers produced an explosion of subcommittees, staffers, roll calls, and money spent to run Congress. The quality of legislation was not commensurately enhanced.

The Legislative Reorganization Act of 1970 had done away with "teller votes," a quaint congressional custom meant to hide from the public and lobbyists the members' votes on amendments to legislation. Members would line up in the aisles, two lines for aye and nay, and march toward the Speaker's rostrum, where clerks would clap their shoulders as they passed and tally the votes in duck-duck, goose-goose manner. Unrecorded were the votes of individual members, who then could say they had been for or against such and such a controversial matter as exigency pressed.

In 1973 the House installed an electronic voting system. Just as fax machines proliferated the amount of the nation's paperwork and portable phones redoubled the number of phone calls, electronic voting tempted Congress to hold more sessions and cast more votes. The system was developed by Frank Ryan, a doctor of mathematics and a former quarterback for the Cleveland Browns. Members swiped a magnetic card, much like a credit card, through a voting device at their desks. Previously forty-five minutes were allowed for voting, but Ryan decided to allot just fifteen minutes because, after all, that was all the time required for a quarter of football. In practice, the leadership holds voting open for as long as needed to round up straying members.

To accommodate the Tuesday Through Thursday Club, the number of paid trips home enjoyed by each congressman was increased to twelve a year, compared to one when Rostenkowski started, and then to eighteen. The suspension calendar, containing routine matters not requiring a congressman's attendance, was expanded from every other Monday to every Monday and Tuesday, at the Speaker's discretion.

Still at work, reformers forced more proceedings into open sessions under "sunshine" rules. Hearings traditionally were open, but committee "markups," when bills actually get drafted, usually were closed. By 1975 even most of the House-Senate conference committees were pried open.

Reformers further ordained disclosures of members' financial holdings, income, and campaign contributions. Three days before a new rule would require him to disclose rental income from 2150 North Damen, Rostenkowski transferred title to the building to his daughters. Meanwhile, during this period, goo goo groups such as Common Cause started keeping close tabs on lobbyists' contributions, in particular those made to members of Ways and Means, although within a decade the amounts of money that so alarmed reformers in the 1970s would seem like small potatoes.

So the post-Daley, post-Watergate Congress was a changed creature from the one Rostenkowski had grown up in. Wilbur Mills did not consent even to have any subcommittees. Subs would just multiply the workload without advancing the cause of consensus, Mills held, not unreasonably, though his real motive probably was a refusal to fragment his authority. Mills would not report a bill to the floor without achieving bipartisan backing on the order of a 23–2 committee vote. The bill then was almost certain to pass the full House without amendments, safeguarding the committee's prestige and ensuring that fiscal bills would be more conservative than the sentiment of the House as a whole.

Promptly after his 1974 debacle, Mills retired from Congress, entered treatment for alcoholism, and sought no vindication. He was a public servant of substance, and it is a shame that he now is remembered mainly for capering with a stripper. In any event, his departure triggered the creation of Ways and Means subcommittees. Rostenkowski took the health care chair.

The issue had engaged him back in the Springfield years, and during the 1960s he and Daley would beat the drums for various presidential health insurance proposals. Nixon, in his 1974 State of the Union address, proposed a weak form of national health care that drew Rostenkowski's endorsement. (Despite his reputation as a conservative, Nixon, father of the Environmental Protection Agency, the Occupational Safety and Health Administration, a wage-price freeze, and abandonment of the gold standard, was far from conservative on domestic policies.) Under Ford, Rostenkowski tried and failed to impose a 1 percent tax on group health premiums to finance health care for the unemployed. There was a recession.

Rostenkowski held hearings on this proposal and indeed always insisted on public hearings even when presidents and Speakers thought them superfluous and dilatory. In a tiny Ways and Means hearing room, he sat next to an interested senator, Lloyd Bentsen of Texas (the 1988 Democratic vice presidential nominee), banged the gavel, folded his arms, leaned his abdomen into the table, and peered over black-rimmed glasses threatening to fall off the end of his nose. After three tedious hours, a witness offered "off the record" praise for the committee members who had stayed around for "lasting so long." Rostenkowski would have none of that. "Why don't you put it on the record," he said.[10] He might belong to the Tuesday Through Thursday Club, but he would demonstrate his capacity for endurance.

The subcommittee approved Rostenkowski's plan 9–3. The legislation ultimately failed under a tangle of turf wars in the House and Senate, conservative opposition, and the refusal of big labor to allow the insurance industry a primary role in running national health care. Consistently during the decades-long national health battle, Rostenkowski insisted that any public program would have to be paid for, an inconvenient fact from which President Clinton would avert his eyes. Carter, throughout his term, was determined to contain hospital costs. The endeavor suffered under his unhappy relations with Congress.

O'Neill, a cartoonish, cigar-puffing, yarn-telling Boston pol in size 52-

long suits, whose grandfather had immigrated during the Great Famine, was mystified and repelled by the Carter White House. "They came up here and they didn't understand us Irish politicians or Italian politicians or Jewish politicians from the urban areas," he said, less than three months after Carter took office. "The average Southerner is a sweet talker and a charmer and charismatic, a smooth type that can skin you alive with sweetness and kindness. Politics are different in the North. There's a terseness and a toughness and an infighting." [11]

Rostenkowski would second that observation. He had been among the national Praetorians summoned to President-elect Carter's conferences in Plains, Georgia, where he "nearly had tears in his eyes," Rostenkowski reported, when talking of his mandate to reorganize and simplify the federal government. But by May 1977, Rostenkowski was furious with the president. "I've been the most loyal nice guy," he said. "I've told Tip and some of the guys not to be angry. Well, tonight that came to a screeching halt. I'm going to make sure they know they said 'no' to Danny Rostenkowski." Carter's sin: he had refused an invitation to speak to Democrats in Chicago. When Carter was governor, he despised the state legislature, an attitude he carried to Washington. "I see him at breakfast," Rostenkowski fumed, "and he tells me how we're going to work together, and then I turn on the television a few days later and I see 'Peanuts' sitting at the counter with some cotton picker and he's telling them how awful it is that we [Congress] took the weekend off." [12] An insult to the Tuesday Through Thursday Club!

Rostenkowski felt especially wronged because he had asked only one personal favor from the new president, a modest one at that. He wanted to give Kenneth Sain, Daley's deputy mayor, a job as regional director of Health, Education, and Welfare. Carter, who espoused a strong cabinet, turned the matter over to his HEW secretary, Joseph Califano. Califano had been chomping on apples with Larry O'Brien when Rusty stormed into the room and demanded justice at the 1972 convention. Secretary Califano kept the HEW job dangling for seven months, ignoring Rostenkowski's queries. Finally the congressman informed the HEW secretary, "I didn't see any need for my subcommittee to move on anything on health for them" [13]—the Pennsylvania Avenue equivalent of a declaration of war.

A veteran of the Johnson White House, Califano was no naif about political patronage, although he chose to strike that pose in relating the Sain incident in his memoirs.[14] Why, the man was unqualified for the job! Califano gave it to a Chicago nonmachine alderman.

Several weeks later, Rostenkowski confronted Carter in the White House and warned he would be a one-term president unless he could start rewarding his friends. "The fact is that I can come out and tell you this because the shape you're in, you can't hurt me," Rostenkowski said.[15] Soon after, Carter declared his first year in office a major success, except that Congress was holding up his energy bill.

The distance between Carter and urban, white ethnics in Congress went beyond the regional, social, and political: it was religious. Carter's born-again Southern Baptism fascinated reporters who covered Carter's appearances at fundamentalist and black churches as anthropological visits to exotic cultures, as though they had never heard country preaching before, which they probably hadn't. Still, the topic of the cultural gulf between Catholics and Protestants remained taboo, an unspoken issue since the election of Kennedy. Bringing up the importance of religious divisions in public life made reporters and editors nervous; did it not violate the hallowed separation of church and state? It did not make such as Rostenkowski and O'Neill nervous. It nettled them.

"Do you notice," Rostenkowski asked the Speaker after one of Carter's Tuesday breakfasts with the leadership, "that he never asks any of the Catholics to say the prayer?"

"Come on, Danny," O'Neill said. "You know those Protestants are professionals. They pray so beautifully."[16]

Tip's comment was not sarcastic. In the church Tip and Rusty grew up in, mass was celebrated in Latin, and laymen rarely took the lead in formal prayer. For small-town Protestants, the impromptu asking of divine blessings came naturally. O'Neill really did wonder at this facility. At the White House, after the men held hands around a table and one of the Protestants said grace, Mondale, O'Neill, and Wright would whisper to one another, impishly grading the effort on a scale of one to ten.

Rostenkowski and O'Neill were the only Catholics in the seven-member leadership delegation. Rostenkowski's observation that Carter didn't ask the Catholics to pray quickly got back to the White House, as in Washington of course it would. A week later, O'Neill encountered Rostenkowski at a restaurant and said, "Danny, tomorrow morning you'll be called upon to say grace."

"Don't be silly. We've been through all that, remember? He only calls on the Protestants."

"You never know," O'Neill shrugged.

In the morning, Carter said, "Danny, you'll say the prayer today."

Rostenkowski astounded everyone in the room by smoothly offering up a prayer of elegance and eloquence. Wright said it would have done justice to the Archbishop of Canterbury. This comparison was freighted, perhaps unknown to Wright, with irony. Would a Catholic kid from Milwaukee Avenue be puffed by association with the Archbishop of Canterbury?

Back on the hill, Rusty told Tip, "When you said the president would call on me, I was sure you were kidding. But at five in the morning I woke up and started worrying. I said to myself, that big Irish son of a buck always knows what's going on. So I went into the other room and sat down and wrote out a prayer. I couldn't get back to sleep, so I had plenty of time to get it right." [17]

In May 1978, Rostenkowski finally dragooned Carter into speaking to a Democratic fund raiser in Chicago. As part of his antipolitician stance, Carter had "depomped" the White House, forbidding his aides to whip around town in limos. As a result, a Ways and Means hearing was delayed because a Treasury Department official could not find a cab—to the congressmen, a shocking insult to the Hill and to Treasury as well. Under depomping, Carter also had spurned the playing of "Hail to the Chief" and "Ruffles and Flourishes" at public appearances. Rostenkowski told Carter that the Cook County Democrats were going to play "Hail to the Chief."

Carter said, "We're not doing that."

Rostenkowsi said, "I think the people deserve it. 'Hail to the Chief' is spine-chilling."

Sure enough, when Carter walked into the Conrad Hilton ballroom, the band played, "dum dum ta-dum, ta-tum-dum ta-dum-ta-dum-tum." The crowd rose in a prolonged ovation, thrilling Carter. "He grew to about seventeen feet tall," Rostenkowski said. He leaned over and whispered to the president, "It's just like penicillin, isn't it?"[18] Thereafter, "Hail to the Chief" was played at Carter's occasions of state.

The revival of pomp did little to improve the president's legislative scorecard. He sought tax increases for energy and health programs, regarding their merits as self-evident and disdaining the grubbiness of trading horses for them.

Rostenkowski had been delving into the tax code since the Nixon-Ford era. In fact, some reformers considered him quite the taxpayers' watchdog on Ways and Means—as a rule, the House was more hostile to shelters and tax breaks for the wealthy than was the Senate. However, Rostenkowski held the standard view of the tax code, that it was a fine instrument for managing the economy. The code is "almost like a living organ . . . a living, breathing part of our economy," he said.[19] In 1976, after three years of work, Congress passed a fifteen-hundred-page "tax reform" bill that did little but make the tax structure more complex. It would take Rostenkowski another decade to realize that the "living organ" was a living monster.

Discussing the bill in 1975, Rostenkowski said of Ford's proposal for an across-the-board tax rebate: "I don't see the point of giving some guy who makes $40,000 a year another $1,000 that he'll just put in the bank."[20] There was a perfect formulation of the attitude of the political class toward taxation. Allowing "some guy" to keep some of his own money amounted to "giving" it to him. The unspoken credo of the political and media elite was *send more money to Washington*. For backing this credo under the Reagan, Bush, and Clinton administrations, Rostenkowski won consistent raves from the *New York Times* and the *Washington Post*.

In Carter's first year, Congress passed the Tax Reduction and Simplification Act of 1977. Taxes were not reduced. They were not simplified. A separate law drastically increased the schedule of Social Security payroll taxes. Carter said that the legislation guaranteed the solvency of Social Security until 2030. He was off by forty-seven years. In 1983 Congress raised payroll taxes again.

In the Carter years, Rostenkowski was inclined to favor health and energy taxes, especially one of his own hobbyhorses, a higher gasoline tax. In May 1977, Ways and Means rejected Carter's five-cent standby gas tax along with Rusty's three-cent tax to fund public transit and energy research. Rosty then tacked a four-cent tax onto the omnibus energy bill. House members did not want to sell the tax to their constituents, energy crisis or no, unless most of it would go for highway repairs. It was rejected in August, 370–52. "Some day soon, we in Congress are going to have to pass a very substantial tax on gas," Rostenkowski insisted.

In February 1978, Rostenkowski announced to the hospital lobby that Ways and Means would shelve Carter's mandatory controls on hospital cost increases. Califano, in charge of the bill for the administration, was stunned—Rostenkowski himself had introduced the bill the previous year (along with a substitute bill of his own). The Chicagoan admitted he was still smarting over the Sain affair, but more important, he believed there was really no enthusiasm for the legislation. Califano soon took revenge by chiding Rostenkowski in a speech to newspaper editors.

And so it went for the rest of the Carter administration. In March 1978, Rostenkowski sold the most tickets for a congressional campaign fund-raising party. Senate Majority Leader Robert Byrd of West Virginia wore his red vest, played the fiddle, and sang bluegrass. The House leadership followed by telling jokes about Carter and his team of Georgians. O'Neill said a guy took a slug of Billy Beer, marketed by the president's brother, and immediately sent the stuff off to a lab for analysis. In due course, the doctor reported, "Sorry, but your horse has diabetes." [21]

The next month Carter called Chairman Ullman, Rostenkowski, and a third Ways and Means member to the White House to discuss the perennial bill of every modern presidency for "tax reform." Carter was somber. "He has never been talked to as candidly as he was this morning," the third member said. "We tried to explain to him he had no constituency in the Congress or in the country for these reforms." [22]

Actually, a major bill was passed in November. As a conventional Democrat, Carter had aimed tax relief at lower-income taxpayers and tried to close loopholes for the rich. The bill Congress finally passed, during the year of a tax revolt triggered by California's Proposition 13 ballot initiative to cut property taxes, was designed to stimulate investment more than to redistribute income. Amazingly, a Democratic Congress reduced the tax on capital gains (profits on the sale of assets). A new politics of economic growth was supplanting the old politics of redistributing wealth.

Rostenkowski put a stamp on the bill at the behest of a golfing buddy, Arnold Palmer. The golf pro appeared in the House cloakroom to tell Rostenkowski, "Congressman, we've got to do something about the tax code."

"What do you mean we?"

"We've got to fix it. It's ridiculous."

"I'll fix it when you get me on the golf course and give me a playing lesson." Palmer laughed, but Rosty got the lesson.[23]

At 4:00 A.M. after a long conference committee weekend markup of the bill, Rostenkowski proposed killing a provision to end the deduction for country club dues. He traded it for something the Senate wanted, and, presto, the bill was approved and businessmen golfers slept soundly.

Playing at the next Bob Hope Golf Tournament in Palm Springs, California, Rostenkowski and O'Neill were invited to a party thrown by Hollywood types. Rostenkowski, delighted to meet the actress Mary Martin, told her, "You know, when I came back from Korea, I must have seen 'South Pacific' a dozen times. To me, you've always been a great star."

Martin said, "Thank you, but I'm not a star any longer. These days it's my son [Larry Hagman] who's the real star. You know, from 'Dallas,'" the popular television series.

"No, I've never been to Dallas, so I never met the guy." Turning to O'Neill, Rostenkowski said, "But you've been there, Tip. Do you know Mary's son?"

O'Neill claimed that Rostenkowski liked to tell this story, too, except that in his version, it was *Tip* who committed the gaffe.[24]

After Daley died, Rostenkowski and his Loop and labor backers entertained the notion of his becoming mayor. The city council had installed in the seat Michael A. Bilandic, a political dullard although he was the alderman from Daley's own Eleventh Ward. Keane, by telephone from prison, helped to ordain the succession.[25] The swift seating of Bilandic foreclosed the ascension of the city council president pro tempore, who had a claim to the mayoralty. However, he was black.

To make sure the new mayor would not enjoy Daley's dual dictatorship over city hall and the Democratic party, the party chair was given to Dunne. Bilandic was not even a committeeman—the Eleventh Ward seat was held by the late mayor's son, Rich. Dunne was handsome and distinguished looking, personable, the rare big shot who did not screen his calls through secretaries but answered his own phone. He also could match anyone in Cook County for wiliness.

A special election would be held in 1977 to fill the last two years of Daley's term, and much of the establishment wanted Rostenkowski. "Bankers, business leaders, labor leaders" asked him to run, he said. "There's still a grand horizon for me," he said in his Rayburn Building office with a flourish of his arm. The gesture ended ambiguously with a hand pointing to the portrait of Daley on an antique table under the lighted portrait of FDR.[26]

Pucinski thought his time had come and challenged Bilandic, as did a black state senator, Harold Washington. Bilandic won. The machine ruled. Rostenkowski backed Bilandic and occupied himself with getting federal pork for the proposed Deep Tunnel flood control project and the Crosstown Expressway.

Bridgeport still had its arms around Rostenkowski, or vice versa. On Friday evenings, home from Washington, he drove down to Daley's old neighborhood to meet pals for dinner at Sophie's Wagon or maybe at Schaller's Pump, the local landmark tavern founded by the grandfather of Daley's law partner. The gang usually included two or three businessmen and Jack Parker, the city hall paymaster. Parker never learned to drive, so Rusty would pick him up for weekend golf outings and then drive him home. "That's a damn good friend," Parker said.[27] Loyalty and friendship: the machine's cardinal virtues.

A friend from Rosenkowski's district, Anthony "Micky" Ramirez, a five-foot-six, tattooed former marine, a firefighter, was hired by the congressman to moonlight as his photographer. He shot ward dinners, Rostenkowski with his military academy appointees, Rostenkowski family weddings, and parties at the Wisconsin lake home. Rosty liked to throw "theme" parties—a Hawaiian luau, a Western "ranch" with a chuckwagon.

Ramirez was paid about twenty thousand dollars in congressional staff money from 1977 to 1986. He cashed the checks and handed the cash to Nancy Panzke, manager of the congressman's district office, who placed it in a manila envelope marked "Photos." Ramirez was given spot wages at seven and a half dollars an hour.

When the indictments hit the fan in 1994, indicating Ramirez was a public employee illegally paid for personal services, he, apparently alone of the fourteen alleged ghost payrollers, did not hire a defense attorney. He figured he had done nothing wrong. "The FBI told me they weren't looking to get anything on me," he said. "I don't want to say I'm a good guy or nothing like that, but I don't want to get in no trouble. That's why I kept all my receipts."[28]

Rostenkowski did not trouble himself unduly about financial disclosures, although his questionable practices were getting increasing exposure. In July 1977, reporter Chuck Neubauer, then with the *Tribune*, struck. He said Rostenkowski for seven years had rented his congressional district office at 2148 North Damen, a building owned in a secret land trust by his sisters, Gladys and Marcia. The sisters' building also housed the insurance business set up in 1967 by Dan and LaVerne. Rostenkowski said he had no interest in his sisters' building, although Cook County records indicated he held a one-third ownership as a bequest from Joe. Nothing came of this.

In August, Neubauer struck again. He disclosed that Rostenkowski had placed on the congressional payroll his personal attorney Leonard Levin (the nominee for his Egyptian Trotting Association stock), developer Dan Shannon, and a Shannon protégé. Levin drew $7,500 a year for advising Rostenkowski's constituents on legal problems in his ward office. Shannon got $3,005 for sixty days of consulting on tax legislation in 1972. During that time, Shannon purchased half of Rostenkowski's interest in a real estate development in the gentrifying Lincoln Park neighborhood. Shannon's protégé got $3,500 for ninety days of public relations consulting. Nothing came of this.

The relentless Neubauer reported in October about apparent governmental favoritism toward a North Side savings bank in which shares were owned by Rostenkowski, Sain, and Forty-fifth Ward committeeman Thomas J. Lyons (later the Cook County chairman). Nothing came of this.

The machine was unconcerned about Bilandic's reelection in 1979 but worried sick about the tax assessor's election in 1978. The assessor when Daley first took office was convicted of income tax evasion. His successor was implicated in a financial scandal and saw thirteen of his aides indicted. That man's successor, Thomas M. Tully, was the subject of a federal investigation into real estate deals he made with developers who got tax breaks from his office. Rostenkowski undertook a mission to calm Tully's jittery nerves and persuade him to seek reelection.

Despite six hours of the Rostenkowski treatment, Tully declined to run. In Chicago, this was equivalent to LBJ's abdication of the presidency in 1968. If the Irish had to choose between holding the mayoralty or the assessor's office, they might have come down for the latter, a superb position from which to raise money and peddle influence. Then something as shocking as Tully's turning his back happened. A Pole, Ted Lechowicz, and a Croation, Ed Vrdolyak, challenged the divine right of Irish to the office and mounted candidacies. Through a spokesman, Rostenkowski said he was for Lechowicz, though not everyone believed he meant it. In due course, Tully's successor was an Irishman, Thomas C. Hynes. As for Tully, he never was indicted. As for Rostenkowski, the usual noises were made about his running for mayor in 1979.

On 31 December 1978, 15 inches of snow fell, hardly anything special in Chicago. Two weeks later another 20 inches fell. By the time of the mayoral primary in February there had been a total of 82.3 inches, enough to drive even Chicagoans mad.

Bilandic awarded a snow removal consulting contract to Kenneth Sain, who thought really hard and duly reported, in so many words: When snow falls from the sky it makes a mess and has to be plowed off the streets. Bilandic also, ill-advisedly, directed rapid transit trains to speed past snowbound stations in black neighborhoods but to stop and pick up Loop commuters in closer-in white neighborhoods.

Bilandic compared the "vicious onslaughts" against his administration to the crucifixion of Christ, the persecution of Jews, the Soviet annexation of Eastern Europe, black slavery in America, and discrimination against Hispanics—a catalogue of victimization. Bilandic's opponent was Jane Byrne, the city consumer affairs commissioner, who objected that a city taxi fare increase had been clouted by Bilandic. The machine remained complacent. Key arteries had been plowed, such as the one in front of Rostenkowski's home, enabling him to back his 1976 Ford Thunderbird out of the driveway. The snowplows had come merely to accommodate a funeral at St. Stan's, he said. Anyway, "I'm not worried [about Bilandic]. The dark clouds of January and February always hover over Chicago."[29] On the eve of the 27 February primary, he predicted Bilandic would win by one hundred thousand votes.

Byrne's upset of Bilandic was portrayed by the Chicago and national media as the aurora borealis, the rising sun, the parting of the seas, and the star in the East. To be sure, the machine had not lost a contested mayoral primary since 1911. However, Bilandic's vote (49 percent) approximated the norm for slated mayoral candidates over the previous quarter century. The difference was that Byrne faced Bilandic one-on-one, while in previous primaries, multiple candidates split the opposition vote. Also, Byrne herself was no reformer but a daughter of the machine.

Although Byrne crowed that she "beat the whole God-damned machine single-handedly," she had a brilliant strategist in Don Rose (it was he who coined the 1968 slogan "The Whole World Is Watching"). Rose believed that the racial issue had kept the machine glued together. But for racial politics, the machine's dissident groups—blacks, Poles, Italians, lakefront liberals—might have combined to overthrow the Irish oligarchy, as Cermak had done in 1931. In time, Rose reasoned, a disaster of some kind would befall the city to unite the dissidents and beat the machine. When the blizzards came in 1979, they proved to be the disaster Rose had predicted. Rose also had an attractive candidate, a five-foot-three blond with the sort of aggressiveness that invariably gets female politicians labeled "feisty" and "scrappy."

Heavy was the blanket of gloom on the machine. The day after the primary, Rostenkowski speculated that it might put up an independent candidate in the April general election. At the next White House breakfast, Carter said, "Danny, what's going to happen to poor Chicago now?"[30] Rostenkowski flew back to Chicago for a Central Committee meeting the next day. One committeeman thundered out of the room rather than "break bread with this woman."[31]

It did not take long for the machine to grow accustomed to her. Soon there was the presidential election to think about. Ted Kennedy challenged Carter for the nomination. Byrne endorsed Carter when he spoke at a Chicago fund raiser for her in October 1979. Two weeks later, she endorsed Kennedy and prevailed on the Central Committee to do likewise. Always overdoing things, including her efforts not to overdo things, Byrne told Carter she was endorsing Kennedy personally, not in her roles as mayor or committeeman, as if that mattered.

Byrne's fandango put Rostenkowski in a painful bind. He still had to work with the White House every day, and moreover, his relationship with

Carter had warmed over the past year. To avoid just such jams as that, Daley always had fielded Chicago delegate slates that were uncommitted. Rostenkowski elected to sidestep the problem by not running for a delegate's spot. "I'll support what the committee has done," he said. "I've always done that. But I've also always run as a delegate on their slate. This time I won't do that."[32] Much later he revealed, "President Carter told me it would hurt him personally if I ran."[33] The appeal to a personal bond is a political weapon deployed only in extremis.

Supposedly neutral, Rostenkowski still managed to signal his leanings. In June 1980, he staged a Washington fund raiser for Rich Daley, a Byrne foe and a candidate for state's attorney. Byrne's fear of Rich went past normal political insecurity into something like clinical obsession. She pressured the machine to slate someone else for state's attorney in the primary, getting Vrdolyak and other machine figures to go along, which Daley considered betrayal and never forgave. After Daley won the primary, the Byrne machine gave him only nominal support in his November race against the Republican incumbent. Thus, Rostenkowski's five-hundred-dollar-a-plate dinner for Daley, attended by Mondale, Byrd, O'Neill, and Strauss, was a major comment on the Chicago scene. Chairman Dunne, not a favorite either of Byrne or Daley but a longtime favorite of Rostenkowski, was dismayed that the congressman did not consult him about throwing the Daley funder. Besides emitting anti-Byrne, pro-Carter signals, Rostenkowski perhaps was putting out a subtler message that he was growing too big for Cook County.

In August at the Democratic National Convention in New York, Rostenkowski sat on stage as the "adviser to the chair," who was Tip O'Neill, fielding phone calls and settling squabbles. The mood of the convention that renominated Carter was grumpy and sour, in contrast to that of 1976. Rostenkowski helped broker a platform compromise between the Carter and Kennedy camps concerning Kennedy's demand for a huge federal jobs program, the sort of fight that consumes the political class for the moment and loses its last particle of significance the instant the convention adjourns. On the final night, at the scene of Carter's acceptance speech, his people recruited passersby off the Manhattan streets to fill Madison Square Garden lest TV cameras show empty seats. Many Kennedy delegates had gone home in a snit.

The Reagan landslide of 4 November booted out of office John Brademas, the Democratic whip, and Al Ullman, the chair of Ways and Means. On election night, O'Neill and Wright phoned Rostenkowski to discuss the obvious: Two powerful posts had opened up for him.

By becoming whip, he would fall in line for ascension to the Speakership he always had coveted. By taking over Ways and Means, he would gain power over fiscal policy. It was a tough call, very tough.

But of one thing he was positive. President-elect Reagan, he asserted confidently, would have to raise taxes on gasoline.

Peter Rostenkowski (*far left*), grandfather of Dan Rostenkowski, receives the *Polonia Restituta* award from Polish premier Ignace J. Paderewski (*seated*) in 1926. (Polish Museum of America)

The house that Peter Rostenkowski built at the corner of Evergreen and Noble streets (*left*), still occupied by Dan and LaVerne Rostenkowski. (*Chicago Sun-Times*)

Joseph P. Rostenkowski, state representative, Thirty-second Ward alderman and committeeman, and boss of "Polish Downtown" for twenty-five years. (Chicago Historical Society)

Illinois state senator Daniel D. Rostenkowski on the eve of his election to Congress at age thirty in 1958. (*Chicago Sun-Times*)

Rostenkowski and his wife, LaVerne, show off their invitation to the 1965 inauguration of President Lyndon Johnson. (*Chicago Sun-Times*)

Rostenkowski charms a Chicago banquet crowd in 1969 while introducing his patron, Mayor Richard J. Daley (*center*). Senator Daniel K. Inouye is seated at right. (*Chicago Sun-Times*)

Rostenkowski loved to have a gavel in his hand. This was his official photograph after he became chairman of the Ways and Means Committee in 1981. (*Chicago Sun-Times*)

This was the Rostenkowski visage that congressional colleagues, corporate CEOs, and labor leaders alike often saw—the scowl, the warily appraising glare. (*Chicago Sun-Times*)

Rostenkowski with Chicago mayor Richard M. Daley, the late mayor's son, in 1992. (Richard Hein, *Chicago Sun-Times*)

Rostenkowski meets with advocates for the disabled before giving a speech in Chicago touting President Bill Clinton's national health care plan in 1994. (Rich Chapman, *Chicago Sun-Times*)

"Rosty" and President Clinton respond to cheers at Wright College in Chicago shortly before the 1994 Illinois Democratic primary. (John White, *Chicago Sun-Times*)

ROSTY'S ROTUNDA

The apportionment of taxes on the various descriptions
of property is an act which seems to require the most exact
impartiality; yet there is, perhaps, no legislative act in
which greater opportunity and temptation are given to a
predominant party to trample on the rules of justice.

— James Madison, *The Federalist*

ROSTENKOWSKI surprised the political realm by rejecting the whip's post for the Ways and Means chair. He was a
lapel grabber, a shout-into-the-telephone fixer, a ward boss, not
a student of macroeconomics. The chairmanship would take
him off the leadership ladder that led to his pole star, the speakership.

Not only that, but the power of Ways and Means was diminished.
Aside from the Democratic members' loss of the authority to assign seats
on other committees, and aside from the general shrinkage of seniority
clout, Ways and Means as a whole was less central to the budget process.
The 1974 reforms had revamped budget writing, creating a Budget Committee that chewed pieces off both Ways and Means and Appropriations.
Previously, Appropriations had spent the money that Ways and Means
raised (yes, an oversimplification).

Some sources believe that O'Neill ordered Rostenkowski to take the
committee chair because liberals in the caucus would not tolerate him
as whip—the taint of Daleyism was sewn into the linings of his jacket.
O'Neill himself was disingenuous in his memoirs, claiming that "Danny"
could not become whip because he was *already* chairman of Ways and
Means.

Certainly, O'Neill had reasons of his own to want Danny in that chair.

Absent Rostenkowski, the chair would be Sam Gibbons of Florida, not an O'Neill crony and moreover not the sort for hand-to-hand combat with his counterparts in the Senate, Republican Bob Dole of Kansas and Democrat Russell B. Long of Louisiana. The House is always trying to best the more prestigious Senate, one of the least understood dynamics of the government.

Rostenkowski said O'Neill and Wright told him he could make his own decision, and probably this was true. To hold that he was coerced into the chairmanship disregards the modern breakdown of party discipline and further ignores the subtle ways in which gigantic political egos negotiate with one another. The explicit personal appeal—do this or you'll hurt me personally, as Carter implored Rostenkowski not to run as a Kennedy delegate in 1980—is rare. That Tip said, Danny, take this chair or else, is unlikely.

"You agonize as to what you should do, what you would like to do," Rostenkowski said. "Maybe even in the autumn of a career, what would you like to have people recognize you as? The chairman of the Ways and Means Committee is a very high-profile and always, quote unquote, powerful person." And then came the clincher. "The whole program of President-elect Reagan's administration will come through the Ways and Means Committee because that is the economic policy maker of the country." [1]

The bright guys, the goo goos, the hotshots of the media, they thought he was a lazy legislator, a Daley machine hack with mediocre brainpower. Who was he to penetrate the interstices of the tax code? He would show them.

Support came from, of all people, Vice President-elect George Bush. Rostenkowski and Bush had become friends as fellow Ways and Means members in the late 1960s, when Bush was a Houston congressman. Rostenkowski's aptitude for friendships with seeming social opposites had been persistent since St. John's. Bush, the WASP preppie son of a U.S. senator from Connecticut, and Rostenkowski, the unpolished kid up from the grit of Milwaukee Avenue, simply liked each other. They shared the masculine milieu of bonhomie, the camaraderie of the boys' club in the treehouse.

Bush told Rusty, look, you're a Democrat we can work with, we'd love to have you heading Ways and Means; together we can craft a tax cut that will benefit all Americans, and so forth. Or as Rostenkowski delicately put it, "He felt he knew me and that it wouldn't be difficult to discuss economic matters with me."[2]

How could Rostenkowski say no when the Speaker of the House and the vice president of the United States appealed both to his ego and to his patriotism? "The more physical thing was the whip job," he allowed. "I would have enjoyed it more. I don't enjoy sitting and listening to testimony."[3] But on 5 December he announced he would take Ways and Means.

O'Neill arranged a sweetener. Reagan had carried in a Republican Senate for the first time since 1954 and the strongest GOP position in the House since 1958. O'Neill swiftly stacked Ways and Means and other key committees in favor of Democrats. The party ratio on Ways and Means had been 3:2. O'Neill made it close to 2:1—twenty-three Democrats and twelve Republicans, even though Democrats held only 56 percent of the House.

Republicans cried bloody murder and tried three times in January 1981 to overturn O'Neill's coup. Once, seeing there were too few Democrats on the floor, O'Neill abruptly adjourned the House rather than call a vote on the issue.[4] Democrats dominated the House from 1955 to 1995, in part by rigging the rules, especially in gerrymandering districts. The media shrugged—these were mere institutional arrangements, not personalities or scandals.

First off, Chairman Rostenkowski had to set the Reaganites straight on something. With the cockiness afflicting all incoming administrations, Reagan's men plotted to introduce the president's tax plan in the Republican-controlled Senate instead of the House. A parliamentary technicality to bypass the Constitutional mandate that all revenue bills originate in the House could easily be effected.

Rostenkowski went to Bob Michel, the new House Republican leader, and Barber F. Conable of New York, the ranking Republican on Ways and Means, and secured an agreement that the Reagan program would be introduced in his committee. He was entirely within his rights. "There is a very jealous bone in every member of the House's body with respect to writing tax legislation," he said.[5]

Okay, said the White House. On his first visit to Reagan's Oval Office,

Rostenkowski promised never to surprise the president, and Reagan said something similar in reply. "We're both new to our jobs," Rostenkowski said. "I'd like to be a success, and I'd like to help you be a success."[6]

Rostenkowski had a second point to set Reagan straight on. The White House fancied a swift passage of the tax plan, but Rostenkowski insisted on full-scale public hearings. The Reaganites had wanted to railroad the bill during the "honeymoon" of all new presidents. "I think President Reagan, as President Carter before him, was unaware of the legislative process," Rostenkowski said later.[7]

Reagan, mindful of Carter's blunders, listened. He was scheduled to present his tax package to Congress on 17 February but put it off a day because Rostenkowski had a commitment to speak to the Economic Club in Chicago. Rostenkowski's ego was puffed.

On 18 February, Reagan's televised address to Congress was a typically sensational media success for him. He wanted a three-year income tax cut of 10 percent a year, as contained in a bill by Representative Jack Kemp of New York and Senator William V. Roth of Delaware (in Capitol shorthand, "10-10-10" or "Kemp-Roth"). The bill also offered faster business writeoffs for depreciation—ten years for buildings, five for equipment, three for trucks ("10-5-3").

The Reaganites also demanded a "clean" bill, 10-10-10 and 10-5-3, nothing else, no amendments, no special tax breaks. If they believed this at all, they were dreaming.

It was a time of high unemployment, high inflation, 20 percent interest rates, bipartisan fear of deficits, and a belief that Reagan meant what he said about slashing social welfare spending. The Reaganite "supply side" theory was that tax reductions would stimulate the economy, which in turn would generate higher revenues despite lower tax rates.

Reagan had campaigned on cutting taxes, cutting social welfare spending, increasing defense spending, and balancing the budget by 1984. The political class took this program as something tantamount to a drug-induced hallucination. Which, considering the refusal of Congress to curtail pork, it was.

Rostenkowski's view of the tax code had evolved; it was not an economic afflatus so much as a destabilizer. "I don't like tinkering all the time with the tax code," said a tinkerer of the tax code. "First we help this group and then that one. We should help business through government tax incentives and then leave it there."[8] He was a probusiness moderate Democrat. Still, he was far from buying supply side.

In his Economic Club speech, he said, "I have no rigid tax or economic philosophy. I have seen too many grand designs fall apart. I don't believe in miracles or the wizards and alchemists who promise them. I doubt that Uncle Sam stands to gain a dollar of feedback revenue for every dollar of new economic activity." He also took the opportunity to preen before a hometown crowd. "Raising all federal revenue and controlling almost half the federal budget falls within the jurisdiction of the Ways and Means Committee. Just about all the matches are stuck in my shoe."[9]

Six weeks later, Rusty met four hundred constituents at the Pulaski Park field house, where they presented heart-tugging tales of privation. Don't cut our food stamps, Medicare, Medicaid, or Social Security, they pleaded. If you cut our benefits by so much as a nickel, we all shall surely die. The Reagan White House, for all its political savvy, did not appreciate the intensity of these pressures on congressmen—Democrats and Republicans alike. "Lobbyists in Washington are one thing," Rostenkowski said. "But you come back here and you are sitting in your office and those are the real lobbyists. They come in off the street and say, 'What are you going to do to me on food stamps?'"[10]

And yet social welfare—modest cuts indeed were imposed—was not the real onus of Reagan's plan. What appalled Congress was that Kemp-Roth would take it out of the tax-writing business for three entire years. Yes, Reagan deserved a chance to put his policies in place, but this was going too far, election mandate or no. How would congressmen justify their existence? Solicit campaign funds from lobbies?

"We are not going to lose control of the economy for three years in the House of Representatives, certainly not in the Ways and Means Committee," Rostenkowski swore.[11] Note the surviving assumption that controlling the tax code amounts to controlling the economy, a distaste for "tinkering" or no. As early as 25 March, Rostenkowski declared Kemp-Roth dead.

The job of congressmen is perennially to sell advantages in the tax code. From the point of view of the buyers of these advantages, whether the seller is a Republican or a Democrat is mostly a matter of indifference.

To be sure, each party has its own roster of friends, roughly speaking, multinational corporations for Republicans and unions and minorities for Democrats. However, all interest groups are biased toward incumbents. They do the selling, not their out-of-office challengers. Republicans were disturbed by Wall Street's support for Lyndon Johnson over Barry Goldwater in 1964; Democrats were dismayed when prominent partisans embraced Nixon in 1972 and Reagan in 1980. There is a single story here. The Johnson Republicans and the Nixon/Reagan Democrats all had investments to protect. They prized stability, but supply side was "a riverboat gamble," as one of Reagan's own men described it.

Thus the political class scorned supply side in 1981. The punditry focused on the ideological conflict between supply siders and liberal tax and spenders, overlooking the three-year political dimension of the struggle except to insist that three straight tax cuts would explode the deficit.

The tax and spenders were ahead, so the White House plotted first to cut a deal with Rostenkowski and then write the "real" bill in the Senate. Toward that end Bush planned a trip to Chicago on 31 March to proclaim what a great guy Rusty was. Rostenkowski would receive the Copernican Award at the Conrad Hilton.

On 30 March Reagan was wounded in an assassination attempt by John W. Hinckley Jr. Bush was confined to Washington but called in a tribute to the Copernican dinner via telephone hookup. Governor Thompson said Danny was "a man of destiny and he still has a long way to go." [12]

Reagan's good-humored, wisecracking recovery from a pistol shot to the chest changed the political scenery. O'Neill found he could not walk through airports without passersby shouting, "Why don't you leave the president alone, you fat bastard!" At O'Hare Airport he was physically accosted by a man whom Rostenkowski had to shoulder block out of the way, after which Rostenkowski always arranged police bodyguards for Tip when he went to Chicago. [13]

Meanwhile, Rostenkowski was having private meetings with the "wizards and alchemists" of supply side—White House chief of staff James A. Baker III, Treasury Secretary Donald T. Regan, Budget Director David A. Stockman, and Bush. Of this quartet, only Stockman was a true believer. On 8 April, Rostenkowski and Conable met with Bush in the White House, where the chairman proposed a one-year tax cut as a substitute for

10-10-10. On 9 April he presented this plan in a speech in Chicago, honoring protocol by calling Secretary Regan first to brief him on it.

No way, said President Reagan. On 7 May, the House passed the Reagan budget resolution, 253–176. The preliminary budget resolution actually has little to do with ultimate appropriations, but the Reaganites chose to make this one a test of Reagan's proposals to cut the budget. The vote was a humiliating rejection of the Democratic leadership. The White House grew even cockier.

On 12 May, the wizards and alchemists met with Reagan in the Oval Office and agreed on a "bait-and-switch" strategy.[14] Kemp-Roth was dead, they thought, but they could still put Rostenkowski in a pincers between Tip's liberals and southern conservative Democrats known as "boll weevils" (formally, the Conservative Democratic Forum with forty-four members).

Toss Danny some sops, "bait," and after the final conference committee bill came up, he would have to "switch" to support it, given the president's popularity. In this scheme the wizards were abetted by a boll weevil, Texan Phil Gramm of the Budget Committee, who regularly snitched to the White House about Democratic strategy sessions (enraged Democrats dumped him from his Budget seat in 1983; he switched parties and sought the GOP presidential nomination in 1996). Reagan assented to bait and switch but refused to accept that Kemp-Roth was dead.

The president's men agreed to keep no notes of the meeting and all but cut their palms with a penknife to swear a blood oath of secrecy. This was Washington. News of the meeting leaked that very afternoon. Reagan went ballistic and repudiated any talk of compromising on a three-year tax cut.

That same day, the White House stupidly proposed benefit reductions in Social Security, which was going broke. Republicans joined Democrats in sprinting away in horror. Democrats took heart—maybe the wizards weren't so smart after all.

With the bait-and-switch exposure and the Social Security fiasco, there was no hope of a deal with Rostenkowski, so the White House calculated: Screw Ways and Means; we'll take it to the House floor. Reagan was assuring Democrats he would not personally campaign against anyone who voted for his tax bill. The wizards started telling reporters, "Rostenkowski is scared to death of a floor fight." Calling what he hoped was a bluff, Rostenkowski said, "If they've got the votes and they want to pass something inflexible, let them pass it. But they're playing a risky game."[15]

Reagan met with O'Neill, Wright, Rostenkowski, Long, and Byrd in the Oval Office on 1 June, a tableau for the media to get pictures and the wizards to play games. Reagan took a hard line, but as the meeting broke up, his aides quietly told Rostenkowski to "keep the door open" for a compromise and not to be as adamant as O'Neill.

The wizards were pursuing the old split-the-opposition, divide-and-conquer strategy. Too clever by half, they characteristically were. Far from splitting the two urban ethnic pols, they precipitated a Rusty/Tip, good-cop/bad-cop game. Even with Tip's bad-cop posture, liberals criticized him for being too soft on Reagan—an indication of the ossification of ideology in Congress. And yet none of this mattered in the end.

Rostenkowski, desperate to preserve the primacy of his committee, kept seeking a consensus bill of Republicans and weevils. His technique was to buttonhole a member in the library off the Ways and Means room in the Longworth House Office Building. The library held an oval mahogany table, ten yards long. Brass plates inlaid along the rim declared the names of successive chairmen, ending with *Dan Rostenkowski, Illinois, 1981–*. Rosty liked to sit in front of this plate when putting the squeeze on.

He might say, what do you want? A tax break for a plant in my district, might be the reply, or campaign funds, or a campaign visit by Ronnie, or by Tip or Ted—whatever. If the item were feasible, the chairman would say, all right, you've got it, but now you have to support the whole package when it hits the floor. No defectors, he growled. The private handshake deal, the soul of the machine, the legacy of Daley and Mills.

But the White House kept picking off the weevils by loading the tax bill with local goodies. Kent Hance of Texas, excited by a summons from Reagan, paid a visit to Wright. "I know what he wants, Mr. Leader," Hance said, adding, "I've never talked to a president one-on-one before. But I'm going to tell him I can't do it. I won't leave you, Mr. Leader."[16]

Yes, he did. He even cosponsored Reagan's bill. At least he was man enough to 'fess up. "You have one consolation, Mr. Leader," Hance told Wright, grinning. "Just remember that time wounds all heels."[17]

Republicans who remember Reagan's first term as the golden age have forgotten how much the true believers resented his consorting with the enemy. Conservative Republican Phil Crane, a Ways and Means member from the northwest Chicago suburbs, said, "If I were Reagan, I wouldn't have a thing to do with those guys. You look at their districts, those ought to be Republican seats. I would say they can go ahead and vote with Tip, and then . . . we'll have a majority in the next Congress."[18]

After his seduction by Reagan, Hance took his chair in the gold-carpeted Ways and Means room to find it oddly lower than the others, nor would it scoot up to the table. Rostenkowski had ordered the casters removed. Later Hance went to Andrews Air Force Base for a Ways and Means junket to China. Somehow his name was off the airplane manifest, and he could not board. "If you're against me, I might as well screw you up real good," as Rostenkowski said on another occasion.[19]

On 15 May, Rostenkowski suggested an eighteen-month to two-year tax cut. Later he said a third year might be tacked on, to be "triggered" only if the economy were sound. Reagan held tough. Conable and Hance put in a bill for 5-10-10, a slight trimming of 10-10-10. I'll take it, Reagan said at the 1 June meeting, but nothing less.

Early that month Ways and Means Democrats voted 21–0 for Rostenkowski's 5-10 plan, but the White House barely noticed. Rostenkowski called Regan to complain that Reagan had reneged on his promise to compromise and—horrors!—was auctioning off votes. Rostenkowski then went home to Chicago, where the president called him Friday morning to say, in his genial manner, that he would fight it out on the floor.

"I just don't think the country can afford to have the legislative and the executive in an auction contest," Rostenkowski said. He was right.[20]

That weekend, 7 and 8 June, became known as the "Lear Jet Weekend," with business executives flying in to tell the wizards the tax advantages they wished in the bill. On Tuesday, Ways and Means began the markup of Conable-Hance as a substitute for Kemp-Roth.

On 7 July, Reagan visited Chicago for a Governor Thompson fund raiser, though the real purpose, Reagan wrote in his memoirs, was to put heat on Rostenkowski, "to point out to his constituents that he held the fate of the tax-cut proposals in his palm. I urged them to write to him: 'If all of you will join with your neighbors to send the same message to Washington, we'll have that tax cut and we'll have it this year.'"[21]

Rusty and Tip were doing what they knew best: legislative politics.

Reagan was doing what he knew best: modern media politics. Network news producers had started calling Rostenkowski for the Sunday "talking heads" public affairs programs, where he often was countered by Dole. Despite this exposure, and despite the lessons in the mass mediation of public affairs taught by Chicago 1968, Rostenkowski still did not get it.

True, he had inklings of what was coming. As early as his Economic Club speech, Rostenkowski said that Reagan "gets to kick off and I get to lead the suicide squad downfield." [22] After Reagan went to Chicago, he said, "My problem is that the president can gear up his army with just one television appearance. That's fighting the Army, Navy, Marines, and Air Force." [23] Reagan generated mail that produced a two-to-three-day backlog of deliveries from the House post office, which had not happened since Watergate. Rostenkowski still did not fully get it. He and Tip, the two old machine pols, were steamrolled.

Meanwhile, Reagan's political operation, led by strategists Lyn Nofziger and Lee Atwater, conducted Luftwaffe divebombing raids on fifty-four critical districts. They induced the congressmen's major campaign contributors to threaten to oppose them in 1982 if they voted against the tax cut.

On the eve of the House vote, both sides thought it too close to call. Reagan spent the entire day on 27 July telephoning fence-sitters and then made another televised address to Congress that night. He "delivered a masterpiece of propaganda," wrote Stockman in 1986. [24] By that time, having left the administration, he did not mean it as a compliment.

After Reagan's speech, the only question was how many candy canes would be hung on the Christmas tree. They were considerable in number. The bill was such a thrown-together mishmash that clerks did not have it ready and printed for handing out on the floor before debate began on 29 July, when the House passed Conable-Hance. The key parliamentary vote was 238–195, the final vote, 323–107. The bill included in its text, as the proposed law of the land, the name and telephone number of a House staffer, Rita Seymour. Someone had scrawled it on a page of the markup draft, which became the final bill by default.

Reagan then won wavering conservatives in the Senate by agreeing to index income taxes against inflation. The Ford-Carter inflation of wages and prices had pushed taxpayers into higher tax brackets, showering Washington with revenues and enabling Democrats to pass the "tax cuts" of the 1970s that really just relaxed the effects of "bracket creep." Dole and Senate Majority Leader Howard Baker of Tennessee imposed indexing, though for fear of deficits it would not be implemented until 1985.

House and Senate conferees met all night on 31 July, when oil-state weevils were captured with the bait of tax breaks for oil. The Senate approved the bill on 3 August, 67–8.

On 4 August, Rostenkowski made a rare declamation on the House floor. He deplored the administration's railroad job on the budget resolution and its end run around Ways and Means, abuses of proper tax-writing procedures that generated a dreadful bidding war. "This process leaves us exhausted and disheartened," he said. "It takes away the incentive members must have to labor long and hard in these halls." The speech was well reasoned and well spoken. Politically it was beside the point. Reagan's presidential mastery of Congress in 1981 surpassed any since LBJ's in 1965 and has not been seen since. "If we accept the president's substitute [bill], we accept his domination of our House for months ahead," Rostenkowski pleaded. "We surrender to the political and economic whim of his White House."[25]

Conable rose to praise Rostenkowski—"Under a lesser leader, [the Democratic effort] would have come apart." Both sides of the aisle gave Rostenkowski a standing ovation.[26] He was gratified but also recognized it as a good-sportsmanship gesture to a loser. The final vote for the Economic Recovery Tax Act of 1981 was 282–95, a formality.

The wizards were sipping champagne with Reagan in the Oval Office when O'Neill placed the traditional courtesy phone call to the president. He had on the line Wright, Rostenkowski, and the whip, Tom Foley of Washington.

"We're all sitting here stunned," O'Neill said.

"I'm a little stunned myself," said Reagan, who thereafter placed congratulatory calls to Bob Michel and others.[27]

The law granted tax breaks to commercial real estate so improvident that they both enabled the construction of Presidential Towers and ensured that, with consequent overbuilding, it could not make money. Further, the rate on capital gains—profits on the sale of assets—was cut from 28 percent to 20 percent. The 10-5-3 depreciation schedule ended up as a complex 15-10-5-3. Violating a Democratic verity, personal income tax rates were reduced across the board, not skewed toward lower and middle incomes.

Detailing further provisions of the act would be otiose because Congress started rewriting it as early as 1982, with Reagan's assent. Quickly it became a Democratic article of faith that the $750 billion in revenues thrown away by the 1981 law caused the mountainous deficits of the 1980s. A mere glance at the public record suffices to show that, after the trough of the recession in 1982, federal revenues increased substantially every year. The deficits derived mostly from overspending.

An academic analyst has calculated that the 1981 tax cuts accounted for one-third of the escalating deficits of the 1980s.[28] Two-thirds were caused by higher spending on social welfare and defense, along with steeper interest payments on the accumulating public debt. Perhaps that schema might be taken as an allotment of liability for the deficits: Reagan one-third, Congress two-thirds.

In his first outing as Ways and Means chairman, Rostenkowski got sucked into a bidding war that he lost. Rostenkowski, the old-line Democrat, worried more about the deficits than did the supposedly green-eyeshade, gimlet-eyed, fiscally conservative Republicans, and he got bloodied for it. Before he even had much time to dress his wounds, the Republican/boll weevil coalition fell apart.

On 24 September, Reagan proposed a second round of spending cuts to trim the projected deficit. His coalition promptly deserted him. Congress will cut taxes but not spending. Stockman, himself a former congressman, professed in his memoirs that this was a shocking revelation to him.

As the recession deepened, the bond and stock markets grew increasingly nervous. The wizards convinced Reagan in 1982 that he had to raise taxes to shrink the deficit. When he heard of this, Rostenkowski figured, for all his jealousy of the prerogatives of his House and his committee, let the Republicans take the fall for this one. The Senate, to use his expression, could have these matches stuck in its shoe.

In March 1982, James Baker called O'Neill to suggest a private meeting the next day at the Speaker's home. O'Neill also invited Chairmen Richard Bolling of Rules, Jim Jones of Budget, and Rostenkowski. However, Rostenkowski was in Hawaii and missed the meeting. When he got back, Baker escorted him to a private talk with Reagan before the president met with other Democratic leaders. "Dutch" Reagan, a downstate Illinois boy, had taken a liking to the beefy Chicagoan.

That night, Rostenkowski and Bolling met in the den of Baker's home with Regan, Michel, and Representative Trent Lott of Mississippi (later the Senate Republican leader). Rostenkowski said what he had been saying publicly, that Democrats wanted to repeal the third year of 5-10-10 and might give up some spending cuts to get it. No way, said the GOPers. The group planned to meet again in a few days for breakfast.

Eventually this group expanded to become what its members called the "Gang of Seventeen." It had to move out of Baker's house into the Indian Treaty Room of the Executive Office Building next to the White House; or Blair House, the diplomatic residence across from the White House; or Bush's mansion. For Washingtonians, the gang kept these meetings exceptionally secret. Actually, there was little to leak—the meetings always broke down over defense, social welfare, or Social Security.

On 29 April, Reagan took to the airwaves with a televised blast against Democratic obstructionism. This was mostly just stagecraft. Again in contrast to the myth of a conservative golden age, Republican divisions between supply siders in the House and tax raisers in the Senate were so fierce that they had to be invited to separate meetings at the White House. Democrats felt other, equally sharp pressures.

They feared that if they voted for a tax increase, Republicans would hammer them for it in the November elections. Reagan offered to provide political cover by writing personal thank you letters to Democrats who supported the tax increase. The Republican National Committee even mounted a four-hundred-thousand-dollar public relations campaign for the tax hikes. In 1981 Reagan promised solidarity with Democrats who voted for his tax cuts. In 1982 he promised solidarity with Democrats who voted for his tax increases. The national myth that Republicans want lower taxes and smaller government, while Democrats want higher taxes and bigger government, stood fast against these facts. Just as it withstood, with barely a shutter flapping in the wind, Reagan's tax increases in the Social Security Act Amendments of 1983, the Deficit Reduction Act of 1984, the Temporary Extension of Tax Laws Act of 1985, the Omnibus Budget Reconciliation Acts of 1986 and 1987, the Airport and Airway Improvement Act of 1987, and the Technical Corrections and Miscellaneous Revenue Act of 1988.

Stockman, a bureaucratic rival of Regan and Baker, opened his own avenue to Rostenkowski that summer, soliciting help for raising excise taxes. Rostenkowski agreed, but only on condition that Reagan appear on television and publicly endorse the bill. That was the end of that.

The 1982 law was crafted by Bob Dole's Senate Finance Committee. It repealed some of the egregious 1981 business giveaways and raised various consumer taxes and fees. Ways and Means did not even draft a bill. Committee Democrats did not want their fingerprints on a tax increase, and committee Republicans wanted the GOP-led Senate to write it. Rostenkowski, jealous of his tax-writing turf, at first resisted his committee's abdication but had to give in. "I wasn't going to put Democrats on the line to increase taxes when through no fault of theirs they had been cut so much in 1981," he later said[29] in a partisan sophistry of the sort he did not often indulge (on the crucial roll call, forty-eight House Democrats had voted for those 1981 cuts).

On 28 July, the House approved Rostenkowski's motion to bounce the issue to the Senate so that it would be decided in a conference committee. Rostenkowski needed White House help for this maneuver. At first Conable and other committee Republicans refused to go directly to conference. Rostenkowski called Baker and demanded backing from at least six of the twelve GOPers for his plan. He got it.

Reagan thought he had made a deal with O'Neill that Congress would cut spending by nearly three dollars for every dollar of new taxes—$284 billion in cuts against $98 billion in taxes over three years. Republicans have complained bitterly that Tip double-crossed Reagan, but Reagan never exerted himself to enforce the deal, and it was moonshine anyway, to wit:

- $108 billion was assigned to lower interest rates on the public debt, which didn't happen.

- Budget director Stockman vouchsafed another "magic asterisk"—his term—for $47 billion in unspecified management savings, which didn't happen.
- More than half the rest would come from defense cuts, which Reagan himself refused.
- The remaining sliver was cuts in social welfare. Congress actually did pare the rate of growth in some of these programs.

The conference version of the Tax Equity and Fiscal Responsibility Act, the biggest peacetime tax increase to that date, passed the House on 19 August, 226–207. Reagan expressed thanks for the "revenue enhancers," daring not call them "taxes."

In December, Congress passed Rostenkowski's proposal to raise the federal gas tax from four cents to nine cents a gallon. Reagan signed it because the revenues were earmarked for road and bridge repairs, and the wizards sold it as a "jobs" bill to ease the recession. Rostenkowski had been right two years earlier—Reagan indeed signed a major gas tax increase.

More than that, Rostenkowski was a player, back in the ring, recovering from the debacle of 1981. Reagan, Baker, and Dole all liked him, worked well with him. Also, as chairman, he benefited from first-rate bean counters and lawyers on the committee staff. In fiscal policy, 1981 had been Reagan's year, 1982 Dole's year; Rostenkowski planned to make 1983 his year.

Expansively, he made peace with Kent Hance, phoning in an endorsement to his fund raiser in Texas. "My respect for him went up 200 percent after that," Hance said.[30] The old Rostenkowski was not entirely suppressed. A California Republican defeated for reelection paid a farewell visit to the chairman with one last request for his district.

"Be nice," he said, "I won't be here much longer."

"That's why I don't have to be nice," Rostenkowski growled.[31]

After the November 1982 election, in which Democrats gained twenty-six House seats, Rostenkowski and a few favored committee members toured Jamaica, Panama, Barbados, St. Lucie, and the Dominican Republic. Far from criticizing this junket, the White House aided it, dispatching presidential assistant Kenneth M. Duberstein as tour guide. Duberstein had been one of the Gang of Seventeen. Upon returning to Washington,

Rostenkowski raised Reagan's Caribbean Basin Initiative from the dead. The trade incentives thereupon passed Ways and Means by a lopsided 28–6 vote.

One of the wizards said that Reagan "likes Rostenkowski and trusts him more than the other [Democratic] leaders. He's gone out of his way to nurture that relationship with little notes and phone calls and other gestures . . . Rostenkowski is the easiest of the Democrats to do business with."[32]

Eventually, a wall of H208 featured a photo of Mount Rushmore, except that Rostenkowski's likeness was pasted alongside the mountainous head of President Washington. Scribbled across the scene was the message, "Dear Danny, It looks good to me. Say hello to George for me." The note was signed, "Ronald Reagan."

The other Democratic leaders were not thrilled by these valentines to the Chicagoan. Democrats kept pushing to repeal or at least curtail the final year of 5-10-10. Rostenkowski's insistence that they lacked the votes caused a rift with O'Neill. Rostenkowski believed the most they could pass was a delay in indexing for inflation.

More important, Rostenkowski struck out on his own on the Social Security issue. Reagan had set up a national advisory commission, chaired by Alan Greenspan (later chairman of the Federal Reserve Board), which produced the usual blah blah. Rostenkowski turned down a chance to sit on the commission because he did not wish to be bound to its recommendations.

Tentatively, Reagan, Dole, and O'Neill started dancing around one another, looking for a deal. "I've got to move," Rostenkowski said. "I've got to have a bill through the House by the end of next March. If I don't, the system goes belly up next June."[33] Sure enough, he launched hearings on 1 February and passed a bill on 9 March by a fairly close vote, 228–202. Ken Duberstein helped assemble GOP votes.

Rostenkowski threw a celebratory dinner party that night. The only Republican invited was Duberstein, whom Rusty hailed as the middleman of the Reagan-Rostenkowski vote-gathering machine. They had accelerated the schedule of Social Security tax increases passed in 1977 and gradually raised the retirement age from sixty-five to sixty-seven by 2027. Rostenkowski received much credit for his part in rescuing the sacred Social

Security system. He had demonstrated once again that Republican executives and Democratic legislators collude to raise taxes and provide pork. What doubtless carried more weight in his mind was that he was emerging as a logical successor to O'Neill as Speaker.

Morton's of Chicago, a famous steak house, opened a restaurant in Washington at 3251 Prospect Street and waited for the crowds to come. Inexplicably, they didn't. The owner called Rusty, who then scheduled a dinner with several people from "downtown"—Washington parlance for K Street lobbyists—who had been seeking an audience.

Thereafter he went to Morton's every night for two weeks straight. Swiftly it became a hangout for Capitol Hill and K Street types. Rostenkowski was a D.C. bigfoot. He had never had a personal press secretary, but the Ways and Means press office put out a press release with a typo calling him "Rosty." Overnight he became Rosty instead of Rusty. He had become not only a bigfoot but, almost in spite of himself, a creature of the Washington media.

Soon Morton's screwed a brass plaque into a wall in an alcove with a round table near the grill that said, "Rosty's Rotunda." It always was held open, reservations or no, waiting throngs or no, for Rosty's possible appearance.

In he would barge, boisterous and jokey, with a retinue of courtiers, and order "see-throughs" (Gibson's gin martinis) and the biggest steak in the house "Pittsburgh style," charred on the outside, pink on the inside. The meal included potatoes and onion rings, finished off by glasses of Chateauneuf du Pape. No wimpy, yuppie swordfish and white wine for him. He consumed cholesterol time bombs nightly without care. At one of his other haunts, the Palm, a caricature on the wall depicted Rosty as obese; he thought it was funny.

K Street underlings, kids out of college, would be assigned merely to arrange these dinners. They began at seven, when Rosty might entertain the table with an impersonation—his LBJ was so on target he could have grown up in Texas—and then proceed to talk shop. Adjournment came promptly at ten, when Rostenkowski retired to the bachelor apartment he called the "Junkyard," there to catch the TV news and go to bed.

A junior lobbyist from Illinois planned a junket for members of the

Illinois Manufacturing Association to crawl around Capitol Hill and hear speeches from Kemp and Kennedy. A lavish welcoming reception was to be hosted by Rostenkowski and Michel in the Rayburn Building. Horrified, the kid learned from the industry group that the invitations had gone out too late. He called Kemp, Kennedy, and others to cancel the event, but through a snafu, Rosty and Michel never got the word. The Ways and Means chairman and the minority leader of the House sat drinking alone in an ornate banquet room, surrounded by teams of formally jacketed bartenders, wondering where everyone was.[34]

A somewhat similar mix-up happened back in the Carter days. Bob Strauss arranged a dinner for the president to schmooze with "the boys," namely, Tip and Danny. Carter and Strauss waited at a table at the Paul Young restaurant, but because of a scheduling error "the boys" thought the dinner was the next night.

By chance, Strauss spied Rostenkowski in a corner and waved him over. He sat down, and the three men had a drink. Then Rostenkowski dumbfounded Strauss by getting up and saying he needed to return to his original table because he was seeing "important people" from Chicago. In Rosty's movable feasts, people from Chicago and old friends were VIPs. Besides, he still thought the dinner with Carter was the next night.

Almost never did Rosty pick up the tab. Once a waiter placed the check at his elbow, only to receive the Rostenkowski Glare. Restaurant staffers liked him—few could help it—but he could be moody and demanding, giving voice to the mean streak that seems to lie, however hidden, in the spleen of every great leader. Rostenkowski was far, far away from the days when he and Michel counted quarters for the special of the day at the Chicken Shack.

He was such a boulevardier that striking a pose as the defender of the little guy against Reagan's giveaways to the rich, as some Democrats urged him and for which O'Neill modeled constantly, would have been problematic. Rostenkowski made no apologies, then or later, certainly not when the *Washington Post* first detailed the extent of his high living.

In June 1982, the *Post* reported that within a five-month period Rostenkowski spent forty-five days at golf tournaments or other gatherings at luxury resorts, paid for by lobbyists or private persons, at which he received personal gifts and campaign donations.[35] Now and then he was accompanied by Michel, who likewise benefited, because lobbyists work both sides of the street. Bob and Rosty golfed with such as former President Ford, who said (to a Chicago reporter), "Danny is a terribly honest, forthright, hardworking, decent individual . . . he doesn't like to lose [at golf] and, quite frankly, he hates to pay [bets] when he does lose." [36] LaVerne often joined Danny on these free trips, sometimes staying extra days after her husband returned to Washington.

In disclosure forms newly required by reformers, Rosty was the champion recipient of "honoraria," fees for speeches often made at the free luxury outings, amounting to $50,898 for 1982 (second was Jack Kemp with $42,880). Listed among Rosty's assets, a minor holding but defiantly still there, was stock in the Egyptian Trotting Association. The chief lawyer for Ways and Means said, "Dan Rostenkowski has been less swayed by special interests in how he votes than any member I know." And he meant it.

The *Chicago Tribune*, a Republican paper that loved Rostenkowski, editorially reprimanded him for living high on lobbyists' tabs. Nothing came of this, in Chicago or Washington.

In February 1983, Mayor Byrne was up for reelection, and the usual vibrations were felt, with Rostenkowski as usual teasing that he would come home to run. When a reporter asked, "Would you consider it a step up to be mayor from House Ways and Means chairman?" Rostenkowski said, "Oh, it might be a lateral move," chuckle, chuckle.[37] As if he would abandon the salvation of the nationally worshiped Social Security to do so.

Still, Rosty did not neglect his home base. If the mayor or the governor called with a request, he usually would comply, even though he disliked Byrne and Thompson was a Republican. In 1981, for example, Thompson sought an amendment to give Illinois more money in a surface transportation safety bill. "He wants it and we're going to try to push it for him," said Rostenkowski, riding the members' elevator to the floor. "And the governor gives me the impression that, 'The only fellow that can do it is you, Dan!'" Grinning and shaking his head, kidding on the square as he stepped off the elevator, he added, "You know, one of those things so that if it's all a total failure, it's all my fault." [38]

Resolutely Rostenkowski protected three giants, the Chicago Board of Trade, the Chicago Mercantile Exchange, and the Chicago Board Options

Exchange. Historically they traded futures contracts on pork, corn, and other farm commodities in a Wild West, boom-and-bust atmosphere. After Nixon's abandonment of the gold standard and other economic shocks of the 1970s, the exchanges took to trading "commodities" such as U.S. Treasury bills, the value of a group or index of stocks, and foreign currencies. By the early 1980s, farm commodities made up only half their total volume.

The futures industry is a prime example of the snarls that can result from federal regulations of markets. The industry was regulated by a toothless agency, the Commodity Futures Trading Commission. The new financial instruments provoked rivalry between the CFTC and the Securities and Exchange Commission over which agency would regulate what and how. In part this was a Chicago-New York fight, with the CFTC in the role of frontier upstart and the SEC as guardian of old Yankee, Wall Street respectability. Meanwhile, state attorneys general cried out that federal preemption prevented them from prosecuting commodities fraud, which was considerable.

Look, the futures industry told Congress, we'll set up an umbrella organization to police ourselves, much as the American Bar Association regulates lawyers or the American Medical Association regulates doctors. Okay, said Congress in 1978.

Three years later, grudgingly, the industry formed the National Futures Agency, with the head of the Merc as president. Washington was dissatisfied, and the Reagan administration proposed a tougher CFTC financed by user fees on futures transactions (similar fees on stock trades had helped set up the SEC in 1934). In Orwellian fashion, Reagan would accept tax increases only if they were called "user fees," leading to the Washington joke that the income tax was a user fee on income.

Look, said the industry, you can't expect us to pay user fees for the CFTC and dues to fund the National Futures Agency at the same time. Rostenkowski spearheaded the House defeat of the user-fee bill in September 1981. Stockman had threatened a presidential veto, but the 319–59 vote persuaded him to forget it.

Rostenkowski stood as an invincible sentinel against futures industry taxes for the next thirteen years. At a 1983 champagne breakfast for the opening of a new Merc complex, he said, "The Merc is to Chicago what oil is to Texas and Oklahoma, what milk is to Wisconsin, and what corn is to Iowa." [39]

And then there was the United States Steel Corporation. The 1980s were terrible for heavy industry. Even after Rostenkowski gave it tax breaks in the 1981 tax law, U.S. Steel announced the shutdown of most of its huge South Works plant, a portal into the middle class for generations of white ethnic workers, located in Ed Vrdolyak's district. U.S. Steel used its tax windfall to buy another corporation, Marathon Oil.

Elected officials at all levels huffed and puffed to save the steel jobs. Rostenkowski and others flew to Pittsburgh in 1983 to meet the U.S. Steel chairman and offer a bouquet of state and local tax concessions. They believed they had won a commitment to build a modern rail mill on the old South Works site.

The company then jerked around the politicians on tax relief demands, and the union jerked them around on benefits and givebacks, until they angered Rostenkowski, a man not safely angered. "They're going to come back to Rostenkowski," he said. "And Rostenkowski's going to be an awful, awful quiet man for a long time"—the same threat of inaction that he had used against Califano and that he would invoke time and again. [40]

Meanwhile, Vrdolyak characteristically represented the union as a lawyer at the same time he pocketed campaign donations from steel executives. The resolution of the fired workers' benefits took an entire decade. The economy of Vrdolyak's district was razed. The rail mill was never built.

And then there was the Chicago Theatre, the spectacular old Loop movie palace into which Rostenkowski had sneaked as a boy. Larry Horist, who ran an old civic group called the "City Club," tried to save the theater from the wrecking ball. He went to H208 to ask Rosty for a small Urban Development Action Grant, a piddling $2.5 million.

There's a problem, the chairman said. Reagan's housing secretary, Samuel R. Pierce Jr., was freezing all requests from Chicago in retaliation for Rostenkowki's opposition to Reagan's "urban enterprise zones" bill. Democrats considered the zones a gimmick that would help businesses escape taxes without addressing chronic inner-city unemployment. Plus, Pierce's department would grumble from time to time about Presidential Towers.

Rostenkowski brightened. "I think I know a way around that," said he, who often found a way around things. He called his old buddy Bush and said, "If I don't get that grant you're gonna have one very pissed off chairman of the Ways and Means Committee for your tax bill."[41]

The vice president called the housing secretary. The housing secretary called Rosty and meekly asked for an appointment in the chairman's office. Sure, Rosty said, and don't forget to bring the papers for the theater grant. As for enterprise zones, Rostenkowski remained opposed. The theater was saved, though, with a combination of public and private money.

During Horist's visit the mayoral race naturally came up. "You know, I probably could become mayor," Rostenkowski mused. "I have to ask myself why . . . I'm one of the most powerful guys in Washington and there's virtually no spotlight on me. I run for mayor, I got every day, every reporter is on my door, second-guessing what I'm doing. And I've got to deal with racial strife, you know, it'll be a black-white race, it'll be ugly. Why would I give this up?"[42]

Rostenkowski's relations with Mayor Byrne were erratic and soon chilly, but then her relations with nearly everyone were erratic and soon chilly, save for such as Vrdolyak and Swibel. Rostenkowski claimed that he first amassed a huge campaign fund to thwart Byrne's implied threats to run somebody against him in the 1982 primary. This was disingenuous. It is true that he did not stage a Washington fund raiser with the K Street crowd until 1982. But his fund was big enough to put up campaign billboards outside his own district, to inform all Chicago of what a big man he was, as early as 1978.

Byrne deposed Dunne as party chairman for Vrdolyak because Dunne supported Rich Daley for mayor. Rostenkowski, with misgivings but still a good party soldier, voted for Vrdolyak over his old friend Dunne.

Byrne angered blacks by dumping black members of the housing authority and the school board for whites. The political class thought she was nuts. Actually, her alienation of blacks was a calculated tactic. She would provoke them into putting up a candidate against her and Daley, thereby splitting the opposition and gaining reelection by a plurality.

It had worked in 1977, when state senator Harold Washington joined Pucinski in futilely challenging Bilandic. Pucinski had dreamed of a Polish-black alliance to topple the Irish oligarchy, but it was never to be. Washington won five South Side black wards for 10 percent of the citywide vote.

Rostenkowski had gotten to know Harold Washington, a fellow payroller in the city corporation counsel's office in the 1950s, after he entered Congress in 1981. Washington represented the First District on the Near South Side, historically the oldest seat of black political power in the country, the domain of the late Bill Dawson.

Washington was a man of charisma, intelligence, and puzzlements. He might charm a crowd with his folksiness, wade into the city council chamber and duke it out passionately with his foes, go home alone to his South Shore bachelor apartment to read weighty books far into the night, and then stay up and brood. White voters and politicians had trouble understanding both his toughness and his political mode.

By 1983 blacks and whites were roughly equal in voting-age population, but whites had a substantial edge in the number of registered voters. Begged by blacks to run for mayor, Washington refused unless tens of thousands of blacks registered to vote. And so, fueled in part by Byrne's perceived insults to the African American community and tub thumped by Jesse Jackson, it happened.

Somewhat as he had been torn between Carter and Byrne/Kennedy, Rostenkowski was torn between Byrne and Daley. He permitted his puppet, Alderman Terry Gabinski, to circulate ballot petitions for Byrne, but as ward committeeman Rostenkowski officially was neutral.

On 30 January, Rostenkowski finally endorsed Daley, drawing a rebuke from Vrdolyak, as if it mattered. Byrne's machine was falling apart, though most of the white ethnics—Annunzio, Pucinski, the rest—endorsed her.

Undaunted, Rostenkowski cut TV commercials for Daley. Byrne, having raised an astounding $10 million for a mayoral race, also aired TV ads, for which Washington lacked money. In this election, TV ad slickness did not count.

Daley, who had flunked the bar exam twice, was so inarticulate in televised debates that critics said he made his father sound Churchillian by comparison. Washington by contrast was crisp and cool, Byrne cranky and shrill. On the Loop elevateds and the trains to the South and West sides, every black passenger—grandmothers, maids, punch press operators, hospital cafeteria workers, the unemployed, little kids, everybody—wore blue Washington campaign buttons featuring a rays-of-a-rising-sun motif. The local media did not notice this outpouring of black pride. Their members generally did not take the Chicago Transit Authority to the South and West sides.

Byrne's strategy boomeranged against her—she and Daley split the white vote, enabling Washington to win the nomination in February with a plurality of 38 percent. The black candidate won 85 percent of the black vote, 16 percent of the Latino vote, and 4 percent of the white vote. In Rostenkowski's ward, the vote was Daley 46 percent, Byrne 39 percent, Washington 15 percent.

Byrne and her white machine were heartbroken and slapped silly. The ensuing campaign against the obscure Republican nominee, attorney Bernard Epton, was nobody's finest hour. Washington, who had served a brief jail term for failing to file tax returns, also was targeted by a poison-pen campaign alleging he was a closet homosexual and pedophile.

Byrne approached Larry Horist about running in the general election as a write-in Republican or independent candidate, but that idea was shot down by the Republican national chairman and by Ted Kennedy.[43] Kennedy and Tip O'Neill endorsed Washington, but Rostenkowski held off.

Poor Walter Mondale had endorsed Daley before Washington said he would run. To make amends with blacks after the primary, he accompanied Washington to a campaign stop at St. Pascal's Church on the Northwest Side on 27 March. They were met by a jeering, hateful crowd and a spray-painted slogan on the church wall: "nigger die." In later years, black leaders would refuse to countenance questions about whether this protest had been staged to galvanize black voter turnout. Perhaps the questions were improper, borne of the cynicism sired by Chicago 1968.

On 17 March, Rostenkowski endorsed Washington, but he did not deploy his precinct captains for the Democratic nominee. Most of the white ethnic committeemen openly or secretly supported Epton. They preferred a Jewish Republican to a black Democrat. On 5 April, Washington barely defeated Epton, 52 percent to 48 percent. The Thirty-second Ward voted for Epton, 56 percent to 44 percent.

Everyone wrote obituaries for the old Daley machine, which once again proved to be premature. The machine gritted its teeth and figured, heck, we worked with Janey, we can work with Harold. Washington ran as the enemy of the machine, but he was no young radical; he was sixty-one years old and had not fully broken with the machine until 1979. After the primary, a peace council was held in the Bismarck Hotel across from city hall. Over breakfast with Washington, the "two Eddies," Vrdolyak and Southwest Side powerhouse Ed Burke, and other aldermen performed the rites of mutual backslaps, jokes, and pledges of unity for the good of the party. Washington took the aldermen's phone numbers and promised to call, but he didn't.

Then, two days before the 29 April mayoral inaugural, the two Eddies and others went to the nation's capital for the official hanging of Rostenkowski's portrait as Ways and Means chairman. William O. Lipinski, a new congressman from the Southwest Side, told the two Eddies he wanted to see them later in his office.

In Lipinski's lair in the Longworth House Office Building, he reported a double-cross was in the making. Alderman Wilson J. Frost, the former president pro tem whose claim to the mayoralty after Mayor Daley died was spurned because he was black, was assembling an alliance of pro-Washington and pro-Daley aldermen to oust the Byrne loyalists from their committee chairs.[44]

Vrdolyak returned to Chicago with enthusiasm to organize a swift countercoup. When Washington presided over his first city council meeting, Vrdolyak and his 28 followers seized every position of leadership in the council. Washington, with his fatal inattention to detail, had been blind sided. In the galleries overlooking the council chamber, black supporters of the mayor pounded on the glass wall and screamed in frustration.

There followed the nationally notorious "Council Wars," with Washington stomped on by a 29–21 council opposition. The *Wall Street Journal* called Chicago "Beirut on the Lake." White aldermen wore lapel buttons bearing the numeral *29*. Terry Gabinski joined the 29 and was rewarded with the zoning committee chair. Washington could not prevail until special aldermanic elections in 1986, ordered by federal courts to redress racial bias in Byrne's 1981 redistricting, gave him a council majority by a single vote.

Rostenkowski's relations with Washington were cool, although both were chunky, jovial sons of the old machine and hard-headed politicians to boot. One night Rosty took Harold on a pub crawl of Northwest Side Polish taverns. Washington enjoyed it so much he told a friend he might try an Italian bar circuit next.[45] Despite these overtures, the white aldermen remained obstructionist.

Although he remained a committeeman, Rostenkowski was largely removed from all this. LaVerne made a rare trip to Washington to pull the drapery off her husband's new portrait in the Longworth Building. The ceremony demonstrated that Rostenkowski's ego had completed the journey from Milwaukee Avenue to Pennsylvania Avenue.

The portrait by a Chicago-area artist, Robert Dewar Bentley, was commissioned by Chicago industrialists and private persons such as Carl Yastrzemski, the Boston Red Sox star. It shows Rosty standing in front of a desk in a dark suit and light blue tie, arms folded, a twinkle in his eyes and a small smile on his lips. Indistinct swatches of gray make up the background. While hardly high art, the portrait is realistic and slightly flattering.

About 250 people showed up for the ceremony, including Daley, Bilandic, Vrdolyak, Burke, Dunne, Mikva, Gibbons, O'Neill, Wright, and Bush. "This is the biggest crowd I've ever seen" at such a "hanging," O'Neill said.[46] However, neither Byrne nor Washington attended. Jim Wright, who fancied himself something of a man of letters, offered this doggerel:

> The corpses of Kennedy, Mondale, and Glenn
> Lie piled in layers
> And so long as I know Rostenkowski will win
> I don't get involved with no mayors.[47]

Bush, whose trait for dry humor is unrecognized, said, "What a fantastic tribute to Rostenkowski, and he isn't even dead yet."

Gibbons, on bad paper with O'Neill and Rostenkowski, said, "He is now one of the pre-eminent citizens of the world."

Rostenkowski several times sniffled and dabbed at his eyes, blurting out at one point, "My parents always wondered if I would ever amount to anything."[48]

8

WRITE ROSTY

But if great princes are rare, how much more so are great
legislators!

—Jean-Jacques Rousseau, *The Concept of the General Will*

A COMMON criticism of the modern Congress is that it is ungovernable. An apparently trivial sumptuary point might illustrate this. Speaker Sam Rayburn required members to appear on the floor wearing business suits and neckties that would not draw stares at any Kiwanis or Rotary banquet. This unwritten rule preceded by many years the televising of the House, when the only spectators were visitors in the cramped galleries. Old Sam's attitude was that members were serious people doing serious business, the people's business, and should dress accordingly. History has not recorded when sport jackets and slacks began to penetrate the sanctum. By now, if a member is just dashing onto the floor for an errand or a quick vote and knows he won't be on camera in the well, he might wear—as one old lion groused upon his retirement—"fishing clothes!"

A more radical criticism is that the modern Congress has more or less stopped legislating. Members spend their days "dialing for dollars" from campaign contributors, posturing before cameras, seeking publicity in hearings, and riding in airplanes. Major laws that still get passed mostly enroll noble ideals in the code books—say, uncontaminated air, water, and topsoil—and leave the details to the regulatory agencies of the executive branch. The subsequent actions of these agencies provide still more opportunities for congressmen to intervene as their constituents' and bank-rollers' Mr. Fix-It.

Article I of the Constitution created Congress as a powerful legislature. Congressmen no longer legislate so much as they proffer the unraveling, for a price—a campaign check or just a constituent's vote—of governmental red tape. Their workaday routines hardly justify the ambition displayed by junior politicians coveting their seats. They jawbone on the phone with bureaucrats and campaign donors, trot down long tiled hallways in one of the House office buildings to catch some kid bearing a videocam with a TV news logo affixed and then drive or take the Metro to the airport to grab a flight to their home district or a colleague's for still more fund raising. Unless they chair an important subcommittee or committee, or at least belong to the majority party, they hold just 1 vote out of 435. This would be a disagreeable occupation for most people.

As the legislative function has steadily diminished under the tyranny of modern media politics and big-money politics, Congress has staked off one area where it still insists on enacting specific, legalistic provisions and is willing to devote the needed time and care: the tax code. To be sure, some fine points are left to the IRS and thence to the U.S. Tax Court. Primarily, though, Congress is in the business of buying and selling tax advantages. As Rostenkowski harrumphed in 1981, the House was loath to abandon "control of the economy" for three years in a row.

It has been thus since at least 1913, when the Sixteenth Amendment permitted a national income tax. Just eight years later, Congress set up the first Tax Simplification Board. "Reforming" and "simplifying" the tax system has been a perennial indoor sport ever since, a game with no final buzzer.

The 1986 law made the system more equitable by lowering tax rates for everybody, ending income taxes for the working poor, and paying for the rate cuts by scrapping or restricting many deductions, exemptions, exclusions, credits, and deferrals. Its surprise passage provoked a champagne party of self-congratulations among the political and media clerisy, jubilant over this rare proof that the government "works" for the public interest after all. The next year, Congress started chiseling away at the law, and by now it is nearly demolished.

Whatever the flaws of the tax reform law of 1986 and Rostenkowski's performance in passing it, he at least legislated. He passed a bill that enjoyed no natural constituency in the ungovernable Congress. Everyone is for "tax reform" in the abstract but chary in the event. Rosty hacked his way through jungles of competing interests to clear pathways to consensus, endured hour upon long hour of hearings and negotiations, meticulously assembled coalitions, buffaloed some of the princes of the House and crowned heads of the Senate, worked himself to near stupefaction, and passed a monumental law—even though it turned out to be mostly a short-lived reform, perhaps not worth the effort. In any case we might imagine the ghosts of the framers of Article I nodding proudly at him. He legislated.

Rostenkowski's triumph was also, with the inevitability of the tragic human condition, eventually his downfall. The blessing carried two curses. First, the 1986 tax law was born of corruption in the sense that, as with the 1981 tax law, it was consummated by the buying and selling of tax and regulatory advantages. Second, it made Rosty a national celebrity. Our culture alternately adores and destroys celebrities. Rosty was adored and then destroyed in a progression he never understood, not even when federal prison afforded ample time for reflection.

To pass the 1986 tax bill, precious to him and to the Republican president, Rostenkowski set up a bourse of tax and regulatory advantages. At that thirty-foot mahogany table in the Ways and Means library, he perfected the techniques he had practiced in the auction of 1981, when he was outbid by Reagan. There was more to the story than this auction, of course, considering Rostenkowski's leadership skills in the postreform Congress. He was sincerely affronted when critics then, and federal prosecutors later, called him "venal." He had legislated.

In 1987, *Wall Street Journal* reporters Jeffrey H. Birnbaum and Alan S. Murray published *Showdown at Gucci Gulch: Lawmakers, Lobbyists, and the Unlikely Triumph of Tax Reform*, the definitive account. There is thus no need here to retell the entire legislative process, as marked by suspense and drama as it was. Instead, this chapter will focus on Rostenkowski's actions, in particular as they related to the culture of corruption. In doing so the narrative will unjustly slight the nearly coequal role played by Senate

Finance Committee Chairman Robert Packwood of Oregon in passing the law, as well as the important roles of James Baker, key congressional aides, and others.

On Near Year's Day 1984, Rostenkowski told Chicago reporters, "You people analyze us as being a commercial enterprise or some cunning confidence operation. I think a great many of us want to do a good job and need your support and your understanding. Sometimes we don't get either." [1]

Three days later, he appeared before Chicago business leaders to endorse a commercial enterprise and a cunning confidence operation. Members of the Chicago Board of Trade and Chicago Board Options Exchange used a device called a "spread" or "straddle" to buy and sell at the same time options or futures on the same stock or commodity. In this way, they could record paper losses in the current tax year while putting off profits to later years when lower capital gains rates would kick in.

The 1981 tax law in effect ended the tax shelter for spreads in futures contracts but neglected to include options contracts. The result was predictable.

In 1984, traders faced assaults on two fronts. The futures industry thought it had a deal with Congress that tax-deferral spreads done before 1981 would not be examined by the IRS. But the IRS was looking into those earlier trades anyway. Meanwhile, a pending bill would bar such tax-deferral trading in the options industry as well.

At the Midland Hotel in the Loop, a member of the 4 January luncheon audience rose to ask Rostenkowski what he could do about this deplorable situation. His reply was a single word. "Legislate." [2]

Before he could attend to that chore, there intervened the matters of tax-exempt municipal bonds, which had nettled Rostenkowski since Presidential Towers, and the March 1984 Democratic primary.

As seen in the discussion of Presidential Towers, the use of tax-exempt municipal bonds, supposedly meant for public works, to boost private development instead had mushroomed. Mayor Byrne even offered an election-year bond in 1983 to benefit a North Side wine store popular with yuppies (that issuance later was revoked). The Treasury, annoyed that such bonds enlarged the deficit, proposed limiting the amounts that cities could issue. Rosty actually tended to agree. He proposed a quota of $150 per resident.

Mayor Washington flew to the capital twice in February 1984 to lobby against the Treasury Department's cap on bonds. He managed to recruit Rostenkowski, a sponsor of the ruling 29 abhorrent to Washington. Rosty and Treasury made a deal. The caps would not apply to facilities owned and operated by cities—to wit, O'Hare Airport—or to bonds floated to build multifamily residential housing—to wit, Presidential Towers. Later, municipal bonds became a sticking point in the 1986 tax bill.

Meanwhile, so many Hispanics were moving into the Thirty-second Ward that Luis Gutierrez thought he should be the Democratic committeeman. Rostenkowski might be aloof from Council Wars, but damn it, he would run his own ward. His crushing of Gutierrez was efficient and ruthless. (In 1992 Gutierrez, by then an alderman, was elected to Congress with the support of Rich Daley in a gerrymandered district neighboring Rostenkowski's.)

Gutierrez, a slightly built thirty-one-year-old, assiduously gathered enough petition signatures to win a spot on the 1984 primary ballot, in itself an insult to Danny. The challenger quit his job as a state social worker to drive a cab, twenty hours a day seven days a week, to build a bank account sufficient to pay his bills long enough to run for committeeman against Rosty. He assumed he would get help from Mayor Washington. He was wrong.

"He told reporters he endorsed me," Gutierrez said philosophically, "but he didn't. But I understand why. He can't. Under the table, his heart is with us. But his mind—that's with Rostenkowski. Who's going to say they are against Danny when he controls all the money coming into this city? When Chicago can't get a light bulb replaced without Danny's cooperation?" [3]

Still, Rosty's precinct captains seemed to be asleep. Gutierrez, campaigning frantically, entertained thoughts that he might upset the overconfident incumbent. On a Saturday shortly before the primary, he went to bed actually believing he would win. Stepping outside his home Sunday morning, he saw that every house on the block except his had a blue and orange Rostenkowski sign taped in the front window. The ward office had spent weeks lining up supporters and then plastered every Hispanic street—the reliable Polish streets were not so favored—with signs in a dark-of-night frenzy.

On the morning of election day, when a typical late-winter mist from Lake Michigan moistened the ward, Gutierrez entered a Hispanic grocery to buy cigarettes and thanked the owner for the Gutierrez poster in the window. Upon exiting, the challenger took another look. The window also held a poster for Rosty. "He's playing it real safe," Gutierrez observed.

Having crushed Gutierrez, Rostenkowski played it safe with the options industry tax issue, as did Bob Dole. Late one night in June—taxpayers filling out their annual 1040 forms would be dismayed to learn how the tax code annually is written by tired, cranky House-Senate conferees in the wee hours—Rosty suddenly offered a clause to protect Chicago commodities traders from tax liabilities. Senate Finance Committee Chairman Dole instantly agreed. And so it came to pass that 333 traders evaded tax payments at an average of $866,000 per trader.

In 1981, Dole had scorned these traders as a Democratic clientele. He even had urged the IRS to pursue abuses of the trading straddle tax shelter. In the ensuing years, the industry poured big bucks into one of Dole's PACs, "Campaign America." Dole became persuaded of the essential role of this industry in the American economy. His change of heart placed a Rostenkowski-Dole provision in the tax law of 1984 inhibiting the IRS from going after straddles prior to 1981, thus voiding many cases in U.S. Tax Court. Technically, the law shifted the burden of proof from the trader to the IRS. This issue also became a sticking point in 1986.

In July 1984, Democrats nominated Walter Mondale at their national convention in San Francisco. Washington and Vrdolyak had agreed on Rosty as the Illinois delegation chairman as a compromise acceptable to supporters of Mondale, Gary Hart, native son Jesse Jackson, and Washington himself, who with a handful of Chicago delegates was pressing for an urban assistance plank.

Dick Daley had controlled the delegation with formal delegation meetings. Rosty saw that the ethnic and political schisms were unbridgeable and dispensed with the meetings—let the delegates party and vote at will; Mondale's nomination was ordained anyway. Rosty had endorsed Mondale in 1983 and was among the party elders summoned in turn by the former vice president to his North Beach, Minnesota, home for consultation before the convention.

In his acceptance speech, Mondale said, "Mr. Reagan will raise taxes and so will I. He won't tell you; I just did." The speech concluded with the traditional balloons and confetti raining on the arena, bands blaring, while the nominee and party leaders pranced and waved on the stage. When this dance bumped Rostenkowski against Mondale, the congressman said, "You've got a lot of balls, pal."[4] Rostenkowski himself persistently called for tax increases through the 1980s, but then he was not running for president. Also, Mondale, widely scorned for promising to raise taxes, was right: Reagan raised them too.

Back in Chicago the next Monday, Rostenkowski had a personal mishap. Leaving his ward office on Damen Avenue for his vacation home in Wisconsin, he drove north on Damen and, starting to turn left onto Fullerton Street, collided with an oncoming southbound car. The other driver, Helen Wing, a widowed sixty-four-year-old flower arranger, was hospitalized with broken ribs and severe lumbar sprain. Rosty spent five days in a hospital, undergoing nasal surgery to set a broken nose. Police issued no tickets.

Two years later, Wing filed a $250,000 lawsuit against Rostenkowski, charging he was drunk at the time of the accident and failed to yield the right of way. Wing said two witnesses would testify that the congressman behaved in an intoxicated manner. However, the doctor who had treated him said, "There was blood all over his face. We were as close to him as possible. Our faces were in his nose. None of us noticed alcohol on his breath."[5] In a deposition in 1987, Rostenkowski denied having consumed any alcohol, drugs, or medicines in the twenty-four hours before the accident. The case was never tried. Wing died in 1990.

In his 1985 State of the Union address, President Reagan repeated a call he had raised during the 1984 campaign for a total overhaul of the tax code. He pledged it would not camouflage a tax increase, nor would it worsen the deficit: it would be "revenue-neutral." What is more, it would relieve the 6 million lowest-paid workers of all income taxes—a provision calculated to be irresistible to Democrats.

The supply-side school still was spouting the efficacy of low marginal tax rates. Supply side is regarded as an invention of a few right wingers in the 1970s, but back in 1958, cinema actor Ronald Reagan had testified before a congressional committee that confiscatory tax rates suppressed the work ethic. Reagan would make enough movies in a year to earn four hundred thousand dollars. After that point, taxes claimed 91 percent of his income, whereupon he said, the heck with it, and took the rest of the year off.

"If I could keep fifty cents on the dollar I earned," he told Congress, "I would be too busy in Hollywood to be here today."[6]

This anecdote about downtrodden movie stars became one of Reagan's favorites, privately retold throughout his presidency. Rosty likewise had a personal anecdote. Three of his daughters were airline hostesses, and the fourth was an office assistant for a machine politician. The appalling sums withheld from their paychecks exceeded, on a percentage basis, the taxes exacted from their corporate bosses.

The tax system had proliferated such a menagerie of deductions, exemptions, exclusions, credits, and deferrals that the public no longer trusted it, feeling justified in efforts to cheat it. This was the national moral problem that Reagan—whatever his blithe ignorance of details of tax policy—perceived. Some of his wizards and alchemists also worried about the economic distortions wrought by a national compulsion to run open-armed into tax shelters.

Despite his daughters' vexations, Rostenkowski was dubious about the prospects of tackling the tax issue after Mondale's landslide defeat. "You won't see a lot of profiles in courage around here," he said.[7]

U.S. Treasury bean counters, showing the courage derived from the blissful state of not having to run for election, prepared an outline of tax reform during 1984. Three weeks after the election, Secretary Regan gave it to Reagan. It was rational and fair and, therefore, politically impossible. Still, the plan that became known as "Treasury I" was a starting point for negotiations.

The next morning, Regan called Rostenkowski to brief him on the plan before releasing it at a press conference, honoring the sacred Washington rites of protocol. Regan assured that it was not set in cement. The media then scanned Treasury I and gave it the horselaugh.

In December, Rostenkowski flew to Chicago for a Loop business roundtable to discuss Treasury I. When the businessmen went ballistic, Rosty was surprised. Didn't they know this scheme, this carpet-bombing destruction of business deductions, would never become law? Rosty deduced that he could appease the lords of the Loop with tax breaks, still pass some version of tax reform, and perhaps ride the resulting hosannas to the Speakership.

During that month, James Baker called secret meetings at his Foxhall Road home with Democratic leader Richard A. Gephardt, Republican leader Jack Kemp, and others. Rosty boycotted these sessions, smelling a trap. He might pass tax reform, but he would not become a Reagan stooge. When Baker coaxed him to come, he said, "Jimmy boy, you're massaging me. I've been handled by better than you, and your hands are cold." [8]

On the day before New Year's Eve, Senator Bill Bradley of New Jersey delivered a tax-reform pep talk to Ways and Means at Rosty's invitation. Normal people outside the Beltway would not grasp the significance of this event. A senator almost never interposes himself in the operations of the House: a taboo breach of custom. But Bradley, a tax-reform advocate, had met with Rosty at a Loop hotel in November at his request. Rostenkowski knew that tax reform would have to be bipartisan and bicameral in Congress, so, sure, come on and drop by, Bill.

Tip O'Neill had more intensive partisan concerns. Tax reform might become a Republican booster rocket to majority-party status, an enduring daydream of the Reaganites, with the GOP seen as the champion of the average taxpayer against the "special interests" that controlled the Democratic party (labor, minorities, women, the elderly). Tip looked around for a Democrat to brace the inexplicably (to him) popular Reagan. Why not Danny? He had just given a well-received speech on tax reform to black-tied CEOs at the Economic Club of New York.

Meanwhile, in March 1985 the Chicago media fell into one of their periodic seizures about Danny coming home to run for mayor. The connection was not noted, but in February, Jim Wright trumped Rostenkowski by declaring he had secured a nearly invincible 184 Democratic pledges to succeed O'Neill, who was retiring. Wright had moved with the quiet thoroughness he had shown at the 1976 convention to become majority leader. Speaker Wright, not Speaker Rostenkowski, apparently would greet the 1987 Congress. So Rosty, thwarted in rising in the House again, toyed with the idea of the mayoralty again, but it was just talk as always.

After the bring-Danny-home fever died down—a *Sun-Times* poll showed Washington would beat him—Rostenkowski remarked with characteristic candor, "I've always said I'd love to be mayor. The question is whether I'd want to run for it. I'd love to be Speaker. The question is whether I'd run for it."[9]

Political office was a bequest from Joe Rusty or Dick Daley, not a prize won by struggle. The machine rationed out offices to its sons, its worthies. But after the reforms of the 1970s Congress no longer was ruled by its version of a machine hierarchy. Rosty, who still ran his committee like an urban ward boss, making secret handshake deals to accommodate competing interests, was an anomaly, an anachronism. He was not about to grub for votes among House members the way Jim Wright did. Could he imagine Dick Daley going hat in hand to his committeemen? No, if he became Speaker it would be by something like acclamation, not by running for it. Rostenkowski often showed political courage, but not the brand of courage needed to run openly for Speaker. In this respect his critics were right—he was just a machine politician.

O'Neill placed a call. Danny, I want you to deliver the Democratic response to Reagan's nationally televised speech on tax reform. Naw, said Danny, I'm not one of those pinstriped, blow-dried guys; get somebody else. Okay, said Tip, I guess I'll get one of our fine Democrats from the Other Body (House code for the despised Senate). Rostenkowski bristled. Better he than one of those pompous fools in the Senate. "Goddamn right I want to do the response."[10]

With only a week to get ready, Rostenkowski secured the services of a consultant from the realm of the modern media politics he detested. A Beltway myth holds that the consultant, Joseph Rothstein, cleaned up Rosty's dese-dem-and-dose Milwaukee Avenue crudities for the benefit of television. In fact, Rostenkowski had a gift for personal rapport and vivid, figurative language, a penchant for mixed metaphors or no. Rothstein pretty much just walked his client through the text, put contact lenses on him, counseled him on the superiority of smiling to frowning, and had him practice reading from a television prompter.

On 28 May 1985, Reagan delivered a Reaganesque Oval Office speech, a hymn to tax reform as "revolutionary." Moments before Reagan approached his "God bless America" coda, when Rosty should have been clearing his throat and giving the speech a final scan before following the Great Communicator, he suddenly leapt to his feet.

"Shit," he said, "I'm not gonna do it!"[11]

To the gaping camera crew in H208, Rosty said, heh, heh, just kidding, and sat back down. The old har-de-har Rosty. "Good evening, I'm Congressman Dan Rostenkowski from Chicago," he said when the red lights blinked on, reading a speech written by his Ways and Means spokesman, John Sherman.

> Trying to tax people fairly: That's been the historic Democratic commitment. Our roots lie with working families all over the country, like the Polish neighborhood I grew up in on the northwest side of Chicago. Most of the people in my neighborhood worked hard in breweries, steel mills, packing houses; proud families who lived on their salaries. My parents and grandparents didn't like to pay taxes. Who does? But like most Americans they were willing to pay their fair share as the price for a free country where everyone could make their own breaks.
>
> Every year politicians promise to make the tax code fair and simple, but every year we seem to slip further behind. Now most of us pay taxes with bitterness and frustration. Working families file their tax forms with the nagging feeling that they're the biggest suckers and chumps in the world. Their taxes are withheld at work, while the elite have enormous freedom to move their income from one tax shelter to another . . .
>
> This time, it's a Republican president who's bucking his party's tradition as protectors of big business and the wealthy. His words and feelings go back to Roosevelt and Truman and Kennedy. But the commitment comes from Ronald Reagan. And

that's so important and so welcome . . . A Republican president has joined the Democrats in Congress to try to redeem this long-standing commitment to a tax system that's simple and fair.[12]

The observation that working-class taxpayers feel like chumps remains true. Without that foresight, Rostenkowski ended with, "Even if you can't spell Rostenkowski, put down what they used to call my father and grandfather—Rosty." He pronounced it "Rusty," as none but he and elderly Chicago committeemen still did. "Just address it to R-O-S-T-Y, Washington, D.C. The post office will get it to me. Better yet, write your representative and your senator. And stand up for fairness and lower taxes."[13]

The eleven-minute speech was a tremendous hit. Reagan, perhaps not comprehending how Rosty had hijacked the issue from him with all that sweet talk (what president could resist comparison with "Roosevelt and Truman and Kennedy"?), called to offer congratulations.

"Mr. President, you know if you're gonna criticize me the first day we start, if you're gonna take shots at this thing as we're proceeding through it, this bill's going nowhere," the chairman said.

"What is it that you want?" Reagan said—the primary question of any politician.

"I don't want you to make any comment on it. I want you to keep your powder dry."[14]

So they made a deal: Reagan would refrain from criticizing the committee's handiwork from the White House, and Rosty would not attack the Reagan proposal outside the walls of Ways and Means.

The next morning, typically, Rostenkowski made the rounds of the TV networks' early news shows and then sped to the Congressional Country Club in Bethesda, Maryland, for golf. Senator Sam Nunn of Georgia, a golfing buddy, complimented him on the "Write Rosty" speech and expressed hope that a bill could be passed that year. Sorry, said Rostenkowski, I'm not going to talk about it at all until it gets out of my committee. Then he whacked the ball on a par-three hole. He made par, not the usual occurrence.

Mail addressed to R-O-S-T-Y flooded the House post office. Not only had he neutralized tax reform as a Republican issue, but he had cemented the primacy of Ways and Means in writing tax law and become a national celebrity to boot. Bill Daley, the late mayor's son, was among those stunned by the performance. "He's never had a tough campaign, so he's never had to use media before," Daley marveled. Rosty allowed, "I must admit, I am on a high."[15]

Rostenkowski already had been a Beltway celebrity, holding court at Rosty's Rotunda or joining the elect who were invited to soirees at Democratic doyenne Pamela Churchill Harriman's mansion, where he happily expostulated on tax policy for the nation's mandarins. The "address it to Rosty" speech made him a national celebrity, an exemplar of a Hollywood type, the likable tough guy. He had said he did not want to run for mayor because it would attract a Chicago spotlight. Now the national spotlight was on him. He gloried in it. It took six years for the media operators to place a dark gel over the spotlight to place in relief his wrongdoings. He never understood the turnaround. He might be better off now, a wealthy retired elder statesman, if his pride had been suppressed enough to have said no to Tip.

"Write Rosty" buttons, passed around by his staff, started appearing on Capitol Hill within days. James Baker sported one on his lapel when he took a seat as the first witness in Ways and Means hearings.

In mid-June, Rostenkowski held a fund raiser (in political parlance, a "funder") with Washington lobbyists (in political parlance, "downtown"). Hundreds of lobbyists wearing expensive Italian loafers (hence, "Gucci Gulch") paid five hundred dollars each to schmooze with the guy who first would get his mitts on the tax bill. Donors were given shrimp, beer, and buttons that said, "I Did Better Than Write Rosty." O'Neill chuckled, "Danny, this is really marvelous. All this for just a little piece of legislation—which might or might not get to the [House] floor."[16] Laughter all around. That the tax laws of the United States were controlled by an old-fashioned machine politician was considered amusing. Good old Rosty.

This funder was thought to be Rosty's unspoken declaration of candidacy for Speaker. Wright was no champion of tax reform, rightly fearing it would undercut oil-state tax breaks. If Rostenkowski got tax reform through, the media accolades might give him an outside shot at the Speaker's chair despite Wright's meticulous gathering of pledges. An improbable twinning of modern media politics and antique machine politics could deliver Speaker Rostenkowski. He was mistaken.

The White House, with its persistent misunderstanding of the legislative process, wanted a bill passed by the end of the year, irking Republicans once again, especially by Reagan's silent complicity with Rosty. "They thought they could work for six months with Rostenkowski and then six hours with us and that would be enough," complained Newt Gingrich of Georgia.[17] Republicans seethed through the summer and fall of 1985, ultimately shocking the White House with an open mutiny.

For his part, Rostenkowski spent the summer before the August recess staging the hearings on which he always insisted. Few people cared. Polls showed scant public interest in tax reform—or, rather, voters did not believe Congress would make the tax system fair. What concerned people much more was deficit reduction, a separate track in Congress.

Shortly after Labor Day, Rosty put thirty-three of his thirty-six committee members on a bus that rolled through the suburban hills to arrive at Airlie House, a luxe convention center in Virginia horse country, for a weekend retreat. Also attending were Baker (now the Treasury secretary, having traded jobs with Regan, now the chief of staff, early in the year); Baker's aide, Richard Darman; and a few economists. It is important to understand how the political class opposed, or at the best cast a cold, suspicious eye on, tax reform. Members from states that produced oil and gas would defend to the death their tax preferences; members from high-tax states in the Northeast would defend to the death the federal deduction for state and local income taxes, and everyone would defend to the death their constituents' deduction for interest payments on home mortgages. The White House wizards figured they could play off the southern oil states against the northern high-tax states, a strategy with limited success. One of the Airlie House savants observed that only three people in the country (Reagan, Baker, and Rostenkowski) were eager for tax reform and that only one of them had a vote in Congress. Not said was that a member of the trio, Baker, took the posture of an aide carrying out a mission for his boss, not that of a true believer. Rosty hoped that the Airlie House confab might forge a rough consensus.

In a sunken living room with a huge picture window overlooking hills with trees on the verge of turning autumn colors, Rostenkowski keynoted the final session. As usual he touted the primacy of Ways and Means, "the

Cadillac of committees." He touted the once-in-a-career chance to write truly historic tax law. And once again he brought up his daughters, struggling to get by while their paychecks suffered deeper tax bites than those that afflicted millionaires. An emotional man, his eyes watered. After this performance, Airlie House broke up with an air of comity.

On 18 September, Ways and Means started to consider a bill, drafted by the committee staff with Rostenkowksi's approval and based on the Reagan administration proposal. Soon the committee decided to start with the existing law, not the staff's draft. This in effect reversed the burden of proof: Members would have to argue *for* eliminating a tax break instead of arguing *against* the elimination of a tax break already included in the draft bill. In short, wiping out tax advantages was made more difficult. It looked as though Rosty already was losing control of his committee over the impossibly tangled issue of tax reform. But the next day the committee reversed course and agreed to work from the Rostenkowski/staff draft. Not until 3 October did the procedural wrangling give way to actual markup.

Rostenkowski closed the committee sessions, having done away in 1983 with the nonsense imposed by goo goos during the 1970s reforms that opened such sessions to the press and public. He was right. When sessions were open, members merely played to the media or the Gucci Gulchers.

Still, members were beholden to the Guccis. Within two weeks they gutted the draft bill. The idea, supposedly, was to close loopholes. In contrast, the committee voted to enlarge a tax shelter for commercial banks having to do with reserves held against bad loans. In 1100 Longworth, an enraged Rostenkowski, a man not safely enraged, threw down his pencil, which bounced on the table while slightly abashed congressmen watched in grim silence. When word of the giveaway leaked out to the hallway, populated with expensively dressed loiterers (Gucci Gulch), a cheer went up.

That night the chairman went home to the Junkyard and wrote a letter to himself. "I wrote myself how lonely and how miserable I was," he told a reporter later. "You know, do people really want reform? I mean, are we all so phony?" [18]

That inscription of loneliness merits comment. It communicated not just his self-image as a solitary proponent of honest taxation while all the hacks around him wanted to sell out, but loneliness in the personal sense. For all their bonhomie, politicians fit the sociologist David Riesman's classic model of "the lonely crowd." They lack true intimacies because personal intimacies always are overlaid by the calculus of personal advancement. With friends in Chicago over late-night drinks, with the medallion hung from his neck engraved with the dates of his wedding and his daughters' births, Rosty's eyes would tear as he reflected on his failings as a father and husband. Had he blundered by never moving LaVerne and the girls to Washington? By talking Daley into sending him to Washington in the first place? For decades now he had retired to his squalid Junkyard apartment to watch the TV news and then go to bed alone. Did voters or the media appreciate his sacrifices? While he could be making really big bucks in the private sector? No. And meanwhile his youngest daughter, Stacy, twenty-four years old, was seriously ill, in need of a kidney transplant.

A few days were needed for Rostenkowski to recover, but recover he did. Entering his favorite sanctum, the library in the rear of 1100 Longworth, he made deals one by one to overturn the egregious bank giveaway. He was abetted by the press, portraying the members as puppets of special interests, in this case Republican special interests (big business, Wall Street) and not Democratic special interests (unions, minorities, women, the elderly), without recognition that most lobbies are pragmatically bipartisan.

Rostenkowski had to give up something. He gave up the proposed elimination of the deduction for state and local income taxes. On 23 October, the committee rescinded the bank break. The next day, Baker heard about the preservation of the state-and-local deduction. Far beyond a mere policy dispute, state-and-local was a showstopper, a potential killer of the Reagan plan. Keeping the deduction would cost revenues the White House was counting on. To make up the difference, the top individual federal tax rate would have to be cranked up past the level Reagan would accept. He demanded a ceiling of 35 percent, apparently forgetting his 1958 reverie of contentment at "fifty cents on the dollar." Baker tracked down Rosty at a member's funder in North Carolina.

"Goddamn, Danny, what did you do to me? How can you do this?"

"Hey, I'm not getting any support from you," Rosty responded, an allusion to White House negligence in securing GOP votes for tax reform. "What the hell do you think I am? You think I'm gonna run up against my Democrats?"

Baker hereupon chastised Rostenkowksi for cutting deals without warning, in violation of his 28 May agreement with Reagan.

Rostenkowsi remarked, "I'm gonna hang up on you, you son of a bitch."

"No, no, no, don't hang up," Baker said. The tone conveyed a warning, not a plea.

Click.[19]

The next morning Baker and Darman continued the shouting match back in the Ways and Means office. Rosty was defiant, refusing to admit he had explicitly dealt away state and local, which he had. Furious, Baker and Darman then went to Andrews Air Force Base near Washington to meet with Chief of Staff Don Regan.

The selection of the out-of-town site in itself tells much about political operations in the capital. Supposedly, the Treasury officials went to Andrews because Regan was stopping through during a trip from New York (for a presidential speech) to Georgia (for golf). The real reason is that Regan did not want news of the secret meeting to leak, not to the press, but to White House Communications Director Patrick Buchanan. A bureaucratic rival of Regan, Buchanan and his allies favored spurning Ways and Means and its evil Democrats altogether. Regan did not want more trouble from Buchanan.

The Andrews oracles were tempted for a moment to adopt the strategy of their famous victory in 1981: screw Ways and Means; we'll take it to the floor. Of course the White House now had nothing like its 1981 power. Reagan had fired up *Air Force One* for a national speaking tour for tax reform, but it fell flat. On 9 October, the president reprised one of his 1981 ploys by visiting Rosty's district in Chicago, but this time he did not ask for public pressure on the chairman.

Realistically, the alternatives at Andrews were to accept what Rostenkowski delivered and then try to fix the bill in the Republican-controlled Senate or else to put the president on stage blaming Democrats for ruining tax reform and pledging to start from scratch, maybe next year. The unhappy oracles decided their best course was to stick with Danny and then direct the Senate to fumigate the bill.

Still, Baker and Darman wanted to signal their disappointment with

Danny, so they stopped sitting in on Ways and Means markup sessions. If this snub bothered Rostenkowski, he did not say so. More pressing was the interminably pesky issue of municipal bonds, the unfading shadow of Presidential Towers, which had opened in Chicago just that year.

As Regan jetted off in the Indian summer skies to the Georgian links, Ways and Means embarked on a rare three-day weekend markup, inflicting tax wounds on trusts and estates, farmers, builders of low-income housing, and timber interests. Rosty had set up bipartisan task forces on knotty issues; a task force would reach a consensus and forward it to the full committee, which usually adopted it with minor changes. This process was efficient by congressional standards. It yielded reforms generally weaker than either the chairman or the White House wanted.

The task force on municipal bonds had one of the toughest jobs, meeting in an inelegant conference room while bond lawyers and lobbyists murmured anxiously in the hall. In effect, members were being asked to defy their mayors and governors, who loved bestowing tax-exempt bonds on businessmen, as well as the securities brokers and lawyers who handled the sales—heavy campaign donors one and all. Proceedings were so fractious that Rostenkowski was impelled to step in to cut the deals himself. Limits were placed on the bonds, with exceptions, naturally—bonds for airport development in Atlanta, urban renewal in California, and so forth.

Ten months after Reagan's State of the Union, the committee actually was moving fast to build a bill. Republican members were miserable in their role as virtual spectators though, and Rostenkowski fretted that the White House was losing them. On 1 November, Gingrich and thirty-seven other conservative Republican members signed a letter asking Reagan to abandon the Ways and Means effort as hopeless.

Rostenkowski called Regan to ask for a meeting with the president. Regan put him off. Rolling out heavy artillery, Rosty threatened to go on the morning news shows and "say that I'm the chairman of the Ways and Means Committee and I can't even get in to see the president of the United States." Obviously, he had learned something about the mass mediation of public affairs.

Regan replied, "Can I get back to you?"

"Don, listen to me, nothing technical," Rostenkowski soothed, trying to dampen the horror that overcame Reagan's men whenever they faced the prospect of their president having to confront specifics of policy. "I want to talk to him about the lack of Republican support, but I promise you there'll be nothing technical."[20]

Soon enough, Rostenkowski rode the elevator upstairs to the White House living quarters—firmly in his own right now, not as Daley's underling—and had coffee with Reagan. Rosty hoped, best-case scenario, that he might persuade Reagan to accept the retention of state and local, nudge up his 35 percent ceiling a couple of points, and whip his Republicans into line. The meeting was friendly, but Reagan conceded nothing.

A few days later, Reagan publicly complained about "some of the waterings-down that are taking place" on the Hill, breaking the keep-the-powder-dry treaty of 28 May. Rostenkowski grabbed a phone.

"What's going on here?"

"Sorry it happened, won't happen again," Reagan said.[21]

Not even a Dan Rostenkowski made a practice of dressing down the president of the United States. That call was a successfully aggressive tactic, but it also was born of fatigue, frustration, and personal worries. Rostenkowski wanted to donate a kidney to Stacy; he and other family members were awaiting the results of blood tests for compatibility.

All the while, Rostenkowski's business and labor supporters were hitting him hard. He and Baker, a Texan "oilie," kept bickering over tax breaks for oil and gas. Inside the committee, markups were steadily rancorous. The committee was taking a beating from the press for its stumbles and sellouts; *Business Week* sneered at "the hapless Rostenkowski."[22] At the same time, Chicago was taking a beating in the press over Council Wars.

As early as March, Rostenkowski had told a labor audience in Chicago that labor had to put its tax breaks on the firing line along with everyone else. He told the same thing privately to AFL-CIO president Lane Kirkland. Disregarding this notice, labor fought relentlessly to keep fringe benefits excluded from taxes. Rostenkowski wanted to tax just one benefit, employer-paid life insurance. Fiercely pressuring Rosty for labor's hands-off position was one of his own disciples, Marty Russo of Chicago's Southwest Side, so close to his mentor that he named his younger son after him.

Corporate America's posture was less uniform. Capital-intensive heavy industry favored current laws and disliked the package that was shaping up. Smaller, labor-intensive service and high-tech businesses liked the new deal. To win key business support, Rosty promised heavy-hitter CEOs at a secret meeting in the Chicago suburb of Northbrook on 6 September that he would hold the top corporate tax rate to 35 percent, down from the existing top rate of 46 percent.

As the markups entered their final days, Rostenkowski learned that no family member was a suitable organ donor for Stacy. As everyone who has endured serious illness in the family knows, the Rostenkowskis were hearing different advice from different doctors as they awaited an available donor.

Plunging ahead with tax reform, Rostenkowski offered a startling simile: "Writing good tax law is like drawing a circle from a bucking horse. The trick is to close the loop." [23] He closed the loop by selling tax breaks to isolated beneficiaries. At 7 A.M. on 22 November, he met with committee lawyers to sift through hundreds of requests from members. At 9:30 A.M., he and the chief counsel, Robert J. Leonard, strolled into the library, sat down with a telephone and a mound of paper, and started the auction.

Calling colleagues one at a time, Rosty awarded tax breaks for waste-treatment plants in New York, sports stadia in five cities, parking garages in South Carolina, and so forth. As in 1981, his message was blunt: I'm giving you this because you've been cooperative, but now that you've got it, you have to support the whole package.

The device for these preferences is called "transition rules." When tax laws change, transition rules govern when, how, and in what cases the changes will apply. In his February speech to the Economic Club in New York, Rosty had assured nervous CEOs, don't worry, there will be transition rules. Sure enough.

Rosty took care of his hometown and state. The final bill in 1986 included tax breaks on industrial development bonds for a new White Sox stadium in a deal made with Governor Thompson; $200 million worth of advantages for an Illinois power company, Commonwealth Edison; liberal breaks for wealthy developers of the North Pier Terminal project in Chicago; preferences for the John Deere farm machinery firm in Moline, Illinois, and for a Chrysler Corporation plant in Belvidere, Illinois; and a special provision for Talman Home Federal Savings and Loan in Chicago, wherein Rosty kept $150,000 of his campaign fund. Another clause made sure that the tax court would heed the break for Chicago commodities traders granted in 1984.

Transition rules are written deliberately to conceal the beneficiaries. For example, the North Pier Terminal provision was defined only as "the rehabilitation of 10 warehouse buildings built between 1906 and 1910 and purchased under a contract dated February 17, 1986."[24] In fairness, such particularity has a purpose beyond cover-up. It prevents taxpayers in similar circumstances from suing for the same relief. Sometimes the specificity can backfire, though. As a favor to a Chicago developer, Rosty bestowed a break on a residential high-rise project that "was the subject of lawsuits filed on June 22, 1984, and November 21, 1985." But the staff listed the dates wrong.[25]

Asked about such secretiveness, Rostenkowski said blandly, "Members of the House have never been forced to divulge the names of constituents on whose behalf they sought transition relief."[26] Thus the antidemocratic nature of the Chicago machine fused easily with the antidemocratic folkways of Congress, for all of its 1970s reforms.

With the transition rules taken care of, a physically and emotionally depleted Rostenkowski hoped to wrap things up in the markup that night. Instead, the hardball of fringe-benefit taxation slammed home. Rosty's protégé Russo asked attorney Leonard the money a mere percentage-point raise in the corporate rate would raise. Over five years, $13 billion, Leonard said. Just enough to pay for keeping all bennies tax free. Russo excitedly delivered this news to fellow Democrats.

Quickly they jumped on Rosty to go to 36 percent, but he was married to his 35 percent pledge of 6 September to the CEOs. "There goes the bill," Rostenkowsi said fatalistically, stood and walked alone into an alcove, leaned against the wall, and wept.

Joseph K. Dowley, his top aide, walked in, a bit sheepishly, to check on him.

"Just leave me alone, Joe," Rostenkowski managed to gargle out.[27]

With Republicans muttering mutiny, meeting separately in 1129 Longworth, Rosty could not afford to lose any Democrats, but they were adamant on fringe benefits. Some, such as Charles B. Rangel of New York, had made pledges of their own—to labor leaders.

Everyone was crestfallen. Rangel said when a dry-eyed Rostenkowski returned, "Mr. Chairman, we've got the votes, but you're our leader. What do you want us to do?" The members rallied around their chairman in his hour of despair—an extreme rarity in the modern Congress.

The compromise was shrewdly Rosty-esque. Rangel would present his fringe-benefit amendment in formal session. Rosty would call for a voice vote and declare it defeated. But if Republicans demanded a roll call—as they were bound to do, out of spite—fringe benefits would win. Whereupon the chairman himself would propose going from thirty-five to thirty-six on corporate. And so it happened.

At 3:30 A.M. on 23 November, Rostenkowski opened the door of 1100 Longworth and told the throngs of reporters and lobbyists in the hall that work on the bill was finished. Later, the traditional celebratory champagne with his colleagues seemed flat. "I was boiling inside," Rostenkowski said.[28]

Ronald Reagan's biggest domestic bill of his second term had cleared its first and highest hurdle, but he remained curiously silent on it. Rostenkowski tried to call, tried to tag along on a presidential trip to California, but the White House kept brushing him off. On 30 November, Reagan called Rosty to complain that Rosty had complained about his lack of response. Not until 4 December—a day after Ways and Means formally reported the bill, 28–8—did Reagan issue a statement, a limp call for the process to go forward. That same day, Jack Kemp tub thumped a GOP revolt against the bill in the House Republican Conference.

Some of Reagan's advisers and their big-business allies believed the committee's handiwork would, in the buzzwords of the time, further "deindustrialize America" and constrain "capital formation." Finally, on 6 December, after an internal White House struggle, the administration gave Rosty the word that Reagan would start rounding up Republican votes for the bill.

Bills enter the House floor only after passing through the Rules Committee, which writes "the rule," setting the time of debate and kinds of amendments, if any, allowed. Without these restrictions, the 435-member House really would be ungovernable (the 100-member Senate is much more free in allowing debate).

On 11 December, the House considered the rule reported by the Rules Committee the previous day, normally a matter of routine. As usual, the tax bill was permitted no amendments, just a Republican substitute bill. Oddly, Republicans were voting nay on the rule. When Rostenkowski discerned the trend, he lunged to the cloakroom for a phone.

"Goddammit," he told Baker, "the rule is going down!"[29]

Which it did. In a coup led by Trent Lott with the support of Rosty's pal Bob Michel, 164 of 178 Republicans voted to humiliate both the White House and the Democratic leadership. The rule failed, 223–202. Tax reform was dead.

Five days later it arose from the dead. Reagan removed himself from Olympus (the White House) to the Rayburn Building to beg his party's legislators to pass the bill, just to move it to the more congenial Senate if nothing else.

Even if all Republicans had snapped to attention and saluted, "Yes, sir, Mr. President," which they did not, the fate of the bill was in the bosom of the Speaker. Some Democrats advised him to leave the bill in its tomb, thereby effectively destroying Reagan's legislative influence for the next three years. O'Neill rejected the advice, but he made Reagan sweat and squirm. Give me fifty more Republican votes, he told Reagan shortly after the rule fiasco, and I'll put the rule to another vote. (O'Neill later claimed he demanded only forty votes, but all other sources hold for fifty.) The White House labored hard for five days and barely assembled the requisite number after Reagan's visit to the Rayburn Building. When Reagan phoned with the happy news, O'Neill gleefully declined to take Reagan's calls until late that night.

The next day, O'Neill made a rare descent from his own Olympus (the Speaker's rostrum) to speak in the well and appeal for "a vote for the working people of America over the special interests."[30] A slightly modified rule was adopted, 258–168. After the stipulated five hours of debate, the 1,379-page bill was approved on a voice vote.

O'Neill then looked to his left, to the Republican side of the aisle, for the usual demand for a roll call. But none came. So the Speaker banged the gavel and declared the bill passed.

Republicans maintained the roll-call omission was a blunder wrought by exhaustion and confusion. An alternative explanation is that they did not want their votes recorded. That way they could tell reporters and goo goos they were pro but their big-business benefactors they were con.

This hardly mattered to the formerly "hapless" Rostenkowski, who went home for Christmas lionized by the media as a master legislator, as in fact he was. Christmas was even sweeter because Stacy had had a successful kidney transplant.

The garden back home needed cultivating. In late December, Rostenkowski refused to endorse Vrdolyak for reelection as Democratic chairman. Rosty's old friend Dunne, one of the few white committeemen who supported Mayor Washington, offered the potential of peace talks in Council Wars if he would retake the chairman's post he had held after Daley died. In the event, Dunne declined to run for chairman in 1986.

A federal judge had ordered special aldermanic elections in seven wards in March 1986 to redress the racial bias in Byrne's 1981 redistricting. The crucial ward was the Puerto Rican Twenty-sixth, where Luis Gutierrez outpolled his machine-backed opponent by just twenty-five votes, necessitating a runoff election. Rostenkowski and other machine bigfeet— Vrdolyak, Daley, Byrne—endorsed the machine candidate. Gutierrez won, and Mayor Washington had a tie-breaking vote over a 25–25 council split, ending Council Wars. The media reported that the machine was dead, really dead this time, forever dead. It was as dead as Dickens's Jacob Marley or Shakespeare's Banquo.

Forty years had passed since Rostenkowski left St. John's for Korea. On the first of June, he attended the fortieth reunion of his class, exhibiting his customary conviviality at a prime rib dinner at a resort in Oconomowoc, Wisconsin. At 1:15 the next morning he was pulled over by a Racine County sheriff's police sergeant near Burlington, Wisconsin, for driving his Cadillac with congressional vanity plates seventy-one miles per hour in a fifty-five zone.

Rostenkowski fumbled trying to find his driver's license. The sergeant asked him to close his eyes and touch his finger to his nose. Then he asked him to walk heel to toe in a straight line. Rostenkowski flunked these assignments. He went to the sheriff's office and refused a sobriety test. Posting a $497.50 bond, he called LaVerne at their vacation home at Benedict Lake to come get him. He was released to her custody.

The next morning, a TV news helicopter and a swarm of reporters accosted Rostenkowski as he played in a charity golf tournament in Wisconsin. He consulted with Bill Daley and agreed to hold a news conference that evening in Chicago, where he expressed contrition.

Two days later, Helen Wing filed her lawsuit from the 1984 accident. Her attorney said the timing was coincidental.

On 9 June, Rostenkowski had his lawyer enter a guilty plea to driving drunk and paid a $555 fine. His driving license was suspended for six months in Wisconsin and a year in Illinois.

Rostenkowski gladly flew to Washington, where Bob Packwood's Finance Committee, against all expectations, had approved serious tax reform, 20–0.

In a road-to-Damascus style of conversion, Packwood had taken an aide to a downscale Irish pub on Capitol Hill that April. Over two pitchers of beer, they decided the House bill was, of all things, too weak. Formerly a defender of loopholes, Packwood now fought to trade them for lower tax rates.

Still, the Senate bill, passed 97–3 on 24 June, tilted toward business more than the House version did. The conference committee was scheduled to meet on 17 July. Rosty led the House conferees and picked his fellows for their loyalty, not their seniority as custom prescribed. The bargaining would be tough; he and Packwood were not close.

During a 1984 conference, Packwood had blurted out that Rosty did not know what he was talking about. The result was predictable: the Rostenkowski Glare followed by rejection of the provision Packwood wanted.

Like Rostenkowski, Packwood was a big, proud man, and a realist. "You're going to have every special interest lobbyist in America trying to hit every conference, saying, 'Save us, save us, save us,'" he prophesied.[31] The next four weeks validated the prediction.

On 12 August, Senator Russell Long of Louisiana had a brainstorm. House and Senate conferees were stalemated, so why didn't Packwood and Rostenkowski huddle by themselves and try to cut a deal? The tactic was unprecedented but seemed to work. For the next few days, the two chairmen and their aides gathered in H208, Rosty's lair, and made substantial progress. They faced a self-imposed deadline of 16 August, before a congressional recess would give lobbyists an opening to pressure lawmakers at home.

Just as in the final Ways and Means markup on November 1995, a last-minute snag threatened to wreck the whole enterprise. The number crunchers revealed an unexpected gap of $17 billion over five years in keeping the projected prereform and postreform revenues even. Dejected, the two chairmen met in H208; getting nowhere, they took a walk through the nearly deserted nighttime Capitol, with portraits and statues of historical figures gazing soberly at them. "Son of a bitch, Bob, I wish it was you, I wish it was me, but it's the Goddamn numbers," Rosty said. Returning to H208 to meet reporters, Packwood said, "He and I almost cried."[32]

Rosty went to the Junkyard and packed to go home the next day. Tax reform was dead. First, though, he and Packwood were scheduled to pose on the Capitol steps at 7:30 A.M. for a *Time* photographer. After many snaps the shooter asked them to jump. At the time, Toyota had a TV ad campaign showing happy car owners jumping, but the magazine wanted the shots for its series of celebrities jumping—the tradition went back to the 1950s and included even a photo of Vice President Nixon jumping. "He must think this is a fucking Toyota commercial," Rostenkowski said, stomping off. Packwood, perhaps disposed to ask "how high," jumped.[33]

Implored by their conferees, the chairmen decided to give it one more shot. They met on the afternoon of Friday, 15 August, and negotiated for twelve hours. Each gave up certain tax preferences and—by implication—the votes of the conferees who demanded them. Finally, early on Saturday, they had a bill. Whether they could sell it to the conference was another question.

The Senate caucus met at midday, argued, recessed, conferred with Rosty, voted 6–4 for the deal, and joined their House counterparts shortly after 9:00 P.M. The conference opened its final session to the cameras, reporting the bill by voice vote, with only two audible nays, shortly before midnight. Rostenkowski leaned forward on the desk and spoke, he hoped, for posterity: "They said out there that it couldn't be done. Well, we've done it. We both compromised at the margin, but clung to our principles. Ladies and gentlemen, the political process worked. The center held."[34]

The political and media classes endorsed and magnified these sentiments. Always before, Congress had revised the tax code piecemeal, incrementally, never across the board. Now, somehow, the people had triumphed. The phrase, "the center held," an allusion to Yeats, informed the vocabulary of commentators.

Only a few public scolds such as Senator Howard Metzenbaum, a liberal Democrat from Ohio, said the bill was misbegotten. On the Senate floor he questioned Packwood tenaciously about the legerdemain for transition rules, in particular one for insurance companies that held so-called deep discount bonds.

Packwood replied, "This was perhaps the last or next-to-last transition rule that Congressman Rostenkowski and I agreed to at 3 or 4 o'clock in the morning. And I must confess that on this one I made a mistake. I thought the request related to one company in which the chairman of the Ways and Means Committee was interested. He said, 'Bob, this is critical to me and it is critical to the person that I am asking for.' He named it. I said, 'Mr. Chairman, I will give it to you.' I did not know at the time that it related to 15 companies." [35]

Later that day, 27 September, the Senate passed the bill, 74–23. The House had done likewise, 292–136, five days earlier. Reagan signed the bill with due South Lawn ceremony on 22 October.

Fourteen tax brackets with rates from 11 to 50 percent were reduced to three: 15, 28, and 33 percent. The top rate on corporate income was cut from 48 percent to 34 percent. Long-term capital gains were treated the same as ordinary income, with the top rate raised to 33 percent from 20 percent.

The liberal impulse to redistribute wealth and the conservative impulse to defend wealth were in rare, perhaps unique, equipoise. Conservatives won lower marginal rates for the rich, while liberals won a broadening of the tax base by denying rich people and businesses their loopholes. Such was the logic of the bill, though the logical appeal might have mattered less than the moral one.

"I said that we're going to take six or seven million people that are poor off the rolls. We're going to do more for the lower end of the tax structure and corporate America is going to wind up paying more in taxes. Those are the arguments that I kind of shamed my colleagues into accepting," Rostenkowski said. [36]

Beyond the appeals of logic or morality lay fear—fear of media condemnation if the lawmakers failed, fear of sanctions by Rostenkowski and his Senate counterparts if they didn't go along, sanctions such as the denial of a transition rule.

The official projection was that the transition rules would forfeit $10.6 billion in revenues over five years. Political scientists hold that the immense deficits of the 1980s constrained congressmen from making proposals that would cost revenues. If $10.6 billion represents constraint, the lack of it would not be pretty.

Another official statistic is that the 1986 law shifted $120.3 billion in taxes from individuals to corporations over five years. Giving up $10.6 billion in transition rules to make a small number of rich people even richer, in exchange for $120.3 billion in relief for consumers, would seem to be a tremendous bargain for the public.

Not really. In the first place, Congress could not resist steadily undercutting the law. There is no twelve-step program for Tax and Spenders Anonymous. Democrats keep pressuring to raise taxes "to make the rich pay their fair share," whereupon Congress starts another merry-go-round of buying and selling tax and regulatory loopholes. Persistently Congress raised general taxes or marginal rates in the Omnibus Budget Reconciliation Act of 1987, the Surface Transportation and Uniform Relocation Assistance Act of 1987, the Technical Corrections and Miscellaneous Revenue Act of 1988, and the Omnibus Budget Reconciliation Acts of 1989, 1990, and 1993.

Further, the transfer of taxes from individuals to business does not in the end save consumers money. Business costs are passed along to consumers. In effect, the corporate income tax is a national sales tax. Still further, income tax relief for lower incomes was offset by ever-increasing payroll taxes for Social Security and Medicare, a nearly perfectly regressive tax.[37]

Nor did business refrain from exploiting its remaining loopholes or seeking and winning new ones. During the 1970s, in round numbers, corporations paid about 25 percent of all income taxes; individuals paid the rest. From 1987 to 1993—after the vaunted 1986 reforms—corporations paid only 18 percent of all income taxes.

Trumpets blared for the 1986 law as a radical reform, but it was in the mainstream of U.S. tax policy. It embodied Marxian economic determinism, the idea that the tax code's scheme of incentives and disincentives regulates public behavior. It continued to favor consumption over savings and debt over assets. An alternative system, taxing consumption instead of income, was never considered. It was explicitly rejected by Rostenkowski and others.

The law had a social-engineering dimension, to rescue economic activity from unproductive tax shelters, and a moral dimension, to restore public confidence in the tax system. In the moral dimension, at least, it failed.

Imagine that you are a reporter going into your editor's office. "Boss, I want to comb through the 858 pages of the Tax Reform Act, plus the appended 886 pages of the conference report explaining it, to unearth the hidden giveaways. The project will take more than a year, during which I won't be writing anything else, and I can't guarantee that in the end the stories will increase our circulation or, what is much more important to you, win a Pulitzer Prize."

Two reporters in the country actually got away with that. Donald L. Barlett and James B. Steele of the *Philadelphia Inquirer* analyzed the 1986 law in a Pulitzer-winning series of articles in 1988. They identified many beneficiaries of the 682 opaque transition rules, including those written by Rostenkowski.

For example, limited partners in the North Pier Terminal redevelopment included among many others the three great-grandchildren of the founder of G. D. Searle & Co., a giant pharmaceutical manufacturer; sixteen other Searle family members; and Abra Prentice Anderson, a Rockefeller heir. The investors were eligible to avoid payment of $12 million in taxes. Rostenkowski declined to comment on these or other disclosures by Barlett and Steele.

However, Rostenkowski never pretended to be doing anything other than what he was doing—making private deals to get legislation passed. As for the giveaways to Chicago and Illinois interests, he had, as in the Presidential Towers affair, the defensible explanation of promoting economic vitality for his constituents.

The paradox of Rostenkowski's corruption is that he stood up to fierce pressures from business and labor to fight for his perception of the common good in the 1986 law, yet at the same time he manipulated the law to benefit a few of his rich pals. The simplistic view that the transition rules were Rosty's payoffs to his campaign donors does not begin to explain the paradox. Everybody, from all segments of the political spectrum, wants to give money to the chairman of Ways and Means. Rosty could hardly doodle on a scratch pad without pleasing one donor and disappointing another. His erasures of millions of dollars in tax obligations for rich friends derived from the machine-taught values of loyalty and friendship and the drive for power to control the political process and its treasury.

The deeds that later got Rostenkowski jailed were, by comparison, picayune. The difference is that the statutory giveaways he wrote were perfectly legal.

The transition-rule preferences for the rich, along with Congress's continual messing with the tax code, did not renew the public's faith in the fairness of the tax system. In terms of Rostenkowski's career, they also did nothing to propel him to the speakership.

The Chicago papers slighted coverage of Rosty's crucial role in passing tax reform, concentrating instead on Presidential Towers and the new White Sox stadium. Miffed, Rosty seized on *Gucci Culch* when it came out, delineating as it did his statesmanship. He sent multiple copies to colleagues, friends, and benefactors. One staffer in the *Chicago Tribune*'s Washington bureau recalls getting copies from Rosty three different times.[38]

9

TALL BOLD SLUGGER

Flinging magnetic curses amid the toil of
piling job on job, here is a tall bold
slugger set vivid against the little
soft cities . . .

— Carl Sandburg, "Chicago"

THE Tax Reform Act was Rostenkowski's greatest triumph, but, with the woeful dialectic of human lives, the remaining years of the 1980s often were unhappy for him. The first misfortune was a family one. On 23 January 1987, Chicago police, acting on an anonymous tip, knocked at the door of a North Side apartment. Invited inside, they saw three people and drugs apparently in plain view. They asked for identification. Dawn Rosten, thirty-four years old, opened her purse and exposed two foil-wrapped packets. Confiscated, they contained a white powder resembling cocaine. She was freed on personal recognizance pending laboratory results.

On 10 March, the charges were dropped. This looks like preferential treatment for a congressman's daughter but probably was not. There were so many cocaine arrests that the lab could not keep up. Hundreds of cases were dismissed for late lab results. In April, Dawn agreed to attend drug rehabilitation classes after the lab reported that her purse had contained .92 gram of cocaine. Alas, it was not the last encounter of a Rostenkowski daughter with a criminal drug offense.

The next misfortune was political. For mayor in 1987, Rostenkowski endorsed Thomas C. Hynes, the Cook County assessor. A patriarch of the Southwest Side Irish cabal, Hynes was tall and distinguished looking like his Near North Side Irish counterpart, Rosty's old pal George Dunne, an apostate who sided with Washington.

To prevent the two-whites-one-black debacle of 1983, the machine with Rostenkowski's support essayed a voter referendum in November 1986 to make mayoral elections nonpartisan, with a one-on-one runoff if no candidate won a majority. Washington thwarted it with a maneuver so clever that even his enemy Alderman Ed Burke admired it. An obscure state law limited referenda to three per election, so the mayor had his city council load up the ballot with three meaningless questions before the machine could act. The machine then resorted to the machine-controlled Chicago Board of Elections, which duly installed the nonpartisan election question, only to be overturned in court.

After all this, the machine arranged a one-on-one, black-against-white primary anyway. Then, on 27 February Washington defeated Jane Byrne with 54 percent of the vote. Shortly before the 7 April general election, Washington's campaign office in Rostenkowski's Thirty-second Ward was destroyed by arson, routine stuff. Hynes and Vrdolyak ran on separate third-party ballots. Hynes recognized the futility and quit the race. Vrdolyak got 42 percent. A respectable Republican candidate, naive enough to believe his party's promises of real money and real support this time, got 4 percent.

Reelected and enjoying his new control of the city council, Washington dumped Terry Gabinski, Rostenkowski's alderman, as chairman of the zoning committee in May. With the ouster came the loss of Rostenkowski's seventy-one-year-old sister Marcia's $32,580 patronage job as committee secretary. The congressman could do nothing but swallow the defeat.

Rosty's unmarried twin sisters, still living in the family home, had long since left their Hawaiian-style singing and dancing careers as Nani and Tani. Marcia had been working for the city since 1941. Gladys went to work for the city council in 1944 and retired in 1986 from the Cook County courts.

On 6 July, Mercy Hospital, which had fixed Rostenkowski's broken nose in 1984, performed an appendectomy. The Ways and Means Committee put out a statement: "The operation was routine with no complications." An aide called from the capital to check up on him, and Rosty said curtly, "What do you want?" Apparently he disallowed the notion that the call was a sincere inquiry about his health and not an overture to a political transaction.[1] (In 1990 Mercy opened a new Rostenkowski outpatient surgery wing underwritten by his fund raising and donations from speaking fees he could not legally keep.)

After the 1986 law, along with these misfortunes, Rosty grew ever more of a grandee, at once more imperious and more peevish, often frowning and bitching. Even though he sought the Mr. Fix-It business, he was tiring of the demands on this personage. He was feeling the pressures of stardom, of celebrity.

The White Sox and the Chicago Bears, the professional football team, kept hitting him up for new stadia. The 1986 tax-exempt bonds break for the Sox was void because of a technicality, and meanwhile the Bears wanted a new palace to replace old, decrepit Soldier Field on the lakefront, just as the Sox wanted to replace old, decrepit Comiskey Park in Daley's neighborhood. Governor Thompson importuned Rostenkowski, as did scores of congressmen wanting tax-exempt bonds for their own pet projects. "People seem to think I can wave a magic wand," Rostenkowski grumbled. "But I didn't create the problem and I don't know that I can solve it."[2] Somehow his foot dragging on the new stadia seemed to follow Washington's dumping of Gabinski.

Among other projects, Washington was plotting a city takeover of Commonwealth Edison, the power monopoly. In October Rosty arranged for federal legislation to prevent it (the issue, once again, was tax-exempt bonds). Rosty went to the fifth floor of city hall on a Friday, so changed from his years of Fridays with Daley, to tell Washington, no way.

On 25 November, Washington was conferring with his press secretary on the fifth floor when his head banged on the desktop at about 11 A.M. At sixty-five, the man who vowed to be mayor for twenty years had suffered a fatal heart attack. The city's grief paralleled that for Daley over an undeniably, for all his flaws, great mayor.

The next day was Thanksgiving. The next day, Friday, Jesse Jackson flew into town from his new Washington base to convene a black conclave on retaining the mayor's seat. The favorite of the "movement" survivors was Alderman Timothy C. Evans, Washington's council floor leader from the poverty-level Fourth Ward on the Near South Side.

Ed Burke remembered when he was twenty-four years old and machine members plotted the succession of his late father as Fourteenth Ward committeeman at his father's very wake in 1968. Burke had the white committeemen convene at the Northwest Side Thirty-fifth Ward home of Alderman Joe Kotlarz (honoring a venerable Chicago tradition, Kotlarz, as a state representative, was convicted on corruption charges in 1997). White aldermen favored Eugene Sawyer, a four-term black alderman from the middle-class black neighborhoods of the Sixth Ward. Sawyer was a quiet, get-along-go-along sort with a soft mumble from his Mississippi upbringing. Obviously, the council meeting to elect Washington's replacement would be interesting.

Washington was buried on a sunless Monday. On a sunless Tuesday the council met at 10:00 A.M. for a memorial service, the mayoral chair draped in black just as at Daley's death. At 5:30 P.M. the council met to choose a successor. The following ten hours and sixteen minutes were perhaps the council's ultimate historical display of farce and disgrace.

Black demonstrators packed city hall and the bordering streets and chanted, "no deal, no deal," which was rather like shouting at a zebra, "no stripes, no stripes!" Young men climbed the outside walls to stand on windowsills ten feet above the ground and lead cheers for Evans. At least one black supporter of Sawyer wore a bullet-proof vest on the council floor.

Inside the council chamber, Sawyer confronted Mary Ella Smith, Washington's longtime fiancée. They hugged and Sawyer's knees literally buckled. His heart was sundered by the Evans/Jackson forces and the white council majority that could make him mayor. Sawyer retreated to his upstairs office with his pastor, and the council ventured into chaos. Sawyer wanted to go home, but his backers would not permit it.[3]

During this interim, Gabinski came within one vote of privately assembling a majority to be chosen mayor, but so did one or two other white aldermen. There had even been talk of getting a Northwest Side alderman to resign, having the acting mayor—an unimportant north lakefront alderman—name Rostenkowski in his place, then electing Rostenkowski mayor. This was just a rumor among many.

Demonstrators in the rear of the chamber took to waving dollar bills at the aldermen. Near midnight, a black alderman on the floor opened her purse, took out a wad of bills, and waved it back. A demonstrator hurled a handful of quarters, some of which struck Gabinski. He had police remove the man, prompting chants of "police brutality!"

Evans overstepped. He told the TV cameras that Sawyer's claim of a majority was a lie. This made Sawyer angry. He reentered the council and took his seat at 12:07 A.M., guarded by police. A white alderman stood atop his desk, waved his arms, and yelled in a vain effort to be recognized by the chair. He stepped down grinning, enjoying himself. By the time the roll call finally was complete at 3:59 A.M., Sawyer was mayor, 29–19. He made a few inaugural remarks, claiming to be a disciple of Washington, but the machine had beaten the reformers one more time. In the ensuing twelve years, the machine never relinquished the mayoralty.

The installation of Sawyer was a prelude to a restoration of the Daley dynasty, but a special election for Richard M. Daley was still two years away. Shortly after Washington died, a reporter noticed an oddity. Nobody was circulating petitions in the Thirty-second Ward for Danny's reelection as committeeman in the March 1988 primary. He called 2111 Rayburn, and Rosty's aide Virginia C. Fletcher said, yes, that's right, he's stepping down. And so Rostenkowski quietly yielded the seat that he and Joe had held since 1936.

Perhaps he had heard enough criticism that he was just a glorified ward heeler. Maybe he thought it past time to cleanse the stain of the machine from his jacket, especially after the mayoral succession spectacle that reporters called "the night of the living dead aldermen." Or maybe he was just consumed with larger concerns. Tax and trade policy chuted through his office constantly, and everybody wanted a piece of him, everybody. Let Gabinski run the ward—he was too busy. Still, Rostenkowski continued to wear a silver and sapphire pinky ring, a patent of the machine.

By 1989, Rosty had one close friend as president of his country and another as mayor of his city. Yet he often was in ill humor. Probably one factor was the enduring obsession of a son of the machine with ethnicity. The moderate northern machine ethnic Democrats were nearly extinct; Rosty did not bother even to learn the names of many junior members, the blow-dried guys. Just about his only remaining mate was John Dingell of Detroit, another hulking Pole who was the son of a powerful pol, but Dingell was a rival, allied with Wright.

There were two recorded instances of alleged anti-Semitism by Rostenkowski. Back in 1981 in a Chicago radio interview, he said he had favored Reagan's sale of high-tech radar planes to the Saudis but voted no for fear of the Jewish lobby.[4] After the predictable protests, he crabbily boycotted that radio program for eleven years. He could be given the benefit of the doubt in the radio remarks but not in another incident years later. In a leadership conference he opposed the appointment of a member to the Foreign Affairs Committee, saying, "There are already four kikes on that committee." The other leaders threw sidelong glances at one another.[5]

And always, always, taxes and budgets and Social Security and Medicare and congressional scandals and campaign funds and lobbyists, lobbyists. The practice of lobbying had changed since he had joined Ways and Means, even since he became chairman. Corporate board chairmen and CEOs used to disdain explicit lobbying as beneath them, grunt-level work for underlings, kids with masters' degrees in business or public administration deputed from K Street to arrange golf junkets, honoraria, dinner at Rosty's Rotunda. With the ballooning dominance of Washington's myriad of subsidizing, regulating, and taxing activities came what might be called "Lear Jet lobbying," "face time" of CEOs with congressional mandarins in Capitol Hill redoubts, say, in Rosty's 2111 Rayburn or—a sign of favor—his H208 sanctum, in the relentless drive to transmute political influence into money.

Mr. Chairman would grant audiences with a brusque, let's-get-down-to-business manner. "I have sat in his office with Stanton Cook and Lee Iacocca," an associate said, referring to the former CEO of the *Chicago Tribune*'s parent company and the former chairman of Chrysler Corporation, respectively. "They go in and see him and they come out fast. He's not a person who will dance you around. It's yes or no."[6]

Again the essential interchange had been learned in the Cook County Democratic Central Committee and the House Ways and Means Committee. What do you want? X. I can get it for you, or I might get it in exchange for Y, or maybe I can get it if you first bring the Speaker or the White House on board, or forget it, no way. Again like Daley, Rostenkowski bestowed a comforting blanket of political cover over loyalists. "I'd like to help you, but the chairman says no and that's it" was an excuse frequently offered lobbyists by congressmen.

It was a weary Rostenkowski who listened to Lech Walesa, who liberated Poland during the historic, the astounding collapse of the Iron Curtain, address a joint session of Congress on 15 November 1989. Rosty had visited Poland in 1987, his first trip there in ten years. Over dinner with colleagues after Walesa's speech Rostenkowski struggled to tell what the occasion meant to Polish Americans. "We were ten thousand feet tall."

The graduate of an Episcopalian prep school went on to deplore all the years he had spent trying to camouflage his Polishness and "Anglo-Saxonize myself," and he started to cry.[7]

Visit any senior senator's or representative's office, and you will see a "power wall" bearing framed photos of the lawmaker in grip and grins with presidents, inscribed and autographed with often dubious presidential affection. Rosty not only had such photos of George Bush in 1211 Rayburn, he had them on the walls of his Chicago home.

In March 1988, Rostenkowski endorsed Massachusetts Governor Michael S. Dukakis for president. At the Democratic National Convention in Atlanta, he made the first of the seconding speeches for Lloyd Bentsen for vice president. Reviewing other events of this convention would be pointless because by then it was little more than a quadrennial, micromanaged television program.

That summer Thompson was granted an audience in H208. Rosty pointed to the portraits on the wall. "Jim, you know what those are? Those are all the [seven] members of the Ways and Means Committee that became president. Next year, one more's going up there."[8] He meant Bush. Thus did the Democratic chairman communicate with the Republican governor who chaired the Bush campaign in Illinois.

By October a curious equanimity had settled over Democratic elders concerning Dukakis's impending defeat by Bush. At the Republican National Convention in New Orleans, Bush famously said, "Read my lips: no new taxes." Republicans took this to heart. Democrats figured he was just mouthing words penned by his speech writer, Peggy Noonan. Democrats were right.

As Bush approached the stage on the east front of the Capitol for his 20 January 1989 inaugural, he spied Rosty in the gallery, waved, and shouted, "Hi, Danny!"—the equivalent of a king of England publicly inviting a knight from the dissident nobility into his Privy Council.

Soon Danny was having lunch with Treasury Secretary Nicholas F. Brady. Bush called and said, "You gotta come down here." So Brady and Rosty went to the Oval Office to greet Bush and his chief of staff, John Sununu. The president said, "John, Nick, could you leave me alone with the chairman, please?" When they exited Bush exulted, "Jesus Christ, Danny, can you believe I'm the president of the United States?" [9]

Thereafter developed something of a ritual. Rosty would urge tax increases. Bush would respond with a favorite, all-purpose one liner, "If you're so goddamned smart, how come you're not the president of the United States?" By 1990 Rosty put kidding aside. "Tell the people that if we don't balance our budget we're going to be number two [to Japan and Germany], and they'll say, 'the hell we will!' If you challenge them, Mr. President, they will accept whatever sacrifice you say is necessary. If you lead, they'll follow."

The degree of mirth in Bush's reply is hard to gauge: "It's easy for you to say." [10]

Rostenkowski's travails were real because the United States budget was crazy. Social welfare and defense and local pork were kept high while congressmen and presidents gamed the tax code and brayed about wanting to balance the budget. Rostenkowski, who was honest after his fashion, despised the hypocrisy. Almost alone among top policy makers in Congress and the White House, the chairman, though a son of the New Deal, worried constantly about the deficits, thought they were a disaster.

He was no professional economist, but he understood the essential dilemma. The people wanted government checks and pothole-free roads, but they did not want large chunks of money withheld from their paychecks. Ways and Means continuously was pressured to squeeze money out of spending programs without ever actually saying no to any organized constituency. So, for example, Congress trimmed payments to Medicare providers here, accelerated the schedule of Medicare payroll taxes there, but would never tell the seniors' lobby, "health care is not free."

No wonder Rostenkowski was querulous and arrogant. He was the chief tax writer of the nation, and every day he heard from conservatives and CEOs, "Give us pork, but cut our taxes." He heard from constituents, too, as in this personal letter to Rosty:

> Dear Congressman:
>   I want to thank you for helping me get my increase in my Social Security payment. I had enough money left last month to buy me a radio. It is so much company to me. I have been here in the nursing home since my dear husband passed away 3 years ago. I had never had any visitors so my new radio means a lot to me. Mrs. ——— who lives in the next room had had a radio since she came here 2 years ago but she would never let me listen to it. She's 85 years old and I will be 83 March 3. Last week her radio fell off the table and broke and she asked me if she could listen to mine and I said fuck you.
>   Sincerely yours, ———[11]

This epistle was circulated all over Washington for a laugh, but its subtext expressed a common attitude. The federal government, among its manifold obligations, ought to provide individual radios to nursing home residents.

Coincident with the Ways and Means movement on tax reform in 1985 Congress had passed the Gramm-Rudman law to phase out deficits until a balanced budget, through spending cuts or tax increases or a combination, was achieved by 1991. If Congress did not so act, automatic, statutory spending cuts would be imposed. It is possible that some congressmen in 1985 actually believed this would happen. The unwritten message of the law was, all right, President Reagan, cuts in defense or increases in taxes— which will it be?

A major bulwark of the two-party system is that it provides a neat, bipolar world for reportage of public affairs. Republicans want lower social spending, higher defense spending. Democrats want the opposite. This fraternity fight was the focus of reporting, while uninterrupted high levels of total spending remained a given.

Republican presidents and Democratic Congresses spent years laboring to undo, dilute, delay, disguise, or evade the terms of Gramm-Rudman.

All this work was easier than admitting they had no intention of seriously cutting spending or raising taxes.

The Republican "revolutions" of 1980 and 1994 promised to shrink the federal government but failed. Government was 22.9 percent of Gross Domestic Product when Reagan took office. It was 22.1 percent when he left. The White House and Congress shed a lot of blood, sweat, and tears and toted many barges and lifted many bales, for the sake of eight-tenths of a percentage point of GDP.

Rostenkowski responded by promoting, time and again, pieces of policy that assembled into a Rostenkowski program: Raise the gasoline tax to increase revenues and encourage conservation. Raise excise taxes and user fees to fund the normal functions of government. Raise payroll taxes to fund Social Security and Medicare. Reduce income taxes for the middle class, but increase them for the upper brackets (soak the rich, but write loopholes into the law to favor many of the rich, those with muscular PACs, but, hey, I am not a sellout to PACs! I only want what is good for Chicago and Illinois and the country. Reelect me because I bring home the bacon. Reelect me because I strive to force fiscal discipline on those nutty Republicans in the White House. Did I not get Congress to repave the Kennedy Expressway in Chicago? Did I not kick George Bush to rescind his stupid "read my lips"?)

By 1990 the financial markets fretted so much over the deficits that Republican leaders approached Rostenkowski to murmur, "Okay, we'll let you raise taxes if you will agree to increase defense."

"We'll *let* you raise taxes? We'll let you raises *taxes*! Huh! That's about the most ridiculous thing I ever heard." [12] The glare, the scrunched-up face, the crossed arms behind the *Dan Rostenkowski, Illinois* plaque on that long table—gestures that congressmen had learned to fear. Rosty would entertain no such idea until President Bush himself urged a tax increase, as indeed he did.

On 6 December 1988, Rostenkowski proposed a gas tax increase and the *New York Times* editorially and typically praised his "courage." That same day, though, the chairman had lunch with President-elect Bush and promised he would avoid embarrassing him over the tax issue for a year, out of friendship, but that's it. One year and no more.

Speaker Wright felt no such obligation as he and his House Democrats kept pressing for taxes. Wright and Rosty circled each other like boxers in a ring, feinting but wary of striking the first blow. Wright had fought Rosty on tax reform, though he did not, at O'Neill's request, make a public show of it. As an oil-state southerner, he naturally opposed gas taxes and favored commodities-trade taxes.

Just as with Speaker Albert, Rosty shared much personal biography with Wright, for all the enmity. Wright, like Rosty, never finished college, dropping out of the University of Texas the day after Pearl Harbor. He was elected to the state legislature at age twenty-three (Rosty, twenty-four) and to Congress in 1954 at thirty-one (Rosty, thirty in 1958). Both men's fathers were hard drinkers and New Dealers. But Wright was Speaker, and Rosty was not.

For a politician, Wright was a bit of a cold fish, a brooder with a tight, off-putting smile and eyes that blazed from under a thicket of brows, whereas Rostenkowski was gregarious. Scratch Rosty, though, and you would find a similar depth and moodiness. By the end of his first year as Speaker, 1987, Wright was being hailed as the strongest Speaker in decades. Rostenkowski was not delighted.

The writing of Reagan's final budgets of 1987 and 1988 was tortuous and quarrelsome, with various tax increases despite Reagan's professed antitax dogma. After the stock market crash of 19 October 1987, the financial markets grew ever more worried about the deficits, although the connection between federal deficits and stock prices is unclear. The crash was an incident from which the market quickly recovered.

Also during this time, Reagan was weakened by the Iran-contra scandal. Wright was winning on budgets and also in his personal interventions in foreign policy toward Central America. Republicans railed against this violation of the separation of powers, but Wright figured, better I than the likes of White House aide Oliver North, the media's central figure in Iran-contra. What really bothered Congress about Iran-contra was not North's diversion of funds from illegal arms sales to Iran to the anti-Communist Nicaraguan contras, a diversion that might or might not have broken an on-again, off-again law against funding the contras. What really bothered Congress was Reagan's contempt for institutions, for his own State Department and for the Foreign Affairs and Intelligence committees of Congress. Wright perceived a hollowness of institutional power and charged into it. He was dominant, although in mid-1988 Common Cause and Newt Gingrich filed ethics charges against him.

In 1987 Wright said forget the gas tax. Rosty countered by making a splash about the gas tax in the *Wall Street Journal* and about trade policy in the *Washington Post*. This is how politicians use the media as a covert messenger service. The message was, heads up, Mr. Speaker, I am still the chairman of Ways and Means! Wright responded with a cold "Dear Danny" letter hand delivered by a page to his office. It was a Monday, so Danny was in Chicago. He had his aide Robert Leonard read it over the phone.

The letter contained a subtle but unmistakable threat that he could be replaced as chairman, a threat that to all previous Speakers Rosty had known was unthinkable. For a Speaker to dethrone a chairman would be like a king beheading a prince. The institutional uproar would be painful to contemplate. Rostenkowski considered the missive for a minute and then muttered, "We're communicating by letter now? Is this what it's come to?" [13]

The trade issue was a particular sore point between them. Typically, Rosty was ideologically neither a free trader nor a protectionist but kept a sharp lookout for a deal. The leadership decided to make trade the top legislative priority of 1987 after the issue of American jobs lost to cheap foreign goods helped Democrats retake the Senate in the 1986 elections. That event also impressed the Reagan administration, which suddenly decided it wanted a trade bill after all, after having buried a House bill in the Senate, then still controlled by Republicans, in 1986.

Despite a general prosperity, the nation was running up record trade deficits and heavy industry was closing plants. Congress wanted to require reprisals against countries—especially Japan—that kept their internal markets effectively closed to American goods while dumping cheap imports here. The bill also would give the president "fast-track" authority to negotiate trade agreements that would be subject to up-or-down votes, but no amendments, in Congress. It was a relatively "clean" trade bill without relief for specific industries such as southern textiles, which would just tie Congress up in sectional competitions.

Roughly speaking, Republicans were free traders and Democrats protectionists. Rosty leaned toward free trade and against Wright. James Baker sang overtures to Rosty that they could write the most sweeping trade bill since 1974, just as they had written tax reform together. Wright did not appreciate this. Neither much, for that matter, did Rosty. In March he suggested creating a cabinet position, secretary of international trade, an uncharacteristic proposal to set up a new bureaucracy. If this was a bargaining chip, it failed—the White House was not interested. Rostenkowski then introduced a bill that toned down the tough retaliatory sanctions sought by Wright and Richard A. Gephardt of Missouri. "I want to get enough votes to pass this bill," Rosty explained.[14]

Gephardt planned to seek the 1988 Democratic presidential nomination on the platform of saving jobs by ending unfair trade practices. His Gephardt amendment, whatever the various versions of it actually said, was regarded as protectionist. Rosty's comments on the amendment had triggered Wright's "Dear Danny" letter. The vote on the amendment became in large part a proxy for the Wright-Rosty feud.

Rostenkowski fought fair. He buttonholed members to argue the merits of the bill and even made a speech on the floor, but he did not twist arms or appeal for votes on personal grounds. On 29 April, the Gephardt amendment passed, 218–214. In losing, Rostenkowski actually had won. He could have defeated the measure by changing two votes, creating a 216–216 tie. Had he really tried, he might have leaned on members hard enough to get two more votes, thus humiliating Wright. The next day's 290–137 vote to pass the entire trade bill was a formality. The whips cheered, but Rosty did not join in. He just sat on the floor, gazing steadily up at the Speaker, eyes hard, jaw clenched.

Both the House and the Senate passed versions of the trade bill by large margins. The conference committee to reconcile the bills was a monster—155 House members and 44 senators—because fourteen House committees and nine Senate committees were involved in the legislation. Before talks got very far, the 19 October stock market crash put the deficit and budget back in the limelight, and the trade bill was delayed until 1988.

The budget summit of 1987 ultimately yielded a two-year deal. The essential agreement was written by Rosty and Senator Bentsen in a face-to-face, six-and-one-half-hour session. The deal proposed to reduce the deficits by $68 billion over two years and raise taxes and user fees $28 billion during that time. Reagan signed the tax increases and continued his antitax rhetoric without embarrassment. An exhausted and cranky Congress sent Reagan the key appropriations bill in the early morning hours three days before Christmas.

By early 1989, Rosty held a trump over Wright with his closeness to Bush. It hardly mattered by then because Wright was "embattled"—media code for "he should quit"—over ethics charges. Both men considered the charges penny-ante, partisan, and media-driven foolishness. Rosty grew closer to the Texan, two old lions licking their wounds together.

Rosty took to strolling into the Speaker's office to reminisce about old Sam Rayburn and the majesty of the People's House, rather in the way that old West Pointers speak of the Corps. "If you leave, Jim," Rosty said, "don't be surprised if I retire." He was interrupted by a catch in the throat, a wetting of the eyes. "Don't be surprised if I don't run again." [15] Of course he did, the media and the blow-dried guys notwithstanding.

The ethics charges were serious enough, but the issue that helped tip the House against its Speaker was a congressional pay raise. Congress contrived to increase its members' salary from $89,500 to $135,000—a 55 percent jump—without actually having to cast recorded votes on the action. In the resulting public revulsion, Wright abruptly switched sides and assisted in killing the raise on 7 February. Some members felt double-crossed.

Rostenkowski placed an op-ed piece in the 12 February *Chicago Tribune* headlined "Congressmen Work Hard and Deserve to Get Top Dollar." He recalled the half-serious bill he had introduced in 1987 to allow a congressman to draw any salary between $89,500 and $135,000—whatever he thought he was worth. "I would sign for the highest end of the scale," Rostenkowski wrote. "It is high time we stopped whipping ourselves."

Many House members, Republicans as well as Democrats, felt they were whipping themselves over ethics. True, some Republicans took the assault on Wright as revenge for the Senate's rejection of Bush's nomination of former Senator John Tower of Texas to be defense secretary. But overall, Washington was dismayed by a sense that partisan attack and counterattack had gone too far.

The House ethics committee hired a Democratic lawyer, Richard J. Phelan of Chicago, to investigate Wright. Democrats soon learned they could take no comfort in Phelan's partisan label because of his almost naked ambition to nail Wright and thereafter run for governor of Illinois (he ran and lost). On 17 April, the committee issued a 91-page report charging Wright with violating House rules sixty-nine times. Phelan issued a separate, far more damning 279-page report.

In essence, Wright was accused of accepting improper gifts to him and his wife from Fort Worth developer George Mallick. Mallick was Wright's sugar daddy much as Daniel J. Shannon was Rosty's. Wright also was charged with scamming the limit on speech fees by pressing bulk sales of his book, *Reflections of a Public Man*, to groups that sponsored his speeches. Whatever Rostenkowski's wrongdoings, he never inflicted on the public such a 117-page compendium of banalities as *Reflections of a Public Man*.

In sorrow, Rostenkowski had said, "I used to be very close to Jim Wright. He's a loner. That's one reason he's got a problem. I think the situation's terrible, embarrassing to the House. Members have talked to me about running against him [for Speaker]. But I don't think I can beat him." [16] I don't think I can beat him—spoken like an heir of machine-bestowed offices.

The spring weekend of the Kentucky Derby found Rosty as usual at Churchill Downs, guest of the racing lobby. Somebody thanked him for some tax break, and he said, "Don't thank me for anything. I didn't do anything for you and if I did I don't want to know about it." [17] An exegesis of this remark might be, "I don't sell out to lobbyists like they say I do, and if you acknowledge some quid pro quo in front of all these people the media and the Republicans might start coming after me the way they are going after Wright." In fact, Rosty did not cave in to big donors, if for no other reason than that he had so many big donors seeking conflicting cave-ins. What he did was reward pals and patrons and those of fellow politicians, especially if they were Illinoisans, Democrat or Republican.

On 26 May, the trauma of the House deepened when Tony Coelho of California surprisingly announced he was quitting as majority whip and resigning from Congress after being implicated in a "junk bond" deal. Rosty considered Coelho an ingrate for allying with Wright after Rosty had promoted him in the leadership; Rosty had started dropping hints about imposing taxes on wine, produced in Coelho's Napa Valley district. But Coelho's ignominious departure was another kick in the stomach for all House Democrats.

On 31 May, Wright announced his resignation in a dramatic, hour-long floor speech. He portrayed himself as a victim of partisan warfare conducted by leaks and a *j'accuse* fervor about the personal ethics of public servants. This was true in a broad sense, although the ethics committee had rejected the specific charges filed by Gingrich.

"All of us, in both political parties, must resolve to bring this period of mindless cannibalism to an end . . . Let me give you back this job you gave me as a propitiation for all of this season of bad will," Wright said, shoulders straight, head high.[18]

On 6 June, Thomas S. Foley of Washington was elected Speaker over Bob Michel on a routine party-line vote. Even a let's-all-be-friends guy such as Michel was moved to deliver a hard-edged speech on the floor. "The distinguished members of the ethics committee," he said, "equally divided from both parties, are neither mindless nor cannibals." He went on to say, "Thirty-five years of uninterrupted [Democratic] power can act like a corrosive acid upon the restraints of stability and comity. Those who have been kings of the Hill for so long may forget that majority status is not a divine right, and minority status is not a permanent condition."[19] The harsh words were a defense, unavailing, against the insurrection of Gingrich and his camp in the GOP.

The bipartisan amity of Michel's and Rosty's car trips home and back in the late 1950s and early 1960s now seemed quaint, innocent, as antique as hula hoops and Davy Crockett coonskin caps. Both parties had sharpened their ideological claws to knife points. Taxes and spending were kept high throughout, though.

On 28 June, his last working day in the House, Wright voted to send $110 million of pork to Texas to begin a superconducting supercollider project.

During that summer, the postmaster of the House post office went to see his supervisor of accounts in a basement office across the street from the

Capitol, closed the door, and asked for two thousand dollars in cash in exchange for a two-thousand-dollar voucher filled out for stamps for Rostenkowski's office.

"Can we do this?" the subordinate wondered.

Sure, said the postmaster, Rosty's our friend. "He takes care of you, he takes care of me, and this is the way he wants it done."[20] That axiom of machine politics would have been appreciated by Dick Daley.

Rosty might have felt gratified at beating the goo goos. Until 1977, congressmen ordinarily "cashed out" the unused portions of their travel, stationery, and district office expense accounts. It was a convenient way to increase their pay without having to vote for a salary increase. Outspoken as usual, Rosty publicly ranted against the reformists' stoppage of this practice. Whether cashing out on postage expenses was allowed was left ambiguous. Rosty saw a loophole and drove through it.

He scarcely thought about the postage scam because he was throwing a $768,000 gala for the bicentennial of the Ways and Means Committee, a Rosty-esque extravagance of ego. The money, mostly from corporations, foundations, and unions, produced an official, slick-paper, four-pound, 526-page history as well as a sixty-minute historical video. After the video depicts the committee handling the problems of a civil war, depression, and two world wars, Rosty appears often on camera expressing the need for more revenues, more revenues. He does not mention more taxes.

The bicentennial banquet on 24 July drew current and past committee members, including Bush. The Democratic chairman told the Republican president in front of everybody that he had halted just "one step short" of endorsing Bush over Dukakis in 1988. Perhaps this is one reason Rosty had quit the Cook County Democratic Committee that year—the machine would not have countenanced an endorsement of the Republican nominee for president.

The diners were given commemorative gold cuff links. A young Rostenkowski protégé, Thomas J. Downey of New York, quipped that the cuff links were the single bicentennial item that did not have Rostenkowski's picture on them. Rosty replied in kind by asking that the cuff links be returned so that the oversight might be corrected.

He was less merry back in Chicago on 17 August when senior citizens angrily mobbed his car. Rosty had gone to the Copernicus Center for the Elderly and Disabled on Milwaukee Avenue to discuss the 1988 Medicare Catastrophic Coverage Act.

Wright had granted, for sentimental reasons, sponsorship of the bill to Claude Pepper of Florida, the eighty-seven-year-old champion of seniors' benefits. This transgression against sacred committee jurisdiction angered both Rostenkowski and Energy and Commerce Committee Chairman John Dingell. After this tiff was over, the bill easily passed Congress, and Reagan signed it with fanfare.

It expanded coverage of medicines and of nursing home, home health, and hospice care. Some of the beneficiaries actually were required to pay for the benefits. The upper-income 40 percent would be taxed up to $800 per person in 1989 and more thereafter. Most of the people crowding the Copernicus Center would have escaped the means test. Catastrophic was a good deal for them. Rostenkowski tried in vain to explain this.

In arrogant disgust, he left the center and entered his chauffeured car. Several dozen folks followed, surrounded the car, and shouted, "Impeach!" and "Rotten-kowski!" They hit the car with picket signs and pounded on the windows. A sixty-nine-year-old woman plopped herself across the hood of the car. Rostenkowski sensed that driving off with an old lady as a hood ornament would be poor public relations.

He got out and walked up Milwaukee Avenue, pursued by a few jeer-ers, and told reporters, "I don't think they understand what the govern-ment's trying to do for them." He cut through a gas station and then ran toward his car, whose driver had managed to break away.[21]

By the end of the year, the act was repealed.

Rostenkowski fared little better with, of all things, his realm of exper-tise, general taxes. Bush insisted on cutting the rate on capital gains to pro-mote investment and juice the economy. Not just an article of Republi-can "theology," this was nearly the totality of Bush's domestic agenda. He was the son of the leader of a blue-chip Wall Street firm who became a U.S. senator. Treasury Secretary Brady had headed a Wall Street firm himself. Bush was far from enamored of Reagan's 1986 tax reform and said during the 1988 campaign that he would open up the tax code. Sure enough. Tax reform treated capital gains and salaries equally at a top rate of 28 percent for most people, 33 percent in some top-bracket cases. Bush demanded 15 percent.

Blaspheming against Democratic theology, Rostenkowski said after a private meeting with Bush in June that he would consider a cap-gains cut as part of a broader tax plan. He promised the president that he would try to craft a bill that would not attract a veto.

Under the latest budget deal, Congress needed to find $5 billion in new revenues. A reduced cap-gains rate temporarily would suck in revenues as asset holders liquidated their locked-up gains to take advantage of lower taxes. After that windfall to the treasury, the long-term revenue effect was a question for theologians. Rosty did not believe in cutting capital gains, did not want to start mucking up tax reform, but he put up a cut-cap-gains trial balloon for Bush's sake. He soon tried to shoot it down.

Republicans and southern Democrats on Ways and Means were flying away with it. They combined to advance a cap-gains cut, which Rosty struggled to bury in committee to prevent a floor fight. Giving up, he allowed the committee to vote on 14 September. The chairman was defeated, 19–17.

Now the matter was up to the new leadership—Foley, Majority Leader Gephardt, and Majority Whip William H. Gray III of Pennsylvania. They lost the floor fight on 28 September, 239–190. The party discipline imposed by Wright had evaporated. But in the end, Bush did not win on capital gains. He was forced to strip it from a necessary deficit-reduction bill to get that bill passed.

Rostenkowski was defeated on another piece of the 1986 bill known as Section 89. Congress did not tax fringe benefits for health for fear that employers would simply drop their health plans for employees. However, Section 89 required that lavish health and life insurance coverage for executives be taxed unless scantily covered wage earners got equal coverage. The result was an IRS tangle and the abandonment of all coverage by some employers anyway. Rosty cared about the health issue, and he also cared about the loss of potential revenues. He put forth a bill to simplify the so-called nondiscrimination features of Section 89.

The small-business lobby was screaming for outright repeal. Rostenkowski used his wiles to contain the issue in his committee, but the Rules

Committee stepped in and took it to the floor. Then he tried to attach his bill to the Bush deficit-reduction bill. "I'm disappointed that the Congress has adopted this mood of just bending to pressure groups," he lamented.[22] On 27 September Rostenkowski pleaded on the floor to save the basic nondiscrimination features. Mr. Chairman was rebuked with an astounding 390–36 vote to repeal Section 89.

With righteous anger following the annulments of catastrophic Medicare and Section 89, Rostenkowski placed an op-ed piece in the 13 October *New York Times* saying, in so many words, screw it, let the automatic spending cuts ordered by Gramm-Rudman kick in, let the banshees howl. Maybe then at last we'll get some honest deficit reduction. Of course the ultimate Bush-Congress budget deal found ways to get around Gramm-Rudman. Rostenkowski wept at the Walesa dinner and went home thinking the next year could only get better.

The new year smashed home with another family misfortune. In June 1990, Gayle Rosten, thirty-three, was arrested in Lake County, north of Cook County, and charged with possession of cocaine with intent to deliver. In September, she pleaded guilty to a lesser charge. Her lawyer said she had no criminal record but had been a heavy drug user. In October, she was sentenced to three years of probation, two hundred hours of community service, and a $2,800 fine. She would violate the probation before it was up. Her father made no public comment, then or later.

Rosty called the White House asking to meet with Darman and Sununu about his child care bill. This was a ruse. On 6 March, he talked with the two aides and then they went to the Oval Office, where Rosty told Bush he would put forth a hard-nosed plan to tame the deficit. The one-year tax reprieve had run out; now Rosty was serious. Just give the plan an honest chance, don't attack it from day one, he asked. The request was cheeky because Rosty had recently given a major speech against a cap-gains cut. Okay, said Bush.[23]

The tolerance with which the White House greeted the Rosty plan distressed Republicans, who correctly inferred that the president was about to renege on "read my lips." Rosty flogged the plan with an 11 March op-ed column in the *Washington Post*, Sunday talk show appearances, an 18 March speech to the advertising lobby in Palm Desert, California, and a

10 May "Rosty Challenge" speech to the National Press Club in Washington. "I've participated in the binge of irresponsibility," he repented, "but no more." From the trunk of his car outside the press club, he handed out blue "Rosty Challenge" caps, made in China.[24]

The plan was, by Washington standards, austere, the core of the Rosty program developed over decades—freeze cost-of-living increases in Social Security and elsewhere; suspend the inflation adjustment to the income tax; raise the gas tax fifteen cents; and for good measure raise taxes on alcohol and tobacco, too, but expand the earned income tax credit for the working poor. "High marks for honesty and courage," intoned the *New York Times*. The proposal was praised, with due partisan restraint, by the likes of Sununu and Dole and even the Business Roundtable (Rosty was a favorite of the Roundtable, which gave him an award in 1987).

In April Rosty had a secret lunch with Bush, secret in the sense that Washington keeps secrets. In early May was held the Gridiron Dinner, a high tribal rite in which the political mandarins abase themselves before the media mandarins. The Gridiron Club is a top-drawer, print-media assembly that performs satirical songs and skits at an annual banquet. Supposedly it is off the record, but, as everyone in Washington knows, nothing is ever really off the record. Even as proud a personage as Nancy Reagan was impelled to prostrate herself before the Gridiron. Early in the Reagan presidency, the media scorned the first lady as a frivolous *nouveau riche* obsessed with buying gilt-edged presidential table settings and wearing free designer dresses. Dutifully Mrs. Reagan went to the Gridiron.

The importance of this investiture into the elect is hard to exaggerate. President Nixon, an amateur pianist, and Vice President Agnew had performed a duet making fun of their "southern strategy." When Nancy's turn came she appeared in an aqua skirt with red and yellow flowers secured by safety pins, topped by an outlandish feathered hat, thus poking fun at her own fashion-plate image. The media leaders were delighted. Diners tend to leave the Gridiron feeling immensely pleased with themselves. Media criticism of the first lady notably abated, at least until Don Regan's memoirs revealed that she scheduled the president's affairs according to astrological charts.

At the 1990 Gridiron, Darman heard a media poohbah impersonating Senator Daniel Patrick Moynihan of New York sing, "I'm much more charmin' than Richard G. Darman," an indisputable proposition. After midnight Rostenkowski clasped Darman across the shoulders and in a loud whisper revealed the news of his "secret" lunch with Bush—a big tax deal was aborning.[25] Surrounding revelers made an instant mental note. Read my lips was dead.

On 6 May, Bush invited the top congressional leadership (not including Rosty) for a Sunday talk about the budget, "no preconditions," that is, never mind read my lips. The president's approval ratings were high after a successful military incursion in Panama, but he feared the deficits and an oncoming recession. Within weeks even Gingrich, gonfalonier of the tax-cut crowd, mused that he might be able to support a tax increase as part of a five-year deficit reduction package. Gingrich's remark much heartened Rosty.

On 21 June, Rosty and Bentsen lunched with Brady and Darman, by now Bush's budget director, in the Treasury secretary's private dining room. On 26 June, the White House quietly posted a sinuous, 131-word statement that effectively rescinded read my lips. That set all the hounds to baying, but in fact Bush's initial budget proposal of 29 January had included $19 billion in new taxes and fees. The 26 June statement reverently capitalized "Bipartisan leadership" and "Bipartisan agreement." Bipartisanship is Washington code meaning the public should not make a fuss when the government raises our taxes or gets us into foreign wars.

In August Iraq invaded and seized Kuwait and Congress recessed. Budget bargaining commenced in September in seclusion at the Andrews Air Force Base Officers Club. Without a budget by 1 October, Gramm-Rudman spending cuts would kick in. A deal was announced by the Andrews oracles with one day to spare. Bush proclaimed it in the Rose Garden and, two days later, made a televised pitch for it. The speech was a flop, and the president did not win over even half his GOP House members.

Yet another humiliation was inflicted on the leadership in the early hours of 5 October when the House killed the summit deal, 254–179. Rostenkowski was accustomed to a divide of Republicans and southern Democrats against northern and western Democrats. This House vote was produced by a coalition of conservative Republicans enraged by the new taxes and liberal Democrats enraged by the trims in social welfare and increases in regressive excise taxes. Just as social forces were breaking up the old urban machines, they were breaking up the old congressional alliances. Congress passed a stopgap budget resolution, but Bush petulantly vetoed it. House Democrats passed a soak-the-rich tax plan, but it was just a gesture. Gingrich Republicans wore bright yellow "Junk the Summit" buttons, another gesture.

Even though congressmen wanted to go home to campaign for reelection they could not reach consensus; the ideological edges were keen—cut cap-gains versus soak the rich. Bush partially shut down the government for lack of funding authorization over the Columbus Day holiday weekend. A new budget package was not ready until late October, less than two weeks before the elections.

Many House Democrats thought "the clearest Democratic hero" was Rostenkowski, the *New York Times* reported.[26] In particular the chairman's protégés Russo and Downey sang hosannas. On the same day that the *Times* reporter wrote this piece, 25 October, ABC's *Prime Time Live* aired an exposé of a recent lobbyist-paid congressional junket to Barbados, showing overweight congressmen, including Rostenkowski, frolicking in the surf. For congressmen trying to enact new taxes and worrying about their institution's 23 percent approval rating in the polls, the timing was inopportune. On the next day, Gayle Rosten was sentenced on drug charges.

After still another late-hours session, the House passed a budget deal near dawn on 27 October, and the Senate followed suit near dusk. Congress adjourned at 1:17 A.M. on 28 October, the longest it had tarried in an election year since World War II. The tax bill was written under the Democratic "fairness," not the Republican "growth," rubric. Bush, seemingly unaware of the political wound he, Sununu, and Darman had inflicted on the Republican party, signed it the day before the 6 November elections.

The agreement promised to reduce the deficit by $496 billion over five years by cutting spending, largely in defense, and raising taxes by $146 billion over five years. There was moonshine, of course—accounting tricks, another "magic asterisk" of $3 billion in unspecified savings, provisions to make Gramm-Rudman go away for a while (until 1995), and purposeful ignorance of the military costs of a possible Persian Gulf intervention. Nevertheless, the 1990 budget deal really did curb the deficit, the benefits of which Bush's successor, Clinton, would enjoy.

Rostenkowski was one of seventeen congressional negotiators, and his importance might have been matched by Michel's. Still, Rostenkowski managed to get out the story that he was the "clearest Democratic hero." And the deal tracked, in broad outline though not in severity, the "Rosty Challenge." The gas tax went up ten cents a gallon, the schedule of Medicare payroll taxes was inflated, the upper bracket paid more in income taxes, and the capital gains rate was unchanged. While he was at it, Rosty and his colleague William O. Lipinski of Chicago's Southwest Side also imposed a three-dollar airport passenger tax to finance Mayor Daley's (ill-fated) plan to build an airport in the city's southeast corner to supplement O'Hare.

Once again, after the horrors of 1989, with an ungovernable Congress or no, Rosty was the man, the tall bold slugger. The Wright scandal of 1989 was followed in 1990, typically, by a House reprimand of a Massachusetts congressman for keeping a male prostitute in his home, the conviction of an Ohio congressman on sexual misconduct charges, the conviction of a New York congressman for extortion, and moreover the national failure of the savings and loan industry and the "Keating Five" savings-and-loan influence-peddling scandal in the Senate. But the tall bold slugger was unharmed. He proceeded to prove it in an eight-month power struggle with Darman over a measly $8 million, or .00057 of 1 percent of the $1.4 trillion federal budget.

This episode will be examined in some detail as a specimen of Washington decision making. On 28 March 1990, Rosty had slipped an $8 million grant for his alma mater, Loyola University, into a conference report on an "emergency supplemental" budget measure. Not even the lobbyists packed in the hallway noticed it. Loyola wanted the money to build a new business school just north of the Loop. On 15 November, a minor White House official, given a budget document for review, spied that tiny giveaway.

The official was puzzled because the secretary of education had recommended that Bush sign the bill even though the secretary was known to oppose such "sole source," pork-barrel grants. It turned out that the undersecretary had used an autopen to sign the secretary's name while the boss was off at a conference in Paris. The undersecretary had been an Illinois state education official.

So the White House aide called the education secretary in Paris and got his chief of staff on the line. No, the secretary had never heard of this; should he be awakened?—it was nearly midnight in Paris. Naw, just tell him in the morning, and let me know what I should do.

At four A.M. Washington time, the aide was called at home. The chief of staff said the secretary was furious. Get the Education Department's budget officer to write another letter to Darman's office and use the autopen to sign the secretary's name. This new letter revokes the do-sign recommendation. Don't tell the undersecretary about it.

Okay, fine. The White House aide employed a bureaucratic maneuver to block the transmittal of the previous do-sign letter at the Oval Office. By the time the new letter was vouchsafed there, Darman's office had gotten wind of it. That afternoon the aide bumped into Darman while crossing the blocked-off street from the Old Executive Office Building to the West Wing of the White House. The encounter was not pleasant. Darman despised scams that he did not perpetrate. The president is not going to veto a bill over an itty-bitty piece of pork for Danny! In Washington, $8 million is infinitesimal. Darman went to Sununu and tried to get the aide fired. Bush signed the bill.

The bill Bush signed *authorized* the $8 million. It did not *appropriate* the money. Much congressional and White House wrangling over budgets concerns this distinction.

Meanwhile, Loyola was displeased because the money was cannibalized from the defense budget. The university feared its business school would be beholden to conduct research for the Department of Defense or, alternatively, that defense research grants to its other departments might be diminished by the amount of the business school grant. Not only that, but the Jesuit Fathers had scruples about taking money from a Pentagon that propped up wicked right-wing Central American dictators.

Agreeably, Rostenkowski switched the money from the Department of Defense to the Department of Education through, of all vehicles, the March 1991 bill to pay for Bush's war against Iraq. Darman stepped in and told Rosty he could not do that because of the 1990 budget covenant. Taking the $8 million from domestic spending would burst the ceiling on domestic spending placed by the budget deal by $7.3 million. The result would be automatic across-the-board cuts of $40 for each $1 million of domestic spending. Do you want this, congressmen? He sent a letter to the leadership asking that question.

Like James Baker, or his predecessor David Stockman, Darman had erected a wall of protection around himself by winning media approval through frequent but shrewd leaks—Sununu and Regan scorned this technique and paid the price. Darman thought he had Rostenkowski and his fellow big spenders on this one. The *New York Times* picked up on the $8 million budget buster in early April.

Rosty, infuriated by Darman's letter and leak, struck back. He met with Darman on 2 April without resolution. A leaker in his own right, he put out word that the real budget buster was not the Loyola grant but $7.5 million given the Library of Congress for books for the blind. Did the White House really want to come out against blind people and higher education? And besides, the cost of administering the automatic spending cuts would exceed the puny 8 mill for Loyola.

The 1990 budget deal emplaced a supposed pay-as-you-go standard—additional spending had to be offset by equivalent spending cuts or added revenues. Meanwhile, Bush wanted to grant most-favored-nation (MFN) trading status—a misnomer meaning the foreign country was treated ordinarily—to the Soviet Union, having won concessions from Moscow on the Jewish emigration issue. Lithuania, Latvia, Estonia, Bulgaria, and Mongolia also were included. Plus, Bush had an "Andean Initiative" to allow duty-free exports from Bolivia, Columbia, Ecuador, and Peru.

How will you cut spending to accommodate the giveaway to Loyola? demanded Darman.

How will you cut spending to accommodate the $41 million in tariff losses from these trade deals? demanded Rostenkowski.

After you, Gaston. No, after you, Alphonse.

And so it went through the summer and fall. Rosty wrote Darman on 26 June and again on 3 September to the effect that the revenue implications must be addressed before Ways and Means could act on the trade bill. As in so many cases, Rosty's toughest sanction was not action but the threat of inaction. The power to say no is often mightier than the power to say yes. On 19 September, Darman replied that MFN for Bulgaria would increase revenues by $1.3 million in the next fiscal year. He ignored the

Soviet Union and said he would get back to the chairman regarding the Andes.

On 19 November, Darman uncharacteristically surrendered. He wrote Rostenkowski that, lo and behold, he had found extra money in the budget and there would be no need for automatic spending cuts, that is, if the committee acted "promptly" on the trade bill. Whereupon Ways and Means reported out the trade bill. Loyola got its business school, and Moscow got its trade benefits, not that the Soviets produced much that America wanted to buy. Oddly, Darman had no comment for the press.[27]

The tall bold slugger had a mostly successful 1991, following his routine reelection in 1990. A poll taken for the Republican National Congressional Campaign Committee had indicated that Rosty might be vulnerable after the Copernicus Center fiasco and amid a general feeling against incumbents and with so many Hispanics displacing eastern and southern Europeans in his district. The party did not even think of putting up a serious challenger.

In 1991 a Republican-written remap of Illinois congressional districts dumped two Democratic incumbents but took care to carve out a district for Rosty. He pondered whether he should run yet again in a new district in 1992.

On 22 January 1991, the chief of the independent Capitol police force called the U.S. Justice Department. Something about the cash drawer of a clerk in the House post office coming up short.

A BIRD SO HIGH

There is never a bird that flies so high it doesn't have to come down to get a drink of water.

—proverb often cited by Joseph Rostenkowski

WHAT seemed to get Danny as much as anything was Wednesday golf. The lobbyists who paid him laud and the blow-dried guys on his committee could be overheard scheduling tee times for Wednesdays. "I could never make a date to play Wednesday golf," Rosty grumbled. "Figure that out. I'm sixty-two years old and I have no control over my own scheduling."[1] Hearings, hearings, lobbyists, lobbyists.

Throughout 1991 he publicly played Hamlet over whether he would retire from Congress after 1992. "When you are sitting in an office like this and men are coming in that you absolutely conclude have far less ability than you do, and they are getting 500,000 or one million dollars a year, you sit and scratch your head and say, 'You know, maybe I won't have to worry about the budget next year. I'll just make 500,000 dollars.'"[2]

He could have done so easily enough. He had seen a string of his high-level aides such as James C. Healey, Joseph K. Dowley, Thomas M. Sneeringer, and John Salmon leave his employ for large salaries as corporate partners, board members, consultants, or lobbyists. Any CEO would have been delighted to pay for Rosty's expertise in the ways of Washington.

Moreover, if he quit in 1992, Rosty could take the money and run, to the tune of $1,052,462. That was the sum standing in the accounts of his two political committees on 30 November 1989. Legally he could convert the money as of that date to his personal use—provided, of course, that he paid taxes on the income—but a reform law prevented congressmen elected in 1992 and after from doing so.

"I could do a lot with that money," he teased a Chicago reporter. "Put it in my pocket. I could give it to the Thirty-second Ward Regular Democratic Organization. I could give it to St. Stanislaus. And I would get a tax write-off . . . Do you know what it's like to meet every day with people who make ten times, a hundred times what you do?"[3] Actually, the reporter did not.

More personal misfortunes struck early in 1991. Robert J. Sulski was a son-in-law of a congressman and nephew of a state legislator; best man at Danny's wedding to LaVerne; godfather of Dawn Rosten; a former assistant state's attorney whose brother, testifying under a grant of immunity in 1956, implicated Sulski in a kickback scheme (there were no charges); picked by Rosty to oust Alderman Prusinski in 1959; later a Cook County judge installed by Rosty who connived with Rosty and Vrdolyak in 1985 to retire as judge in a way that rigged the ballot to elect their selected successor. Sulski died at age sixty-nine.

At St. Joseph Hospital, Alderman Terry Gabinski, age fifty-two, having just been elected vice mayor, a mostly honorary position meaning he would succeed Rich Daley if he died, was connected to life support machines. Gabinski complained of chest pains during a Zoning Committee meeting. He first made sure there were no troublesome items left on the agenda and then called his mentor before consenting to a trip to the hospital. During the call to Rosty, he had a heart attack. Gabinski fully recovered, but surely Rosty was moved to contemplate his own mortality. He went back to Washington to help push Bush's fast-track trade authority with Mexico through the House—this evolved into the NAFTA debate under Clinton.

While weighing all these matters, Rostenkowski thought he should have some fun and invited the entire House for a "Chicago Congressional Weekend." The lawmakers were feted by corporate and civic lobbies, took a dinner cruise on Lake Michigan, heard the Chicago Symphony Orchestra in Grant Park, and watched a Sox game at the new Comiskey Park built by tax-exempt bonds fixed by Rosty and Jim Thompson.

A mid-September good time was had by all, but Rosty faced a 16 December filing deadline to run for reelection. On 11 November, Dick Simpson, a lakefront goo goo, declared that he would run against Rostenkowski or Frank Annunzio or both, whoever emerged from redistricting.

The three Chicago black districts had to be retained—that was a given. The disputed question was whether a Hispanic district should be created, largely from Rosty's own district. Rostenkowski saw the quandary. "I don't see how you are going to satisfy the blacks *and* the Hispanics." As early as March, he had convened a Washington meeting of Chicago party elders at which Lipinski put in a motion that no Hispanic district could rationally be drawn—a truism, as the eventual district for Luis Gutierrez was the ultimate in rococo gerrymander. Politicians are utterly, deadly self-protective about reapportionment. Rosty's meeting was rancorous and inconclusive, and he continued to waver. "I won't jump off the Sears Tower if I don't get [a district]," he said.[4]

Republicans did not heed this. They tried to clear a district for Rosty by tossing Annunzio and north lakefront Representative Sidney Yates into the same district. Jews who regarded Yates's seat as the state's Jewish district rebelled.

Meanwhile, Rosty kept jetting around the country giving speeches to lobbies. The annual report of the House clerk as usual crowned him the congressional champ with $309,850 in speaking fees, $283,000 of which was given to charity. The limits on collecting speech fees did not daunt him.

You can keep $2,000 max, said the goo goos. My fee is $10,000, said Rosty. Once he sat on a panel with Bob Strauss and TV newsman Ted Koppel. Strauss ribbed Rosty about getting just 2 grand when he was getting 10 and Koppel 15. The next time he was slated to appear with Koppel, Rosty said if he gets 15, I'll take 10. The organizer cleared his throat. "Mr. Chairman, the law says you can only take $2,000."

"Wrong. It says I can only *keep* $2,000."[5]

Greed, pure and simple, is no good explanation of Rostenkowski's attitude toward money. Alderman Tom Keane used to say that he wanted money and Dick Daley wanted power and both got what they wanted. Like Daley, Rosty desired power, status, obeisance, more than the mere accumulation of greenbacks. True, Rostenkowski believed high living and luxury were a birthright, a concomitant of high office, but that is not the same thing as money hunger for its own sake. He would quip that he had given a million dollars to charity and if his father knew he would turn over in his grave. But then, old Joe himself was more interested in power than in riches and gave away lots of money to personal and neighborhood causes.

Even Gutierrez, a foe of Rostenkowski, commented, "I think he gives two shits about money."[6] In November 1991 the Illinois secretary of state involuntarily dissolved Confidence Insurance, the business he and LaVerne had set up in 1967, because it had not filed the requisite annual paperwork. But LaVerne continued to collect a small stipend from the dissolved firm.

In a 1993 interview, Rostenkowski said his only holdings were the home inherited from his grandfather and vacation property he had acquired in Wisconsin. He omitted mention of his stock holdings. His comments were reminiscent of Richard Nixon's "Checkers speech" of 1952 when, defending himself against charges of having a slush fund, Nixon said, in effect, if I'm a crook, how come I'm not rich?

Like Nixon and many other national politicians, Rosty lived partly off campaign cash. From his takeover of Ways and Means in 1981 to the end of his career in 1994, Rostenkowski collected $5,514,861 in political donations. This wealth flowed in almost effortlessly, simply by virtue of his chairmanship, and it was habit forming. Much of it, from the vehicle of his America's Leaders PAC, he gave to other congressmen's campaigns to earn their fealty. At the same time, Rostenkowski was troubled, truly, by the enslavement of elected officials to campaign donors.

After struggling with tax reform in 1986, Rosty said, "There was on the part of three or five members, on both sides of the aisle, a definite string attached to some corporate lobbyist outside in the hall. In one instance, a direct link with how much money he could raise in a campaign. That got me nauseated."[7] Rosty was entrenched enough to have such a tender stomach, but it was not so queasy that he stopped taking interest group money himself.

So should he lay down the title *Mr. Chairman* to get rich in the private sector? LaVerne told him, "If you're going to be like your old man and come down without shaving and sit around the house, forget it."[8] In November Rosty said to a Northwest Side business group, "I like the action, but if you're going to leave, why not leave while you're on top? I'm having some sleepless nights over it. I really, honest to God, don't know what I'm going to do."[9]

The public stature of Congress was being cut down even more by still more scandals. The Senate's confirmation hearings of Clarence Thomas to the Supreme Court were a national soap opera of alleged sexual harassment. On the House side, it was revealed that members routinely bounced checks automatically covered by the House bank. The clerisy scolded the public that the overdrafts were not technically bounced checks and that no public funds were lost. The public disregarded these lawyerly distinctions. Congressmen had granted themselves a privilege not enjoyed by private check writers; also, every dollar for congressional operations comes from taxpayers.

Rosty, ever more the grandee, was asked by a *Time* reporter whether he had bounced any checks. He snapped, "None of your damn business! None of your damn business!"[10] In fact, he had not. But the response showed, as did his flight from the Copernicus Center seniors, that he had superordinated himself over his constituency.

The Republican president, George Bush, asked Rosty to stay on for the good of the country. The new Republican governor, Jim Edgar, asked Rosty to stay on for the good of Illinois. The Democratic mayor, Rich Daley, asked Rosty to stay on for the good of Chicago. It is hard to say no when three such eminences appeal to one's ego. But that is not the real reason Rosty hung on to his chairmanship.

The $1,052,462 in political funds up for grabs was an albatross. "If I quit now," Rosty told a reporter, "the obituaries will say, 'He kept the million bucks.'"[11]

No way. The 1992 elections might put a Democrat in the White House. Then national health care could be enacted at last. Rostenkowski would go down in history as no Daley hack but as the giant who wrote fairness into the tax code and bestowed health care on a grateful nation.

On 2 December, Rosty said he would seek reelection. The same day, Annunzio said he would retire rather than challenge Rosty. Annunzio, seventy-six, had been having a hard time and was heartbroken over quitting. He had been bounced as chair of the House Administration Committee and, as chair of a House banking subcommittee, was brushed by the savings and loan scandal.

Mapmakers did the best they could for Rosty, but his new district was problematic. Carved from his old district and parts of Annunzio's and Yates's old districts, less than half its population resided in Rosty's previous fiefdom. It stretched from the Near North Side lakefront, home of yuppies and old money alike, through multiethnic Northwest Side neighborhoods, to suburbs abutting O'Hare. One resident in five, at most, was Polish.

Rostenkowski was impelled for the first time to hire a media consultant and pollster, technicians of the new politics that he despised. Simpson's was no idle threat.

On 12 January 1991, Congress voted to permit Bush to fight a war against Iraq. The resolution was broadly hailed as a reassertion of congressional power over warmaking, as per Article I, Section 8, of the Constitution. It was not. Rather, it affirmed the principle established by Eisenhower's Formosa Resolution of 1955 and LBJ's Tonkin Gulf Resolution of 1964 that a modern president pretty much can take the country into a foreign war whenever he wants. The 1991 resolution, meticulously worded by the White House, did not confront the question of whether a president may wage war without congressional action.

Still, the congressional debate over the use of armed force in foreign affairs was lofty, and Capitol consciences were torn. Rostenkowski was the only Illinois Democrat to vote for war, a salute to his friend Bush and an expression of his lifelong belief in national power.

By July the war was won, and in the next month the Soviet Union started falling to pieces. Bush enjoyed an interlude of near-unanimous acclaim for apparent mastery of foreign policy, but a souring economy and the constraints of the 1990 budget deal soon put the political focus back on Rosty's turf—taxes and spending.

During the period when Bush's approval ratings tipped 90 percent, Rosty pleaded with the president to shift his focus from foreign affairs to the economy. Bush reacted by turning to his wife and joking that the congressman was picking on him.

In truth Rosty did not want another omnibus tax bill. He said the public needed a rest from constant fiddling with the tax code, he said. Habitually he put in another gas tax (five cents), but the proposal died in August in a nasty jurisdictional fight with the chairman of Public Works and

Transportation. In November Rosty proposed a tax cut for the working and middle classes offset by higher taxes on the rich, but his heart was not in it. It was tax legislation for the sake of political posturing, which he disdained, though he did as the leadership, revving up for the 1992 elections, asked.

Bush already had taken a public relations beating by opposing the congressional insistence on extending unemployment benefits. Soon the president endorsed a tax cut hastily drafted by Gingrich and his claque with yet another stab at cutting cap-gains. By now it was late November, and Speaker Foley called the bluff by telling Bush he would summon the House back in session in December to consider it. Never mind, said Bush. Foley countered with a parliamentary trick to embarrass Bush. Congress did not formally adjourn on 27 November when it left town but set the official date at 3 January, allowing a prompt return for a special December session, as if Bush really wanted a showdown he would lose.

All of this was just theater for the media. The real tax issues of 1991 concerned extenders and business write-offs for intangible assets.

Just as Rosty was the king of transition rules, he was king of tax extenders. Extenders are standing tax breaks, so called because Congress renews or extends them for a year, sometimes six months, at a time. Two days before the November adjournment, Rosty called a sudden Ways and Means markup on extenders, having won agreement that the extender bill would not be bogged down on the House or Senate floors with amendments. "Welcome to the season of giving," a jolly Rostenkowski told Gucci Gulchers in the hallway.[12]

The twelve extenders, estimated to cost the treasury $3 billion over five years, included items such as tax-free tuitions granted employees by employers, tax-exempt bonds for state and local governments to underwrite home ownership, a credit for research and development conducted by universities for corporations, and so forth. But don't get too cocky, Rosty told lobbyists, I'll be back in 1992 either to eliminate these loopholes or else to make them permanent. The extender bill passed the House 420−0. Then the members went home. Bush signed the bill without complaint.

The intangibles issue was a deeper swamp. The tax code fixed the depreciation terms for tangibles—machinery, buildings, vehicles. Intangibles were will-o'-the-wisps such as business goodwill, computer software, and mailing lists of reliable customers. A tax break could be claimed for a worn-out truck, but what about an obsolete software program? The code was ambiguous. Intangibles grew more valuable as the service economy displaced the manufacturing economy. Businesses likewise grew bolder about writing them off.

The IRS brooked no such self-interpretations of tax law and ruled that businesses were positing too short an amortization period or claiming assets that deserved no write-off at all. But the Tax Court consistently overruled the IRS. The IRS went to Congress and asked for help. As with many provisions of corporate taxation, fortunes could be won or lost at the margins. Businesses went to Congress and asked for help.

In July Rosty quietly offered a bill to clarify the taxation of intangibles. It set a uniform fourteen-year write-off for nearly all intangibles, including goodwill, which had been disallowed since 1927. The scope of the bill astonished lobbyists, who spent weeks figuring out whether their industry would win or lose under it. Rosty's stated aim was to "provide certainty to taxpayers while eliminating the source of much tax litigation and controversy."[13] The bill also affected Chicago interests such as airline landing rights at O'Hare Airport and city-based cellular phone services.

This and other Rostenkowski bills to simplify parts of the income tax probably had no hope of passage in 1991 or in 1992, which would be an election year. Rosty wanted to get them on the table, showing that he was a serious legislator and not just offering soak-the-rich tax bills to gain headlines and tweak Bush. He held hearings on intangibles and then went home to run for reelection.

On 13 February 1992, four former employees of the House post office were charged with embezzlement. One also was indicted on drug charges.

Dick Simpson had been a lakefront alderman in the 1970s, one of the few independent Democrats who always irritated Mayors Daley and Bilandic but never could beat them. He left the city council to teach political science at the University of Illinois at Chicago and lead the Illinois Coalition Against Reaganomics. Personal ambition aside, he resolved to challenge Rostenkowski out of a civics-textbook, good-government conviction—the people of the new Fifth Congressional District were poorly represented and deserved better.

Unfortunately for Simpson, he had a hangdog, plodding, professorial manner, which did not charm voters. Nevertheless, his campaign against "congressional gridlock and corruption" might well have won had he been able to raise more money.

Back in April 1991, a House postal clerk under investigation had grabbed a few thousand dollars from the cash drawer and fled to Puerto Rico. His father coaxed him home to face the music. The clerk admitted the theft and implicated his co-workers. The Capitol police then sprang surprise audits and found that most of the thirteen clerks were short. There followed jurisdictional disputes among Capitol police, the U.S. Postal Service, the Justice Department, and the House Administration Committee over who should handle the investigation and how. The U.S. attorney in Washington, a Republican, notified of the postal problems in January 1991, was moving in fast. Some of the fingered clerks offered to implicate higher-ups in exchange for leniency.In Chicago the House postal probe sparked the softest of whispers that Rostenkowski would be tainted. Voters paid little mind to such inside-the-Beltway developments, but they were grumpy about government in general.

When the precinct captains in their uniforms of khakis, windbreakers, and Chicago Cubs caps fanned out to circulate Rosty's ballot petitions in wintry December, the unthinkable happened—some voters slammed doors in their faces. The Daley/Rosty troops started to worry for real about the public's antipolitics, anti-incumbents mood.

Rostenkowski actually campaigned, stumping as in the old days and seeking "free media" as in the new days. "The cameras come on, you go from a frown to a smile," he said with a tight smile. Rosty was in real peril but found asking for votes distasteful. "You come home to eat your humble pie," he said. "In Washington it's 'Mr. Chairman this' and 'Mr. Chairman that.' You come home and it's, 'Hey, you!'" [14]

He even appeared on the WMAQ-AM political talk show he had spurned since the "Jewish voters" flap of 1981. "If I have a fault," he allowed, "it's that I have in the last twenty-five years failed to build my image about how effective or how much I can try to do that would make the city more exciting, viable, and I think you are going to see a change in atmosphere from old Danny Rostenkowski." [15] Evidently he thought he had been too humble.

Simpson had calculated he would need to raise $350,000 to win. He raised only $215,500. Rostenkowski spent $1,400,000 in the 1991–1992 election cycle.

On primary election day, 17 March, hundreds of machine workers invaded the Fifth District, all but yanking targeted, promachine voters out of their kitchens to escort them to the polls. Simpson's base, the lakefront, had only 17 percent of the district's population. For all that, Simpson's campaign against Rosty as the lord of "honorariums and free travel and free lunches and backroom deals and payoffs" won 43 percent of the vote. Members of the political class reassured one another that Rosty was invincible.

The machine remembered the 1992 primary as the year the Poles beat the Italians. Rostenkowski elbowed Annunzio into retirement; Lipinski, forced into the same Southwest Side district as Russo, defeated Russo in a typically tough Chicago fight.

At the time, a young man named Michael P. Flanagan was leaving his second stint in the army. A captain in the 1980s, he had rejoined to write the official history of the Third Army's operations in the Gulf War. Now, with exactly one suit to his name, he was looking for a job practicing law. Flanagan's hero was Ronald Reagan, but he took no particular interest in politics.

With timing that did Simpson no good at all, House Postmaster Robert V. Rota resigned two days after the Illinois primary. It was Rota's fifty-seventh birthday.

The House post office (HPO) was a Democratic patronage sink. Rota, from Pennsylvania, postmaster since 1972, was a patronage hire, just like the Chicago sewer commissioner. Sometimes a patronage crumb fell to Republicans; Michel had sponsored the guy who was Rota's driver. Formally elected by the entire House, the postmaster in effect was appointed by the majority party. Back in the 1980s Rota used to quip that he would not inform his successor of all the favors he did for Rosty, "so the next guy won't have to be anything but postmaster."[16] They were little favors but important to Rosty, such as sending a car and driver to pick him up at Washington National Airport on Tuesday mornings. Likely as not, Rostenkowski had played Monday golf in Wisconsin, arisen at 3:30 A.M., and caught the

6:25 flight from O'Hare. Or, likely as not, he arrived from a charity golf tournament in Florida or California or another pleasant clime.

The HPO, one huge mailroom, five branches, and 160 employees, was a sloppily run operation with cash and stamps left lying about. The night shift supervisor drank and slept on the job and sat on allegations of drug dealing in the office.

The HPO functioned as a money laundry for some members. They would deliver an official voucher for stamps and then redeem the stamps for cash. Sometimes they turned in vouchers for cash right away, so that stamps never even changed hands. An outsider might wonder why they needed stamps in the first place. Congressmen get free postage, called the "franking privilege" or "frank," by affixing their signature on official correspondence, though not on personal mail or campaign mailings, a distinction that congressmen tended to blur. The vouchers could have disguised illegal campaign contributions, gifts, gratuities, or bribes.

Rostenkowski and at least six other members used the HPO to skirt a law against receiving campaign checks in their offices. They opened post office boxes at U.S. Postal Service facilities at Union Station or Brentwood near the Capitol. HPO staffers obligingly picked up the campaign checks at the post office boxes and ferried them to the members' offices. Technically, the congressmen might argue, the checks were not received at their congressional offices but merely arrived there by courier. This is the sort of ingenuity that perpetually defeats the goo goos.

Rota and his officers bemoaned the avalanche of mail they were deputed to process, from 250 million to 500 million pieces a year. This was typical bureaucratic inflation of self-importance to gain more funding. The U.S. Postal Service set the figure at 30 million to 50 million, in itself an impressive number for 435 lawmakers. The average member received 250 letters a day and mailed out thousands. These extravagant franks were another device of the incumbent-protection system which helped Democrats control Congress for forty years.

The post office scandal that destroyed Rostenkowski caused real discomfort in the elite media. Unlike the Abscam grafters or the Keating Five senators or the House bank check bouncers or the savings and loan sellouts or the scattered convicted bribe takers or the various sexual miscreants in Congress, Rosty enjoyed the media's affection. Danny had his faults; he could be a bully, but surely he was not a petty thief? Washington scandals usually reach a point of critical mass when the media turn on the subject like a pack of dogs, saying they knew the truth all along, but even when Rostenkowski was indicted the elite media openly mourned.

The House as an institution went haywire trying to handle the scandal. The HPO probe was revealed in late January and early February 1992 by the *Washington Times*, a conservative newspaper that considers itself an antipode to the liberal *Post*. The *Times* reports implied that the Democratic leadership tried to shut the investigation down. The Republican reaction was predictable. Pressured, Foley assigned the Administration Committee to launch an HPO inquiry.

The scandal took a human toll even before the investigations got very far. The sergeant at arms, another officer nominally elected by the House but hired by the leadership, was Jack Russ, forty-six, a Mississippian who left his gas-station business to become a part-time House doorman and then chief page. Named sergeant at arms in 1983, a favorite of Rostenkowski, Coelho, and Wright, he was in charge of the Capitol police and the House bank and incidentally gave members their monthly paychecks. Not only did he countenance members' rubber checks at the House bank, but he bounced his own checks there. Foley, not a Russ patron, told him in 1989 to end the check bouncing, but he did not, to the eventual dismay of Foley and many others.

Early in 1992, Russ was shot in the face. He told police he was walking his dog on Capitol Hill at night when he was mugged by two men, one of whom put a gun in his mouth, while the other grabbed his wallet and Rolex watch, then shot him through the left cheek. Police found no suspects, gun, or bullet.[17]

On 12 March, Russ resigned. On 19 March, Rota resigned. On 20 March Rostenkowski offered to pay Rota's legal defense bills. "Remember, I always got my stamps"—stamps, not cash—Rosty told him, according to the eventual indictments. His administrative assistant and scheduler, Virginia Fletcher, allegedly drove Rota to a pay phone in Virginia to call the chairman to elude possible bugs on Washington phones.

Fletcher, then forty-seven, who often greeted callers to her boss with a cheery, "Why, he was going to call you!" had been constrained to give up a sideline business the year before. She had worked for Rosty since 1963 and in 1987 started selling clothing as a home-based fashion consultant in the manner by which Tupperware is sold. Financial disclosure forms showed she had made $93,054 over five years. She sold to friends, fellow staffers, and women tax lobbyists with business before the committee. In 1991 Rosty told her, look, some people might say you are capitalizing on your relationship with me. She quit selling clothes, and Rosty increased her salary to make up for the loss.

On 9 April, amid a typical partisan uproar following the disclosure that Foley's wife and chief of staff, Heather, had been called to testify before the grand jury, the House voted to put nonlegislative services under a professional administrator, supposedly ending patronage. On 17 April, the chief postal clerk was indicted for possession of cocaine and concealment of embezzlement.

On 6 May, sealed subpoenas were issued for six years of the office expense records of Rostenkowski and Pennsylvania Representatives Joseph Kolter and Austin J. Murphy (from whose district Rota came). On 14 May, the subpoenas were made public and Republicans screamed to Foley, why are we being kept in the dark?

Later that month, James C. Smith, the HPO supervisor of accounts, implicated the three congressmen in a cash-for-stamps scheme. A Rosty patronage hire, Smith was a friend of Virginia Fletcher and decorated the office Christmas tree every year in 2111 Rayburn. Smith said he gave cash to Rota, who gave it to the three members. "That's ridiculous," Rostenkowski snorted.[18] Smith was called before the grand jury. Rosty and the two Pennsylvanians then personally were subpoenaed to testify.

On 22 July, a deadlocked Administration Committee issued separate reports on the postal mess. Witch hunt! cried Democrats. Cover-up! cried Republicans. Rostenkowski claimed total exoneration. Republicans said the case was far from closed—key witnesses would not testify.

The House voted 414–0 to turn over the Administration Committee's task force records to the Justice Department and the House ethics committee (formally, the Committee on Standards of Official Conduct), but the House did not even consider making the task force materials public. The House protects its own.

Rostenkowski refused to testify before the grand jury, asserting his Fifth Amendment right against self-incrimination and denouncing a "fishing expedition and political witch hunt." Kolter, Murphy, Rota, Smith, and the HPO chief of staff, Joanna G. O'Rourke, also refused to testify.

The press went to the House clerk, pored over voluminous Statements of Disbursement—the House would not computerize or simplify them—and reported that Rostenkowski was the champ, just as he always was with speaking fees, buying $24,776 in stamps over six years. "I mail a lot . . . Overseas mail, you've got to put stamps on," he explained.[19]

In September, Chief of Staff O'Rourke was charged with misusing public resources, the Justice Department's first clear indication that post office favors for congressmen might have involved congressmen in criminal offenses. When the media understood that the post office scandal tracked the bank scandal, with many fewer miscreants but with a lord of the House under suspicion, Rosty was dogged, every step he took, by concentric circles of junior media members with boom mikes and video cameras—surely one of the worst ordeals the country inflicts on high officials engulfed by scandal. Senior media members do not deign to perform this "body watch." Rosty, a natural talker, was constrained by his lawyers to shut up, in itself probably an ordeal for him. Democratic whips at their weekly meetings started noticing that he was skipping them, likewise the monthly luncheons of the Illinois delegation. Rostenkowski scarcely troubled himself to campaign for reelection.

On 3 November, Rostenkowski was reelected over a Republican nobody, a Bosnian immigrant and small businessman who listed his ballot name as Elias R. "Non-Incumbent" Zenkich. Zenkich spent all of eighty-three thousand dollars and held Rosty to 57 percent of the vote. Again the political establishment congratulated itself on Rosty's permanence. Shrewder pols noticed that 43 percent of the district's Democrats did not want Rosty even against an unpopular goo goo, Simpson, and 43 percent of the electorate did not want him even against a Republican joke, Zenkich. Further, underscoring the district's erosion of automatic Democratic voting, Clinton carried the district with just 51 percent.

Bill Clinton unseated President Bush. The Illinois primary had been critical to his clinching the Democratic nomination; his state chairman was Bill Daley, who incidentally was on the board of Rosty's America's Leaders PAC, and top aides to Rich Daley had helped run Clinton's campaign. Clinton courted and flattered Rostenkowski much as Rostenkowski had courted and flattered his mentors Dick Daley, Hale Boggs, and Lyndon Johnson. Clinton saw Rostenkowski as the thaumaturge for national health care just as he had been for tax reform.

On 13 December, the *Chicago Sun-Times* swung the first of its many hammers against Rosty, reporting that since 1986 he had paid himself and his sisters seventy-three thousand dollars in rent from his campaign fund for an office in a storefront owned by the family at the rear of the family home. The office appeared to be a mail drop and nothing more.

Enraged, Rosty invited two local TV stations to tour the office but refused entry to the *Sun-Times*. A reporter for the paper knocked on his door and asked to gain entrance. He angrily shoved her twice.[20] She was pregnant. Perhaps her winter coat concealed the condition. In any case the incident was not good public relations. Rosty had called the cops when she and a photographer drove up and parked on Noble Street. A squad car arrived and asked the reporter and photographer for identification. The TV cameras that day shot what appeared to be a storage room.

On 21 December, the paper published a letter from Rosty in which he stated, "[M]y staff and I have spent many hours in an honest effort to respond to insatiable demands from the *Sun-Times*." This was incorrect. Since 11 September, reporters had tried to interview him, with the payoff of one brief phone conversation on 9 December. The letter continued, "The *Sun-Times* has created a circus of suspicion and sensationalism and would like me to perform as a trained bear."

He was no trained bear, but he was still Mr. Chairman. "Several times a week," he said, "I respond to requests from the [incoming] Clinton administration on issues of tax, economic or health policy in an effort to help the new administration create a program that will benefit the American people."[21]

In Washington, U.S. Attorney Jay B. Stephens read the paper's account of Rostenkowski's phony office with interest. He referred it to the grand jury.

Early in 1992, the leadership had enlisted Rostenkowski once again to push a tax bill he did not believe in. Bush, in his State of the Union speech, proposed yet another cap-gains cut, along with accelerated depreciation for new business investment and measures to promote home buying. In a gambit of election-year politics, Bush challenged Congress to pass his plan by 20 March. Rosty craftily had Gephardt introduce the Bush plan at once, just to demonstrate that it would not attract Republican votes. Meanwhile, Democrats drew up their own standard soak-the-rich tax bill.

Funny thing was, the Democratic bill did not attract Democratic votes either. Chronic deficits and the 1991 recession had dissolved ideological lines over budget policy, even as the partisan rhetoric grew harsher. The leadership had to struggle to win Democratic votes to impose higher taxes on the rich to finance a tax cut for the middle class. Redistributionist "fairness" no longer was the ruling rubric for the party; members were bending toward the "economic growth" rubric. After all, Democrats and Republicans alike were drinking from the same PAC cups. Hours before the scheduled vote on the bill on 27 February, the whips told the leadership they could not assemble a majority.

The leadership leaned on members hard, arguing that House Democrats could not trample on their party's election-year banner of tax cuts for the middle class. Rosty offered a substitute amendment, with sweeteners for the real estate industry and other parts of the economy, which narrowly carried, 221–210. This was perhaps the last legislative coup that Rosty pulled off. The scandal was chipping away at his time and his effectiveness.

In terms of tax policy, it hardly mattered. The Democratic bill was designed to draw a Bush veto, and it did. That fall, Clinton campaigned on a middle-class tax cut plank, but he did not mean it.

With Clinton's election Mr. Chairman was delighted with the prospect of working with a Democratic president after twelve years of Republican presidencies. Clinton promised not only national health care but head-on tackles of the tax, deficit, and budget problems. "I'll do my damnedest to see that he succeeds," Rosty said.[22] In December Clinton removed himself from Little Rock conferences long enough to appear with Danny in his Chicago district.

After a president takes the oath of office, he slips inside the Capitol for a private lunch with the leaders of Congress before launching the inaugural parade. At his first such luncheon, Clinton pointed to Rosty and told LaVerne, "He's my man."[23]

Still the scandal cut at Rosty's innards. He told an interviewer, "My stomach is hamburger. What's next? They're sprinkling this so-called infield with subpoenas. Thirty-four years in public service, and some ya-hoo in the post office is saying you took money. I never even thought of those things." [24] The record shows that he did. Soon he was telling his young friend Tom Downey, with pain arising from fathoms, "They've sub-poenaed my children!" [25]

Four days after Clinton's 20 January inaugural, the *Sun-Times* slammed Rostenkowski again. The reporting team of Chuck Neubauer and Mark Brown, assisted by Michael Briggs in the paper's Washington bureau, set the pace for national reporting on the Rostenkowski scandal from 1992 to 1994. Neubauer and Brown revealed that Rostenkowski had leased three vehicles from a north suburban car dealer with taxpayer funds and, when the leases expired, took personal ownership of the vehicles. The insurance was paid by the congressman's campaign committee, although the com-mittee did not own or lease any cars.

In Washington, U.S. Attorney Jay B. Stephens read the paper's account of the car scams with interest. He referred it to the grand jury.

Also in January, the *Washington Post* reported that the IRS was under-taking a "net worth" investigation of Rosty's lavish lifestyle. He was con-fronting not just embezzlement charges on the stamp scams but, down the road, possible tax evasion and racketeering charges. Rosty did his best to keep up his normal bluster and confidence. Shortly before Clinton's inau-guration he threw a bash at a Chicago steakhouse, roistering with such as Eddie Vrdolyak, Terry Gabinski, and members of the city's cafe society. Later when House Democrats held their annual retreat, which Rosty usu-ally skipped as an affair for junior members and beneath him, he showed up at Johns Hopkins University in Baltimore, joined the conga line, and then climbed upon a chair and "conducted" the dance music. [26]

Bill Daley marveled, "He works, he goes to dinner, he eats fifteen-ounce steaks five nights a week. You wonder why the guy's alive. That's all he does." [27] This is conjecture, but perhaps Rostenkowski was buoyed be-cause he had acquired some reasons for optimism that the case would be dropped.

Prosecutor Stephens had grown up on an Iowa farm, was an underling for the Watergate prosecution, and had been appointed U.S. attorney for the District of Columbia by Reagan in 1988. He set up a public corruption unit that nailed Washington Mayor Marion S. Barry Jr. in a drug sting.

Stephens observed that Barry, congressmen, and other public officials under investigation tended to regard criminal proceedings as a dimension of politics, a political problem to be overcome with political methods. As a prosecutor, Stephens was not supposed to respond in kind, though he had political ambitions himself and did not always resist the temptation.

Stephens' HPO case followed standard procedure. His lawyers would warn witnesses that they should "flip"—courthouse jargon for pleading guilty to lesser charges and cooperating with the investigation in exchange for leniency—because their protector, the big fish, was going down. The federal lawyers started hearing from witnesses that they had no need to cooperate because within three months this case would be shut down. How do you know that? the lawyers asked. Don't worry, we know. There were rumors, never proven, about calls from White House aides to Webb Hubbell, the number-three official at Justice and a former law partner of Hillary Rodham Clinton, concerning the Rostenkowski case.

On 23 March, Attorney General Janet Reno held her first news conference and announced the summary firing of all ninety-three U.S. attorneys. Whenever the White House changes parties, the new president installs his own U.S. attorneys, but the process normally takes months or years as pending cases are concluded and recruits are sought. This has nothing to do with Rostenkowski, Reno insisted. Cynical Washington and cynical Chicago believed otherwise. So did Stephens, who complained in the *Washington Post* that his ouster could disrupt a case on the verge of "a critical decision" concerning "allegations of financial fraud involving Mr. Rostenkowski." Other Republicans suggested that Reno's move was aimed not just at Stephens but also at a U.S. attorney in Little Rock inclined to pursue the Whitewater matter.

The chairman apparently had at least a temporary reprieve and could be counted on to push Clinton's deficit-reduction package. The media as one called it "a bold plan"—headlines everywhere proclaimed a "bold plan," but it was not. It was a hodgepodge of tax increases, which would restrain the economy; spending reductions, which also according to Keynesian theory would restrain the economy; and spending increases, which would stimulate the economy, inflate the deficit, and withal keep the pork flowing. Previous presidents had done the same but not on Clinton's scale.

Senator Daniel P. "Pat" Moynihan was the new chair of Senate Finance, and reporters were amused by the Pat and Danny duo. They wrote profiles matching the New York intellectual and the Chicago ward boss and exchanged the joke that Moynihan had written more books than Rosty had read.

Rosty always called the senator "Dan," not "Pat," explaining, "How can a Dan whose name is Dan view another Dan as though that wasn't his name?" Moynihan asked a House member to "tell him my name is Pat. He can remember an Irish name, for heaven's sake."[28] Better, perhaps, than Moynihan understood.

Actually, the two were not enemies. Moynihan was a Harvard savant but also a big-city liberal politician. They had fought over a tax break that benefited art museums in the 1980s, and then Moynihan helped open the pork barrel for repaving the Kennedy Expressway in time for Rosty's 1992 primary. A grateful Rosty then gave Pat the arts tax break.

In March Rosty took Ways and Means to a retreat in Austin, Texas, to discuss the Clinton package. The committee was a new creature. Rosty's pals Russo and Downey had been defeated for reelection; indeed, there were fourteen departures through defeat, retirement, or candidacies for the Senate. The spine of the committee, Democrats at the middle level of seniority, was gone. Rosty looked for new members who would stick with him and cast the tough votes and found this species was dying out.

Jim Traficant of Ohio sought a seat and enlisted, of all people, Chicago Bears coach Mike Ditka to lobby Rosty for him. Traficant and Ditka had played football together at the University of Pittsburgh. "Over my dead body," said Rosty.[29] In time he assembled a panel of loyalists, not mavericks such as Traficant, but the committee was not combat tested.

In May, shortly before the committee vote on Clinton's plan, the president, Rosty, and Bill Daley had dinner at a Chicago restaurant. Clinton had recruited Daley to push the North American Free Trade Agreement through Congress, a consolation prize after Clinton had falsely promised the brothers Daley that Bill would be secretary of transportation. The mood at the dinner was good humored and optimistic. Ways and Means passed the budget plan 24–14 along straight party lines.

Later that month, the House passed the Clinton package, 219–213. In June the Senate passed a somewhat different bill, 50–49. In both cases, not a single Republican voted aye, the first time in memory a major budget bill received zero bipartisan support. Presumably Rostenkowski and Moynihan would cut the necessary deals in the conference committee in the fall, but in the meantime the Chicagoan hoped to turn his legislative skills to national health care.

On 19 July, Rota flipped. This was disastrous news for Rostenkowski, House Democrats, and Clinton. It meant an indictment of Rostenkowski was inevitable, just a matter of time. Then Rostenkowski would have to relinquish his chair, either as required under House Democratic rules or as a provision that Justice surely would demand under any plea bargain. The interim U.S. attorney, J. Ramsey Johnson, obviously had not softened the investigation. Perhaps Rosty had followed the sad pattern of Jim Wright and so many others, hanging on to a feeling of invulnerability and indispensability, viewing the investigation as an extension of politics more than of criminal justice.

Rota pleaded guilty to one count of conspiracy and two counts of embezzlement for helping members pilfer cash through stamp scams. The Justice Department said $21,300 was taken by a member identified only as "Congressman A," but clearly Rostenkowski, and $9,300 by "Congressman B," clearly Kolter. Murphy was not charged.

With courage and audacity, Rosty carried on as usual. The next day he and Moynihan lunched with Clinton, and the president made a point of inviting in the cameras. That night Stephens appeared on ABC's *Nightline* to discuss the case, renewing his charge that the White House had stalled it. This was broadly regarded as bad form, and Stephens ended up not running for the Senate in Virginia after all.

The House was crestfallen on both sides of the aisle. Bob Michel said, "By golly, I've known the guy for more than twenty-five years. I can't believe he'd do any such thing. It's just not like our Danny." [30] Jack Brooks of Texas, like Rosty a man of the 1950s more than the 1990s, told a female reporter, "It's just a cloud. It's not a rain cloud, honey. It's a light cloud." [31] A tax lobbyist said, "If the headlines read, 'Rosty carrying Madonna's baby,' it couldn't be more off the wall." [32]

A light cloud or no, the House soon fell into partisan uproar. On 22 July, amid much shouting on the floor, the GOP accused Democrats of concealing embezzlement and demanded the release of the 1992 Administration Committee transcripts. The Gingrich strategy was to invalidate the entire Democratic Washington establishment as corrupt, and Democrats thoughtfully gave him lots of ammunition. Prosecutors, mindful that Oliver North's conviction was voided by publicity from the Iran-contra hearings, asked to keep the records sealed. The House so voted, mostly along party lines.

Rosty had other concerns. On 23 July, his office tracked down Robert S. Bennett in Boston at the college orientation of a daughter. Bennett caught the next flight to Washington. Late that night, he and his partner Carl Rauh were hired as Rosty's new legal defense team. Rosty had fired his previous lawyers, Stanley M. Brand, Abbe Lowell, and Judah Best.

Brand, former chief counsel for the House, and his partner Lowell specialized in ethics cases. Best had brokered the plea bargain for Vice President Spiro Agnew in 1973. They were first-rate lawyers but inexpert in media politics; their advice was, keep your mouth shut and you won't get in more trouble. Bennett was as savvy, tough, and high-priced as Washington litigators came. His clients included former Defense Secretary Caspar W. Weinberger, an Iran-contra defendant, and Democratic elder statesman Clark Clifford, snared in a banking scandal. Bennett incidentally was the brother of social conservative William Bennett, Reagan-Bush cabinet officer and compiler of the best-selling *Book of Virtues*.

The day after he was hired, Bennett had Rosty appear before the cameras to declare that he had committed no crime. He read a statement and took no questions. Two days later Clinton appeared at a Democratic funder in Chicago and declared once again that he needed Rosty at his side, prompting a standing ovation.

By now the media were riding to hounds. The *New York Times* editorially called on Rostenkowski to step down as chairman. In Chicago, the *Tribune* disclosed that two of Rosty's daughters had paid jobs at the Chicago Board of Trade at the same time they worked as flight attendants. At the *Sun-Times*, editors were sensitive to criticism that they were harassing a giant over peccadillos. They assigned Neubauer and Brown to tabulate just how much money Rostenkowski allegedly had stolen.

Their report on 25 July was headlined, "$600,000 in Questions." The particulars: $76,843 in stamp purchases since 1978; $141,440 since 1987 in leases, expenses, and insurance for vehicles to which he eventually acquired title; $73,000 in rents for a phony Noble Street campaign office owned by him and his sisters; and $329,350 in rents since 1970 for family-owned storefronts at 2148-50 North Damen, offices for the congressman, Gabinski, and the ward Democratic headquarters. As it turned out, the $600,000 estimate was conservative.

On 1 August, Gayle Rosten was pulled over by Chicago police for driving through a stop sign. As the officers approached, the occupants of the car were "fidgety," they said. A packet of white powder fell from between the front seat passenger's knees. Rosten then shoved something into her waistband. After the ensuing search, she and her two passengers were charged with possession of cocaine. On 1 October, a Cook County judge without explanation dismissed charges against all three.

Also in October, Eric H. Holder Jr. was sworn in as the new U.S. attorney for the District of Columbia. Rostenkowski's office payroll records were subpoenaed; some turned out to be missing. Kolter was indicted for stealing more than forty thousand dollars in stamp and stationery purchases.

On 5 November, a Cook County grand jury reinstated charges against Gayle Rosten. Rosten was scheduled to be arraigned on 18 November, but she was out of town on her airline job. In Lake County, a judge extended the term of her probation by six months. On 12 April 1994, a Cook County judge ruled that police had had no probable cause to stop Rosten's car the previous August. That had the effect of voiding the drug charges. On 5 May, the charges formally were dropped. The Republican state's attorney's office did not appeal.

Rostenkowski was laboring to keep up appearances on Clinton's health plan, gaveling hearings to order in September 1993. He put up a brave front, but legal fees for himself and his associates, including Virginia Fletcher and Nancy Panzke, who were granted immunity from prosecution and thus compelled to testify, were depleting his campaign funds. Meanwhile, he faced a threatening March 1994 Democratic primary. There was talk that he would retire to fight the charges full time, but he needed the title of *Mr. Chairman* to leverage contributions. In August he had set up a legal defense fund with James Healey, a former longtime aide whose father had served with Rosty on the Commerce Committee in the early 1960s, as coordinator. Rosty's net worth might have exceeded $2 million—

ambiguous disclosure forms do not permit a more exact figure—but lawyers could consume that and more—again, surely one of the worst penalties the culture inflicts on public figures engulfed by scandal. Could he not leave an estate for his girls? The Justice Department was saying he was a bird that flew high and came down to drink from an ethical cesspool. And yet observers of the health care hearings might have thought he was Mr. Chairman, unmolested.

In December the *Sun-Times* revealed that Rostenkowski's office payroll was inspirited by "ghosts," employees who did not show up for work. His pal Tom Downey took him out to see a movie, *In the Line of Fire*, with Clint Eastwood as a Secret Service agent guarding the president. Rosty had always identified with movie tough guys such as John Wayne and Clint Eastwood—once, asked if he wanted be mayor, he said he would rather be John Wayne. Downey drove him back to the Junkyard; they parked and talked about Washington, how it had changed, how buildings had come and gone, statesmen had come but mostly gone. Even a young guy such as Downey could see it. Suddenly, Rosty blurted out, "Jesus, Tom, this is awful, it's killing me. When I go to bed I think of, first of all, my image in the future. What are they gonna say about Danny Rostenkowski?"[33]

What are they gonna say about Danny?

Hillary Rodham Clinton flattered him, joked that, as a native of suburban Park Ridge, she was now his constituent in the new Fifth District. She concluded phone calls by saying, "I love you, Danny." During his 1994 primary battle, she offered to stand by and fly in to campaign for him at a moment's notice, if he thought it would help.[34] She was not needed because her husband did the job.

A BLADDER FULL OF WIND

"Your might," said she, "is scarce a thing to dread;
"For power of every mortal man but is
"Like to a bladder full of wind, ywis.
"For with a needle's point, when it is blown,
"Prick it, and all the pride of it comes down."

— Chaucer, "Second Nun's Tale," *Canterbury Tales*

THE culture of mass media has so constricted attention span and memory that an effort is needed now to recall what a disaster, what a fiasco and blunder and misbegotten failure the Clinton health plan actually was. Whatever its substantive merits, it was presented in a form sure to be spurned by Congress, even a Democratic one.

Clinton assumed, not foolishly, that congressmen would love to brag in their retirement about how they had created universal health insurance just as their predecessors had created Social Security and Medicare. But as a small-state governor, Clinton did not understand the modern Congress. The institutions of party and congressional discipline had been displaced by media politics and interest group PACs. Employers did not want mandated health payments, doctors did not want cost controls, insurers did not want to be nationalized, and their PAC beneficiaries, Republicans and Democrats alike, did not want to cross them.

In relying on Rostenkowski, Clinton and his wife overvalued a personality against institutions. The "reform" president thought he needed a machine politician to pass his bill. The tax code is so arcane that Rosty could cut the internal congressional deals to rewrite it. Health care, though, presses on everyone directly and tactically. The lobbies were armed and blazing away long before the Clintons could draft a bill. Not even Rosty at the height of his powers, his legal problems aside, could have passed their monstrosity through the House.

The health care industry's lobbies are not monolithic, but Mrs. Clinton in effect made them so by excluding them from the construction of the White House plan through most of 1993. The president announced on 25 January that his wife would head a panel to draft legislation. Rosty, who sometimes called the Clintons "the kids," muttered, "I couldn't do that to my wife."[1] Mrs. Clinton reasoned that the medical-industrial complex had invented the present, intolerable system and therefore could not be trusted to reinvent it. She and the Clintons' friend and policy adviser Ira Magaziner fashioned the White House plan while consistently blowing self-imposed deadlines for its release.

Magaziner liked to advise congressmen that he did not know political process but he could tell them about policy. This was an insult. Congressmen understood that process and policy are conjoined twins. Only (in Washington jargon) "policy wonks" and "propeller heads" thought they were separate. Capitol Hill took to calling Magaziner "The Iratollah."

Still, in 1993 the notion was in the air that national health care was an idea whose time at last had come. Early in 1992 President Bush, documenting once again his bedrock faith in manipulations of the tax code to produce desired social ends, had proposed a scheme of tax credits and deductions to make medical care affordable for everyone. The Democratic Congress, sensing a recapture of the White House, never even considered it. Some of the GOP high command kept telling Bush the issue was a loser for Republicans and he should ignore it anyway. He could not possibly outbid Democrats on social welfare. The media focused the issue through the convenient Republican-versus-Democrat lens, slighting the news that both parties now were more or less creatures of K Street lobbies and law firms.

Early in 1993, Mrs. Clinton took Magaziner to visit Rosty on the Hill. She said her husband would be washed up politically if he failed to enact health care in his first year. The chairman was the man, they couldn't do it without him, and so forth. Rosty told her to her face to fire Magaziner. Also, she needed to sit down with her adversaries such as David Bromberg, longtime lobbyist for the Federation of American Health Systems. After this session Rosty called his "Rosty's Rotunda" pal Bromberg and told him to expect a call from Hillary. But Mrs. Clinton did not take the chairman's advice.[2] That call was not placed until August, and then it was an invitation, rejected, for Bromberg to join the president at a PR stunt.

The day after Clinton was elected, Bromberg had retained lawyer/lobbyist Thomas Hale Boggs to help him combat national health. Bromberg and Boggs are Washington types. Boggs is the son of Rosty's old mentor Hale Boggs and the brother of Cokie Roberts, television newscaster and wife of pundit Steven V. Roberts, former editor of the *Harvard Crimson*; the couple are members of political journalism's royalty. Bromberg is an ambulatory stereotype of the fast-talking, hustling New Yorker. Every other year he and his wife staged a "scavenger hunt" party in which a dozen or more power couples whipped around the city in limousines provided by the hosts, clutching whimsical clues to whimsical "treasures." Such capering illustrates official Washington in its small-town, frat-boy and sorority-gal mode.

Rostenkowski shook his head. "Hillary is a very intelligent girl and a very aggressive young lady," he said. "But she and Bill Clinton had no idea how to use the power of the president and first lady"[3]—the same judgment he had made upon the ascension of another southern governor, Jimmy Carter.

Late in February, Magaziner went up the Hill to meet the key Democratic leaders and chairmen. The Clintons fancied they could pass deficit reduction and health care alike in 1993. "You guys don't get it," Rosty told Magaziner. "You can't send up another tax," meaning two tax increases in the same year, one for deficits, one for health care.[4] Magaziner took this as another irksome impediment of mere process.

Meanwhile, Rosty was cutting side deals with White House congressional liaison Howard Paster concerning deficit reduction. A member from Oklahoma had garnered enough votes to kill Clinton's new energy tax unless it were watered down. Give that oil-state congressman what he wants, Paster told Rosty in effect, or else I'm dead meat and then you will have to deal with Lloyd Bentsen.[5] Rosty got the point. Bentsen, now Clinton's treasury secretary, had been Rosty's enemy as chairman of Senate Finance. So Rosty caved to the Oklahoman's wishes.

But the "BTU" tax on British thermal units was still in trouble. One day Rosty, Paster, and Clinton lunched at the White House in Bentsen's absence. When Bentsen heard of this, he demanded that the president anoint him as the administration's sole voice on tax policy. After the usual Clinton fumbling, it came to pass. Clinton then horsewhipped House Democrats into voting for the BTU tax, only to abandon it abruptly when it encountered Senate opposition. House members who had put their careers on the line for the new president vowed never to be "BTU-ed" again. The mood of Washington was slowly, subtly turning against the Clintons and their health care castle in the clouds.

After the perils-of-Pauline passage of deficit reduction that summer, Clinton finally presented his health plan in a televised speech to a joint session on 22 September. Shortly before the speech Rosty went to the White House, where Clinton assured him the projected costs and savings were granite hard, the bean counters and propeller heads had crunched them time and again. Clinton's ensuing speech was a public relations smash, but, unlike Reagan's first-term PR triumphs, it did not translate into passing laws. The actual legislation was not introduced until 20 November. The administration explained the delay by saying the propeller heads had been still "scouring" the numbers.

Clinton never fronted the fundamental question: Is health care a right or a service? If a right, then we should go ahead and nationalize it. If a service, then private industry will rule. Clinton proposed, in effect, nationalizing private industry without taxes through nests of bureaucratic entities and imposed costs on businesses. He thought it was a moderate compromise. It was just a mess.

On 28 September, Rostenkowski made a fool of himself, as did others, by fawning all over Hillary Rodham Clinton during her testimony before Ways and Means. The middle-aged, white males behaved as though it were remarkable that a Yale-trained lawyer who had spent months boning up on the subject could speak knowledgeably about health care without whispering with aides or consulting notes, as male witnesses often did. Rosty gushed, "I think in the very near future, the president will be known as your husband. 'Who's that fellow? That's Hillary's husband.'"[6]

For her part, Mrs. Clinton displayed estimable political skills. "I am here as a mother, a wife, a daughter, a sister, a woman," she declared, and never lost a molecule of poise.[7] Rosty went out and told the press that health care would be passed.

The administration fanned out its mouthpieces across the county to pitch the plan. A meeting of Treasury official Roger Altman with the *Chicago Sun-Times* editorial board may be taken as typical. The Clinton-Magaziner plan was an impossibly, almost satirically complex scaffold of regional health alliances that would purchase massive collective policies with employers paying at least 80 percent of the premiums; thereby, universal coverage would be attained by 1999 without new taxes. The newspaper editors asked whether the alliances would not politicize health care. "It's just purchasing," Altman shrugged, "that's not political."[8] The Chicagoans exchanged glances. Somewhere, Dick Daley laughed heartily.

Rostenkowski was dishonest in the "thou shalt not steal" sense, but he was honest about policy. The Congressional Budget Office (CBO), a creation of the mid-1970s reforms, was assigned to do a nonpartisan, impartial numbers crunch. Some lawmakers, including Senator Kennedy, pressured the head of the CBO to tilt the numbers Clinton's way lest babies die, widows starve, and breadwinners suffer. Not Rosty; neither Moynihan. The two chairmen told CBO, give us real numbers, we'll worry about the politics.[9]

Fortified by Danny and Pat, the young CBO chief shot straight. CBO reported that the plan would be costlier at first than Clinton estimated, but, if implemented, it would lower national health costs in the long run.

Rostenkowski concluded that he needed to deliver a message to the thick-skulled Clintons. They held that the systemic savings wrought by the plan would finance it without a tax increase—a mirage. Rosty chose the vehicle of two speeches, first to the Health Insurance Association of America, meeting at a hotel near O'Hare Airport, then to the Harvard School of Public Health in Boston.

Just before his 19 January 1994 speech to the health insurers, Rosty met with seven Fifth District constituents in wheelchairs representing an advocacy group for the disabled. Five days earlier, they had stormed his North Damen Avenue office and were told to wait out on the sidewalk if they wanted to see their congressman. That is not a tempting invitation in Chicago in January even for the able-bodied. Rosty's campaign handlers told him he had to give them a photo op—no more arrogant brush-offs like the Copernicus Center fiasco. Seated on a metal folding chair with his overcoat across his lap in a North Side studio apartment, the chairman looked grim and uncomfortable. The advocates said he was a puppet of insurance industry PACs. No, I'm not, he said (and, really, he wasn't), and be assured that your input will be heard.

Then he went to the O'Hare Westin hotel and told the insurance industry it had better get with the program. Since 8 September this lobby had been airing "Harry and Louise" television commercials portraying a fictional couple delineating the evils of Clintoncare. That TV spot probably was as influential as the Bush campaign's Willie Horton ad of 1988. Rosty let them have it. "If you oppose the process, you will lose," he said, and in case they didn't understand, added, "Your messages are becoming the Willie Horton commercials of the health care campaign—they're increasing the heat of the debate without adding any light."

There followed quintessential Rosty-ness. "It is time to make a deal. But making a deal implies a willingness to compromise . . . It requires you to abandon the high-profile outside game you've become so good at and instead embrace an intense, but private, inside game." [10]

Ah: the handshake deal behind closed doors, the heart of Dick Daleyism—Clinton's regional alliances need not drive smaller insurers out of business, hell, no! In fact, if they would play ball, they could get government protections to survive well into the next century! Didn't they get it?

The president of this lobby of small and midsized insurers was Bill Gradison, like Bromberg, Boggs, and the Robertses, a Washington type. As an Ohio congressman, he had been the ranking Republican on Ways and Means. Now he lobbied his former colleagues, shared with them dinners, golf at Burning Tree, Redskins games at RFK Stadium. "We are ready to sit down with whomever he [Rostenkowski] designates," Gradison said cheerfully. [11] He did not worry too much. The "outside game" of television and PACs was shouldering aside the "inside game" of machinated deals.

For once in his career Rostenkowski felt compelled to wait until he was nominated for reelection before he called for a national tax increase. At his 22 April Harvard speech, he said, never mind what Clinton says, national health care will require a "broad tax increase." Not only that, but the regional health insurance purchasing alliances probably were dead. "I just don't see my colleagues embracing, quote unquote, larger government."[12] Why not, he wondered, expand the existing Medicare program to cover the uninsured? This was precisely what the Clintons did not want. Medicare reimbursed doctors and hospitals for medical bills without the cost-saving incentives of private insurance, which was pushing the nation into health maintenance organizations and other forms of so-called managed care. Rostenkowski was facing indictment on criminal charges, but he still was telling the president and his wife that he knew how to pass health care and they did not.

Back on 15 March, the health subcommittee of Ways and Means had voted out Clintoncare, the first congressional unit actually to vote on the plan. This was the same day as the Illinois primary.

The House Office Supply Service in the basement of the Longworth Building, known as the "stationery store," was not open to the public, and, typically, members listed their purchases only as a quarterly "Stationery Allowance Charged" amount, not itemized.

On 6 January, Rostenkowski sent the chairman of the House Administration Committee two checks totalling $64,728.62. On 1 February came another check for $17,366.54. The money reimbursed the stationery store for bowls, mugs, plates, china, crystal models of the Capitol, clocks, magnifying glasses, picture frames, chairs, cameras, albums, keychains, commemorative booklets, and luggage obtained from 1988 to 1993.

In a lengthy letter, Rostenkowski explained that the objects "were used as gifts to officials both abroad and in this country," to people who "counseled, assisted or supported my activities in public service," and to "charities in my district to use as items at fund-raising auctions." In the main, he said, "These are expenses that I would not have incurred but for the fact that I am a Member of Congress. Nevertheless, so that there can be no question about these items, I have decided that I personally will reimburse the House for them." Actually, about $46,000 of the money came from his campaign fund. "Out of an abundance of caution," he tacked on 10 percent to everything, the surcharge he "recently learned" was added to purchases for nonofficial purposes.[13]

All of these gewgaws formed, so to speak, a geometry of ego, tangible bunches of artifacts attesting to the importance of Mr. Chairman. He loved handing out stuff bearing his name. During his committeeman races, he used to shower the district with tiny Rosty-emblazoned sewing kits. After thirty-five years of golf outings, some of his friends had a whole shelf of golf sweaters embroidered with "Rosty" (provided by his campaign, not the House). His PAC spent thousands of dollars a year on these sweaters — no surprise; the committee also spent thousands in "consulting fees" to golf pros who accompanied him on the links.

Stephens had developed the stamps, rents, and cars aspects of the case. Holder was pursuing a new one, ripoffs from the stationery store. Perhaps Rosty and Bennett thought the reimbursements would keep that dog chained. However, returning stolen money is not a legal defense. Whatever the legal benefit, the checks belittled the chairman. Here was a man who wrote legislation worth billions, his friends said, being hectored over a lousy eighty-two grand worth of thingamajigs.

In February the *Sun-Times* disclosed that Rosty's stationery purchases had included handcrafted maple chairs with handwoven seats, with a stencil of the Capitol on the backrest and Rosty's name inscribed. The manufacturer suggested a retail value of $1,080; the government bought them wholesale at $379. Some of Rosty's friends in Chicago proudly acknowledged receiving these gifts; some refused to comment.[14] His true friends kept them in their offices even after he went to jail.

Gingrich went to Foley and demanded an ethics investigation. Foley set it in motion, but Justice once again asked the House to hold off. Gabinski's wife, Celeste, cited for contempt for refusing to testify before the grand jury, finally testified in mid-February. Rosty told reporters, "She was a great employee. I'm sorry I lost her when she got married." Then why, a reporter asked, did she stay on the payroll for five years after her 1987 marriage? "She didn't," he said, and walked away.[15] Rosty was paying legal bills for Terry and Celeste Gabinski, Fletcher, Panzke, and others. He was having difficulty focusing on reelection — he didn't install phones in the campaign office until a month before the primary. Clinton decided to give him a lift, egged on by David Axelrod, Rosty's and Daley's Chicago-based media consultant.

The machine is not ideological. The first principle of the machine is self-protection. The second is self-aggrandizement. The question for the machine was whether Rostenkowski would be indicted before or after the primary. The investigation, in the tradition of Washington probes of official wrongdoing, seemed to be taking forever. When indicted, or when he copped a plea, Rosty might resign forthwith, or else he might choose not to run for reelection to concentrate on his defense, or he might even run again. In any event, the machine needed to keep the Fifth District seat.

Simpson was running again. A forty-five-year-old state senator, John J. Cullerton, a member of a family that had held political offices in Chicago since 1881, and a member of a law firm that handled tax assessment appeals, announced his candidacy. Cullerton thought he couldn't lose. If Rosty dropped out, he could beat Simpson. If Rosty ran, Cullerton would cut into Simpson's vote, thus ensuring Rosty's renomination and earning the gratitude of the machine, which thereby would slate Cullerton for Congress in 1996, when Rosty likely would be retired or jailed.

Accordingly, Cullerton aimed his attacks against Simpson, not the incumbent. In fact, he claimed at first that he would leave the race should Rostenkowski decide to run. But then ambition got the best of him. Emboldened by polls showing Rosty's weakness, Cullerton started running against Rosty. Daley and the White House were angered.

On 28 February, Clinton stood at Rostenkowski's shoulder at a Chicago school and all but showered him with rose petals, stopping just short, for the sake of protocol, of an outright endorsement (presidents normally do not interfere in local primaries). Republican Governor Jim Edgar felt no such compunction and flatly endorsed Rosty. Clinton also dispatched his labor secretary to appear with Rosty and Mayor Daley at the opening of a new jobs center—Rosty brings home the bacon! was his campaign theme.

Simpson kept hammering away with a "Cancel Rostenkowski" campaign, a play on the stamp scandal. Although Rosty never engaged Simpson personally, his campaign put out the word that he was a liberal flake. Cullerton joined in with gusto.

In 1989 Simpson had published *The Politics of Compassion and Transformation*, which his opponents now derided as the ravings of a New Age whacko. Cullerton sent mailings to voters ridiculing the book. One, headlined "The Twilight Zone," featured the book jacket photo of Simpson standing in clerical robes (he is an ordained United Church of Christ minister) in front of a large "Nuclear Weapons Free Zone" sign. Another piece highlighted out-of-context quotes such as, "I tried various techniques of self-discovery from psychotherapy and Progoff Life Context Journal to past life regressions." Neither brochure mentioned Cullerton, except for the tiny "paid for by" bug required by law.

Simpson was not surprised to learn how rough and nasty Chicago politics can get, but he was dismayed at the lack of a one-on-one shot at Rostenkowski. "When they did the direct-mail attack on me so my [poll] numbers started dropping," he said, "Cullerton actually thought for a while there he could win. He then got over-enthusiastic for his own good." [16]

Simpson charged that Cullerton was an apprentice Rostenkowski, another backroom wheeler and dealer. He also tried without success to run on women's and seniors' rights, term limits, and other issues. But the only real issue was Rosty. In the end, Cullerton and Rostenkowski fired away at each other in TV ads while Simpson could afford only a few radio spots.

A week before the election, Rosty spoke at the Polish American Museum near his home. "Your support and your faith in me is more valuable than any political victory could be," he said, choking back tears. He added, "In the final analysis, the sum of any one person's life can be found in who their friends are . . . I say to myself, 'Danny, you're a lucky son-of-a-gun. You're a darn lucky son-of-a-gun.'" Mayor Daley was there; so was Governor Edgar. [17]

On 15 March, the Daley machine went pedal-to-the-metal for Rostenkowski, deploying as many as eight hundred precinct workers. Rosty helped his cause by spending $1,047,000. Cullerton spent $412,000. Simpson spent $261,000.

The vote: Rostenkowski 50 percent, Cullerton 30 percent, Simpson 14 percent. Two minor candidates got the rest. Bill and Hillary Clinton, Al Gore, and Jim Edgar made the traditional congratulatory phone calls to the winner.

And then there was the Republican primary. Despite Rosty's lackluster showing in the Democratic primary, Michael Patrick Flanagan's nomination for the GOP spot in November was regarded as a formality. "Feeble" is too strong a word for the Chicago Republican party. In the Democratic primary, 93,246 votes were cast (a relatively low turnout); in the Republican, 10,108.

Drawing unemployment benefits because his law practice was going nowhere, Flanagan had spent much of 1993 hanging out in neighborhood bars, playing darts. An old buddy from high school ROTC, Greg Liadis, and a few other pals joined him one night that summer at Ray's Chili and Suds on Lincoln Avenue. Liadis had just returned from a trip to Washington, where he was stunned by the immensity of the federal establishment. With a simile that would impress Chicagoans, he said, "The Department of Agriculture is three buildings that look like the Merchandise Mart." [18]

So while they tossed darts, the friends griped about Clinton and big government. Flanagan was the only lawyer, and somebody suggested he might do something about it, like maybe run for Congress. Two weeks after walking out of Ray's pub, Flanagan decided to run. The candidacy was kept quiet for a time, not that anybody would have noticed.

There was no Republican primary race to speak of, no debates, rallies, phone banks, polls, news conferences, or commercials. Flanagan had four opponents, including "Non-Incumbent" Zenkich and three other nobodies. They campaigned by visiting GOP ward committeemen—some of whom were ringers for the Democratic machine—and enlisting family and friends as volunteer workers.

The Fifth District was a mix of Anglos, Poles, Italians, Irish, Asians, and others; there were few blacks and the Hispanics were sliced off into a district gerrymandered for Gutierrez. The good Irish name of "Michael Patrick Flanagan" on the ballot no doubt attracted votes, even though the Irish composed only 15 percent of the district. Throughout Chicago, voters were accustomed to selecting Irish candidates—another legacy of Dick Daley and his predecessors.

Flanagan spent about five thousand dollars and won a plurality of 38 percent of the vote to 21 percent for Zenkich. Flanagan lived three blocks outside the district but moved in upon winning the nomination.

The morning after the primary, a reporter called the Cook County Republican headquarters seeking a phone number for Flanagan. The office did not have a number. The county chairman had never even met the guy. "He's the candidate in the Fifth, right? He's the congressional candidate, isn't he?" [19]

On 31 May, again with timing unhelpful to Simpson, Rostenkowski was indicted on seventeen felony counts. The depth and breadth of the charges surprised even his enemies.

Cop a plea, said counselor Bennett. They've got you. I can get you off with just six months in prison and a fine if you plead guilty to just one felony and resign from Congress. The fine would be $150,000, minus the $82,095 you already coughed up for the stationery store. Plus, they'll drop the cases against your friends and employees. This proposed deal was leaked to the *New York Times*, presumably to enhance the pressure on Rosty to acquiesce.

The managing editor of the *Sun-Times* was new to Chicago, unschooled in politics, and, like media executives all over the country, in awe of the *New York Times*. She demanded that the *Sun-Times* get the plea-bargain story. Neubauer, Brown, and others insisted it would not happen; Rosty did not have it in his makeup to plead out. The reporters prevailed after contentious internal debate.

U.S. Attorney Holder gave Rostenkowski and Bennett a deadline of 31 May—cop a plea by then, or take a sweeping indictment. With one week to go, Rosty presided over a health reform hearing, joined the leadership in a health care meeting with Clinton and then went out to dinner with pals, where he was his usual self, holding court and telling stories. Some left the dinner believing he would fight to the last unpersuaded juror.

On 3 May, Clinton had hired Bennett to defend him in a sexual harassment case brought by Paula Corbin Jones, a former Arkansas state employee. Republicans were not alone in their concern over the coloration this move put on the Rosty case. The president's personal lawyer was cutting a deal for a key congressman with the president's Justice Department. Rosty himself was not happy with Bennett's acquisition of that new client.

Rosty spent the final days huddled with family and friends. Friends such as Marty Russo urging him to go to trial probably did not understand all the goods that Justice had on him. They saw the problem as political more than criminal. On their side of the argument, the government's case was not unassailable. Parts of it could be challenged because statutes of limitation had expired, for one thing. For another, Rosty's aides, even those granted immunity, would stand by him. What was most important, Rosty could not bring himself to accept that he had committed felonies. He told

Russo, "Wait a minute. I didn't do this."[20] On 26 May Rosty and Bennett talked in private. Then Bennett called Holder and said, no deal.

On 30 May, a haggard, sad-faced Rosty issued a statement: "Federal prosecutors threaten to indict me if I fail to plead guilty to a series of crimes I did not commit. [They had demanded a plea to one count only.] I will not make any deals with them . . . I strongly believe that I am not guilty of these charges and will fight to regain my reputation in court."[21] Rostenkowski said he would give up the Ways and Means chair but seek vindication at the polls in November.

The next day, Holder, forty-three years old, a son of immigrants to Queens from Barbados, coolly and crisply professional, presented the charges at a news conference. "In essence," he said, "this indictment alleges that Congressman Rostenkowski used his elective office to perpetrate an extensive fraud on the American people . . . This is not, as some have suggested, a petty matter. This is conduct that was not ever acceptable."[22]

As a rule, the more charges that prosecutors throw at a defendant, the weaker their case; the fewer, the stronger. Multiple charges are a device to induce a plea bargain. But these seventeen charges were plangent with vivid specifics of wrongdoing. The plea bargain already had been spurned. Only a rare jury would acquit on all seventeen.

Holder said fourteen ghost workers were paid $529,200 over a twenty-one-year period for doing little or no official work while providing personal services for Rosty such as cutting the grass at his Wisconsin home or keeping the books at Confidence Insurance. The indictments listed the ghosts only by number, but the *Sun-Times* promptly named them in the next morning's editions.

Further, Justice charged Rostenkowski with $101,767 in a fraud to get seven personal vehicles disguised as "mobile district offices," with $1,800 in House-paid parking garage fees tossed in for good measure. Also, he was accused of pocketing $49,300 in stamps-for-cash scams and taking $42,200 in stationery store items. In total, the chairman allegedly misused $724,267. Of this sum, $668,000 came from taxpayers and $56,267 from campaign funds.[23]

The government leveled no charges on Rosty's practice of paying himself and family members rents for family-owned property. Nor did it accuse him of income tax evasion. Some, until they read the forty-eight-page indictment, took the latter omission as a sign of weakness in the government's case. Rather, it was a deliberate act to keep the trial in Washington. In a previous prosecution of a Louisiana congressman, the defendant exercised his right to be tried in the jurisdiction where his tax returns were filed, whereupon a hometown jury acquitted him. Holder was not about to let Rosty move the trial to Chicago.

The indictment highlighted the paradox of a big man who stole little dollars. Perhaps the explanation is simpler than Capitol casuists made it out to be. The pickings were easy; Rosty believed he was entitled to them, and nobody except a few goo goos had ever cared anyway. The principle had been laid down by Hinky Dink and Bathhouse John: Steal in small increments, and nobody gets hurt. And it isn't really stealing, anyway. It's all in the family.

Some of the ghost payroll money could be seen as favors dispensed by a machine godfather—for instance, $3,200 to help put Sulski's son through college. But for the most part, Rosty's use of ghosts seemed petty, abusive, tyrannical. Roger A. Kopacz, an electrical inspector, married Kristie Rosten in 1980. Before joining the family, Kopacz was required to hand over most of his $10,400 ghost pay to Rotenkowski as cash kickbacks. (The couple was divorced in 1990.)

In another specimen of machine money churning, the son of a state senator got $48,400 in ghost pay over three years while Rosty's daughters Stacy and Dawn received $48,000 from the senator's payroll. The arrangement was transitory. In 1984 the senator, James A. Nedza, was defeated for reelection as Hispanics took over his Thirty-first Ward. In 1987 Nedza was convicted of extortion, racketeering, and tax fraud.

Count six of the indictment accused Rostenkowski of obstructing justice by tampering with a witness. An employee of the House sergeant at arms had engraved brass plates and affixed them to fifty crystal models of the Capitol for Rosty to give away. The plates were engraved with the first names of the recipients, a word of sentiment such as "friendship," and the names of Danny and LaVerne. The chairman allegedly told the engraver not to reveal his work to investigators. This charge was deadly because federal sentencing guidelines require harsher punishments for obstruction convictions.

Rostenkowski made no comment. His Ways and Means press secretary left a message on the answering machine: "We have no statements to issue, we have no schedule, we have no bananas." Washington mourned the chairman's fate. Al Hunt of the *Wall Street Journal* said Washington "will not see his like again."[24] Russell Baker of the *New York Times* said he was "under indictment for everything from mopery to failing to wash the ring out of the bathtub."[25] Jon Margolis of the *Chicago Tribune* scorned the "'pygmies' trying to bring down a 'giant.'"[26] David S. Broder of the *Washington Post*, the most respected and respectable of the pundits, wept over his keyboard: "[T]he reaction is one more of tears than of anger. Maybe that's just a reflection of the stunted moral character many citizens impute to the capital. I prefer to think that it is Washington's appreciation of the rarity of people like Rostenkowski with a passion not just to win elections but to govern." Broder went on to praise Rosty's "statesmanship" in pressing President Bush on the 1990 budget deal.[27] In the Washington establishment, increasing taxes equates with statesmanship. Reducing spending does not equate with statesmanship.

A throwback who was caught in a time warp and did not keep up with changes in the rules—this was the received judgment. Although in many ways an anachronism, Rosty was more of an exemplar, an imago of what the rest of the country hated about Washington, the excesses and nuisances and abuses of big government and its celebrity masters. After his 1985 TV speech, Rosty became a kind of heartland hero for shooting straight on taxes. He looked like a guy sitting at the bar of the local VFW or American Legion hall. If you served in World War II or Korea, he looked like your gunnery sergeant. But now, ever scowling, grown fleshier and more arrogant, he looked like another entrenched and crooked politician.

As is common, the public disagreed with the punditry. A national Gallup poll taken 3–6 June showed that 47 percent considered the charges "very serious," not mere bending of the rules. A majority, 54 percent, thought that from "about half" to "nearly all" congressmen were "guilty of the same kind of corruption." A majority, 55 percent, also felt Rosty should have no influence over health-care reform while the charges were pending.

On 2 June, Rosty walked into Ways and Means and received a standing ovation, twice, from the committee. That same day, he fired Bennett. Two days later, he hired a Chicago lawyer, Dan K. Webb.

Jim Thompson had assembled a cadre of Republican federal prosecutors in Illinois. Every year, eight of the "Thompson Youth," who had gone on to top-drawer law firms or public offices, took a fishing trip to Canada or Costa Rica. The group included three former U.S. attorneys, among them Samuel K. Skinner, who became chief of staff to President Bush, and Webb. Webb ended up at Winston and Strawn, a golden Loop firm which had hired Thompson after he left the governor's office (and Walter Mondale after he left the vice presidency.) As U.S. attorney, Webb had put a string of Cook County judges in jail under the "Operation Greylord" sting of the 1980s. The presiding federal judge was another Thompson crony; he and Webb juggled court dates so their families could vacation together (an appeals court later frowned on this). As an assistant to the Iran-contra special prosecutor, Webb had pretty much destroyed the credibility of Oliver North. Webb had a boyish face and a diffident manner at trial that masked relentless drive and preparation. Now, at forty-eight, he was Rosty's defense attorney. "There are not going to be any deals," he said.[28]

Representative Sam Gibbons of Florida was no weakling. He had parachuted into France on D Day and had challenged Tip O'Neill for Speaker, which is one reason Tip wanted Rosty to take the Ways and Means chair over Gibbons in 1981. Gibbons had just returned from France for the fiftieth anniversary ceremonies for D Day when, thrilled, he took over the committee chair on 7 June. The gilded "Mr. Rostenkowski" nameplate was off the door, but Gibbon's nameplate was not yet affixed, nor did he have a key to H208. A staffer had to be summoned to open the door. Rosty emerged from the ensuing meeting to say, "Sam Gibbons is the chairman and I'll do everything I can to help him." He paused, smiled, and added, "*acting* chairman."[29] He fancied a restoration and continued to attend the leadership meetings. The prickly Gibbons was no deal maker, and Clinton lamented his ascension, but Clinton's health bill was in intensive care anyway.

Holder told the House, okay, go ahead and release your findings about the House post office now if you want. The House voted 399−2 for a GOP resolution to release the Administration Committee's transcripts from 1992. The 3,293 pages startled nobody. Mainly they delineated the HPO's eagerness to please Rosty, even covering his office phones when his staff was off at a party or stamping his name on calendars mailed to his constituents. In August the ethics committee decided once again not to investigate Rosty for fear of undercutting the court proceedings.

On 10 June, Rostenkowski was arraigned and pleaded not guilty. Webb filed motions to dismiss the indictments on constitutional separation-of-powers grounds—only the House could adjudicate alleged violations of its rules. This was a delaying tactic. A district judge rejected Webb's argument in October, and the Supreme Court threw out such a defense in another congressman's case early in 1995.

Rosty appeared on *Face the Nation* on CBS on 12 June and tried manfully to talk about health care while the moderator kept asking about the indictments. "You know, in Chicago," Rosty said, "we have a very unusual association with people that work for us, I mean, they're our friends as well, and I'm suggesting that my employees worked forty hours a week when they were on the payroll." [30]

During all this time, Senate Minority Leader Bob Dole probably was the critical figure for national health insurance, more than Rostenkowski, indictments or no. Clinton's claim to a historic presidency died not with a bang but a whimper. On 26 September Senate Majority Leader George Mitchell of Maine admitted the obvious. There would be no health bill. Neither body came within a country mile of voting on it.

The election race between Rostenkowski and Flanagan was one of the oddest in Chicago memory. Both candidates virtually vanished from the public stage. Presumably, Rosty was hoarding his funds to pay legal bills. Also, in the language of political consultants, it was feared that campaign publicity would only "drive up his negatives." It was not as though he needed to increase his name recognition. Thus his general election strategy was the opposite of his primary election strategy.

As for Republicans, they accepted the prevailing wisdom that voters loved pork so much they would hold their noses and vote for Rosty. The National Republican Congressional Campaign Committee, which funds candidates, wrote Flanagan off. Nor did any conservative front groups target the district, although Rosty became a poster boy for the national movement to limit congressional terms. The national pundits all said Rosty would be reelected. In the high traditions of punditry, none of them later examined how they got it so wrong or even confessed that they *were* wrong.

The campaign was a silent contest of generations as much as a contest of issues, including the ethics issue. Time was, Rosty was the youngest participant in machine conclaves. At a 1994 Rosty funder at Cubs' sportscaster Harry Caray's restaurant, a donor observed that, at fifty-three, he was the youngest in the room. Rostenkowski, born in 1928, was politically formed by the New Deal and World War II. Flanagan, born in 1962, was politically formed by the fall of Nixon in 1974, the fall of Saigon in 1975, and the humiliation of the Iran hostage crisis of 1979–80. The two candidates had vastly different attitudes toward the national government.

Flanagan was a lawyer but hardly a yuppie. The son of "Roosevelt Democrats," he spoke in the "dese-dem-and-dose" idiom of the Northwest Side. He was single, chubby, an unabashed chain-smoker, and nearly broke. Other than his army years, volunteer work at a local AIDS clinic was the whole of his record of public service. With his unfashionable, nerdy glasses and 1970s-style bushy moustache, he presented himself as an ordinary guy from the neighborhood, fed up with the rottenness in Washington.

Dutifully, Flanagan made the circuit of neighborhood coffees, civic club luncheons, and "free media" appearances on local public affairs programs. He attacked the excesses of big government but not Rostenkowski personally. He saw there was no need to spotlight his opponent's ethics problems—the media would handle that job.

Rosty stayed away from the media, paid or free. During the primary campaign, he put out ten mailings to voters, slickly printed in vivid blue, green, and red (prepared by Annunzio's son-in-law, a print-medium consultant). He sent out only one mailing against Flanagan. Its stark black cover with contrasting white and red type portrayed Flanagan as a dangerous, radical conservative. On the back, Rosty appealed for the chance to clear his name. One of Rosty's advisers called the low-profile campaign a high-risk strategy. Perhaps it was the wisest choice under the circumstances.

The *Tribune*, the dominant newspaper, endorsed Rostenkowski of course, but so did the *Sun-Times*, editorially sneering at its own reporters' revelations of the incumbent's thefts. Both papers said he was an indispensable civic asset. Rosty's performance at the *Sun-Times* editorial endorsement meeting was a virtuoso smash of charm and swagger as he spun stories about Dick and Lyndon. He simply wowed the editors.

Larry Horist, a combative, maverick conservative political consultant who advised Flanagan, turned the campaign. He perceived the vulnerability exposed by Rosty's defeat of a joke "Non-Incumbent" in 1992 by just fourteen points, followed by the fact that fully half the Democrats in the 1994 primary did not want him. The Flanagan campaign lacked money for professional polling, so Horist pressed for a telephone poll conducted by volunteers.

The results indicated that Rostenkowski was doomed. Through an Illinois congressman, Horist forwarded the poll to the National Republican Congressional Campaign Committee. The committee did not believe it, commissioned its own scientific poll, did not believe it, and commissioned another.

Convinced at last, the committee dropped $55,000 into the district for a last-minute Flanagan TV buy. The sum (the legal maximum) was not impressive, but the mere fact of its arrival made a media splash.

By the Friday before the Tuesday election, Democratic ward committeemen knew the race was lost. It showed in their faces and body language, though for the record they said otherwise. They had seen the private Democratic polls. Rostenkowski said after the election that his polling support once was as low as 29 percent and never exceeded 40 percent.[31]

In the final days, at the groceries and shopping malls and senior centers and block clubs of the Fifth District, Democratic precinct workers were nowhere in sight. The abdication of the machine remains somewhat mysterious still. Where were Rich Daley, Bill Daley, and their political mastermind, former state senator Jeremiah Joyce? Probably the explanation is that Rostenkowski personally was devastated by the indictments. "Jesus, this is awful, my stomach is hamburger." Jim Thompson said, "When the heart goes out of the candidate, the heart goes out of the organization."[32] Rosty suggested another reason—the machine had given up on its weak candidate for governor against Jim Edgar.

Flanagan spent $113,000 and won 54 percent of the vote. Rostenkowski spent $695,000—not a large amount next to his estimated $3,000,000 in legal fees—and got 46 percent of the vote. Flanagan was part of the Republican Risorgimento of 1994, which took control of the House for the first time since 1954.

On election night, Rostenkowski was dignified and stoic in defeat. At Flanagan's victory celebration, when supporters started jeering Rostenkowski, the congressman-elect scolded, in fine Milwaukee Avenue-ese, "Hey, nunna dat, nunna dat!"[33]

The congressman-elect moved into Rosty's own Junkyard in southwest Washington, renting from his defeated opponent in a move the media found hilarious, to the incomprehension of both men. "I'm working very hard to deflate this myth that he's an arrogant, overbearing son of a bitch," Flanagan said, "because he's not. I have found him to be affable. His advice was to take care of the people."[34] Soon Flanagan told a friend that he hated to turn on the lights in the apartment to see "the bright orange plastic chairs sprouting from the green rug," decor "right out of the 1960s."[35]

On 29 November, Rosty and Michel, who was retiring, cast their last votes in the House in favor of a General Agreement on Tariffs and Trade. In a farewell speech, Rosty said, "More than thirty years ago, I came to Washington with one goal in mind, to help govern by writing good law. It has been a great privilege to serve in the House, but I am especially proud to leave today with this vote. I wish you well and truly hope in the days ahead you [he meant Republicans] will put your minds first to the task of governing. That is why the American people send us here."[36]

Rostenkowski's campaign fund was down to its last $354,000. His legal defense fund raised and spent $1,400,000, with prominent industrialists such as Donald Trump and other celebrities donating the maximum of $5,000. (Incidentally, Rosty's defense fund raised more than the Clintons' Whitewater fund did.) Sitting on his desk were legal bills for at least $230,000 from ten law firms for his staffers and associates, plus his own tab approaching $400,000. "If I had spent half a million dollars more [on the campaign], maybe I would have lost by a smaller percentage," he reasoned. He received a federal pension of $96,462. But, "I don't think I have enough to cover [the legal bills]," he said.[37]

"I know that LaVerne will insist that I shave in the morning and put on a suit and tie and get out of the house," he added in remembrance of Joe Rusty. He set up Danross Associates Inc., consultants in "legislative and governmental affairs," working at first out of the North Michigan Avenue office of Michael Segal, head of Near North Insurance, former business partner of George Dunne, investor with Rosty in Wisconsin real estate, and all-around machine fixer. Later Rosty moved the office to his building on Damen Avenue and rented another in a Virginia suburb. Legally, an ex-congressman cannot lobby his former colleagues for a year, but he may consult. "I'm amazed that you can get paid for the advice that I was just giving away for absolutely nothing," Rosty said.[38] Government documents in the investigation of the Hotel Employees and Restaurant Employees International Union later indicated that union president Edward T. Hanley, an old Rostenkowski friend, had provided Danross a $50,000 consulting fee for a single memo.

On 13 December, James E. Nedza, son of the former state senator, was indicted for perjury and obstruction of justice in the investigation of Rostenkowski. In April 1995 Nedza copped a plea. The pressure on lesser figures to flip was escalating.

In October 1995, Rosty held a five-hundred-dollar-a-person defense funder at Galleria Marchetti in the newly fashionable River North area. Nearly all the Chicago establishment fixtures showed up. They believed Mr. Chairman had been railroaded out of office by overzealous prosecutors and the scandal-obsessed news media. Rosty was resolutely upbeat, but Jim Thompson felt a tangible sadness in the room. He thought, "Oh, my God, this is a terrible thing that is happening." He turned to a young associate at his side and said, "You'd better think about the lessons to be learned from all of this."[39] But neither Big Jim nor the associate was exactly sure of what the lessons were.

In his 1995 State of the Union address, President Clinton pronounced that the era of big government was over. Paddy Bauler, or Joe Rusty, or H. L. Mencken, or Will Rogers, or Lyndon Johnson, or Dick Daley, or Danny Rostenkowski might have laughed at this obvious falsehood and how seriously the clerisy took it.

Rostenkowski wrote letters to the editors of prominent newspapers, defending big government against Republican critiques and specifically his own running of Ways and Means and efforts to control entitlement spending. He was fashioning himself as an elder statesman, giving a speech at Yale, donating his archives to Loyola and receiving an honorary doctorate therefrom. He attended the opening of the *Chicago Tribune*'s new Washington bureau and was his old story-telling self. "I think it would have been terribly frustrating for me to be reelected and then to be powerless" in a GOP-controlled Congress, he rationalized.[40] Later he called a *Sun-Times* reporter to needle him, "you were wrong" about whether a provision he had slipped into a bill would save Chicago some O'Hare costs as he and Daley intended.[41]

He continued to employ Fletcher in Arlington and Panzke at the Damen Avenue office. The latter fielded calls from his former constituents asking favors of their congressman, ignorant that he was gone. Voters had wanted to chasten him but "I don't think anyone thought he'd really lose," she mused.[42] The head of Cook County Hospital openly grieved that, without Rosty, she had no clout to get grants for her AIDS clinic.

The legal process rumbled along. Rosty petitioned to move the trial to Chicago. Shortly after Nedza entered his plea bargain, another indictment came down. Robert L. Russo was accused of lying to the grand jury to cover up his ghost job. Russo had been granted immunity, but immunity is no protection against perjury. Next, Rosty took his motion to throw out the charges on constitutional grounds to the D.C. appellate court, which did not welcome it. In May he got a break when a Supreme Court ruling in a separate case narrowed the application of "concealing a material fact," which made up four of Rosty's seventeen counts. But in November, the motion to move the trial to Chicago was rejected.

Russo went on trial in Washington in late October. He was a full-time city Water Department worker who had lived next door to Rosty in an apartment owned by Rosty's family. From 1976 to 1987, he was paid ninety thousand dollars, supposedly to clean the Damen Avenue office, but the money really was for his wife, Irene, to clean Rosty's homes in the city and Wisconsin. Now fifty-eight, a resident of Wisconsin, suffering from Parkinson's disease and walking shakily with a cane, relying on a public defender because Rostenkowski stopped paying his legal bills, Russo was not an ideal witness for the defense. Neither were Roger Kopacz or Gayle Rosten.

First the government called Joanna Hojnowski, who actually did clean the Damen Avenue office, above which she lived, for $100 to $200 a month from 1971 to 1985. Informed that congressional records listed her 1978 annual rate of pay at $27,527, she slapped her hand to her forehead and said, "I've got hot flashes. Where did the money went? Somebody was getting rich on my account."[43]

Testimony revealed how Rostenkowski used Damen Avenue as a hiring hall. He would rotate relatives and neighborhood folks on and off the payroll for months at a time, sometimes collecting each worker's pay for the whole year while dribbling out cash to one and all. Hojnowski said she cashed her government checks at Panzke's request and handed her the cash. She put it in a drawer and gave her a portion of it. Panzke, granted immunity and not charged, said she kept records that matched Hojnowski's payments to the amount of her checks. The government did not dispute this.

Kopacz, who also had lived next door to Rostenkowski, told the court he did not know of anyone but the Russos who cleaned his former father-in-law's homes. Prosecutors slyly tried to bring up Kopacz's own ghost income, but Judge Norma Holloway Johnson ruled it irrelevant to Russo's case.

Gayle Rosten's ensuing testimony was confused and flustered. The flight attendant contradicted herself about the extent of the Russos' cleaning. She could not remember the name of her boss when she had a patronage job at O'Hare in the 1970s, whom she worked with at Damen Avenue in the 1980s, or whether she was paid by cash or check.

On 8 November, the jury found Russo guilty after two days of deliberations. He hugged Irene in the hallway while she wept. His was the tenth scalp taken by the Justice Department in what had started as a probe of a little skimming in the House post office. For the record they said otherwise, but Rostenkowski's lawyers were terribly discouraged by the Russo verdict. Unless he wanted to spend every nickel he owned on lawyers, Rosty had to think about copping a plea. Webb put out a feeler about a plea agreement.

In December Flanagan staged a press party at the Junkyard because so many reporters had asked to see it. No reporters showed up because they did not care any more. The Republicans already were losing the public relations war, forcing government shutdowns in budget confrontations with Clinton.

Also in December, Anthony J. "Busy Busy" De Tolve, a member of the old West Side Bloc related by marriage to Sam Giancana, who had served with Rosty in the Illinois General Assembly in the 1950s, died. His obituary was buried in the papers. The West Side Bloc hardly was remembered any more. Corruption these days was so much more sophisticated.

In February Rosty practiced spin control on "Larry King Live" on the Cable News Network, an almost compulsory rite for the publicly disgraced. He said: "Danny Rostenkowski, chairman of House Ways and Means Committee, walked into a room and was the most popular person and felt—felt that, you know, he was in charge. And then all of a sudden you get these allegations and you start to withdraw. So you—from the day that you get the bad press you start to become a prisoner."[44]

Outside the courthouse in Washington, a spring afternoon's rain fell. Rostenkowski, who did not have a hat, asked Webb, "Are we goofy enough to stand in the rain?" The answer was, "We have to." And out of the courthouse they plodded to front the ranks of video cameras and boom mikes on the sidewalk.[45]

Haltingly, with rain splattering the sheet of paper, Rosty read a statement: "I'd like to emphasize that I pled guilty to the least serious charges set forth in this indictment . . . I personally have come to accept the fact that sometimes one person gets singled out to be held up by law enforcement as an example . . . I realized I could not put my family, my former congressional employees, and my friends [pause, gulp] and supporters in Chicago through this trauma [pause, swallowing his words] and agony of a trial in Washington, D.C."[46]

He had stood, hands in pockets, before Judge Johnson for forty-five minutes and in a raspy whisper said only, "[Y]es, your honor," and, "[N]o, ma'am" to her questions. The guilty plea had been signed on 27 March, but this institutional theater was held on 9 April. Justice had shoved subpoenas on his family members and associates in March to appear at trial in May, surely jacking up the pressure on him to plead out. Rostenkowski pleaded guilty to mail fraud for sending congressional payroll checks to his district office on 28 April 1990 to pay for personal or political service and to sending a check to Lenox China on 14 January 1992 drawn on House funds for personal gifts. Pointedly, he did not admit any stamp or vehicle scams.

Judge Johnson accepted the plea and then delivered a tongue-lashing for his betrayal of the public trust. She sentenced him to seventeen months in jail and a $100,000 fine, reduced by the $82,095 he already had repaid the House. Under the original seventeen counts, he could have received up to six years; under the thirteen after the Supreme Court "concealing a material fact" ruling, up to five.

Officialdom grieved. A Republican elder told a reporter, "What happened to Danny is the same thing that happened to Nixon. The rules changed and they didn't."[47] Such an opinion could not survive scrutiny of the record in either man's case.

Not every Democratic machine member at the curbstone level shed tears over the bier, though. One ward leader said, "He was Mr. Big. He didn't need us until he got in trouble a few years ago, and then he was Mr. Nice Guy all of a sudden, like he was best friends with everybody."[48]

In his remarks to reporters, Rosty was defiant, unrepentant, almost combative. He laid out two lines of defense.

The rules changed, and I, busily writing landmark legislation, did not bother to keep up with them.

It is true that House ethics rules after the post-Watergate reforms have proliferated to the point of asininity. The House ethics code now runs for hundreds of pages of legalese. Imagine belonging to an institution that needs that much rococo script to instruct you in how to be honest. House members had to declare, under penalty of criminal sanctions, the value of a T-shirt of the kind that civic groups always proffer guest speakers. After Gingrich took over he had the House forbid gifts to members and staffs, period. An Ohio woman, helped by her congressman's staff in a passport problem, sent staffers a small box of homemade candy as a thank you in 1995. It instantly was returned, in horror, as contraband. House rules now prohibit common courtesy.

It is also true that some of Rosty's practices, such as cashing out the unused portions of office and stationery allowances, used to be legal, indeed almost encouraged. That these actions were outlawed without his notice is questionable. Rostenkowski was the type who would grab Marty Russo and with avuncular sternness straighten his necktie. In short, he was no Reaganesque big-picture delegator but a detail man, a micromanager of both substance and appearances.

His peculations amounted to strolling past the newsstand every morning and sweeping off the quarters on the counter into his pocket. No matter the proliferation of rules, a formal proscription against sweeping off the quarters is irrelevant for an honest person. The briar patch of rules can be as thick as reformers like, and such as Rosty still will find ways to get around it. That is why a remnant of the Chicago machine survives, regardless of how often the media say it is dead.

Further, it is true that Rostenkowski's thefts were penny-ante. He was accused of stealing about three-quarters of a million dollars, which is relatively nothing next to the multimillion-dollar tax breaks he regularly wrote into the tax code for his pals and contributors—perfectly legally. Ward heelers have been eclipsed by PACs whose money is necessary to buy TV spots. As in the Presidential Towers affair, the public has not decided exactly what, in the media and PAC age, constitutes public corruption.

To the PACs, Democratic and Republican are brand names like Ford and Chevrolet, models that have some emotionally committed loyalists but are basically identical. Systemic corruption by PACdom has been institutionalized by post-Watergate reformers, zealots to regulate and codify politics, just like the Chicago respectables in the era of Stanley Kunz and Joe Rusty. Throughout his career, Rosty expressed scorn for the regulators and codifiers. We may sympathize with his puzzlement: Guys on my committee sell out to PACs all the time, and they are coming after me for postage stamps?

The rules changed, the system changed, the climate changed. But scamming postage stamps is still scamming postage stamps.

I was singled out by prosecutors as a big fish, but most congressmen do the same things.

Again, there is truth in this. Among Nixon, Agnew, Wright, and Rostenkowski, only Rostenkowski went to jail. His persona was precisely of the magnitude to invite efforts to jail him, falling just under the altitude of national iconography that makes jailing unthinkable. Consider if Rosty had been Speaker—would not a resignation from office have sufficed? As it was, Mr. Chairman was such a tempting target for prosecutors that not even a helpful Democratic White House could thwart them.

Conversely, Rosty's election defeat worked in his favor. No longer in office, he was thus a smaller trophy for prosecutors, who may then have felt more inclined to accept a plea offer.

As for the everybody-does-it defense, certainly many congressmen abuse the privileges of office, but few pad the payroll with outright personal valets. Rosty's statement said, "I do not believe that I am any different from the vast majority of the members of Congress and their staffs who have experienced enormous difficulty in determining whether particular services by Congressional employees should be classified as Congressional, political or personal."[49] Some Republican holdovers in Clinton's Justice Department indulged the fantasy of granting Rosty immunity from further prosecution, then compelling him to testify and name all these congressmen he said he knew about: congressmen so befuddled about the difference between honesty and theft, a distinction blurred by, of all people, the goo goos with their ever-expanding book of rules.

Rostenkowski grew up in the Depression gangster era in Chicago, acquainted with the political murders of Mosinski and Switaj and numerous others. Then, in his professional career, he was acquainted with the Orville Hodge scandal; the Evan Howell scandal; Illinois racetrack stock scandals; the Joe Rusty ghost-payrolling scandal; the indictments of Illinois Governors Stratton, Kerner, and Walker (jailed for bank fraud after leaving office); episodic Chicago police scandals; episodic Cook County judiciary scandals; frequent and constant aldermanic jailings too numerous to list, likewise the convictions of Illinois state legislators; serial convictions of his patron Dick Daley's close associates; the Adam Clayton Powell congressional scandal; various Kennedy sex scandals; the Kennedy-Johnson-FBI-CIA abuse-of-power scandals; the Bobby Baker congressional scandal; the Watergate scandal; the Abscam congressional sting; the Iran-contra scandal; the national savings and loans scandal; the Jim Wright scandal; continual destruction of congressmen for graft, theft, or sexual stupidity; continual destruction of presidential assistants for charges ranging from cocaine ingestion to slipshod banking to unwise professional associations; the House bank scandal; the House post office scandal; the Senate's Keating Five scandal; the Whitewater scandal . . . We now will draw a curtain of modesty across this parade of trespasses, which could be extended. The point is that Dan Rostenkowski never believed he was vulnerable to criminal prosecution and still does not believe he committed felonies, though he will admit to breaking a few House rules.

Evidently, Rostenkowski fell into the trap that snared Jim Wright and so many others, the assurance that he was so important and powerful that the rules did not apply to him. He made his own way, his own rules, and goo goos were just goo goos.

The evening after appearing before Judge Johnson, Rosty paid a farewell visit to "Rosty's Rotunda" at Morton's along with Gayle Rosten, Fletcher, and Fletcher's lawyer, Nancy Luque. Then it was back to Chicago to await assignment to a federal prison. Clinton called to wish him well; so did Bush, who invited him to visit at his summer home in Kennebunkport, Maine, when the ordeal was over.

One night he had dinner downtown with three Chicago journalists who had become friends over the decades. He gave each a bag containing a large beer mug with his name on it, a candy dish with his name on it, and a picture of the Capitol. The gifts connoted a clear message—*I am unchastened.*

Entry to prison was delayed when he was diagnosed with prostate cancer. The secretary of the army gave permission for Rosty to be treated at Walter Reed Army Medical Center in Washington, where he had a radical prostatectomy on 17 May. The operation was successful, and Rosty went to Wisconsin to recuperate.

Rosty asked to be sentenced to a minimum security work camp at Oxford, Wisconsin, near his Wisconsin home. Because of his recent surgery, he was assigned instead to a prison hospital at Rochester, Minnesota—seven ugly, boxy, red-brick buildings on a sixty-four-acre compound that used to be the state's mental hospital. He turned himself in at 1:48 P.M. on 22 July, twelve minutes before deadline. He was Mr. Chairman. They called him Federal Prisoner Number 25338-016.

EPILOGUE

THE guards, as Bureau of Prisons regulations stipulated, put Number 25338-016 on a bus in leg irons and handcuffs attached to a belly chain around his waist. That belly had considerably diminished during his five months at Rochester. Rosty ate prison food, not steaks and gin, walked eight miles a day, and even did pushups. In phone calls, the Korean veteran told friends that prison was just like the army except that there was no marching.

The bus rolled 150 miles in the midwestern December, east and then south along Interstate 90 to Oxford in central Wisconsin. Rosty was glad to be transferred from Rochester, surrounded by walls topped with barbed wire, although there was no watchtower and he slept in a dormitory, not a cell. Oxford has no walls, barbed wire, guard dogs, or steel bars, no stock Hollywood sounds of doors clanging. The prison sits on four hundred well-tended acres with elms and sumacs. Rosty worked seven and a half hours a day at landscaping and other chores at a starting pay of twelve cents an hour. He joined 153 other inmates who slept in four-man cubicles with no doors. Chicagoans joked that Rosty had reserved a suite for himself— one bed for his body, three for his ego.

A fellow inmate was a colleague from Illinois General Assembly days, Fred B. Roti, serving four years for rigging zoning and civil court cases as

First Ward alderman. Another inmate was the former personnel director for a Republican Cook County sheriff, serving thirty months for hiring ghost payrollers and fixing employment exams.

Friends were contacted by the Bureau of Prisons: Will you accept telephone calls from inmate Rostenkowski? Of course. Doing fine, losing weight, looking forward to seeing you again. He did not invite visits. He did not believe he had committed crimes and did not want to be seen as a felon in jail. Not even family members were allowed to visit.

Panzke still functioned as his Chicago secretary, taking dictation for letters over the phone. Guards sometimes pulled him off the phone because other inmates were waiting. Rosty would scowl but did not make a fuss. He had told LaVerne he was determined to earn time off for good behavior. Which he did.

On 19 August 1997, Rosty was released to a Salvation Army halfway house in Chicago. The next day he had a hernia operation at Loyola University Medical Center. After recovering, he was allowed to leave the halfway house daily to work a job, namely the revival of his consulting business, but he had to be back by 9:00 P.M. daily. Friends who took him out to dinner scrupulously observed the curfew. Reprising "Rosty's Rotunda," he told stories and held court.

On 15 October, Rosty was released after 451 days in federal custody. He walked out a rear door at two minutes after midnight and sped away in a waiting car to avoid the media. At dawn a reporter drove to Pulaski Park across from Rosty's house. Just before Rosty went to jail, this reporter had hidden in the men's room of the park field house, watching for Rosty to emerge for the morning walk of his dog, "Black." When Rosty did so, the reporter left the men's room and accosted him for an interview. He hoped to repeat this success and suspected that Rosty secretly hoped reporters would be out there, just to show he was still important. But, as pilots tell the control tower when unable to spot another aircraft, "no joy." The reporter gave up and left.

Rosty sent out a form letter on Danross Associates stationery dated 22 October:

> I write not only to let you know I am back in Chicago, but to report on some of the lessons I learned as part of my Oxford edu-

cation. While I wouldn't recommend my withdrawal from society to anyone as a pleasant experience, it was not entirely negative. Some even say it builds character. Others say I had a more than ample supply of character to begin with.

One of the things I learned is that it is a real challenge to have to rely on your personal resources without the supportive environment that many of us have become so accustomed to. I've read more books in the past ten months than I read in the previous ten years. I've lost some weight and gotten back in shape. In many senses, I am healthier now than I have been in years.

Another lesson is that bureaucracies all have a certain mindless logic. I'll reserve my critique of America's criminal justice system for another day. I do believe that a strong case can be made for doing things better. Incarceration isn't a country club—and it shouldn't be. But, things could be changed to yield a more positive result for American society generally. The taxpayers could get more for their money in a redesigned system.

But the most important thing I've learned, once again, is the value of friendship. Despite my isolation and despite the boredom of my daily life, I was constantly cheered by friends—people like you—who took the trouble to stay in touch. When I was in Congress, I was often tempted to merely count the mail rather than read it. In recent months, I've had ample opportunity to read your notes. They were, in every case, positive. It was reassuring to learn that our friendship was not dependent on my official position. Learning that has been a very positive experience and I thank you for writing.

In the months ahead, I hope to have a chance to visit. I'm back in my office on Noble Street, operating Danross Associates. I'm confident I still have some positive contributions to make and am ready to make up for lost time.

Thanks for your friendship during the past year. I appreciate it. In the months and years ahead, I hope we can have many opportunities not only to share memories of our past experiences, but to create new memories as well.

Sincerely, Dan[1]

He then penned a personal note such as, "Get ready for dinner, see you soon."

Far from hanging his head and slinking off to obscure retirement, Rosty slowly and carefully intromitted himself back onto the public stage as an elder statesman. The Washington media welcomed him back with open arms. They liked Rosty, and the nature of his crimes did not offend them. In a lengthy report on his rehabilitation, *Newsweek* said there was no evidence he had lined his own pockets—a stretch.[2]

On 15 November 1997, Terry Gabinski showcased Rostenkowski as the guest of honor at a seventy-five-dollar-a-ticket funder for the Thirty-second Ward. Approaching his seventieth birthday, Rosty once again was greeted by hundreds of folks with deliciously non-Anglicized surnames who lined up to get their pictures taken with him and play do-you-remember-the-time-when. It was much like the Polish National Alliance award dinner in February 1995. It was held at the White Eagle, across Milwaukee Avenue from St. Adalbert's Cemetery.

NOTES

SELECTED BIBLIOGRAPHY

INDEX

NOTES

The following abbreviations are used for frequently cited sources in the notes:

AP	Associated Press
CDN	*Chicago Daily News*
CHS	Chicago Historical Society
CQ	*Congressional Quarterly*
CST	*Chicago Sun-Times*
CT	*Chicago Tribune*
DR	Dan Rostenkowski
MBC	Museum of Broadcast Communications
NYT	*New York Times*
SJR	*State Journal-Register* (Springfield, IL)
WP	*Washington Post*
WSJ	*Wall Street Journal*

1. Big Joe Rusty

1. "Held in Mystery Slaying of Two," *Chicago Daily Times*, 8 August 1938.

2. "Harried Bookies in 32nd Need a Law, Ald. 'Rusty' Thinks," *CDN*, 18 October 1936.

3. This account of the Mosinski and Switaj murders derives from contemporary newspaper reports and files of the Chicago Crime Commission. Histories of the gangster era in Chicago are numerous, but for a former mayor's candid observations, see Byrne, *My Chicago*, 131–32.

4. "Paddy Bauler Dead? Well, Listen to This," *CST*, 24 March 1977.

5. Williams and Duffey, *Chicago's Public Wits*, 111.

6. Steven V. Roberts, "A Most Important Man on Capitol Hill," *NYT Magazine*, 22 September 1985, 49.

7. DR, interview with the author, 4 February 1995.

8. "Kunz and Son Freed by Jury in Bribe Case," *CT*, 28 February 1930.

9. Kantowicz, *Polish-American Politics in Chicago, 1888–1940*, 63.

10. Ibid., 27.

11. Ibid., 211.

12. Renkiewicz, *The Poles in America 1608–1972*, 66.

13. Ibid., 97.

14. Ibid., 98.

15. "Rostenkowski Profile," AP, 1 June 1994.

16. "Kunz Coercing WPA Men, Says Rostenkowski," *CT*, 28 March 1936.

17. "Polonja Wziela Thumny Udzial w Pogrzebie s.p. Piotra Rostenkowski ego," *Dziennik Chicagoski*, 28 June 1936; translated from Polish for the author by Sabina Ligisz of the Polish Museum of America in Chicago.

18. Quoted in "Report on Aldermanic Candidates in Run-off Elections April 1, 1947," Citizens' Association of Chicago, in Joseph P. Rostenkowski file, *CST* library.

19. "M.V.L. Report," *CDN*, 2 February 1935.

20. "32nd Ward—Joseph P. Rostenkowski Preferred," *CDN*, 23 February 1935.

21. Mary Borden, "Chicago Revisited," *Harper's Magazine*, April 1931, 489.

22. Interview with the author, 4 February 1995. The informant asked not to be identified.

23. Barak Goodman, producer, "Daley: The Last Boss," broadcast on WTTW-TV, Chicago, 22 January 1996, video at CHS.

24. John J. Hoellen, interview with the author, 26 April 1995.

25. Tom Drennan, interview with the author, 9 June 1995.

26. "Chicago Sun Aldermanic Questionnaire," in Joseph P. Rostenkowski file, *CST* library.

27. "The 30th and Wards," *CST*, 9 February 1955.

28. Douglas, *In the Fullness of Time*, 93.

29. Ibid., 94.

30. James C. Kirie, interview with the author, 23 January 1997.

31. Ibid.

32. "Rostenkowski Applauded at Portrait Event," *CST*, 28 April 1983.

33. "Inaugural Throng Solemn as It Hears President's Words," *NYT*, 21 January 1941.

34. "Rostenkowski New 'Mayor's Man' in House," *CT*, 24 May 1964.

35. Tom Drennan, interview with the author, 9 June 1995.

36. "Rostenkowski New 'Mayor's Man' in House," *CT*, 24 May 1964.

2. A House for All Peoples

1. Waring, *History of the 7th Infantry Division*, 98.

2. Robert H. Michel, interview with the author, 3 September 1996.

3. Incidentally, Lovelette does not recall this encounter. Judy J. Lovelette, letter to the author, 19 January 1997.

4. "Rostenkowski New 'Mayor's Man' in House," *CT*, 24 May 1964.

5. Arthur Siddon, "Chicago's 'Big Man in Washington' Looms Even Bigger Now," *CT Magazine*, 7 December 1980, 30.

6. John Camper, Cheryl Devall, and John Kass, "The Road to City Hall," *CT Magazine*, 16 November 1986, 36.

7. Siddon, "Chicago's 'Big Man in Washington,'" 30.

8. Ibid, 34.

9. "Rostenkowski New 'Mayor's Man' in House," *CT*, 24 May 1964.

10. "Springfield Ain't Safe, Stranger," *CDN*, 9 February 1957.

11. George W. Dunne, interview with the author, 23 October 1995.

12. *Journal of the [Illinois] Senate*, 30 June 1955, 2351–52.

13. *Journal of the [Illinois] House of Representatives*, 7 January 1953, 4–13.

14. Paul Simon, as told to Alfred Balk, "The Illinois Legislature: A Study in Corruption," *Harper's*, September 1964, 72.

15. "Illinois Legislature Ends Session Ahead of Schedule," *SJR*, 28 June 1953.

16. The Census Bureau's definitions and categories of ethnicity are inconstant. Only first- and second-generation Irish were so labeled, undercounting successive generations in the city.

17. *CT*, n.d., quoted in "City's Irish: From Famine to Fortune," *CST*, 17 March 1995.

18. *Chicago Evening Post*, 9 September 1868, quoted in McCaffrey, *Textures of Irish America*, 19.

19. Sullivan, *Legend*, 150.

20. Hirsch, "Martin F. Kennelly," in Green and Holli, eds., *The Mayors*.

21. Gleason, *Daley of Chicago*, 194.

22. Charles A. Freeman, interview with the author, 27 April 1995.

23. Biles, *Richard J. Daley*, 43.

24. Glazer and Moynihan, *Beyond the Melting Pot*, 260.

25. Reedy, *From the Ward to the White House*, 49.

26. Royko, *Boss*, 40.

27. "Chicago News Conference," WMAQ-AM, 1 January 1984, audiotape at CHS.

28. "Clouter with Conscience," *Time*, 15 March 1963, 35.

29. Biles, *Richard J. Daley*, 144.

30. O'Neill, *Man of the House*, 9.

31. For a development of this argument, see Sowell, *Ethnic America*, 274–95.

32. Lindberg, *Quotable Chicago*, 133.

33. For this insight I am indebted to Alan Ehrenhalt. See his *Lost City*, 40–41.

34. Ibid.

35. Ibid.

36. "Rusty Plans to Rebuild," *CDN*, 7 April 1955.

37. "5 Idle Workers Cost City $17,000," *CDN*, 3 April 1952; see also Merriner, "Fathers, Sons, and Unholy Ghosts," *Illinois Issues*, July 1996, 18–21.

38. James C. Kirie, interview with the author, 23 January 1997.

39. Reeves, *A Question of Character*, 133. For another perspective on JFK at the 1956 convention, see Gorman, *Kefauver*, 82–83, 262–63.

40. Gorman, *Kefauver*, 263.

41. "Panes Broken in Prusinski Ward Office," *CT*, 23 March 1956.

42. Albert, *Little Giant*, 326.

43. Edward Pree, Illinois General Assembly Oral History Program, 1983, 110–11.

44. Thiem, *The Hodge Scandal*, 223.

45. "Spector of Hodge Haunts Legislators," *SJR*, 10 January 1957.

3. If Danny Says It's True

1. This account of the congressmen's commuting is based on interviews with Robert H. Michel, 3 September 1996, and Calvin Collier and Harold Collier, 9 January 1997.

2. Arthur Siddon, "Chicago's 'Big Man in Washington' Looms Even Bigger Now," *CT Magazine*, 7 December 1980, 36.

3. Jack Reynolds, interview with the author, 29 August 1996.

4. As quoted in "Endpapers," *Harvard Magazine*, January-February 1996, 106.

5. John F. Kennedy Jr., unpublished remarks noted by the author, 9 April 1996.

6. Farber, *Chicago 68*, 115.

7. O'Donnell and Powers, *Johnny, We Hardly Knew Ye*, 174.

8. Sullivan, *Legend*, 150.

9. Ibid.

10. Ciccone, *Daley*, 37.

11. Ibid., 45.

12. Ibid., 44.

13. Reeves, *A Question of Character*, 214.

14. Lemann, *The Promised Land*, 166.

15. Nixon, *RN: The Memoirs of Richard Nixon*, 223.

16. Kallina, *Courthouse over White House*.

17. James C. Kirie, interview with the author, 23 January 1997.

18. Reeves, *President Kennedy*, 110.

19. Reeves, *A Question of Character*, 165.

20. Ibid.

21. Reeves, *President Kennedy*, 110.

22. "Kennedy Insists Nations U.S. Aids Help Themselves," *NYT*, 29 April 1961.

23. Philip J. Rock, interview with the author, 5 August 1996.

24. "The Making of Mr. Chairman," *CST*, 2 June 1994.

25. Weinberg, "Rostenkowski," videotape.

26. Ibid.

27. "O'Brien-Birthday," AP, 30 April 1958.

28. Albert, *Little Giant*, 216.

29. Ciccone, *Daley*, 181.

30. Gleason, *Daley of Chicago*, 186.

31. Ciccone, 183.

32. "Rostenkowski! The Name Rings with Political Magic," *CDN*, 13 April 1968.

33. DR, remarks to the Ravenswood Industrial Council, Chicago, 8 November 1991.

34. This rendering is a composite of several tellings of the anecdote. See especially Weinberg, "Rostenkowski," videotape.

35. "Rep. Rostenkowski Runs Scared in 8th District," *CST*, 2 October 1966.

36. "Memorandum," O'Brien to Johnson, EX LG/Chicago, 7:25 P.M., 11 August 1965, Lyndon B. Johnson Library and Museum, Austin, TX.

37. Sullivan, *Legend*, 175.

38. Newton N. Minow, "Voice of the People," *CT*, 16 September 1996.

39. "U.S. Aides Map Steps to Crush Anti-Draft Move," *CST*, 17 October 1965.

40. DR, "Is Patriotism Necessary?" CHS, Rostenkowski file.

4. The Whole World Is Watching

1. Ciccone, *Daley*, 222; and O'Connor, *Clout*, 194. See also "How Mayor Got 1968 Convention for City," *CT*, 10 October 1967.

2. "Illinois House Bloc Proves Pain to LBJ," *CDN*, 16 December 1967.

3. Ciccone, *Daley*, 237.

4. "Few Chicagoans See President on Secrecy-Shrouded Trip Here," *CT*, 2 April 1968.

5. "Sees Spur for Civil Rights Law," *CST*, 9 April 1968.

6. Biles, *Richard J. Daley*, 144.

7. Ibid., 146.

8. "Lyndon Lets His Quips Do the Talking," *CT*, 25 April 1968.

9. William "Fishbait" Miller, *Fishbait*, 281–82.

10. O'Neill, *Man of the House*, 214.

11. Albert, *Little Giant*, 181.

12. The ensuing chronicle draws heavily on Sautter and Burke, *Inside the Wigwam*, 243–72, and *National Party Conventions 1831–1988*, *CQ*, Washington, D.C., 1991, 115–17.

13. Dedmon, *Fabulous Chicago*, 379.

14. Mimi Keane, interview with the author, 17 September 1997.

15. Steven V. Roberts, "A Most Important Man on Capitol Hill," *NYT Magazine*, 22 September 1985, 49.

16. Royko, *Boss*, 181.

17. Biles, *Richard J. Daley*, 160.

18. Albert remained strangely complacent about Chicago 1968. See *Little Giant*, 306.

19. *NYT*, 24 August 1968, reprinted in *NYT Magazine*, "Chicago, Where All America Was Radicalized," 14 April 1996, 118.

20. "Rostenkowski . . . on his city, his party, his mayor." Lerner Newspapers, *North Town*, Chicago, 17 December 1968.

21. Royko, *Boss*, 191.

22. Dedmon, *Fabulous Chicago*, 382.

23. Barry, *The Ambition and the Power*, 12.

24. Biles, *Richard J. Daley*, 170–71.

25. Rakove, *Don't Make No Waves*, 97.

26. Baker, *The Stevensons*, 464; and Ciccone, *Daley*, 294.

27. Albert, *Little Giant*, 326.

28. O'Neill, *Man of the House*, 218. See also Albert, *Little Giant*, 327.

29. "How Rostenkowski Missed the Next Rung Up," *CST*, 24 January 1971.

30. Barry, *The Ambition and the Power*, 22.

31. Jackson, *Honest Graft*, 47.

32. Arthur Siddon, "Chicago's 'Big Man in Washington' Looms Even Larger Now," *CT Magazine*, 7 December 1980, 36.

33. O'Neill, *Man of the House*, 219.

34. Kahn and Majors, *The Winning Ticket*, 1.

35. DR, "Letter to the Editor," *Chicago Today*, 2 May 1971. See also "Democratic Whip Asks U.S. Pullout," *NYT*, 30 March 1971.

36. "Rostenkowski Says Reds Use New Left," *CT*, 17 March 1970.

37. "Daley's Machine Set to Snub Rules," *CST*, 18 March 1972.

38. Ciccone, *Daley*, 231.

5. Pigs Get Fat

1. *Report of the National Advisory Commission on Civil Disorders*, 1, 4.

2. "Bare Rostenkowski's Secret Stock Windfall!" *Chicago Today*, 29 September 1971.

3. "Rostenkowski Future Periled by Track Deal," *CST*, 4 October 1971.

4. James R. Thompson, interview with the author, 5 August 1996.

5. See Garment, *Scandal*, 115. For a review of the racetrack scandal, see Hartley, *Big Jim Thompson*, especially 42–45, 52–53, 110–11.

6. James R. Thompson, interview with the author, 5 August 1996. See also Byrne, *My Chicago*, 231, and Hartley, *Big Jim Thompson*, 43.

7. Unpublished remarks noted by the author, March 1976.

8. Raymond R. Coffey, interview with the author, 9 January 1997.

9. For a discussion of Swibel's actions and the use of tax-exempt bonds for private development, see Ross Miller, *Here's the Deal*, especially 43, 82, 150.

10. "Presidential Towers Rise on Government Subsidies," *CT*, 18 December 1983.

11. "Rostenkowski Bill Saves Pal Millions," *CST*, 20 November 1983.

12. "Ways and Means: The Committee, Taxation with Representation." Washington: York Associates Television, video, 1989.

13. "Council Panel Stalls Funds for Presidential Towers," *CST*, 30 January 1987.

14. "Rosty Defends Tax Break for Towers, " *CST*, 23 May 1990.

15. James R. Thompson, interview with the author, 5 August 1996.

6. The Tuesday Through Thursday Club

1. O'Neill, *Man of the House*, 245.

2. "Nixon in Precarious Position: Illinois Reps," *CT*, 23 October 1973.

3. O'Connor, *Requiem*, 132.

4. "Ford Would OK Nixon Immunity," *CT*, 8 August 1974.

5. "It's Official: Daley to Run," *CT*, 10 December 1974.

6. O'Connor, *Requiem*, 102.

7. "Rostenkowski's Clout Giving Up," *CDN*, 8 December 1976.

8. "IOU Votes Helped Wright Win Democrats' No. 2 House Post," *CDN*, 7 December 1976.

9. Kahn and Majors, *The Winning Ticket*, 1–2.

10. "A Day with Rostenkowski's Committee on Health," *Lerner Booster Newspapers*, 26 March 1975.

11. "The Speaker Takes a Look at His House: 'I Love This Job,'" *NYT*, 5 April 1977.

12. "Rostenkowski's Mad at 'Peanuts,'" *CT*, 6 May 1977.

13. "Carter Stymied by Ways and Means of Congress," *CDN*, 16 December 1977.

14. Califano, *Governing America*, 148–50.

15. "Carter Stymied by Ways and Means of Congress," *CDN*, 16 December 1977.

16. O'Neill, *Man of the House*, 315–16; and Wright, *Balance of Power*, 276–77.

17. O'Neill, *Man of the House*, 315–16; and Wright, *Balance of Power*, 276–77.

18. "Look Who's Flirting with Pomp," *CST*, 27 August 1978.

19. "Rostenkowski Fearful of Tax-Veto 'Mistake,'" *CDN*, 28 March 1975.

20. "Ford Challenged by Democrats on Economic Policy," *CT*, 15 January 1975.

21. "Fund-raising Democrats Eat, Drink, and Sing Blues," *CT*, 20 March 1978.

22. "Carter Is Warned Tax Bill He Wants Won't Be Enacted," *NYT*, 21 April 1978.

23. Tom Callahan, "Golf and Grief in Washington," *Golf Digest*, June 1997, 174.

24. O'Neill, *Man of the House*, 291.

25. Mimi Keane, interview with the author, 17 September 1997.

26. "Rostenkowski Rebuffed Mayor Bid—For Now," *CDN*, 12 February 1997.

27. "The Making of Mr. Chairman," *CST*, 2 June 1994.

28. "One 'Ghost' in Indictment Goes Public," *NYT*, 2 June 1994.

29. "Emotional Bilandic Rips Foes," *CST*, 15 February 1979.

30. Byrne, *My Chicago*, 272.

31. Ibid.

32. Drew, *Portrait*, 22.

33. "Rostenkowski the Peacemaker," *CST*, 15 August 1980.

7. Rosty's Rotunda

1. Weinberg, "Rostenkowski," videotape.

2. "He's Able to Give a Little," *NYT*, 14 December 1980.

3. "New Role for Rostenkowski Gets Him into the Thick of House Power," *CQ*, 16 May 1981, 863.

4. Philip M. Crane, interview with the author, 5 September 1996; see also "GOP Disputes Ways and Means Lineup," *CQ*, 31 January 1981, 219.

5. "Kup's Show," WTTW-TV, 21 February 1981, video at MBC.

6. "This Time, the Spotlight May Flatter Rostenkowski," *NYT*, 6 March 1983.

7. "Chicago News Conference," WMAQ-AM, 7 June 1981, audiotape at CHS.

8. "When He Talks, the Tax Watchers Listen," *CT*, 27 August 1980.

9. DR, "Not So Fast, Mr. President," *CT*, 22 February 1981.

10. DR, "Kup's Show," WTTW-TV, 20 February 1981, video at MBC.

11. Ibid.

12. "1,000 Turn out for Rostenkowski," *CST*, 1 April 1981.

13. O'Neill, *Man of the House*, 351.

14. See Stockman, *The Triumph of Politics*, 234–45.

15. "Rostenkowski: No Three-year Tax Cut," *CST*, 5 April 1981.

16. Wright, *Balance of Power*, 263.

17. Ibid.

18. Connelly and Pitney, *Congress' Permanent Minority?*, 116.

19. Strahan, "Dan Rostenkowski," 200.

20. "Chicago News Conference," WMAQ-AM, 7 June 1981, audiotape at CHS.

21. Reagan, *An American Life*, 286.

22. DR, "Not So Fast, Mr. President," *CT*, 22 February 1981.

23. "Democrats Seek Public's Support to Counter Reagan Tax Proposal," *NYT*, 7 July 1981.

24. Stockman, *Triumph of Politics*, 263.

25. DR, "Rostenkowski on Circumvention of Legislative Process on Tax Bill," *CQ*, 22 August 1981, 1578.

26. "Rostenkowski Wins Admiration in Defeat," *CT*, 30 July 1981.

27. Von Damm, *At Reagan's Side*, 204.

28. James Poterba, Massachusetts Institute of Technology; see Susan Dentzer, "Bob Dole: Now, Reagan Redux?", *U.S. News and World Report*, 10 June 1996, 61. For another economic analysis of the 1981 tax law, see Witte, *The Politics and Development of the Federal Income Tax*, 220–43.

29. "Rostenkowski Seeks More Influential Role," *CQ*, 29 January 1983, 194.

30. *CQ*, 29 January 1983, 195.

31. "Briefing," *NYT*, 13 December 1982.

32. "A Hand Reaches for the Hot Potato of Social Security," *NYT*, 7 January 1983.

33. Ibid.

34. Larry P. Horist, interview with the author, 8 May 1996.

35. "Golfing No Handicap for Rostenkowski," *WP*, 6 June 1982; and "Life in the Tax Lane: Staff Gets Trips, Too," *WP*, 7 June 1982.

36. Weinberg, "Rostenkowski," videotape.

37. "Chicago News Conference," WMAQ-AM, 16 April 1982, audiotape at CHS.

38. Weinberg, "Rostenkowski," videotape.

39. Tamarkin, *The Merc*, 290.

40. "US Steel Reneged, Rostenkowski Says," *CT*, 30 December 1983.

41. Larry P. Horist, interview with the author, 8 May 1996; and Brown, "Rosty: The Clout Is Gone," *Illinois Issues*, December 1994, 14.

42. Horist, interview with author, 8 May 1996.

43. Ibid.

44. "Paralysis of Power," *CT*, 2 September 1984.

45. Rivlin, *Fire on the Prairie*, 277.

46. "Two Worlds of Rostenkowski," *CT*, 28 April 1983.

47. "Rostenkowski Applauded at Portrait Event," *CST*, 28 April 1983.

48. "Rostenkowski 'Hanging,'" AP, 27 April 1983; and "Two Worlds of Rostenkowski," *CT*, 28 April 1983.

8. Write Rosty

1. "Chicago News Conference," WMAQ-AM, 1 January 1984, audiotape at CHS.

2. "Rostenkowski's Tax Hints Offer Brighter Options for Traders," *CST*, 5 January 1984.

3. "Thirty-second Ward David Wakes Up Goliath," *CT*, 21 March 1984.

4. Birnbaum and Murray, *Showdown at Gucci Gulch*, 35.

5. "Aide Spurns Suit's Claim Rosty Drunk in '84 Crash," *CST*, 6 June 1986.

6. Barlett and Steele, *America*, 58.

7. Greider, *Who Will Tell the People*, 95.

8. "Dan Rostenkowski's Old Ways," *WP Weekly Edition*, 15–21 April 1996.

9. "Rostenkowski Holds Back on Vrdolyak," *CT*, 28 December 1985.

10. Birnbaum and Murray, *Showdown at Gucci Gulch*, 96.

11. Ibid., 98.

12. Ibid., 98–99.

13. Ibid.

14. Smith, *The Power Game*, 549–50.

15. "'Dear Rosty' Letters Are Pouring In," *CST*, 1 June 1985.

16. Stern, *Still the Best Congress*, 11.

17. Connelly and Pitney, *Congress' Permanent Minority?*, 48.

18. Smith, *The Power Game*, 550.

19. Ibid., 552.

20. Birnbaum and Murray, *Showdown at Gucci Gulch*, 142.

21. Smith, The Power Game, 552–53; see also "Cool It, Rosty Tells Reagan," *CST*, 7 June 1985.

22. "Washington Outlook," *Business Week*, 21 October 1985, 51.

23. "Briefing," *NYT*, 7 November 1985.

24. "The Great Tax Giveaway," *Philadelphia Inquirer*, 13 April 1988.

25. Jacob Weisberg, "Finding the Fix," *New Republic*, 24 March 1986, 22.

26. Barlett and Steele, *America*, 204.

27. Smith, *The Power Game*, 554.

28. Birnbaum and Murray, *Showdown at Gucci Gulch*, 151.

29. Ibid., 165.

30. Ibid., 174.

31. "Behind the Scenes in Tax Bill Drama," *NYT*, 16 August 1986.

32. Birnbaum and Murray, *Showdown at Gucci Gulch*, 273.

33. Ibid., 274; see also "Packwood's Tax Expertise Pays Off in New Capitol Life," *CT*, 6 April 1997.

34. "Elation and Nostalgia on Capitol Hill," *NYT*, 18 August 1986.

35. *Congressional Record-Senate*, 27 September 1986, S13907.

36. Strahan, *New Ways and Means*, 148.

37. Whether the corporate income tax functions as a national sales tax, and if so to what extent and at what point in the business cycle, is debated by economists. We hold here with the commonsense view.

38. Raymond R. Coffey, interview with the author, 9 January 1997.

9. Tall Bold Slugger

1. Peter Carlson, "Dan Rostenkowski Goes Down in History," *WP Magazine*, 17 October 1993, 34.

2. "Feud Could Block New Sox Stadium," *CT*, 14 May 1987.

3. Alderman Richard F. Mell, interview with the author, 4 April 1989.

4. "Chicago News Conference," WMAQ-TV, 18 October 1981, audiotape at CHS.

5. Barry, *The Ambition and the Power*, 95.

6. "The Making of 'Mr. Chairman,'" *CT*, 2 June 1994.

7. "For the Chairman of a Powerful Committee, the House Is No Longer Home," *NYT*, 20 November 1989.

8. James R. Thompson, interview with the author, 5 August 1996.

9. Another oft-told DR anecdote; e.g., Iris Krasnow, "Power Drive," *Chicago*, November 1991, 119.

10. Duffy and Goodgame, *Marching in Place*, 229.

11. Jackley, *Hill Rat*, 193.

12. DR, interview with the author, n.d., 1990.

13. Barry, *The Ambition and the Power*, 179.

14. "House and Senate Pass Omnibus Trade Bill," *1987 CQ Almanac*, 640.

15. Ibid., 741.

16. Ibid., 650.

17. Barlett and Steele, *America*, 215–16.

18. "Wright Becomes First Speaker to Resign," *1989 CQ Almanac*, 40.

19. Ibid.

20. "Rostenkowski's Postage Buys Rose After 'Cash-outs' Ended," *CQ*, 31 July 1993, 2021.

21. "Rostenkowski Finds He Still Answers to People," *CT*, 20 August 1989.

22. "Section 89 Tax Rules Repealed in 1989," *1989 CQ Almanac*, 345.

23. Darman, *Who's in Control?*, 242–43.

24. "Fighting the Deficit Too Bravely," *NYT*, 13 March 1990.

25. Darman, *Who's in Control?*, 249–50.

26. "The Struggle in Congress," *NYT*, 26 October 1990.

27. See Kolb, *White House Daze*, 58–66; "Lawmaker's Aid to Alma Mater Skews U.S. Budget," *NYT*, 3 April 1991; and "Miffed, Rostenkowski Holds Up Bush Trade Bills," *CT*, 1 October 1991. Darman ignored this episode in his memoirs.

10. A Bird So High

1. "The Power and the Glory," *CQ*, 12 January 1991, 73.

2. Ibid.

3. "Rosty Weighs His Future," *News Star*, 13 September 1991.

4. "Pols Lose Ground in Stand Against Hispanic District," *CST*, 7 April 1991.

5. Barry, *The Ambition and the Power*, 95.

6. Iris Krasnow, "Power Drive," *Chicago*, November 1991, 144.

7. Jackson, *Honest Graft*, 135.

8. "Rostenkowski's Role," AP, 6 May 1993.

9. DR, unpublished remarks to the Ravenswood Industrial Council, Chicago, 8 November 1991.

10. *Time*, 14 October 1991, 19.

11. DR, interview with the author, n.d., 1991.

12. "Tax 'Extenders' Clear at Session's End," *1991 CQ Almanac*, 107.

13. Hill Poised to Revamp Rules on Business Write-offs," *CQ*, 14 September 1991, 2599.

14. "Rosty Eats 'Humble Pie' at Home," *Los Angeles Times*, 14 March 1992.

15. "The Reporters," WMAQ-AM, 15 March 1992, audiotape at CHS.

16. Barry, *The Ambition and the Power*, 99.

17. *Time*, 16 March 1992, 28.

18. "Post Office Patronage Worker Ties Members to Stamp Scam," *CQ*, 23 May 1992, 1415.

19. "The Top 20," *CQ*, 3 October 1992, 3009.

20. "Rosty Guides Office Tours," *CST*, 15 December 1992.

21. DR, "A Reply from Rostenkowski," *CST*, 21 December 1992.

22. "Rostenkowski's Challenge: Delivering for Clinton," *CQ*, 6 February 1993, 255.

23. Ibid.

24. "Rostenkowski Seeks 'Trophy' for Health Care," *NYT*, 28 January 1993.

25. "Rostenkowski's Woes Spotlight the Decline of House's Old School," *WSJ*, 23 July 1993.

26. Ibid.

27. "Congress: The Private Agonies of Chairman Rosty," *Newsweek*, 24 May 1993, 26.

28. Gloria Borger, "Congress's New Odd Couple," *U.S. News & World Report*, 21 December 1992, 48.

29. "Ohio Democrat Continues His Crusade Against the IRS," *WSJ*, 12 November 1996.

30. "The Trouble with Rosty," *Time*, 2 August 1993, 28.

31. "Prosecutors Reported Seeking to Widen Inquiry on Rostenkowski," *NYT*, 21 July 1993.

32. "Oh, Danny Boy: Pipes Really Calling Now," *Crain's Chicago Business*, 26 July 1993.

33. Carlson, "Dan Rostenkowski Goes Down in History," 41.

34. Johnson and Broder, *The System*, 411.

11. A Bladder Full of Wind

1. Johnson and Broder, *The System*, 111.

2. Clift and Brazaitas, *War Without Bloodshed*, 93–94.

3. Ibid.

4. Bob Woodward, *The Agenda: Inside the Clinton White House*. New York: Simon & Schuster, 1994, 147.

5. Ibid., 217; and Birnbaum, *Madhouse*, 37–38.

6. "Rostenkowski Twinkles over 'Marvelous Witness,'" *CST*, 29 September 1993.

7. Ibid.

8. Roger Altman, unpublished remarks to the *CST* editorial board, August 1993.

9. Johnson and Broder, *The System*, 284.

10. "Rostenkowski Pitching Hardball on Health Care," *CT*, 20 January 1994.

11. Ibid.

12. "Rostenkowski Seeks Tax Increase to Pay for Health Care," *NYT*, 23 April 1994.

13. "Rosty Reimburses U.S. $82,000 for Purchases," *CST*, 11 February 1994.

14. "Rosty Bought Crystal, Chairs at House Store," *CST*, 13 February 1994.

15. "Rosty Jury Hears Gabinski's Wife," *CST*, 17 February 1994.

16. Dick Simpson, interview with the author, 29 August 1996.

17. "No Holiday from Politics for Wistful Rosty," *CST*, 8 March 1994.

18. Steve Johnson, "Mr. Flanagan Goes to Washington," *CT Magazine*, 15 January 1995, 14.

19. "Republicans Choose an Unknown to Beat Rosty," *CST*, 17 March 1994.

20. Richard Lacayo, "Gloom Under the Dome," *Time*, 13 June 1994, 51.

21. "Congressional Statement Vowing a Fight," *NYT*, 31 May 1994.

22. "U.S. Indicts Rostenkowski in Broad Corruption Case; He Is Out of Key House Post," *NYT*, 1 June 1994.

23. For details, see "United States v. Daniel D. Rostenkowski," U.S. District Court for the District of Columbia, 31 May 1994, Criminal No. 94-0226.

24. Quoted in Andrew Ferguson, "The Rosty Man," *National Review*, 27 June 1994, 72.

25. Russell Baker, "Good Man on a Bad Scene," *NYT*, 18 June 1994.

26. Quoted in "Corruption, Too, Is in the Eye of the Beholder," *NYT*, 12 June 1994.

27. David Broder, "Why Washington Grieves," *WP*, 2 June 1994.

28. "Rosty Hires a New Attorney," *CST*, 5 June 1994.

29. "Replacing Rosty," AP, 8 June 1994.

30. "Rosty: Staffers Worked Full Jobs," *CST*, 13 June 1994.

31. Steve Johnson, "Mr. Flanagan Goes to Washington," 14.

32. James R. Thompson, interview with the author, 5 August 1996.

33. Richard Roeper column, *CST*, 10 November 1994.

34. Steve Johnson, "Mr. Flanagan Goes to Washington," 20.

35. Mike Sneed column, *CST*, 9 February 1995.

36. "Rosty Casts Final Vote, Says Goodbye," *CST*, 30 November 1994.

37. "Rosty Says He's Short of Cash," *CST*, 21 November 1994.

38. "Former Congressman Dan Rostenkowski," "Larry King Live," 27 February 1996, transcript supplied by Cable News Network, 7.

39. James R. Thompson, interview with the author, 5 August 1996.

40. "Rosty Refuses to Look Back in Anger," *CST*, 31 May 1995.

41. "Capitol Letters," *CST*, 17 July 1995.

42. "Office of the Living Dead," *Time*, 13 March 1995, 38.

43. "Payroll Record Shocks Rosty Cleaning Lady," *CST*, 27 October 1995.

44. "Former Congressman Dan Rostenkowski," "Larry King Live," 27 February 1996, transcript supplied by Cable News Network, Inc., 7.

45. "Washington Wire," *WSJ*, 12 April 1996.

46. "Rostenkowski Pleads Guilty to Mail Fraud," *NYT*, 10 April 1996.

47. Steve Neal column, *CST*, 9 April 1996.

48. "Deal Brings Sadness, Satisfaction," *CT*, 9 April 1996.

49. "Rostenkowski Pleads Guilty to Mail Fraud," *NYT*, 10 April 1996.

Epilogue

1. A copy of the letter was given to the author by a friend of Rostenkowski's who asked not to be identified.

2. "Rosty's Difficult Winter," *Newsweek*, 12 January 1998, 36–37.

SELECTED BIBLIOGRAPHY

Albert, Carl, with Danny Goble. *Little Giant*. Norman: University of Oklahoma Press, 1990.

Allswang, John M. *A House for All Peoples: Ethnic Politics in Chicago 1890–1936*. Lexington: University Press of Kentucky, 1971.

Baker, Jean H. *The Stevensons: A Biography of An American Family*. New York: W. W. Norton, 1996.

Barlett, Donald L., and James B. Steele. *America: Who Really Pays the Taxes?* New York: Simon & Schuster, 1994.

Barry, John M. *The Ambition and the Power: The Fall of Jim Wright, A True Story of Washington*. New York: Viking, 1989.

Biles, Roger. *Big City Boss in Depression and War: Mayor Edward J. Kelly of Chicago*. DeKalb: Northern Illinois University Press, 1984.

———. *Richard J. Daley: Politics, Race, and the Governing of Chicago*. DeKalb: Northern Illinois University Press, 1995.

Birnbaum, Jeffrey H. *Madhouse: The Private Turmoil of Working for the President*. New York: Times Books, 1996.

Birnbaum, Jeffrey H., and Alan S. Murray. *Showdown at Gucci Gulch: Lawmakers, Lobbyists, and the Unlikely Triumph of Tax Reform*. New York: Random House, 1987.

Brashler, William. *The Don: The Life and Death of Sam Giancana*. New York: Harper & Row, 1977.

Brown, Mark. "Rosty: The Clout Is Gone." *Illinois Issues*, December 1994.

Byrne, Jane. *My Chicago*. New York: W. W. Norton, 1992.

Califano, Joseph A. *Governing America: An Insider's Report from the White House and the Cabinet*. New York: Simon & Schuster, 1981.

Ciccone, F. Richard. *Daley: Power and Presidential Politics*. Chicago: Contemporary Books, 1996.

Clift, Eleanor, and Tom Brazaitas. *War Without Bloodshed: The Art of Politics*. New York: Scribner, 1996.

Conable, Barber. *Congress and the Income Tax*. Norman: University of Oklahoma Press, 1989.

Selected Bibliography

Connelly, John F. Jr., and John J. Pitney Jr. *Congress' Permanent Minority? Republicans in the U.S. House*. Lanham, MD: Rowman & Littlefield, 1994.

Darman, Richard. *Who's in Control? Polar Politics and the Sensible Center*. New York: Simon & Schuster, 1996.

Dedmon, Emmett. *Fabulous Chicago: A Great City's History and People*. New York: Atheneum, 1983.

Douglas, Paul H. *In the Fullness of Time: The Memoirs of Paul H. Douglas*. New York: Harcourt, 1972.

Drew, Elizabeth. *On the Edge: The Clinton Presidency*. New York: Simon & Schuster, 1994.

———. *Portrait of an Election: The 1980 Presidential Campaign*. New York: Simon & Schuster, 1981.

Duffy, Michael, and Dan Goodgame. *Marching in Place: The Status Quo Presidency of George Bush*. New York: Simon & Schuster, 1991.

Ehrenhalt, Alan. *The Lost City: Discovering the Forgotten Virtues of Community in the Chicago of the 1950's*. New York: Basic Books, 1995.

Erie, Steven P. *Rainbow's Edge: Irish-Americans and the Dilemmas of Urban Machine Politics, 1840–1985*. Los Angeles: University of California Press, 1988.

Farber, David. *Chicago 68*. Chicago: University of Chicago Press, 1988.

Garment, Suzanne. *Scandal: The Culture of Mistrust in American Politics*. New York: Times Books, 1991.

Giancana, Antoinette, and Thomas C. Renner. *Mafia Princess: Growing Up in Sam Giancana's Family*. New York: William Morrow, 1984.

Glazer, Nathan, and Daniel P. Moynihan. *Beyond the Melting Pot*. Cambridge: MIT Press, 1964.

Gleason, Bill. *Daley of Chicago: The Man, the Mayor, and the Limits of Conventional Politics*. New York: Simon & Schuster, 1970.

Gorman, Joseph Bruce. *Kefauver: A Political Biography*. New York: Oxford University Press, 1971.

Gove, Samuel K., and Louis H. Masotti, eds. *After Daley: Chicago Politics in Transition*. Urbana: University of Illinois Press, 1982.

Greider, William. *Who Will Tell the People: The Betrayal of American Democracy*. New York: Simon & Schuster, 1992.

Grimshaw, William J. *Bitter Fruit: Black Politics and the Chicago Machine 1931–1991*. Chicago: University of Chicago Press, 1992.

Hartley, Robert E. *Big Jim Thompson of Illinois*. Chicago: Rand McNally, 1979.

Hirsch, Arnold H. "Martin F. Kennelly: The Mugwumps and the Machine." In Holli and Green, eds., *The Mayors: The Chicago Political Tradition*. Carbondale: Southern Illinois University Press, 1987.

Holli, Melvin G., and Paul M. Green. *Bashing Chicago Traditions: Harold Washington's Last Campaign*. Grand Rapids, MI: William B. Eerdmans, 1989.

———, eds. *The Mayors: The Chicago Political Tradition*. Carbondale: Southern Illinois University Press, 1987.

Jackley, John L. *Hill Rat: Blowing the Lid Off Congress*. Washington: Regnery Gateway, 1992.

Jackson, Brooks. *Honest Graft: Big Money and the American Political Process*. New York: Alfred A. Knopf, 1988.

Jamieson, Kathleen Hall. *Dirty Politics: Deception, Distraction, and Democracy*. New York: Oxford University Press, 1992.

Johnson, Haynes, and David S. Broder. *The System: The American Way of Politics at the Breaking Point*. New York: Little, Brown, 1996.

Kahn, Melvin A., and Frances J. Majors. *The Winning Ticket: Daley, the Chicago Machine, and Illinois Politics*. New York: Praeger, 1984.

Kallina, Edmund F. Jr. *Courthouse over White House: Chicago and the Presidential Election of 1960*. Orlando: University of Central Florida Press, 1988.

Kantowicz, Edward R. *Polish-American Politics in Chicago, 1888–1940*. Chicago: University of Chicago Press, 1975.

———. "Polish Chicago: Survival Through Solidarity." In Melvin G. Holli and Peter d'A. Jones, eds., *The Ethnic Frontier: Group Survival in Chicago and the Midwest*. Grand Rapids, MI: William B. Eerdmans, 1977.

Kennon, Donald R., and Rebecca M. Rogers. *The Committee on Ways and Means: A Bicentennial History, 1789–1989*. Washington: Government Printing Office, 1989.

Kleppner, Paul. *Chicago Divided: The Making of a Black Mayor*. DeKalb: Northern Illinois University Press, 1985.

Koenig, Rev. Msgr. Harry C., ed. *A History of the Parishes of the Archdiocese of Chicago*. Chicago: The Archdiocese of Chicago, 1980.

Kolb, Charles. *White House Daze: The Unmaking of Domestic Policy in the Bush Years*. New York: Free Press, 1994.

Lemann, Nicholas. *The Promised Land: The Great Black Migration and How It Changed America*. New York: Alfred A. Knopf, 1991.

Lindberg, Richard C. *Quotable Chicago*. Chicago: Wild Onion Books, 1996.

McCaffrey, Lawrence J. *Textures of Irish America*. Syracuse: Syracuse University Press, 1992.

Merriner, James L. "Fathers, Sons, and Unholy Ghosts." *Illinois Issues*, July 1996.

Miller, Ross. *Here's the Deal: The Buying and Selling of a Great American City*. New York: Alfred A. Knopf, 1996.

Miller, William "Fishbait," as told to Frances Spatz Leighton. *Fishbait: The Memoirs of the Congressional Doorkeeper*. Englewood Cliffs, NJ: Prentice-Hall, 1977.

Nixon, Richard. *RN: The Memoirs of Richard Nixon*. New York: Grosset & Dunlap, 1978.

Nozick, Robert. *Anarchy, State, and Utopia*. New York: Basic Books, 1974.

O'Connor, Len. *Clout: Mayor Daley and His City*. Chicago: Henry Regnery, 1975.

———. *Requiem: The Decline and Demise of Mayor Daley and His Era*. Chicago: Contemporary Books, 1977.

O'Donnell, Kenneth P., and David F. Powers, with Joe McCarthy. *Johnny, We Hardly Knew Ye*. Boston: Little, Brown, 1972.

O'Neill, Thomas P. Jr., with William Novak. *Man of the House: The Life and Political Memoirs of Speaker Tip O'Neill*. New York: Random House, 1987.

Selected Bibliography

Poles of Chicago 1837–1937: A History of One Century of Polish Contributions to the City of Chicago, Ill. Chicago: Polish Pageant, 1937.

Rakove, Milton L. *Don't Make No Waves, Don't Back No Losers: An Insider's Analysis of the Daley Machine.* Bloomington: Indiana University Press, 1975.

———. *We Don't Want Nobody Nobody Sent: An Oral History of the Daley Years.* Bloomington: Indiana University Press, 1979.

Reagan, Ronald. *An American Life.* New York: Simon & Schuster, 1990.

Reedy, George. *From the Ward to the White House: The Irish in American Politics.* New York: Charles Scribner's Sons, 1991.

Reeves, Richard. *President Kennedy: Profile of Power.* New York: Simon & Schuster, 1993.

Reeves, Thomas C. *A Question of Character: A Life of John F. Kennedy.* New York: Free Press, 1991.

Renkiewicz, Frank, ed. *The Poles in America 1608–1972: A Chronology & Fact Book.* New York: Oceana Publications, 1973.

Report of the National Advisory Commission on Civil Disorders. New York: E. P. Dutton, 1968.

Rivlin, Gary. *Fire on the Prairie: Chicago's Harold Washington and the Politics of Race.* New York: Henry Holt, 1992.

Royko, Mike. *Boss: Richard J. Daley of Chicago.* New York: Signet, 1971.

Sabato, Larry J., and Glenn R. Simpson. *Dirty Little Secrets: The Persistence of Corruption in American Politics.* New York: Times Books, 1996.

Sautter, R. Craig, and Edward M. Burke. *Inside the Wigwam: Chicago Presidential Conventions 1860–1996.* Chicago: Wild Onion Books, 1996.

Simpson, Dick. *Winning Elections: A Handbook of Modern Participatory Politics.* New York: Harper Collins, 1996.

Smith, Hedrick. *The Power Game: How Washington Works.* New York: Random House, 1988.

Sowell, Thomas. *Ethnic America: A History.* New York: Basic Books, 1981.

Stern, Philip M. *Still the Best Congress Money Can Buy.* Washington: Regnery Gateway, 1992.

Stockman, David A. *The Triumph of Politics: Why the Reagan Revolution Failed.* New York: Harper & Row, 1986.

Strahan, Randall. "Dan Rostenkowski: A Study in Congressional Power." In Lawrence C. Dodd and Bruce I. Oppenheimer, eds., *Congress Reconsidered*, 5th edition. Washington: CQ Press, 1993.

———. *New Ways and Means: Reform and Change in a Congressional Committee.* Chapel Hill: University of North Carolina Press, 1990.

Sullivan, Frank. *Legend: The Only Inside Story about Mayor Richard J. Daley.* Chicago: Bonus Books, 1989.

Tamarkin, Bob. *The Merc: The Emergence of a Global Financial Powerhouse.* New York: HarperCollins, 1993.

Thiem, George. *The Hodge Scandal.* New York: St. Martin's Press, 1963.

Selected Bibliography

Travis, Dempsey J. *"Harold": The People's Mayor*. Chicago: Urban Research Press, 1989.

Van Der Slik, Jack R. *One for All and All for Illinois: Representing the Land of Lincoln in Congress*. Springfield, IL: Sangamon State University, 1995.

Von Damm, Helene. *At Reagan's Side: Twenty Years in the Political Mainstream*. New York: Doubleday, 1989.

Wade, Richard C. "The Enduring Chicago Machine." *Chicago History* 15:1, 1986.

Waring, Paul C. *History of the 7th Infantry Division (Bayonet Division)*. Tokyo: Dai Nippon Printing, 1967.

Weinberg, Tom, producer/director. "Rostenkowski." Film broadcast on WTTW-TV, Chicago, 2 February 1981.

Williams, Kenny J., and Bernard Duffy, eds. *Chicago's Public Wits: A Chapter in the American Comic Spirit*. Baton Rouge: Louisiana University Press, 1983.

Witte, John F. *The Politics and Development of the Federal Income Tax*. Madison: University of Wisconsin Press, 1985.

Wright, Jim. *Balance of Power: Presidents and Congress from the Era of McCarthy to the Age of Gingrich*. Atlanta: Turner, 1996.

INDEX

Index

Index

Index

Index

Index

Index

taxes, Illinois, 70, 73

taxes, U.S.: on capital gains, 159, 196, 219, 240–41, 264; on consumption, 221; on corporate income, 212–14, 219–20, 316n. 37; deductions, 208–9, 211; depreciation allowances, 136, 170, 178, 264; earned income credit, 194, 200, 219; on energy, 147, 275–76; excise, 232; "extenders," 256; on gasoline, 158–59, 166, 181, 232, 234, 246, 255; on health plans ("Section 89") 241–42; indexed for inflation, 176–77; on intangible assets, 256–57; payroll, 220; on personal income, 27, 104, 116, 194, 208–9, 219; "transition rules" of, 212–13, 219, 220–22; user fees, 186, 232, 236. *See also* commodities trading, regulation and proposed taxation of

Tax Reduction and Simplification Act of 1977, 158

Tax Reform Act of 1986, 221, 223

Teague, Olin E. "Tiger," 120, 129

television and politics, 105, 111–13, 229, 273, 278

Thompson, James R. "Big Jim": as governor of Illinois, 131, 138, 140, 175, 225, 251; and Rostenkowski, 141, 229, 291, 293; as U.S. attorney, 126–30, 287

Time, 64, 218, 254

Tisci, Anthony, 88–89, 135

Truman, Harry, 41, 94

Tully, Thomas M., 162–63

Ullman, Al, 134, 159, 166

Vietnam War, 39, 90, 101–2, 105, 112

Vrdolyak, Edward R.: political career of, 145, 147, 163, 165; and Presidential Towers, 138, 140

Vrdolyak, Victor, 138, 140

Walesa, Lech, 229

Walker, Daniel J., 124–25, 131, 299

Wall Street Journal, 191, 195, 234, 287

Washington, Harold: death of, 225–26; as mayor of Chicago, 133, 139, 224–25; political career of, 42–43, 161; and Rostenkowski, 192, 197

Washington Post, 234, 242, 261; and Rostenkowski, coverage of, 184–85, 266, 267; —, editorial praise for, 158, 287

Washington Times, 261

Ways and Means Committee, U.S. House: bicentennial celebration of, 239; powers of, 93, 146–47, 167; reforms of, 146; Republicans on, 169, 174, 210, 214–15; Rostenkowski, jealousy of prerogatives of, 169, 171, 177, 180, 206–7; —, as chairman of, 136, 166–71, 222, 241, 276, 286–87; —, as member of, 93, 149, 159

Webb, Dan K., 287–89, 295, 296

Wendt, Kenneth R., 44, 49, 73, 87

West Side Bloc, 21, 46, 49, 71, 73

Wicker, Tom, 111, 113

Wing, Helen, 199, 217

Wolek, John "Donkey Ears," 9, 11, 12

Works Progress Administration, 24, 56

Wright, James C. "Jim": ethics problems of, 236–38, 298; political career of, 125, 149, 150, 156; and Rostenkowski, 92–93, 166, 233–34, 236–37; as Speaker of the House, 233, 241

Yates, Sidney, 252, 255

Zenkich, Elias R. "Non-Incumbent," 263, 283

James L. Merriner, former political editor and columnist for the *Chicago Sun-Times* and the *Atlanta Constitution*, has covered national politics for twenty-five years. He graduated *magna cum laude* from Harvard University and holds a master's in communications from the University of Pennsylvania. With Thomas P. Senter, he coauthored *Against Long Odds: Citizens Who Challenge Congressional Incumbents*.